The Grounded Instruction Librarian:

Participating in the Scholarship of Teaching and Learning

Edited by
Melissa Mallon, Lauren Hays, Cara Bradley,
Rhonda Huisman, and Jackie Belanger

Association of College and Research Libraries
A division of the American Library Association
Chicago, Illinois 2019

Library of Congress Control Number: 2019943314

Contents

SECTION I. PEDAGOGICAL CONTENT KNOWLEDGE/SIGNATURE PEDAGOGY

SECTION II. SoTL THEORY

SECTION III. SoTL RESEARCH

Acknowledgments

The editors would like to thank the Association of College & Research Libraries (ACRL) Student Learning and Information Literacy Committee, and the ACRL leadership (particularly, Rhonda Huisman), for their continued support and encouragement in the publication of this book.

We would also like to thank Erin Nevius, Content Strategist at ACRL and editor extraordinaire. Her enthusiasm and ideas are so welcome, and her input has helped make this book a success!

Melissa would like to thank her co-editors (Lauren, Jackie, Cara, and Rhonda) for their amazing work on this manuscript—their expertise, ideas, questions, and love of teaching and learning has made editing this book an extremely fun and invigorating project. Melissa would also like to say thanks to all of our creative and smart librarian colleagues for their support and excitement about the librarian SoTL movement.

Cara thanks Melissa, Lauren, Jackie, and Rhonda for welcoming a Canadian librarian as part of the team, and for their passion about SoTL and librarianship, which was evident in every discussion held about this project. She also thanks her supervisor of many years, Colleen Murphy, for giving her the freedom and confidence to pursue her scholarly and professional interests.

Jackie would like to thank her co-editors for opening up new ways of thinking about teaching and learning through SoTL, and her colleagues at the University of Washington Libraries for their support and encouragement.

Lauren would first like to thank Margy MacMillan for introducing her to SoTL! She is not sure what direction her career would have taken without Margy's influence, but she knows it would not be nearly as fun. She also wants to thank her co-editors who made editing this book tremendously rewarding. Their expertise, organization, enthusiasm, and support were always evident.

Rhonda would like to thank the writing team (Cara, Jackie, Dr. Lauren, and Melissa) for agreeing to take a risk (remember that first email?) on creating a wonderful, comprehensive, and innovative collection of works from our peers and colleagues. Thanks to ACRL for continuing to provide opportunities for diverse and evolving professional resources like this collection. Special thanks to Margy MacMillan and Emma Coonan for your SoTL expertise, and finally thanks to all of the librarian educators, teachers, instructors, facilitators, and guides who are part of and grounded in the SoTL library community—for those that are new to SoTL, we truly hope this will be inspiring and help to shape, understand, and reflect on your practice.

Foreword

The book in your hand represents an exciting moment in academic librarianship. Collectively, the work explicitly recognizes the deep connections between the Scholarship of Teaching and Learning (SoTL) and the scholarly work of librarians. Individually, the essays and case studies demonstrate a remarkable range of how these connections support and strengthen our contributions to academic and student learning. SoTL provides a way of grounding our scholarly teaching within theories of learning both established and developing. It is a framework for contextualizing the learning we see (or don't) through research conducted across the disciplines and a portal through which we can enter wider discourses about teaching. In turn, participating in SoTL work, from informal discussions to publication, showcases our expertise in teaching to the broader academic community and perhaps helps us see ourselves differently.

In writing this preface, I'm drawing on many sources, not least rich conversations with Peter Felten and Joan Ruelle as we worked on our essay on professional development. We talked a lot about why reading, research, and writing in SoTL were important, often coming back to a central question: What does SoTL work bring that differentiates it from other engagement with scholarship? From our Google Doc record of conversations, synchronous and asynchronous, comes a statement that ultimately didn't make it into our piece but that answers the "Why SoTL?" question for me:

> SoTL provides a useful framework and communities of practice in which to rethink academic librarianship—to claim and recognize the authentic scholarship happening in libraries.... In librarianship, professional development is often understood as development of the individual professional. SoTL can be a meaningful pathway for both development of the individual professional and the profession as a whole.

SoTL certainly made a difference in my development. Although I had dabbled around the edges of SoTL since 2007, it was the 2010 Symposium on SoTL in Banff that changed how I thought about my work as a librarian. The questions presenters were asking resonated

and the approaches opened up new possibilities. Most of all, I was drawn to the cross-disciplinary discussions that happened after the presentations and continued over meals and walks in the snow. You could feel the desire for mutual understanding across boundaries as scholars explained their disciplines' values and codes and compared terminologies and epistemologies. Articulating the assumptions I made and the meanings I saw for a non-library audience required me to think through my project with more critique and clarity than any other stage in the research process had and challenged me to think about my work from fresh perspectives.

The welcoming community I found at the symposium engaged me with SoTL in a way that reading papers hadn't. Engaging in SoTL led me to a deeper commitment to understanding student learning and using that knowledge effectively in the classroom. The case studies in this book reveal that I am not alone in seeing SoTL as a means to do better research or in appreciating it as a way of facilitating better learning for the students I work with.

Over the next few years, I became more involved in SoTL associations and conferences but met very few fellow librarians engaging in these generative venues. On the flip side, while SoTL researchers were always welcoming, often they were somewhat surprised to see librarians there and curious about what we could offer to the conversation. In the literature, it seemed like there were two solitudes. Papers in SoTL journals, even when based on aspects of learning that librarians know well (e.g., undergraduate research, integrating source material) rarely cited work by librarians. SoTL work in the library literature was rarely labeled explicitly as such, and rarely drew on SoTL work outside of library journals. We have much in common, but it is only relatively recently that we have become part of each other's communities and conversations, as Cara Bradley noted in 2009 when SOTL as a term first hit mainstream academic library literature.[1]

Since then, there has been a steady growth in references to SoTL in library discussions and publications. Key writers and thinkers in academic librarianship (many of whom have contributed to this book) have also worked deliberately to explicitly link SoTL and library scholarship, building a growing community around #librariansotl. In the past three years, there have been presentations on SoTL at key conferences including LOEX, LIW, and ALA Midwinter; within ACRL, support for SoTL is evident in the packed room for the panel on SoTL at ACRL 2017, a dedicated website, two webinars, and the launch of this book. There has been an increasing number of library presentations at SoTL gatherings, including the Symposium on SoTL, the SoTL Commons, and the annual International Society for the Scholarship of Teaching and Learning (ISSOTL) meetings. The 2017 ISSOTL conference saw a record number of presentations and posters by librarians at the premier event in the field, and there is more work in the pipeline for ISSOTL 2018. Recently, the ISSOTL Board approved a SIG for Information Literacy that will foster ongoing conversations. It has been wonderful to watch SoTL and library scholarship come together, share strengths, and develop new ideas reflective of both fields.

This book marks the state of the integration of SoTL and academic librarianship in 2018 and lays the groundwork for the future. The essays by leading SoTL scholars, both within and outside librarianship, draw connections between our work and SoTL as manifested in the theories we use, the teaching we do, the research we conduct, and the professional development we undertake that leads to growth across these aspects of our work. The case studies in each section provide vivid illustrations of the differences this work makes in practice across a range of academic settings, disciplines, and purposes. Each case study also shows the process of SoTL integration, the many paths into this work taken by librarians. We see the effects of personal relationships that develop into collaborations, the impacts of teaching and learning centers that foster communities of practice, and the determination of individuals to explore new academic territories. We understand the questions that led researchers to engage with SoTL and the changes SoTL work made to the questions they asked. We note how external drivers like the Association of College & Research Libraries (ACRL) *Framework for Information Literacy for Higher Education*, institutional initiatives, and concerns around assessment sparked engagement with SoTL. We are presented with evidence that participating in SoTL benefits librarians, libraries, institutions, and higher education. Above all, we learn how SoTL work changes how others see us and how we see ourselves.

—Margy MacMillan

ENDNOTES

1. Cara Bradley, "The Scholarship of Teaching and Learning: Opportunities for Librarians," *College & Research Libraries News* 70, no. 5 (2009): 276–78.

BIBLIOGRAPHY

Bradley, Cara. "The Scholarship of Teaching and Learning: Opportunities for Librarians." *College & Research Libraries News* 70, no. 5 (2009): 276–78.

Introduction to the Scholarship of Teaching and Learning

What is SoTL?

The Institute for Scholarship of Teaching & Learning at Mount Royal University defines the Scholarship of Teaching & Learning (SoTL) as the "the developing field of original research and scholarship about teaching and learning practice specifically in the context of higher education. It is conducted by scholars from a variety of disciplinary backgrounds, who are interested in understanding student learning, innovations in teaching practice, and transformation of higher education.[1]" SoTL can be further characterized as

- focused on student learning, grounded in context, methodologically sound, conducted in partnership with students, and publicly disseminated;
- inclusive and unified by its potential to have an impact in the classroom and to contribute to the production of knowledge and ongoing improvement in teaching and learning; and
- diverse in discipline, theory, methodology, and method.[2]

The phrase "think globally, act locally" has been widely adopted by environmental groups to express the need to take local action to make large-scale change, but the cases in this book also demonstrate the relevance of the sentiment to the scholarship of teaching and learning. The cases are each "local"—that is, situated in a specific time and place, an essential characteristic of SoTL work. Each tells a unique story about students, learning, and librarians, and presents a distinct definition and description of SoTL in the process. The "global" aspect of SoTL emerges in the authors' decisions to share their work with the larger librarian and SoTL communities. In doing so, they contribute to a larger understanding of librarian teaching and student learning, having an impact far beyond the lives of students in a specific classroom. The cases, when read together, also move librarians and other educators toward a much richer and holistic definition and understanding of SoTL than that which can be provided in a single case. It is together, as a community, that we are continually defining SoTL.

Why Should You Care?

While not directly connected, the practice of SoTL is a natural fit within the many frameworks of information literacy. Due to its inclusion of threshold concepts, the Association of College and Research Libraries (ACRL) *Framework for Information Literacy for Higher Education*, in particular, is a logical partner for SoTL research:

> Many educational and discipline-specific theories undergird SoTL research, including threshold concepts. Due to this, librarians may benefit from familiarizing themselves with SoTL studies for the purposes of enhancing information literacy instruction, particularly when working with the *Framework for Information Literacy for Higher Education*. Understanding student learning both in general and in a discipline-specific context can help librarians tailor instruction to meet the needs of students.[3]

Librarians can use this connection, as well as their expertise in information literacy, to connect with faculty to explore SoTL projects as well as to embark on answering their own SoTL questions about student learning.

The editors do want to take care to note, however, that incorporation of the ACRL *Framework* (nor any other "official" information literacy guiding document) is not a necessary component in SoTL work. Many institutions may not have adopted use of the ACRL *Framework* or may still be in the process of figuring out how it works for them. The beauty of SoTL is that, as a practice, it is flexible and adaptable to many different institutional and disciplinary contexts, student populations, and learning environments. The editors hope the case studies in this book will inspire readers to embark on their own SoTL journeys and encourage readers to "think outside of the box" when it comes to embracing SoTL projects.

Book Sections

This book is divided into four sections: Pedagogical Content Knowledge/Signature Pedagogy, SoTL Theory, SoTL Research, and SoTL as Professional Development. While there is overlap among the sections in terms of many key themes and discussions of foundational work in SoTL (such as O'Brien's Compass, for example), each section engages SoTL through a different lens and provides readers with a sense of the varied ways SoTL is currently being "done" in academic libraries in North America and Europe. Each section begins with a foundation chapter from SoTL leaders that discusses central questions, highlights important theories and literature, and introduces the SoTL-in-practice chapters that follow. The practical chapters highlight work at the more local level. These take a range of forms, such as case studies from specific institutions, reflections on individual participation in SoTL work, or explorations of a particular topic or theme. For ease of reference, these SoTL-in-practice contributions are referred to as "case studies" in the book, in the sense that they are examples demonstrating the application of SoTL principles, though not all adhere for the format for a formal research case study. The number of practical chapters varies across sections, which can be taken as an indication of the current state of SoTL in librarianship: while it is clear that many librarians have fully embraced SoTL Research and its attendant professional development opportunities, there is still much for the profession to explore in terms of signature pedagogies. The diverse nature of these SoTL-in-practice chapters highlights the richness of work already underway in academic libraries and points the way to abundant possibilities for the future.

PEDAGOGICAL CONTENT KNOWLEDGE/ SIGNATURE PEDAGOGY

Pedagogical content knowledge and signature pedagogies are two topics that have been minimally explored in information literacy and librarianship. Shulman[4] described signature pedagogies as those ways of teaching that instruct students on the values, ways of thinking, and habits of a profession. Shulman also defined pedagogical content knowledge which is the combining of discipline-specific pedagogy and content.[5]

Anthony Ciccone, in the forward to the book *Exploring More Signature Pedagogies* writes:

> When we ask this question of alignment between the knowledge, skills, and dispositions we want to develop in our students and the pedagogy we currently use, we ask perhaps the most crucial question we can ask as academic professionals. In so doing, we question the values of our field, the way we teach, and what and how students learn. We create a research agenda for teaching and learning in the field that is grounded in what we value for our students.[6]

In the foundation chapter, Hays writes that the section "introduces the concepts of signature pedagogies and pedagogical content knowledge in hopes of promoting further conversation about each in the fields of librarianship and information literacy." This section opens the door for continued conversation about the alignment of pedagogy with content. The editors also hope that from this work a signature pedagogy for information literacy will emerge to help students develop information-literate habits.

SOTL THEORY

In her foundation chapter for the Theory section of this book, Nancy Chick writes that the "question of theory in the scholarship of teaching and learning (SoTL) is contentious and confused one. The field has been criticized for allegedly being atheoretical and undertheorized, and practitioners have been criticized for not identifying the theoretical frameworks that influence their specific projects."

These words could just as easily have been written about library and information studies, with practicing librarians often uneasy about identifying the theoretical frameworks informing their practice, and research confirming that a significant portion of LIS research lacks a theoretical underpinning.[7]

Given this reluctance to engage with theory, it makes sense to ask whether efforts to "theorize" the discipline are worthwhile. Chick answers this question, citing research demonstrating that "the quality of students' learning is affected by the teacher's conceptions of *what teaching and learning mean*—or the teacher's theoretical framework." Her choice of wording here is significant for librarians; most instruction librarians have consistent conceptions of teaching and learning that impact their classroom practices, even if they haven't *named* these conceptions. Theory is the next step of articulating these conceptions in the context of the wider learning landscape, and becoming, as Chick requests, "*explicitly intentional.*"

SoTL is an inviting landscape in which to take this next step of articulating and engaging with theory because of the lack of prescribed theoretical traditions. SoTL is situated in the disciplines so that in addition to educational theory (which one would expect to find), it also encourages theoretical approaches from across disciplines. The cases in the Theory section of this book offer a glimpse of the possibilities this presents and serve as models for the ways in which theoretical approaches from many fields can inform SoTL research by librarians.

SOTL RESEARCH

The Scholarship of Teaching and Learning (SoTL) is really no different than other areas of research within academic libraries; it provides a framework for studying and observing a group of the campus community (in many cases, students), which in turn allows researchers to gather valuable data in order to improve the subjects' experience and connection with the library. SoTL research is ideal for librarians teaching information literacy because it not only encourages a more in-depth study of student learning, it allows for a more holistic investigation of one's own teaching. Embarking on SoTL research projects also has the added benefit of providing librarians with the opportunity to engage in deeper partnerships with faculty members, which may result in a more systematic integration of information literacy skills or, at the very least, a richer learning experience for students.

As discussed in other sections of this book, Scholarship of Teaching and Learning projects are designed to expand upon and, ideally, answer the classic "who, what, why" questions, which are best posited by O'Brien, in her SoTL Compass:

- "What will my students be learning and why is it worth learning?
- Who are my students and how do students learn effectively?
- What can I do to support students to learn effectively?

- How do I know if my teaching and my students' learning have been effective?[8]

O'Brien's Compass has provided a template for many SoTL research projects, encouraging educators to pause, reflect, ask questions, and make changes to their pedagogical method. However, while this framework has been influential in guiding many SoTL projects within higher education (a great deal of which are referenced in this book), published examples of SoTL research projects is sparse in the field of library and information science.

The editors of this book, as readers might guess, are confident that academic librarians have an important and necessary voice in the world of pedagogical research. In the foundation chapter for the SoTL Research section, Emma Coonan aims to "show how and why engaging in SoTL research is beneficial for librarians and library staff, and to be candid about the challenges and rewards that the practice involves." Coonan's argument that the confluence of librarians' "expertise … position within the academy, and … involvement with information literacy" make them ideal candidates to lead and partner in student-learning-focused research projects. The case studies in the Research section further support this argument, covering a variety of information literacy-focused research projects, many of which were completed in partnership with faculty members. Through their thorough questioning and hypothesizing, the case study authors in this section go a long way toward establishing academic librarians as essential participants in the SoTL conversation.

SOTL AS PROFESSIONAL DEVELOPMENT

As Felten, MacMillan, and Ruelle write in their foundation chapter, SoTL is a "form of professional development" and is an "evidence-based approach to professional development for everyone who teaches in academic settings." Individuals participate in SoTL in order to improve teaching and learning. In educational development, SoTL is seen as a key component of the field. Indeed, Felten and Chick recently posited that SoTL may even be a signature pedagogy for the field of educational development.[9]

To develop professionally, instructors need to understand their own teaching and their student learning. Without this knowledge, professional development may be sought in areas not needing improvement. Through SoTL, teachers can gain insight into what is working, what is happening, what could be happening, and what is possible.[10] In turn, this knowledge should impact the growth of instructors.

One of the benefits of SoTL as professional development is that it enables librarians and faculty to collaborate and find common ground, both in terms of shared language and goals for improved student learning. Additionally, SoTL provides a shared space for all members of higher education. SoTL puts librarians firmly in wider higher education professional networks for the mutual benefit of librarians and instructors. This has the power to transform both librarians' own professional practice as well as that of those outside the library we partner with. As Felten, MacMillan and Ruelle write in their foundation chapter:

In librarianship, professional development is often understood as the development of the individual professional (through participation in training, webinars, and professional societies). Through collaborations, communities of practice, and the literature, the common language of SoTL integrates library-based teaching more firmly into the wider discussions in higher education, raising our profile as teachers and scholars even as it deepens our practice."

The case studies in this section offer a variety of rich ideas for ways librarians might partner with instructors, Centers for Teaching and Learning, and each other to engage in professional development activities that enable us to "broaden our horizons, our networks, our concepts of teaching, learning, and research, and our sphere of influence."

ENDNOTES

1. "What is Scholarship of Teaching and Learning (SoTL)?, " Mount Royal University Institute for Scholarship of Teaching and Learning, accessed June 11, 2018, http://www.mtroyal.ca/ProgramsCourses/FacultiesSchoolsCentres/InstituteforScholarshipofTeachingLearning/index.htm.
2. Peter Felten, "Principles of Good Practice in SoTL," *Teaching & Learning Inquiry: The ISSOTL Journal* 1, no. 1 (2013).
3. Lauren Hays and Melissa Mallon, "Keeping Up With… The Scholarship of Teaching and Learning," *American Library Association*, September 19, 2017, http://www.ala.org/acrl/publications/keeping_up_with/sotl.
4. Lee S. Shulman, "Those Who Understand: Knowledge Growth in Teaching," *Educational Researcher* 15, no. 2 (1986): 52.
5. Shulman, "Those Who Understand," 6.
6. Anthony A. Ciccone, Forward to *Exploring More Signature Pedagogies: Approaches to Teaching Disciplinary Habits of Mind*, ed. Nancy L. Chick, Aeron Haynie, and Regan A. R. Gurung (Sterling, VA: Stylus, 2012), xiii.
7. Lynne McKechnie and Karen E. Pettigrew, "Surveying the Use of Theory in Library and Information Science Research: A Disciplinary Perspective," *Library Trends* 50, no. 3 (2002).
8. Mia O'Brien, "Navigating the SoTL Landscape: A Compass, Map and Some Tools for Getting Started," *International Journal for the Scholarship of Teaching and Learning* 2, no. 2 (2008): 4.
9. Peter Felten and Nancy Chick, "Is SoTL a Signature Pedagogy of Educational Development?," *To Improve the Academy: A Journal of Educational Development* 37, no. 1, (2018).
10. Pat Hutchings, "Introduction," in *Opening Lines: Approaches to the Scholarship of Teaching and Learning* (Menlo Park, CA: Carnegie Foundation for the Advancement of Teaching, 2000), 5.

BIBLIOGRAPHY

Ciccone, Anthony A. Forward to *Exploring More Signature Pedagogies: Approaches to Teaching Disciplinary Habits of Mind*, ed. Nancy L. Chick, Aeron Haynie, and Regan A. R. Gurung (Sterling, VA: Stylus, 2012), xiii.

Felten, Peter. "Principles of Good Practice in SoTL." *Teaching & Learning Inquiry: The ISSOTL Journal* 1, no. 1 (2013): 121–25. http://dx.doi.org/10.2979/teachlearninqu.1.1.121.

Felten, Peter and Nancy Chick. "Is SoTL a Signature Pedagogy of Educational Development?," *To Improve the Academy: A Journal of Educational Development* 37, no. 1, (2018).

Hays, Lauren, and Melissa Mallon. "Keeping Up With… The Scholarship of Teaching and Learning." American Library Association. September 19, 2017. http://www.ala.org/acrl/publications/keeping_up_with/sotl Accessed June 20, 2018.

Hutchings, Pat. "Introduction," in *Opening Lines: Approaches to the Scholarship of Teaching and Learning* (Menlo Park, CA: Carnegie Foundation for the Advancement of Teaching, 2000), 5.

McKechnie, Lynne, and Karen E. Pettigrew. "Surveying the Use of Theory in Library and Information Science Research: A Disciplinary Perspective." *Library Trends* 50, no. 3 (2002): 406–17. http://muse.jhu.edu/journal/334.

Mount Royal University Institute for Scholarship of Teaching and Learning. "What is Scholarship of Teaching and Learning (SoTL)?" Accessed June 11, 2018. http://www.mtroyal.ca/ProgramsCourses/FacultiesSchoolsCentres/InstituteforScholarshipofTeachingLearning/index.htm.

O'Brien, Mia. "Navigating the SoTL Landscape: A Compass, Map and Some Tools for Getting Started." *International Journal for the Scholarship of Teaching and Learning* 2, no. 2 (2008): Article 15. https://doi.org/10.20429/ijsotl.2008.020215.

Shulman, Lee S. "Those Who Understand: Knowledge Growth in Teaching." *Educational Researcher* 15, no. 2 (1986): 52.

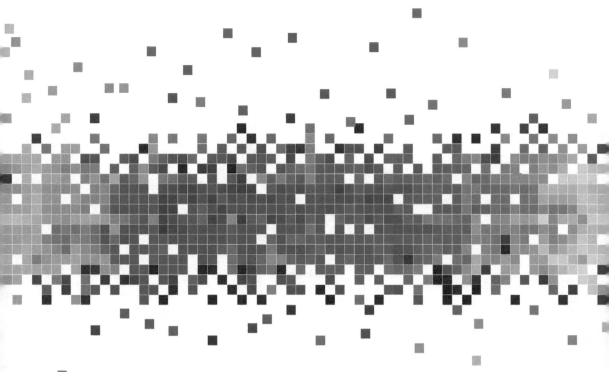

Section I
Pedagogical Content Knowledge/Signature Pedagogy

Examining Information Literacy Instruction through Signature Pedagogies and Pedagogical Content Knowledge

Lauren Hays

Discussions of pedagogy in librarianship typically center on the teaching of information literacy and how the teaching of information literacy is applied in academia.[1] The Association of College and Research Libraries defines information literacy as "the set of integrated abilities encompassing the reflective discovery of information, the understanding of how information is produced and valued, and the use of information in creating new knowledge and participating ethically in communities of learning."[2] On many college and university campuses, librarians serve in the role of expert in information literacy, and they help move students toward thinking like a person who is literate in information.[3] While conversations in post-secondary education circles about teaching and learning have become more common,[4] it is still easy to think about pedagogy generally instead of focusing on and studying specific teaching strategies. For example, many instructors regularly use pedagogical methods such as think-pair-share, jigsaw, lecturing, and the Socratic method. How, though, do educators know if certain pedagogies are those most suited for teaching content in courses? Are some pedagogies better suited for specific subjects than others? How do instructors ensure alignment between their pedagogies and learning outcomes?

Pedagogical content knowledge and signature pedagogies both attempt to help instructors answer the above questions. This section introduces the concepts of signature pedagogies and pedagogical content knowledge in hopes of promoting further conversation about each in the fields of librarianship and information literacy. Additionally, this chapter poses many questions about pedagogical considerations for teaching information literacy. What this section does not do is identify the best way to teach information literacy or identify one signature pedagogy in information

literacy. However, the authors of the case studies presented in this section share multiple pedagogies that may lead the field to develop a signature pedagogy from combined perspectives or, at minimum, identify certain pedagogies that do work better than others. Through SoTL research, a broader and deeper understanding of the ways to teach information literacy will develop.

Signature Pedagogies

Shulman[5] first described signature pedagogies as those ways of teaching that enculturate students into a profession. Understanding the pedagogies that are signature to a field helps observers understand what is valued among the field's members. Additionally, "signature pedagogies are important … because they are pervasive."[6] In other words, they are widely used teaching strategies that help create disciplinary thinkers. About signature pedagogies, Shulman writes, "They implicitly define what counts as knowledge in the field and how things become known. They define how knowledge is analyzed, criticized, accepted, or discarded. They define the functions of expertise in a field, the locus of authority, and the privileges of rank and standing."[7] Importantly, signature pedagogies highlight what is valued in a field.[8] Shulman expands on this principle, writing,

> A signature pedagogy has three dimensions: surface structure, deep structure, and an implicit structure. Surface structures consist of concrete, operational acts of teaching and learning, while deep structures reflect a set of assumptions about how best to impart a certain body of knowledge and know-how. The implicit structure includes a moral dimension that comprises a set of beliefs about professional attitudes, values, and dispositions.[9]

Examples of signature pedagogies include clinical rounds and bedside reporting for medical students,[10] as well as the case-dialogue method for law students.[11]

Still, signature pedagogies will not automatically create a disciplinary scholar. Instead, as Chick describes, the purpose of signature pedagogies is that "in lower-level courses [they] will help students begin to recognize, value, practice, and internalize" the concepts of the discipline.[12] Then, in upper-division courses, "students [will] participate in unpacking the discipline" through the process of "unpack[ing] it further themselves."[13] These pedagogies are widely used because they have been proven to work.[14] They help students learn what is expected of them in a discipline. Studying signature pedagogies in a discipline may improve teaching and learning because it will ask instructors to examine the habits, thoughts, and actions that students in the subject need to develop.[15] For newer fields and subjects, experts are still developing signature pedagogies. In the field of information literacy, many pedagogies are used, discussed, and debated, but a signature pedagogy has not been identified. Some signature pedagogies cross disciplines, some float between disciplines, some signature pedagogies may require adapting to suit a variety of methods, and some signature pedagogies may require creating new hybrid or unique methods.

As Shulman points out, instructors often teach the way they were taught.[16] So, how are librarians taught information literacy? How are librarians taught to teach? The instruction of information literacy is somewhat unique for signature pedagogies because librarians are not teaching students to become librarians the way biology professors are teaching students to become biologists. Instead, librarians are teaching information literacy, a core skill of librarianship, but it is only one of the disciplinary ways of thinking of librarians.[17] Consequently, information literacy instruction is uniquely situated. Signature pedagogies are developed in the professional fields,[18] so it is easier to make a connection between signature pedagogies and academic fields with a job attached to them.[19] However, when librarians teach information literacy, they are still teaching habits of mind that are needed for an information-literate person.

INFORMATION LITERACY AS CROSS DISCIPLINE

The focus of signature pedagogies was first on professions and then on specific disciplines. Therefore, understanding the signature pedagogies that cross disciplines, such as information literacy, is not always clear. Upon reflection, the following questions arise about signature pedagogies in information literacy for librarians: (a) How do librarians teach a student to think as someone who is information literate? (b) What teaching methods should be used to move students' mental thought processes from someone who is not information literate to someone who is? (c) How do signature pedagogies look different in an academic subject that is not strictly its own discipline? Further, researchers argue that thinking is always about something and therefore cannot be separated from the content.[20] Can information literacy, then, be separated from the discipline in which the information is written? Clearly, information literacy, similar to rhetoric and composition, crosses disciplines. However, rhetoric and composition are commonly seen as their own disciplines too.

Of course, while rhetoric and composition are often seen as disciplines, teaching writing and communication often happens outside the bounds of those strict disciplinary frames (e.g., embedded in classes not specifically called out as rhetoric or composition). In addition, to develop signature pedagogies in the subject of information literacy, librarians need to ask themselves if there are different signature pedagogies for information literacy in different disciplines. For example, is there a signature pedagogy for teaching about primary sources in history? Is there a signature pedagogy for teaching about medical texts? Or, on the other hand, will a signature pedagogy work broadly to instruct on elements of information literacy no matter the discipline within which the information is embedded? Answering these questions about signature pedagogies through Scholarship of Teaching and Learning (SoTL) research will lead the field to a better understanding of what is needed by teachers to help students develop literacy in information.

Understanding signature pedagogies in other disciplines can also benefit librarians who embed information literacy in a curriculum. Examples of signature pedagogies in other disciplines include critique in the arts and inquiry-based labs in the sciences.[21] Understanding the pedagogies used in other disciplines to create habits of mind exposes librarians to the core disciplinary values required in order to teach a subject that blends with the core discipline.[22] Knowing how students are introduced to the discipline can help librarians tailor information literacy lessons to the needs of the discipline. In a sense, disciplinary experts value specific ways of thinking and, by extension, scholars in each discipline value specific ways of thinking about information. Knowing how disciplinary scholars teach core concepts can help librarians more fully embed information literacy in discipline-specific curricula.

Signature pedagogies are irrevocably tied to threshold concepts, or core concepts, in a field. In order to teach core concepts, it benefits instructors to be able to name them. Additionally, if there are core concepts that make a subject what it is, then that begs the question, "What are the best ways to teach the core concepts?" One option would be to use the process of decoding the disciplines to help librarians reflect on their own thinking regarding information literacy. Decoding the disciplines is "a framework that facilitates serious thinking about the difficulties students face in a particular field and about strategies to help them overcome these challenges."[23] Engaging in decoding may lead to discoveries about signature pedagogies.[24] Regarding the cross-disciplinary nature of information literacy, Ward asks, "What, for example, are the critical information skills required in the field of anthropology? How best can the library teach them?"[25] The information literacy field needs to ask these types of questions.

INFORMATION LITERACY AS INTERDISCIPLINARY

While information literacy as a cross-disciplinary behavior focuses on viewing information literacy from within different disciplines, information literacy as an interdisciplinary subject means that methods from a variety of subjects are integrated. As previously stated, signature pedagogies primarily focus on the habits of mind necessary for a specific discipline; however, the book *Exploring More Signature Pedagogies: Approaches to Teaching Disciplinary Habits of Mind* includes a section on interdisciplinary signature pedagogies.[26] Inclusion of these interdisciplinary subjects and pedagogies demonstrates how certain habits of mind can cross traditional academic subjects. For example, Nowacek and Mountin wrote of "reflection in action" as an Ignatian signature pedagogy for Jesuit education, wherein professors develop experiences, create reflection opportunities, and support action for their Jesuit students.[27] Furthermore, Hassel and Nelson offer practices in feminist pedagogy as a model in the interdisciplinary field of women's studies.[28] Similar examples of signature pedagogies for interdisciplinary fields may serve as a model for the development of a signature pedagogy in information literacy.

Information literacy is taught and learned in a variety of contexts. While librarians are often positioned as information literacy experts, students also learn information literacy from others, such as faculty and peers. With subjects that are taught over a range of disciplines, teaching and learning scholars must ask themselves, "How does this subject look both generally and situated contextually within a broader discipline? What skills from other disciplines need to be integrated into the instruction of information literacy?" The answers to these questions will help develop a signature pedagogy for information literacy.

INFORMATION LITERACY AS A DISCIPLINE

Johnston and Webber posit that information literacy is a discipline.[29] As information literacy grows and develops as a recognized subject in higher education, a greater understanding should develop of how best to teach it. However, information literacy as a separate discipline is not universally accepted. Webber and Johnston describe it as a "soft applied discipline" and state that it should at least be seen as a separate subject.[30]

Authors of the Association of College & Research Libraries (ACRL) *Framework for Information Literacy for Higher Education* identified core concepts, or a framework, for information literacy. Authors in other studies have identified threshold concepts in information literacy.[31] Based on these inconsistencies, a definitive list of information literacy's core concepts does not yet exist; nevertheless, using previous studies such as the aforementioned ACRL *Framework* and international information literacy standards (e.g., *The SCONUL Seven Pillars of Information Literacy* and *The Alexandria Proclamation on Information Literacy and Lifelong Learning*) can help librarians move toward identifying the core concepts necessary for a person to be literate in information.

Bruce, Edwards, and Lupton identified six frames in their work that they pose as required for information literacy education.[32] The frames are:

- Knowledge about the world of information (content frame)
- A set of competencies or skills (competency frame)
- A way of learning (learning to learn frame)
- Contextual and situated social practices (personal relevance frame)
- Power relationships in society and social responsibility (social impact frame)
- A complex of different ways of interacting with information (relational frame)[33]

The six frames suggest habits of mind with which pedagogies may align.

Others see information literacy as one part of the broader literacy paradigm.[34] Given the connection between information literacy and other literacies recognized by the education profession, signature pedagogies may develop, or relate closely, to ones already being used by literacy instructors. As Ham and Schueller point out, in the last few decades there has been a shift away from teaching a new language as solely grammar to teaching "communicative competence"[35] or "knowing when and how to say what to whom."[36] In other words, language instructors teach the "grouping of underlying assumptions about the nature of language rather than a single narrowly defined method."[37] Likewise, librarians want to teach students about the nature of information instead of narrowly focusing on a single document. Learning and using the variety of pedagogies employed throughout the landscape of literacy shows promise for the instruction of information literacy.

EXPLORATION OF SIGNATURE PEDAGOGIES IN INFORMATION LITERACY

Although this chapter expresses the need for an exploration of signature pedagogies in information literacy, it should be noted that Otto suggests that both the reference interview and the library instruction session are signature pedagogies within librarianship.[38] Furthermore, Chick also muses that the reference interaction might be a signature pedagogy for the field of librarianship.[39] One must, of course, consider the possible differences between signature pedagogies for librarianship and information literacy. Overlap may exist, but there might also be unique ways to consider how the signature pedagogies in the broader discipline of librarianship can be brought to bear upon the subject of information literacy. Signature pedagogies in librarianship may not have a direct relationship with those pedagogies used to teach information literacy. Further SoTL research is needed.

Additionally, Willson found "that giving independent research time in [information literacy instruction] sessions, with scaffolding, is an effective use of class time."[40] In other words, teaching students how to search and then letting them practice may be a pedagogy that helps students develop habits of mind that help them access information. Habits of mind can be both skill-based and conceptual. Someone well-versed in information literacy is going to both do certain things as well as think about information in a certain way. Separating the required skills from the necessary ways of thinking creates a false dichotomy in information literacy. For example, physicians must know both how to think as a medical doctor and how to practice the skills needed to see patients. Signature pedagogies can teach both skills and concepts—both are necessary for learning. Yet, signature pedagogies focus on the mental thought processes necessary to be competent in a discipline; therefore, librarians must recognize that the teaching of skills at the exclusion of teaching how to think about information will lead to the use of pedagogies that do "not reflect the ways of knowing and doing" for an information-literate person.[41]

Importantly, it is also possible that a signature pedagogy in information literacy could be derived from critical theory, and many librarians have recently connected critical theory and information literacy.[42] As Elmborg notes, librarians must create "a critical practice of librarianship—a theoretically informed practice" to move the field forward.[43] This focus would help librarians concentrate on the literacy aspect of information literacy.[44] Given information literacy's place in academia and the Alexandria Proclamation's definition of information literacy, which states that information literacy "comprises the competencies to recognize information needs and to locate, evaluate, apply and create information within cultural and social contexts,"[45] using pedagogies that help students situate information contextually and culturally may very well help them develop information literacy habits of mind that harken to the work of critical theorists. Lupton and Bruce suggest that literacy is culturally situated.[46] Thus, information literacy, because it is a form of literacy, also exists within a society.

SIGNATURE PEDAGOGIES AND THE SCHOLARSHIP OF TEACHING AND LEARNING

Good teaching embraces different styles, modes, and pedagogies. Often, the reason different ways of teaching work well is because of the requirements of each discipline.[47] Thinking about signature pedagogies helps researchers examine what is done, how and why it is done, and whether or not it works. Signature pedagogies connect the ideas discussed in a class with the skills needed by practitioners of that discipline.[48] Perhaps the reason some pedagogies work in some courses and not in others is because it is a signature pedagogy borrowed from another discipline that clashes with what is needed for students in a different course. Exploring signature pedagogies helps teachers define their outcomes and develop pedagogical content knowledge (discussed in the next section). Exploring signature pedagogies also helps teachers consider the habits and skills that are needed in their field and how they teach those habits of mind to their students.[49]

SoTL is inextricably linked to signature pedagogies.[50] As librarians engage in SoTL through research and inquiry about the teaching and learning that occurs in their classrooms, they will come to understand what pedagogies form information literacy habits of mind. From this SoTL work, signature pedagogies will develop. Librarian engagement in SoTL will lead to a deeper understanding of how students develop information literacy skills and perhaps even of what specific ways of thinking and acting indicate a person is information literate. To reiterate, understanding how students develop as information-literate individuals will lead to the development of signature pedagogies that teach the habits of mind needed for information literacy.

As the field of information literacy progresses, it continues moving toward signature pedagogies. Discussions of pedagogy among librarians demonstrate that they are developing signature pedagogies for information literacy. In many ways, though, information literacy is still coming of age due to the ever-evolving nature of information, and therefore signature pedagogies are likely to change. Pedagogies that work today to move students to disciplinary habits of mind may not work in the future. Thus, continued SoTL research to stay abreast of the field's core concepts and determine how students learn those concepts is necessary for instructors of information literacy.

Pedagogical Content Knowledge

Lee Shulman introduces the idea of pedagogical content knowledge.[51] Pedagogical content knowledge is the combination of the knowledge of pedagogy and the knowledge of content. When teachers know what pedagogy best aligns with the specific content they teach, they have developed pedagogical content knowledge.[52] The overlap between pedagogy and content is unique in each discipline. How the overlap is best demonstrated in each context can be learned and understood through SoTL research and reading.

As mentioned earlier, decoding the disciplines is a process useful for the understanding of habits of mind. Decoding is also important for helping instructors develop pedagogical content knowledge.[53] When instructors understand their own thought processes, they will have an easier time teaching students who are new to the field.

Recent literature includes technology with pedagogical content knowledge to create technological, pedagogical, content knowledge. While it is important that technology aligns with pedagogy and course content, technology should not be separate from pedagogy. Technology use should be integrated into the fabric of a course. This is particularly true for the field of information literacy because technology is often the medium through which information is disseminated. Further SoTL research on the role of technology in pedagogical content knowledge—particularly in information literacy—is needed.

While signature pedagogies are important and necessary to help students develop in a field, they can also be used inappropriately. At times, other pedagogical methods are needed to teach a concept, but professors can easily fall back on the pedagogies in which they were taught.[54] Consequently, gaining pedagogical content knowledge may further support the teaching of habits of mind and core concepts in the field when signature pedagogies are not enough.

Pedagogical content knowledge does not negate the importance of understanding pedagogy broadly or the ability to use different pedagogies, but pedagogical content knowledge does emphasize the importance of an alignment between *what* is being taught and *how* it is being taught. For example, if one were teaching a class where the learning outcome is that the students will be able to find information, he or she might show students how to use a database and provide time for them to use the database themselves. The learning outcome is for the students to learn to find their own information in the database—pedagogy and content knowledge must align. Therefore, students need to learn *how* to search the database to find information. How aligns with doing. All instructors must ask the following: (a) Do our pedagogies match our learning outcomes? and (b) Do our pedagogies fit the discipline in which the information resides?

There are similarities between critical thinking and information literacy, and exploring the literature on critical thinking may serve as an initial place to consider pedagogical content knowledge for information literacy. Much research supports the difficulty of teaching critical-thinking skills.[55] As Schlueter writes, "Thinking … is always about *something*."[56] Similarly, information is always about something. Information cannot be separated from the context in which it exists. The context includes both what the information is about and the medium in which it is published/housed. As Norris points out in *Thinking About Critical Thinking*, "There is no scientific legitimacy to [the] claim that critical-thinking ability involves ability to control for content and complexity, ability to interpret and apply, and ability to use sound principles of thinking. If anything, scientific evidence suggests that human mental abilities are content and context bound, and highly influenced by the complexity of the problems being addressed."[57]

SIGNATURE PEDAGOGIES AND PEDAGOGICAL CONTENT KNOWLEDGE IN ACTION: CASE STUDIES

It is important to note that while SoTL work focusing on signature pedagogies and pedagogical content knowledge does emphasize content and the instructor, the student is ultimately what is most important. The learning that occurs by students is what is valued—not the ability of the instructor to use a certain pedagogy. However, when teachers know what pedagogies might lead to greater student learning through the development of habits of mind in a discipline, the likelihood exists for increased student learning. SoTL emphasizes local context and unique students. SoTL work is rarely generalizable. Still, what is learned by making that work public ultimately benefits the students.

Discussion of signature pedagogies breaks new ground in information literacy. The cases in this section highlight common ways information literacy is taught. Kuglitsch and Roberts share a model for pedagogical content knowledge in information literacy instruction, and Smiley helps readers see how to frame library sessions around disciplinary information literacy. Additionally, Houtman's case study asks readers to consider how librarians learn to teach—an insightful piece because the way discipline experts are enculturated into the field is often how they teach their own students. Understanding commonalities of teaching practice and how librarians are taught themselves opens the door for continued conversations about signature pedagogies in the subject of information literacy. Studying the questions Houtman poses will help grow pedagogical content knowledge and signature pedagogies in information literacy.

Additionally, throughout this section, the case study authors give examples of pedagogical content knowledge. The authors highlight successful pedagogical methods used to teach information literacy. Their SoTL work moves the field forward as these librarians study and reflect on their pedagogical methods in order to improve student learning. Pedagogical content knowledge is not new to librarianship, but the construct has not previously been used to frame the contemplation of content and pedagogy. These case studies help introduce a new way of thinking about the instruction librarians do.

ENDNOTES

1. Susan Ariew, "How We Got Here: A Historical Look at the Academic Teaching Library and the Role of the Teaching Librarian," *Communications in Information Literacy* 8, no. 2 (2014): 209; Rebecca Albrecht and Sara Baron, "The Politics of Pedagogy: Expectations and Reality for Information Literacy in Librarianship," *Journal of Library Administration* 36, no. 1-2 (2002): 72; Lisa O'Connor, "Information Literacy as Professional Legitimation: The Quest for a New Jurisdiction," *Library Review* 58, no. 7 (2009): 493.
2. Association of College & Research Libraries, *Framework for Information Literacy for Higher Education* (Chicago, IL, 2016), 3.
3. Lori Townsend, Amy R. Hofer, Silvia Lin Hanick, and Korey Brunetti, "Identifying Threshold Concepts for Information Literacy: A Delphi Study," *Communications in Information Literacy* 10, no. 1 (2016): 30.

4. Mary Taylor Huber and Pat Hutchings, *The Advancement of Learning: Building the Teaching Commons* (Stanford, CA: The Carnegie Foundation, 2005), 3.

5. Lee S. Shulman, "Those Who Understand: Knowledge Growth in Teaching," *Educational Researcher* 15, no. 2 (1986): 52.

6. Shulman, "Those Who Understand," 54.

7. Ibid.

8. Anthony A. Ciccone, foreword to *Exploring More Signature Pedagogies: Approaches to Teaching Disciplinary Habits of Mind*, edited by Nancy L. Chick, Aeron Haynie, and Regan A. R. Gurung (Sterling, VA: Stylus, 2012), xiii.

9. Lee S. Shulman, "Signature Pedagogies in the Professions," *Signature* 134, no. 3 (2005): 52–59.

10. Shulman, "Signature Pedagogies," 52.

11. Lendol Calder, "Uncoverage: Toward a Signature Pedagogy for the History Survey," *The Journal of American History* 92, no. 4 (2006): 1360.

12. Nancy L. Chick, "Unpacking a Signature Pedagogy in Literacy Studies," in *Exploring Signature Pedagogies: Approaches to Teaching Disciplinary Habits of Mind*, ed. Regan A. R. Gurung, Nancy L. Chick, and Aeron Haynie (Sterling, VA: Stylus, 2009), 48.

13. Chick, "Unpacking a Signature Pedagogy."

14. Anthony A. Ciccone, foreword to *Exploring Signature Pedagogies: Approaches to Teaching Disciplinary Habits of Mind*, edited by Regan A. R. Gurung, Nancy L. Chick, and Aeron Haynie (Sterling, VA: Stylus, 2009), xiii.

15. Shulman, "Signature Pedagogies," 58.

16. Ibid., 57.

17. Aeron Haynie, Nancy L. Chick, and Regan A. R. Gurung, "Signature Pedagogies in the Liberal Arts and Beyond," in *Exploring More Signature Pedagogies: Approaches to Teaching Disciplinary Habits of Mind*, ed. Nancy L. Chick, Aeron Haynie, and Regan A. R. Gurung (Sterling, VA: Stylus, 2012), 4.

18. Shulman, "Signature Pedagogies," 56.

19. Haynie, Chick, and Gurung, "Signature Pedagogies in the Liberal Arts," 7.

20. Daniel T. Willingham, "Critical Thinking: Why Is It So Hard to Teach?," *Arts Education Policy Review* 109, no. 4 (2008): 17.

21. Angela Bauer-Dantoin, "The Evolution of Scientific Teaching within the Biological Sciences," in *Exploring Signature Pedagogies: Approaches to Teaching Disciplinary Habits of Mind*, ed. Regan A. R. Gurung, Nancy L. Chick, and Aeron Haynie (Sterling, VA: Stylus, 2009), 236; Helen Klebesadel and Lisa Kornetsky, "Critique as Signature Pedagogy in the Arts," in *Exploring Signature Pedagogies: Approaches to Teaching Disciplinary Habits of Mind*, ed. Regan A. R. Gurung, Nancy L. Chick, and Aeron Haynie (Sterling, VA: Stylus, 2009), 102.

22. Ciccone, foreword to *Exploring More Signature Pedagogies*, xiii.

23. David Pace, *The Decoding the Disciplines Paradigm: Seven Steps to Increased Student Learning* (Bloomington, IN: Indiana University Press, 2017), 4.

24. Pace, *The Decoding the Disciplines Paradigm*, 21.

25. Dane Ward, "Envisioning the Fully Integrated Library," *The Chronicle of Higher Education* 63, no. 20 (2017): A44.

26. Nancy L. Chick, Aeron Haynie, and Regan A. R. Gurung, eds., *Exploring More Signature Pedagogies: Approaches to Teaching Disciplinary Habits of Mind* (Sterling, VA: Stylus, 2012), 129.

27. Rebecca Nowacek and Susan Mountin, "Reflection in Action: A Signature Ignatian Pedagogy for the 21st Century," in *Exploring More Signature Pedagogies: Approaches to Teaching Disciplinary Habits of Mind*, ed. Nancy L. Chick, Aeron Haynie, and Regan A. R. Gurung (Sterling, VA: Stylus, 2012), 129.

28. Holly Hassel and Nerissa Nelson, "A Signature Feminist Pedagogy: Connection and

Transformation in Women's Studies," in *Exploring More Signature Pedagogies: Approaches to Teaching Disciplinary Habits of Mind*, ed. Nancy L. Chick, Aeron Haynie, and Regan A. R. Gurung (Sterling, VA: Stylus, 2012), 150.

29. Bill Johnston and Sheila Webber, "As We May Think: Information Literacy as a Discipline for the Information Age," *Research Strategies* 20, no. 3 (2005): 109.

30. Sheila Webber and Bill Johnston, "Information Literacy: Conceptions, Context and the Formation of a Discipline," *Journal of Information Literacy* 11, no. 1 (2017): 162.

31. Amy R. Hofer, Lori Townsend, and Korey Brunetti, "Troublesome Concepts and Information Literacy: Investigating Threshold Concepts for IL Instruction," *portal: Libraries and the Academy* 12, no. 4 (2012): 402; Townsend et al., "Identifying Threshold Concepts," 33.

32. Christine Bruce, Sylvia Edwards, and Mandy Lupton, "Six Frames for Information Literacy Education: A Conceptual Framework for Interpreting the Relationships between Theory and Practice," *Innovation in Teaching and Learning in Information and Computer Sciences* 5, no. 1 (2006): 1.

33. Bruce, Edwards, and Lupton, "Six Frames," 6.

34. Susan Boyce, "Information Literacy and School Librarianship: A Critical Look at Pedagogy and Profession," in *Reality Bytes: Information Literacy for Independent Learning*, ed. S. La Marca and M. Manning (Victoria, Australia: School Library Association of Victoria, 2004), 16.

35. Jennifer Ham and Jeanne Schueller, "Traditions and Transformations: Signature Pedagogies in the Language Curriculum," in *Exploring More Signature Pedagogies: Approaches to Teaching Disciplinary Habits of Mind*, ed. Nancy L. Chick, Aeron Haynie, and Regan A. R. Gurung (Sterling, VA: Stylus, 2012), 29.

36. Diane Larsen-Freeman, *Techniques and Principles in Language Teaching* (Oxford, UK: Oxford University Press, 2000), 121.

37. Ham and Schueller, "Traditions and Transformation," 29.

38. Peter Otto, "Librarians, Libraries, and the Scholarship of Teaching and Learning," *New Directions for Teaching and Learning* 2014, no. 139 (2014): 78.

39. Nancy L. Chick, "Applying SoTL [webinar]," *Student Learning & Information Literacy Committee, Association of College and Research Libraries,* 2017.

40. Rebekah Willson, "Independent Searching During One-Shot Information Literacy Instruction Sessions: Is It an Effective Use of Time?," *Evidence Based Library and Information Practice* 7, no. 4 (2012): 53.

41. Chick, "Unpacking a Signature Pedagogy," 44.

42. James Elmborg, "Critical Information Literacy: Implications for Instructional Practice," *The Journal of Academic Librarianship* 32, no. 2 (2006): 193; Michelle Holschuh Simmons, "Librarians as Disciplinary Discourse Mediators: Using Genre Theory to Move toward Critical Information Literacy," *portal: Libraries and the Academy* 5, no. 3 (2005): 299.

43. Elmborg, "Critical Information Literacy," 198.

44. Ibid., 195.

45. International Federation of Library Associations and Institutions, "Alexandria Proclamation on Information Literacy and Lifelong Learning," (2005), para. 4.

46. Mandy Lupton and Christine Bruce, "Windows on Information Literacy Worlds: Generic, Situated and Transformative Perspectives," in *Practising Information Literacy: Bringing Theories of Learning, Practice and Information Literacy Together*, ed. Annemaree Lloyd and Sanna Talja (Wagga Wagga, Australia: Centre for Information Studies, 2010), 3.

47. Gary D. Poole, Lynne Taylor, and John Thompson, "Using the Scholarship of Teaching and Learning at Disciplinary, National and Institutional Levels to Strategically Improve the Quality of Post-Secondary Education," *International Journal for the Scholarship of Teaching and Learning* 1, no. 2 (2007): 1.

48. Poole, Taylor, and Thompson, "Using the Scholarship of Teaching," 4.
49. Regan A. R. Gurung, Nancy L. Chick, and Aeron Haynie, eds., *Exploring Signature Pedagogies: Approaches to Teaching Disciplinary Habits of Mind* (Sterling, VA: Stylus, 2009), xvii.
50. Ciccone, foreword to *Exploring Signature Pedagogies*, xiv.
51. Shulman, "Those Who Understand," 6.
52. Ibid.
53. Haynie, Chick, and Gurung, "Signature Pedagogies in the Liberal Arts," 2.
54. Shulman, "Signature Pedagogies," 57.
55. Willingham, "Critical Thinking," 17.
56. J. Schlueter, "Higher Ed's Biggest Gamble," *Inside Higher Ed* (2016), para. 12.
57. Stephen P. Norris, "Thinking About Critical Thinking: Philosophers Can't Go it Alone," in *Teaching Critical Thinking: Dialogue and Dialectic*, ed. John E. McPeck (New York: Routledge, 1990), 70.

BIBLIOGRAPHY

Albrecht, Rebecca, and Sara Baron. "The Politics of Pedagogy: Expectations and Reality for Information Literacy in Librarianship." *Journal of Library Administration* 36, no. 1-2 (2002): 71–96. https://doi.org/10.1300/J111v36n01_06.

Ariew, Susan. "How We Got Here: A Historical Look at the Academic Teaching Library and the Role of the Teaching Librarian." *Communications in Information Literacy* 8, no. 2 (2014): 208–24.

Association of College and Research Libraries. *Framework for Information Literacy for Higher Education* (2016). Retrieved from http://www.ala.org/acrl/standards/ilframework.

Bauer-Dantoin, Angela. "The Evolution of Scientific Teaching within the Biological Sciences." In *Exploring Signature Pedagogies: Approaches to Teaching Disciplinary Habits of Mind*, edited by Regan A. R. Gurung, Nancy L. Chick, and Aeron Haynie, 224–43. Sterling, VA: Stylus, 2009.

Boyce, Susan. "Information Literacy and School Librarianship: A Critical Look at Pedagogy and Profession." In *Reality Bytes: Information Literacy for Independent Learning*, edited by S. La Marca and M. Manning, 16–32. Victoria, Australia: School Library Association of Victoria, 2004.

Bruce, Christine, Sylvia Edwards, and Mandy Lupton. "Six Frames for Information Literacy Education: A Conceptual Framework for Interpreting the Relationships between Theory and Practice." *Innovation in Teaching and Learning in Information and Computer Sciences* 5, no. 1 (2006): 1–18. https://doi.org/10.11120/ital.2006.05010002.

Calder, Lendol. "Uncoverage: Toward a Signature Pedagogy for the History Survey." *The Journal of American History* 92, no. 4 (2006): 1358–70. http://dx.doi.org/10.2307/4485896.

Chick, Nancy L. "Unpacking a Signature Pedagogy in Literacy Studies." In *Exploring Signature Pedagogies: Approaches to Teaching Disciplinary Habits of Mind*, edited by Regan A. R. Gurung, Nancy L. Chick, and Aeron Haynie, 36–55. Sterling, VA: Stylus, 2009.

———. "Applying SoTL [webinar]." *Student Learning & Information Literacy Committee, Association of College and Research Libraries*, 2017. Retrieved from http://acrl.libguides.com/slilc/sotl.

Chick, Nancy L., Aeron Haynie, and Regan A. R. Gurung, eds. *Exploring More Signature Pedagogies: Approaches to Teaching Disciplinary Habits of Mind*. Sterling, VA: Stylus, 2012.

Ciccone, Anthony A. Foreword to *Exploring Signature Pedagogies: Approaches to Teaching Disciplinary Habits of Mind*, edited by Regan A. R. Gurung, Nancy L. Chick, and Aeron

Haynie, xi-xvi. Sterling, VA: Stylus, 2009.

———. Foreword to *Exploring More Signature Pedagogies: Approaches to Teaching Disciplinary Habits of Mind*, edited by Nancy L. Chick, Aeron Haynie, and Regan A. R. Gurung, ix-xiii. Sterling, VA: Stylus, 2012.

Elmborg, James. "Critical Information Literacy: Implications for Instructional Practice." *The Journal of Academic Librarianship* 32, no. 2 (2006): 192–99.

Gurung, Regan A. R., Nancy L. Chick, and Aeron Haynie, eds. *Exploring Signature Pedagogies: Approaches to Teaching Disciplinary Habits of Mind*. Sterling, VA: Stylus, 2009.

Ham, Jennifer, and Jeanne Schueller. "Traditions and Transformations: Signature Pedagogies in the Language Curriculum." In *Exploring More Signature Pedagogies: Approaches to Teaching Disciplinary Habits of Mind*, edited by Nancy L. Chick, Aeron Haynie, and Regan A. R. Gurung, 27–41. Sterling, VA: Stylus, 2012.

Hassel, Holly, and Nerissa Nelson. "A Signature Feminist Pedagogy: Connection and Transformation in Women's Studies." *Exploring More Signature Pedagogies: Approaches to Teaching Disciplinary Habits of Mind*, edited by Nancy L. Chick, Aeron Haynie, and Regan A. R. Gurung, 143–55. Sterling, VA: Stylus, 2012.

Haynie, Aeron, Nancy L. Chick, and Regan A. R. Gurung. "Signature Pedagogies in the Liberal Arts and Beyond." In *Exploring More Signature Pedagogies: Approaches to Teaching Disciplinary Habits of Mind*, edited by Nancy L. Chick, Aeron Haynie, and Regan A. R. Gurung, 1–11. Sterling, VA: Stylus, 2012.

Hofer, Amy R., Lori Townsend, and Korey Brunetti. "Troublesome Concepts and Information Literacy: Investigating Threshold Concepts for IL Instruction." *portal: Libraries and the Academy* 12, no. 4 (2012): 387–405. http://doi.org/10.1353/pla.2012.0039.

Huber, Mary Taylor, and Pat Hutchings. *The Advancement of Learning: Building the Teaching Commons*. Stanford, CA: The Carnegie Foundation, 2005.

International Federation of Library Associations and Institutions. "Alexandria Proclamation on Information Literacy and Lifelong Learning" (2005). Retrieved from https://www.ifla.org/publications/beacons-of-the-information-society-the-alexandria-proclamation-on-information-literacy.

Johnston, Bill, and Sheila Webber. "As We May Think: Information Literacy as a Discipline for the Information Age." *Research Strategies* 20, no. 3 (2005): 108–21. http://dx.doi.org/10.1016/j.resstr.2006.06.005.

Klebesadel, Helen, and Lisa Kornetsky. "Critique as Signature Pedagogy in the Arts." In *Exploring Signature Pedagogies: Approaches to Teaching Disciplinary Habits of Mind*, edited by Regan A. R. Gurung, Nancy L. Chick, and Aeron Haynie, 99-120. Sterling, VA: Stylus, 2009.

Larsen-Freeman, Diane. *Techniques and Principles in Language Teaching*. Oxford, UK: Oxford University Press, 2000.

Lupton, Mandy, and Christine Bruce. "Windows on Information Literacy Worlds: Generic, Situated and Transformative Perspectives." In *Practising Information Literacy: Bringing Theories of Learning, Practice and Information Literacy Together*, edited by Annemaree Lloyd and Sanna Talja, 4–27. Wagga Wagga, Australia: Centre for Information Studies, 2010.

Norris, Stephen P. "Thinking About Critical Thinking: Philosophers Can't Go It Alone." In *Teaching Critical Thinking: Dialogue and Dialectic*, edited by John E. McPeck, 67–74. New York: Routledge, 1990.

Nowacek, Rebecca, and Susan Mountin. "Reflection in Action: A Signature Ignatian Pedagogy for the 21st Century." *Exploring More Signature Pedagogies: Approaches to Teaching Disciplinary Habits of Mind*, edited by Nancy L. Chick, Aeron Haynie, and Regan A. R.

Gurung, 129–42. Sterling, VA: Stylus, 2012.

O'Connor, Lisa. "Information Literacy as Professional Legitimation: The Quest for a New Jurisdiction." *Library Review* 58, no. 7 (2009): 493–508. http://doi.org/10.1108/00242530910978190.

Otto, Peter. "Librarians, Libraries, and the Scholarship of Teaching and Learning." *New Directions for Teaching and Learning* 2014, no. 139 (2014): 77–93. http://doi.org/10.1002/tl.20106.

Pace, David. *The Decoding the Disciplines Paradigm: Seven Steps to Increased Student Learning.* Indiana University Press, 2017.

Poole, Gary D., Lynne Taylor, and John Thompson. "Using the Scholarship of Teaching and Learning at Disciplinary, National and Institutional Levels to Strategically Improve the Quality of Post-Secondary Education." *International Journal for the Scholarship of Teaching and Learning* 1, no. 2 (2007): 1–16. Retrieved from https://digitalcommons.georgiasouthern.edu/cgi/viewcontent.cgi?article=1038&context=ij-sotl.

Schlueter, J. "Higher Ed's Biggest Gamble." *Inside Higher Ed* (2016). Retrieved from https://www.insidehighered.com/views/2016/06/07/can-colleges-truly-teach-critical-thinking-skills-essay.

Shulman, Lee S. "Those Who Understand: Knowledge Growth in Teaching." *Educational Researcher* 15, no. 2 (1986): 4–14.

———. "Signature Pedagogies in the Professions." *Signature* 134, no. 3 (2005): 52–59.

Simmons, Michelle Holschuh. "Librarians as Disciplinary Discourse Mediators: Using Genre Theory to Move toward Critical Information Literacy." *portal: Libraries and the Academy* 5, no. 3 (2005): 297–311.

Townsend, Lori, Amy R. Hofer, Silvia Lin Hanick, and Korey Brunetti. "Identifying Threshold Concepts for Information Literacy: A Delphi Study." *Communications in Information Literacy* 10, no. 1 (2016): 23–49.

Webber, Sheila, and Bill Johnston. "Information Literacy: Conceptions, Context and the Formation of a Discipline." *Journal of Information Literacy* 11, no. 1 (2017): 156–83. https://doi.org/10.11645/11.1.2205.

Ward, Dane. "Envisioning the Fully Integrated Library." *The Chronicle of Higher Education* 63, no. 20 (2017): A44.

Willingham, Daniel T. "Critical Thinking: Why Is It So Hard to Teach?" *Arts Education Policy Review* 109, no. 4 (2008): 21–32.

Willson, Rebekah. "Independent Searching During One-Shot Information Literacy Instruction Sessions: Is It an Effective Use of Time?" *Evidence Based Library and Information Practice* 7, no. 4 (2012): 52–67. http://dx.doi.org/10.18438/B85323.

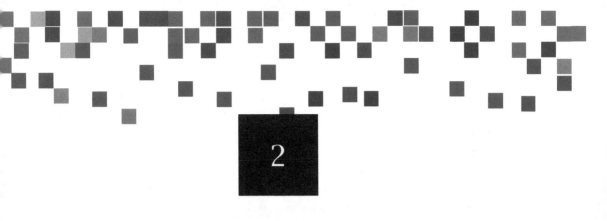

2

Asking "Good Questions" about How Academic Librarians Learn to Teach

Eveline Houtman

"How do academic librarians learn to teach?" This question holds personal importance for many librarians. "Where do you develop those [teaching] skills?" asks one new librarian. "Your first job? I think we're supposed to miraculously know it. That's been my experience."[1] Many new librarians feel unprepared for teaching. This may hold true for more established librarians as well[2] as they take on new roles or are asked to rethink the ways they teach.

The question also holds importance for the profession. A wide array of professional programs and activities exists in support of librarians learning to teach: courses in library schools, the Immersion program offered by the Association of College and Research Libraries (ACRL), webinars and workshops, conferences, local supports such as peer mentoring or communities of practice, scholarly publishing on information literacy instruction, and more. Despite this, the perhaps uneasy question persists: "How do librarians *actually* learn to teach?" Other questions may arise: "How *should* librarians learn?" or "How can we best support librarians learning to teach?" These are practical questions. More broadly, as Shulman suggests, "if you wish to understand why professions develop as they do, study ... their forms of professional preparation."[3]

This chapter explores the *research* questions we might ask to better understand and support academic librarians' professional preparation for their teaching role. The scholarship of teaching and learning "invites faculty [and librarians!] ... to ask good questions about their students' learning."[4] In examining how academic librarians learn to teach, librarians are positioned in the role of student or learner. What "good questions" could we ask about *their* learning? Of course, the connection to librarians' own students' learning also remains; the underlying assumption is that as librarians learn to teach, their teaching improves, which leads to improved student learning.

In search of good research questions to ask, this chapter draws on the field of education, specifically the research on teacher education and teacher learning. Stepping outside our own field offers us fresh perspectives and may challenge our assumptions. Library instruction has already borrowed heavily from the field of education, including teaching techniques, models of instructional design, learning theories, and broad approaches to teaching, such as learner-centered pedagogy[5] or critical pedagogy.[6] The library and information studies (LIS) literature has largely not turned to the education literature on teacher learning, however; librarians are more likely to consult the higher education literature on faculty learning.[7] It may be that librarians see the contexts and experiences of K-12 teachers' learning as too far removed from librarians' contexts and experiences. However, education's large and well-resourced research base has produced extensive research on teacher learning beyond what LIS can accomplish, and many questions do transfer from one context to another. In particular, more than any other field, the field of education has investigated questions related to professional development and professional learning.[8]

The sheer size of the literature on teacher education and teacher learning may also be daunting to librarians: where to start? In approaching this literature, the author has made no attempt to be exhaustive, instead drawing on selected review articles and handbooks on teacher education and learning. The SoTL research questions inspired by this literature are also not intended to be exhaustive; it is hoped that they *are* useful and generative of further ideas.

Focusing on Programs and Activities

One way to think about how librarians learn to teach is to focus on the programs and activities designed to support their learning. This is the main focus, for example, of the research questions suggested by the ACRL's Instruction Section regarding librarians' instruction-related continuing education.[9]

What should librarians know or be taught about teaching and *where* should they be taught are two practical questions that arise within this perspective (similar questions are addressed in the teacher education literature[10]), which have also led to research questions. In 2008, an ACRL task force tackled the *what* question by reviewing the LIS literature; it produced the ACRL's *Standards for Proficiencies for Instruction Librarians and Coordinators,*[11] an exhaustive list of the skills instruction librarians need and presumably are expected to acquire. Westbrock and Fabian's research[12] uses these proficiencies to investigate *where* librarians learn to teach, finding that most proficiencies are learned on the job. Where their participants believe they *should* learn their pedagogical skills, however, is at library school.

A number of studies do investigate library school course offerings on instruction, which typically are not particularly extensive—often just one elective course in a two-year degree, offered irregularly, with little experiential learning.[13] Other studies describe locally developed courses for practicing librarians[14] or on-the-job programs such as a peer mentor program[15] or a community of practice that allows library instructors to learn together.[16]

Given the variety of educational and professional development programs and activities related to instruction, the question arises of what is actually effective in supporting librarians' development as teachers. In fact, the ACRL Instruction Section's first suggested research question is: What are the most effective ways for a librarian to learn fundamental methodologies and pedagogies?[17] This then begs a further question: How should effectiveness be evaluated? Since the overarching aim of these activities and programs is to improve librarians' teaching—and therefore student learning—research questions might be:

- How do the programs and activities change librarians' teaching practices?
- What elements (if any) do librarians incorporate into their teaching?
- Why do librarians not incorporate other elements?

Changes in teaching (and even more so changes in student learning) may be difficult to observe and evaluate, however. In the field of education, Desimone instead proposes measuring the core features of effective professional development as established through research consensus in the field.[18] The five core features she identifies for teachers' professional development are:

1. Content focus. Activities should focus on subject matter content and how students learn that content.[19] The latter relates to pedagogical content knowledge,[20] which combines knowledge of the content with knowledge of how to teach it.

2. Active learning. In the context of teacher learning, this might involve observing an expert teacher or being observed themselves.[21]

3. Coherence. This relates to the extent to which teacher learning is consistent with their previous knowledge and beliefs, and with their educational context.[22] Beliefs and contexts will be discussed further in the next section of this case study, which focuses on professional learning.

4. Duration. Research shows effective professional development requires a sufficient amount of time, including the span of time over which the activity occurs. Suggested duration includes twenty hours or more of contact time with activities spread over a semester, or a more intensive program spread over a few days with follow-up over the semester.[23]

5. Collective participation. Interaction with colleagues is a powerful form of learning.[24]

Research questions involving these core features from the field of education might include:

- How do LIS programs and activities (in general or specific instances) measure up to these core features of effective professional development for teachers? Which are the most effective, based on these criteria?
- Based on the results of the above evaluation, are these measures actually useful in the LIS context?

The issue of *coherence* may be particularly pertinent at this time as the shift from the ACRL's *Information Literacy Competency Standards for Higher Education*[25] to its *Framework for Information Literacy for Higher Education*[26] asks librarians to reconceptualize their information literacy instruction. Research questions could include:

- Looking specifically at professional development related to the *Framework*, how have issues of coherence/lack of coherence with previous practice been addressed?
- Taking the issue of coherence into account, how can programs and activities better support learning in this area?

There are broader, conceptual questions we might ask about professional development programs and activities. For one, how do we as a profession conceptualize the educational and professional development practices involved in learning to teach? The desire to learn at library school suggests widespread approval of a model where teacher knowledge and skills are transmitted through coursework lasting perhaps a semester. On-the-job programs suggest a model that involves collaboration and collegiality. What other models do we/ should we employ?

Again, what should librarians learn about teaching? This is less settled than it may once have seemed. The ACRL's *Standards for Proficiencies* document,[27] with its atomized list of skills was rescinded in 2017; it has been replaced by a document outlining the *Roles and Strengths of Teaching Librarians*.[28] What does this say about our conceptions of teacher knowledge in LIS? Do we need or want a common understanding in the profession of the teaching knowledge necessary for practice?

More broadly still, what is the purpose of our professional development programs? What are our goals, our values, our objectives? What does "improving teaching" even mean?

One way to turn these conceptual questions into research questions is to start with existing programs and activities to examine the thinking underlying their design.[29] This could involve, for example, examining the LIS literature, local professional development initiatives, or activities emanating from a professional organization, such as the ACRL. Research questions might include:

- Looking at current programs and activities, what are their goals, values, and objectives?
- What knowledge and skills are valued?
- Explicitly or implicitly, how do these programs and activities conceptualize "improved teaching?"
- Looking across different programs and activities, what patterns or trends are evident?
- What do these patterns or trends tell us about how learning to teach is conceptualized in the profession?

Researchers should probably not expect to find unified conceptions in the profession on any of these issues. They may well find a variety of conceptions that are in conflict with one another.[30] Such research, however, will allow them to map the terrain as a basis for further research and discussion.

Focusing on Professional Learning

Another way to think about how librarians learn to teach is to focus on their learning. This reflects broader trends: within higher education, the focus is shifting from teaching to learning;[31] in research on professional development, the focus is shifting from content and programs to professional learning experiences.[32]

Research on learning has demonstrated that learners are active co-constructors of knowledge, rather than passive recipients of knowledge. In addition, learners create their own understandings "based upon the interaction of what they already know and believe and the ideas with which they come into contact."[33] The importance of previous knowledge and beliefs has already been mentioned above when considering the *coherence* of a program. Librarians may feel uneasy at the use of the term *beliefs* in a professional context,[34] but in fact it is in use in a wide range of fields, together with a host of alternative or related terms such as conceptions, perspectives, values, personal theories of practice, and many more.[35] Broadly speaking, according to psychologist Bandura, "people's level of motivation, affective states, and actions are based more on what they believe than on what is objectively true."[36]

There has been extensive research in the field of education on teacher beliefs,[37] which may be defined as "teachers' implicit assumptions about students, learning, classrooms, and the subject matter to be taught."[38] Teacher beliefs play an important role in teachers' learning and development; teacher education programs often take great efforts to uncover students' prior beliefs so that these do not interfere with learning new ways of thinking about teaching.[39]

What do we already know about librarians' beliefs related to teaching? There has been little research in the area, so these beliefs may need to be inferred from the literature or from librarians' statements and actions. A fundamental question relates to the role of teaching within the profession: are teaching and learning to teach seen as important and valuable? The librarian who believes the answer is *no* may cut themselves off from professional learning in the area. Library school students often fail to take the instruction courses available to them because they do not recognize their importance and value.[40]

There are tensions between views of library instruction as skills training[41] or "point-and-click" demonstrations and views of library instruction as the teaching of concepts or critical-thinking skills.[42] Librarians may view instruction variously as a presentation,[43] as a performance,[44] or as a co-investigation with their students of "the political, social, and economic dimensions of information, including its creation, access, and use."[45]

Research questions might then include:

- What beliefs about teaching underpin librarians' teaching practices?
- What beliefs about their teaching roles underpin librarians' teaching practices?
- How do these beliefs influence how they learn to teach and how they choose and experience professional learning?
- How do beliefs about teaching develop? How do they change?

Closely related to teacher beliefs is teacher identity.[46] A number of LIS studies have investigated teacher identity in academic librarians. Through survey research, Davis,

Lundstrom and Martin find that 83 percent of their respondents (n = 245) agree or strongly agree with the statement, "I consider myself a teacher."[47] Walter, who explores teacher identity through a small narrative study, finds a strong commitment to the centrality of teaching among his participants to the point that it colors all their work. They recognize that not all librarians are equally engaged with the teaching role, however.[48] Austin and Bhandol find more ambiguity in their small-scale narrative study, conducted in the United Kingdom; they characterize their participants as variously "buying into, playing out and resisting the teacher role."[49]

Professional identity is always entwined with personal identity.[50] As Klipfel and Cook write, "*Who we are as people matters* in the context of learning."[51] Affect plays a role in librarians' views of both teaching and of themselves as teachers.[52] In addition, professional identity may be entwined with the politics of identity, with the social, historical, and political forces that shape an individual.[53]

- How does librarians' teacher identity develop? How does it change?
- How does librarians' teacher identity influence how they learn to teach and how they choose and experience professional learning?
- What role does affect play in librarians' teacher identity? What role does it play in their professional learning?
- What role do the politics of identity play in how librarians experience learning to teach?

Professional learning is experiential.[54] The actual experience of teaching is always a key part of learning to teach: "practice makes practice."[55] Librarians report both positive and negative experiences in their teaching.[56] Negative experiences may, in fact, have a greater impact on their learning as the dissonance these provoke can lead to changes in beliefs and practice.[57]

- How do librarians learn to teach through their experiences with teaching?
- How do negative teaching experiences lead to learning and change?
- What supports would help librarians turn negative experiences with teaching into learning experiences?

Teachers also come to teaching with another kind of experience: they have spent thousands of hours in the classroom as a student watching their own teachers in action; Lortie calls this "the apprenticeship of observation."[58] Faculty members, for example, often become enculturated in their discipline or profession's particular teaching methods—in what Shulman calls their signature pedagogies[59]—through observation of teaching. Librarians, on the other hand, may never have experienced information literacy instruction as a student; they lack this form of experience.

- How do librarians become enculturated in information literacy instruction?
- How do they identify and learn its signature pedagogies?
- What experiences can take the place of an "apprenticeship of learning" as a student?

Reflection is also a key component of professional learning, particularly critical reflection that questions the assumptions brought to the work.[60] The importance of reflection for practice is recognized in the LIS literature.[61]

- How does reflection on their teaching practice contribute to librarians' learning to teach?
- What supports or hinders the development of a critical reflective practice with regards to teaching?

Professional learning is always situated and mediated by context.[62] Context might include the classroom, the students, colleagues, faculty, resources (including time for professional learning), the institutional culture, the professional culture, and the broader culture.

- How do the librarians' contexts enable or constrain their teaching and their learning to teach?
- How do their contexts influence their beliefs about their teaching?
- How do librarians learn to teach through interactions with colleagues?

Professional learning for teaching happens over time.[63] For K-12 teachers, the stages of teacher learning are more formalized: there is pre-service learning (or initial education), teacher induction programs that provide support in the first year(s) of teaching (librarians will appreciate the fact that new teachers also often feel unprepared to teach), and in-service learning for practicing teachers. Librarians also have different learning needs at different stages of their career. Certainly, the most intensive learning usually takes place as librarians start to teach, often under stressful conditions, with varying levels of support.

- What supports most help new librarians in learning to teach?
- How do the learning needs of instruction librarians change over their career?
- How do their learning strategies change over their career?

Finally, professional learning is complex and holistic. Learner, context, and learning are always interrelated; professional learning is embedded in practice.[64] Attendance at an ACRL Immersion program, an interaction with a student, reading a challenging information literacy article, or a light bulb moment in the shower may all be perceived by the librarian as a significant learning experience. Webster-Wright designates this lived experience of continuing to learn as a professional as "authentic professional learning."[65]

- What do academic librarians see as their most significant learning experiences relating to teaching?
- What supports or hinders authentic professional learning?

Conclusion

For an academic librarian just starting to teach, learning to teach may be seen as a relatively simple matter: learn some techniques, maybe a bit about students and how they learn, observe some colleagues, and go. However, the more that librarians teach, the more they may realize how much there is to learn about teaching. The learning becomes an ongoing process.

Likewise, for a practitioner-researcher first researching how librarians learn to teach, the research questions may seem relatively straightforward and uncomplicated, perhaps where and what librarians learn. As the researcher digs deeper, they may realize that how librarians learn to teach is more complex than originally thought. New research questions emerge to reflect this.

Involvement in the scholarship of teaching and learning starts with asking "good questions" about people's learning. This chapter suggests a number of research questions about how academic librarians learn to teach, and there are likely many more that could be asked. They all point to one overarching question, however: What really matters to how librarians learn to teach? And from there we can ask: What does academic librarians' professional preparation for teaching tell us about what matters to the profession?

ENDNOTES

1. Eveline Houtman, "'Trying to Figure It Out': Academic Librarians Talk about Learning to Teach," *Library and Information Research* 34, no. 107 (2010): 36, http://www.cilipjournals.org. uk/ojs/index.php/lir/article/view/195 (site discontinued).

2. Jenny Hall, "Developing Teaching Best Practice—Pedagogy, Preferences, and Professional Development," *International Information and Library Review* 49, no. 1 (2017), https://doi.org/1 0.1080/10572317.2017.1270692.

3. Lee S. Shulman, "Signature Pedagogies in the Professions," *Daedalus* 134, no. 3 (2005): 52, https://doi.org/10.1162/0011526054622015.

4. Lee S. Shulman, foreword to Thomas Hatch, *Into the Classroom: Developing the Scholarship of Teaching and Learning* (San Francisco: Jossey-Bass, 2005), ix.

5. See for example Kevin Michael Klipfel and Dani Brecher Cook, *Learner-Centered Pedagogy: Principles and Practice* (Chicago: ALA Editions, 2017).

6. See for example Maria T. Accardi, Emily Drabinski, and Alana Kumbier, eds., *Critical Library Instruction: Theories and Methods* (Duluth, MN: Library Juice Press, 2010).

7. See for example Scott Walter, "Instructional Improvement: Building Capacity for the Professional Development of Librarians as Teachers," *Reference & User Services Quarterly* 45 (3), no. 3 (2006).

8. Ann Webster-Wright, "Reframing Professional Development Through Understanding Authentic Professional Learning," *Review of Educational Research* 79, no. 2 (2009), https://doi. org/10.3102/0034654308330970.

9. Association of College and Research Libraries, Instruction Section, "Research Agenda for Library Instruction and Information Literacy," accessed October 20, 2017, http://acrl.ala.org/ IS/instruction-tools-resources-2/professional-development/research-agenda-for-library-instruction-and-information-literacy/.

10. Marilyn Cochran-Smith, Sharon Feiman-Nemser, and D. John McIntyre, eds., *Handbook of Research on Teacher Education: Enduring Questions in Changing Contexts*, 3rd ed. (New York: Routledge, 2008).

11. Association of College and Research Libraries, "Standards for Proficiencies for Instruction Librarians and Coordinators," 2008, http://www.ala.org/acrl/files/standards/profstandards.pdf.

12. Theresa Westbrock and Sarah Fabian, "Proficiencies for Instruction Librarians: Is There Still a Disconnect between Professional Education and Professional Responsibilities?," *College & Research Libraries* 71, no. 6 (2010), http://crl.acrl.org/index.php/crl/article/view/16120/17566.

13. Kimberly Davies-Hoffman, Barbara Alvarez, Michelle Costello, and Debby Emerson, "Keeping Pace with Information Literacy Instruction for the Real World: When Will MLS Programs Wake up and Smell the LILACs?," *Communications in Information Literacy* 7, no. 1 (2013), http://www.comminfolit.org/index.

php?journal=cil&page=article&op=viewFile&path%5B%5D=v7i1p9&path%5B%5D=159; Heidi Julien, "Education for Information Literacy Instruction: A Global Perspective," *Journal of Education for Library & Information Science* 46, no. 3 (2005); Loyd G. Mbabu, "LIS Curricula Introducing Information Literacy Courses alongside Instructional Classes," *Journal of Education for Library & Information Science* 50, no. 3 (2009), https://www.jstor.org/stable/40732579.

14. Davies-Hoffman et al., "Keeping Pace with Information Literacy Instruction"; Hall, "Developing Teaching Best Practice."

15. Janet L. Goosney, Becky Smith, and Shannon Gordon, "Reflective Peer Mentoring: Evolution of a Professional Development Program for Academic Librarians," *Partnership: The Canadian Journal of Library and Information Practice and Research* 9, no. 1 (2014).

16. Malia Willey, "Library Instructor Development and Cultivating a Community of Practice," *Advances in Librarianship* 38 (2015), https://doi.org/10.1108/S0065-2830(2012)0000035004.

17. ACRL Instruction Section, "Research Agenda."

18. Laura M. Desimone, "Improving Impact Studies of Teachers' Professional Development: Toward Better Conceptualizations and Measures," *Educational Researcher* 38, no. 3 (April 1, 2009): 183, https://doi.org/10.3102/0013189X08331140.

19. Desimone, "Improving Impact Studies," 184.

20. Lee Shulman, "Those Who Understand: Knowledge Growth in Teaching," *Educational Researcher* 15, no. 2 (1986): 9.

21. Desimone, "Improving Impact Studies," 184.

22. Ibid.

23. Ibid.

24. Ibid.

25. Association of College and Research Libraries, *Information Literacy Competency Standards for Higher Education*, http://www.ala.org/ala/mgrps/divs/acrl/standards/standards.pdf.

26. Association of College and Research Libraries, *Framework for Information Literacy for Higher Education*, 2016, https://doi.org/10.1080/00049670.1995.10755718.

27. Association of College and Research Libraries, "Standards for Proficiencies."

28. Association of College and Research Libraries, "Roles and Strengths of Teaching Librarians," 2017, http://www.ala.org/acrl/standards/teachinglibrarians.

29. Cheryl Amundsen and Mary Wilson, "Are We Asking the Right Questions?: A Conceptual Review of the Educational Development Literature in Higher Education," *Review of Educational Research* 82, no. 1 (2012), https://www.jstor.org/stable/41408679.

30. Gloria Dall'Alba and Jörgen Sandberg, "Educating for Competence in Professional Practice," *Instructional Science* 24, no. 6 (1996).

31. Paul Ramsden, *Learning to Teach in Higher Education*, 2nd ed. (London, UK: RoutledgeFalmer, 2003).

32. Webster-Wright, "Reframing Professional Development."

33. Virginia Richardson and Peggy Placier, "Teacher Change," in *Handbook of Research on Teaching*, ed. Virginia Richardson, 4th ed. (Washington, DC: American Educational Research Association, 2001), 916.

34. Amy VanScoy, "Reference Librarians' Personal Theories of Practice: A New Approach to Studying Reference Service," in *Creating the Reference Renaissance: Current & Future Trends*, ed. M. L. Radford and R. D. Lankes (New York: Neal-Schuman, 2010), http://www.amyvanscoy.net/uploads/5/7/7/9/5779319/vanscoy_refren_chapter_6.pdf.

35. M. Frank Pajares, "Teachers' Beliefs and Educational Research: Cleaning up a Messy Construct," *Review of Educational Research* 62, no. 3 (January 1, 1992), https://doi.org/10.3102/00346543062003307.

36. Albert Bandura, *Self-Efficacy: The Exercise of Control* (New York: W.H. Freeman, 1997), 2.

37. See for example Helenrose Fives and Michele Gregoire Gill, eds., *International Handbook of Research on Teachers' Beliefs* (New York: Routledge, 2015).

38. Dona M. Kagan, "Implications of Research on Teacher Belief," *Educational Psychologist* 27, no. 1 (1992): 66, https://doi.org/10.1207/s15326985ep2701_6.

39. Virginia Richardson, "The Role of Attitudes and Beliefs in Learning to Teach," in *Handbook of Research on Teacher Education*, ed. J. Sikula, 2nd ed. (New York: Macmillan, 1996).

40. Davies-Hoffman et al., "Keeping Pace with Information Literacy Instruction."

41. Emily Wheeler and Pamela McKinney, "Are Librarians Teachers? Investigating Academic Librarians' Perceptions of Their Own Teaching Roles," *Journal of Information Literacy* 9, no. 2 (2015), https://doi.org/10.11645/9.2.1985.

42. Troy A. Swanson and Heather Jagman, eds., *Not Just Where to Click: Teaching Students How to Think about Information* (Chicago: Association of College and Research Libraries, 2015).

43. Houtman, "'Trying to Figure it Out.'"

44. Julia Furay, "Stages of Instruction: Theatre, Pedagogy and Information Literacy," *Reference Services Review* 42, no. 2 (June 3, 2014), https://doi.org/10.1108/RSR-09-2013-0047.

45. Eamon Tewell, "Putting Critical Information Literacy into Context: How and Why Librarians Adopt Critical Practices in Their Teaching," *In the Library with the Lead Pipe*, 2016, http://www.inthelibrarywiththeleadpipe.org/2016/putting-critical-information-literacy-into-context-how-and-why-librarians-adopt-critical-practices-in-their-teaching/.

46. Carol R. Rodgers and Katherine H. Scott, "The Development of the Personal Self and Professional Identity in Learning to Teach," in *Handbook of Research on Teacher Education: Enduring Questions in Changing Contexts*, ed. Marilyn Cochran-Smith, Sharon Feiman-Nemser, and D. John McIntyre, 3rd ed. (New York: Routledge, 2008).

47. Erin Davis, Kacy Lundstrom, and Pamela N. Martin, "Librarian Perceptions and Information Literacy Instruction Models," *Reference Services Review* 39, no. 4 (2011): 691, https://doi.org/10.1108/00907321111186695.

48. Scott Walter, "Librarians as Teachers: A Qualitative Inquiry into Professional Identity," *College & Research Libraries* 69, no. 1 (2008), http://crl.acrl.org/content/69/1/51.short.

49. Trevor Austin and Janine Bhandol, "The Academic Librarian: Buying Into, Playing Out, and Resisting the Teacher Role in Higher Education," *New Review of Academic Librarianship* 19, no. 1 (January 2013): 15, https://doi.org/10.1080/13614533.2012.740438.

50. Rodgers and Scott, "The Development of the Personal Self."

51. Klipfel and Cook, *Learner-Centered Pedagogy*, xv. Emphasis in the original.

52. Kaetrena Davis, "The Academic Librarian as Instructor: A Study of Teacher Anxiety," *College & Undergraduate Libraries* 14, no. 2 (2007), https://doi.org/10.1300/J106v14n02_06; Heidi Julien and Shelagh K. Genuis, "Emotional Labour in Librarians' Instructional Work," *Journal of Documentation* 65, no. 6 (2009), https://doi.org/10.1108/00220410910998924.

53. Rodgers and Scott, "The Development of the Personal Self." See also Jorge R. Lopez-McKnight, "My Librarianship Is Not for You," in *Topographies of Whiteness: Mapping Whiteness in Library and Information Studies*, ed. Gina Schlesselman-Tarango (Sacramento, CA: Library Juice Press, 2017).

54. Webster-Wright, "Reframing Professional Development."

55. Deborah P. Britzman, *Practice Makes Practice: A Critical Study of Learning to Teach*, rev. ed. (Albany, NY: State University of New York Press, 2003).

56. Julien and Genius, "Emotional Labour."

57. V. Darleen Opfer and David Pedder, "Conceptualizing Teacher Professional Learning," *Review of Educational Research* 81, no. 3 (July 21, 2011), https://doi.org/10.3102/0034654311413609.

58. Dan C. Lortie, *Schoolteacher: A Sociological Study* (Chicago: University of Chicago Press, 1975), 61.

59. Shulman, "Signature Pedagogies," 52.
60. Webster-Wright, "Reframing Professional Development."
61. Michelle Reale, *Becoming a Reflective Librarian and Teacher: Strategies for Mindful Academic Practice* (Chicago: ALA Editions, 2017).
62. Webster-Wright, "Reframing Professional Development."
63. Sharon Feiman-Nemser, "Teacher Learning: How Do Teachers Learn to Teach?," in *Handbook of Research on Teacher Education: Enduring Questions in Changing Contexts*, ed. Marilyn Cochran-Smith, Sharon Feiman-Nemser, and D. John McIntyre. New York: Routledge, 2008.
64. Webster-Wright, "Reframing Professional Development."
65. Ibid., 705.

BIBLIOGRAPHY

Accardi, Maria T., Emily Drabinski, and Alana Kumbier, eds. *Critical Library Instruction: Theories and Methods*. Duluth, MN: Library Juice Press, 2010.

Amundsen, Cheryl, and Mary Wilson. "Are We Asking the Right Questions?: A Conceptual Review of the Educational Development Literature in Higher Education." *Review of Educational Research* 82, no. 1 (February 21, 2012): 90–126. https://www.jstor.org/stable/41408679.

Association of College and Research Libraries. *Information Literacy Competency Standards for Higher Education*, 2000. http://www.ala.org/ala/mgrps/divs/acrl/standards/standards.pdf.

———. "Standards for Proficiencies for Instruction Librarians and Coordinators," 2008. http://www.ala.org/acrl/files/standards/profstandards.pdf.

———. *Framework for Information Literacy for Higher Education*. 2016. https://doi.org/10.1080/000 49670.1995.10755718.

———. "Roles and Strengths of Teaching Librarians," 2017. http://www.ala.org/acrl/standards/teachinglibrarians.

———. Instruction Section. "Research Agenda for Library Instruction and Information Literacy." Accessed October 20, 2017. http://acrl.ala.org/IS/instruction-tools-resources-2/professional-development/research-agenda-for-library-instruction-and-information-literacy/.

Austin, Trevor, and Janine Bhandol. "The Academic Librarian: Buying Into, Playing Out, and Resisting the Teacher Role in Higher Education." *New Review of Academic Librarianship* 19, no. 1 (January 2013): 15–35. https://doi.org/10.1080/13614533.2012.740438.

Bandura, Albert. *Self-Efficacy: The Exercise of Control*. New York: W.H. Freeman, 1997.

Britzman, Deborah P. *Practice Makes Practice: A Critical Study of Learning to Teach*. Rev. Albany, NY: State University of New York Press, 2003.

Cochran-Smith, Marilyn, Sharon Feiman-Nemser, and D. John McIntyre, eds. *Handbook of Research on Teacher Education: Enduring Questions in Changing Contexts*. 3rd ed. New York: Routledge, 2008.

Dall'Alba, Gloria, and Jörgen Sandberg. "Educating for Competence in Professional Practice." *Instructional Science* 24, no. 6 (1996): 411–37.

Davies-Hoffman, Kimberly, Barbara Alvarez, Michelle Costello, and Debby Emerson. "Keeping Pace with Information Literacy Instruction for the Real World: When Will MLS Programs Wake up and Smell the LILACs?" *Communications in Information Literacy* 7, no. 1 (2013): 9–23. http://www.comminfolit.org/index.php?journal=cil&page=article&op=viewFile&path%5B%5D=v7i1p9&path%5B%5D=159.

Davis, Erin L., Kacy Lundstrom, and Pamela N. Martin. "Librarian Perceptions and Information Literacy Instruction Models." *Reference Services Review* 39, no. 4 (2011): 686–702. https://doi.org/10.1108/00907321111186695.

Davis, Kaetrena. "The Academic Librarian as Instructor: A Study of Teacher Anxiety." *College & Undergraduate Libraries* 14, no. 2 (2007): 1–24. https://doi.org/10.1300/J106v14n02_06.

Desimone, Laura M. "Improving Impact Studies of Teachers' Professional Development: Toward Better Conceptualizations and Measures." *Educational Researcher* 38, no. 3 (April 1, 2009): 181–99. https://doi.org/10.3102/0013189X08331140.

Feiman-Nemser, Sharon. "Teacher Learning: How Do Teachers Learn to Teach?" In *Handbook of Research on Teacher Education: Enduring Questions in Changing Contexts*, edited by Marilyn Cochran-Smith, Sharon Feiman-Nemser, and D. John McIntyre. New York: Routledge, 2008.

Fives, Helenrose, and Michele Gregoire Gill, eds. *International Handbook of Research on Teachers' Beliefs*. New York: Routledge, 2015.

Furay, Julia. "Stages of Instruction: Theatre, Pedagogy and Information Literacy." *Reference Services Review* 42, no. 2 (June 3, 2014): 209–28. https://doi.org/10.1108/RSR-09-2013-0047.

Goosney, Janet L., Becky Smith, and Shannon Gordon. "Reflective Peer Mentoring: Evolution of a Professional Development Program for Academic Librarians." *Partnership: The Canadian Journal of Library and Information Practice and Research* 9, no. 1 (2014): 1–24.

Hall, Jenny. "Developing Teaching Best Practice—Pedagogy, Preferences, and Professional Development." *International Information and Library Review* 49, no. 1 (2017): 59–64. https://doi.org/10.1080/10572317.2017.1270692.

Houtman, Eveline. "'Trying to Figure It Out': Academic Librarians Talk about Learning to Teach." *Library and Information Research* 34, no. 107 (2010): 18–40. http://www.cilipjournals.org.uk/ojs/index.php/lir/article/view/195 (site discontinued).

Julien, Heidi. "Education for Information Literacy Instruction: A Global Perspective." *Journal of Education for Library & Information Science* 46, no. 3 (2005): 210–16.

Julien, Heidi, and Shelagh K. Genuis. "Emotional Labour in Librarians' Instructional Work." *Journal of Documentation* 65, no. 6 (2009): 926–37. https://doi.org/10.1108/00220410910998924.

Kagan, Dona M. "Implications of Research on Teacher Belief." *Educational Psychologist* 27, no. 1 (1992): 65–90. https://doi.org/10.1207/s15326985ep2701_6.

Klipfel, Kevin Michael, and Dani Brecher Cook. *Learner-Centered Pedagogy: Principles and Practice.* Chicago: ALA Editions, 2017.

Lopez-McKnight, Jorge R. "My Librarianship Is Not for You." In *Topographies of Whiteness: Mapping Whiteness in Library and Information Studies*, edited by Gina Schlesselman-Tarango, 261–70. Sacramento, CA: Library Juice Press, 2017.

Lortie, Dan C. *Schoolteacher: A Sociological Study*. Chicago: University of Chicago Press, 1975.

Mbabu, Loyd G. "LIS Curricula Introducing Information Literacy Courses alongside Instructional Classes." *Journal of Education for Library & Information Science* 50, no. 3 (2009): 203–10. https://www.jstor.org/stable/40732579.

Opfer, V. Darleen, and David Pedder. "Conceptualizing Teacher Professional Learning." *Review of Educational Research* 81, no. 3 (July 21, 2011): 376–407. https://doi.org/10.3102/0034654311413609.

Pajares, M. Frank. "Teachers' Beliefs and Educational Research: Cleaning up a Messy Construct." *Review of Educational Research* 62, no. 3 (January 1, 1992): 307–32. https://doi.org/10.3102/00346543062003307.

Ramsden, Paul. *Learning to Teach in Higher Education*. 2nd ed. London, UK: RoutledgeFalmer, 2003.

Reale, Michelle. *Becoming a Reflective Librarian and Teacher: Strategies for Mindful Academic Practice*. Chicago: ALA Editions, 2017.

Richardson, Virginia, and Peggy Placier. "Teacher Change." In *Handbook of Research on Teaching*, edited by Virginia Richardson, 4th ed., 905–47. Washington, DC: American Educational Research Association, 2001.

Rodgers, Carol R., and Katherine H. Scott. "The Development of the Personal Self and Professional Identity in Learning to Teach." In *Handbook of Research on Teacher Education: Enduring Questions in Changing Contexts*, edited by Marilyn Cochran-Smith, Sharon Feiman-Nemser, and D. John McIntyre, 3rd ed., 732–55. New York: Routledge, 2008.

Shulman, Lee S. Foreword to *Into the Classroom: Developing the Scholarship of Teaching and Learning*, vii–x. San Francisco, CA: Jossey-Bass, 2005.

———. "Signature Pedagogies in the Professions." *Daedalus* 134, no. 3 (2005): 52–59. https://doi.org/10.1162/0011526054622015.

———. "Those Who Understand: Knowledge Growth in Teaching." *Educational Researcher* 15, no. 2 (1986): 4–14.

Swanson, Troy A., and Heather Jagman, eds. *Not Just Where to Click: Teaching Students How to Think about Information*. Chicago: Association of College and Research Libraries, 2015.

Tewell, Eamon. "Putting Critical Information Literacy into Context: How and Why Librarians Adopt Critical Practices in Their Teaching." *In the Library with the Lead Pipe*, 2016. http://www.inthelibrarywiththeleadpipe.org/2016/putting-critical-information-literacy-into-context-how-and-why-librarians-adopt-critical-practices-in-their-teaching/.

VanScoy, Amy. "Reference Librarians' Personal Theories of Practice: A New Approach to Studying Reference Service." In *Creating the Reference Renaissance: Current & Future Trends*, edited by M. L. Radford and R. D. Lankes, 115–28. New York: Neal-Schuman, 2010. http://www.amyvanscoy.net/uploads/5/7/7/9/5779319/vanscoy_refren_chapter_6.pdf.

Walter, Scott. "Instructional Improvement: Building Capacity for the Professional Development of Librarians as Teachers." *Reference & User Services Quarterly* 45 (3), no. 3 (2006): 213–18.

———. "Librarians as Teachers: A Qualitative Inquiry into Professional Identity." *College & Research Libraries* 69, no. 1 (2008): 51–71. http://crl.acrl.org/content/69/1/51.short.

Webster-Wright, Ann. "Reframing Professional Development Through Understanding Authentic Professional Learning." *Review of Educational Research* 79, no. 2 (2009): 702–39. https://doi.org/10.3102/0034654308330970.

Westbrock, Theresa, and Sarah Fabian. "Proficiencies for Instruction Librarians: Is There Still a Disconnect between Professional Education and Professional Responsibilities?" *College & Research Libraries* 71, no. 6 (2010): 569–90. http://crl.acrl.org/index.php/crl/article/view/16120/17566.

Wheeler, Emily, and Pamela McKinney. "Are Librarians Teachers? Investigating Academic Librarians' Perceptions of Their Own Teaching Roles." *Journal of Information Literacy* 9, no. 2 (2015): 111–28. https://doi.org/10.11645/9.2.1985.

Willey, Malia. "Library Instructor Development and Cultivating a Community of Practice." *Advances in Librarianship* 38 (2015): 83–100. https://doi.org/10.1108/S0065-2830(2012)0000035004.

3

Scholarship of Teaching and Learning and Transfer of Information Literacy Skills

Rebecca Kuglitsch and Lindsay Roberts

Introduction

One of O'Brien's four points of reference that form a compass for navigating SoTL is "What will my students learn, and why is it worth learning?" If information literacy (IL) instructors apply the second part of this question, most would say that it is so that students can critically participate in scholarship, their careers, and their personal lives.[1] Another point on O'Brien's compass asks, "How do I know if my teaching and students' learning has been effective?" If librarians are successful in their teaching, students will transfer skills from the library classroom to work and personal contexts. Thus, an understanding of transfer theory enhances IL scholarship of teaching and learning.

Classic transfer theory describes the application of knowledge from one context to another after a new skill is learned.[2] This kind of transfer is often thought of as aligning with two sets of concepts:

- Low road and high road transfer
  - o low road—engaging automatic behaviors and adjustments to routine knowledge or activities
  - o high road—which requires "mindful abstraction of skill or knowledge from one context for application in another"[3]
- Near and far transfer
  - o near transfer—transfer when contexts share visible similarities
  - o far transfer—in which transfer occurs between different contexts

Typically, but not invariably, near transfer and low road transfer are aligned, while far transfer and high road transfer are aligned. For successful transfer of IL, instructors would want to encourage high road and far transfer in particular. But even as many IL instructors

appreciate the importance of this, implementing teaching strategies that promote transfer can be a challenge.

By broadening IL focus from procedural skills to foundational concepts, the Association of College and Research Libraries' (ACRL) *Framework for Information Literacy for Higher Education* primed the authors to address some of these challenges, build teaching practices by integrating active learning, and consider how to promote transfer of learning.[4] Specifically for the authors, the ACRL *Framework* sparked discussion of IL issues that both supersede and contain disciplinary concerns, as transfer theory recommends. The ACRL *Framework* also addresses the affective side of IL, suggesting a way to talk about IL as an opportunity to engage in curiosity, persistence, and joyful inquiry, qualities that are often assumed to be tacitly understood by experts but not always discussed with students. Moreover, it explicitly calls for a special emphasis on metacognition, aligning with the emphasis on metacognition in transfer theory.[5] Thus, the authors find similarities between priorities in the *Framework* and transfer theory that can promote transfer of IL skills.

As illustrated in table 3.1, this case study draws from literature related to transfer theory, workplace learning, and the authors' challenges and opportunities of teaching IL for transferring learning to answer the following questions: How can IL instructors situate transfer theory, metacognition, and workplace learning within the specialized context of pedagogical content knowledge (PCK) for IL? How can they encourage the transfer of IL skills across disciplinary boundaries and into applied contexts? What specific classroom practices that can extend classroom interactions help learners use IL skills within their applied contexts and cultivate a mindset and affect for transferring IL strategies to contexts beyond a specific course assignment or one-shot session?

Table 3.1. Themes that Enhance Transfer

Preparation for Learning	Active Learning	Metacognition & Reflection	Social Learning
Transfer requires a solid understanding of initial material (National Research Council, 1999)	Solving problems over memorizing facts; learning with understanding vs. procedural knowledge (Bransford and Schwartz, 1999, p. 64)	Mindful abstraction, identifying general principles from specific situations (high road). (Salomon and Perkins 1989, p. 124-5; National Research Council, 1999; Barber, 2012; Billing, 2007)	Invite conversations with students which can foster reflection (Barber, 2012)
Actively bridge contexts for and with students (Barber, 2012)	Extensive and varied practice (low road). (Salomon and Perkins, 1989, p 124) Knowledge taught in multiple contexts is more transferable (National Research Council, 1999)	Strategy training with metacognitive reflection (Billing, 2007, p. 508; Perkins and Salomon, 1988)	Teach within a social context. Students can practice explaining their learning to other students (Billing, 2007, p. 509-511)

Preparation for Learning	Active Learning	Metacognition & Reflection	Social Learning
Concrete examples boost relevance (Bransford and Schwartz, 1999, p. 64)	Problem-based or project-based learning strategies (Bransford and Schwartz, 1999, p. 64)	Use modeling and coaching to encourage meta-cognitive skills (Billing,2007, p. 509)	Teacher appreciation of prior knowledge facilitates transfer (Bransford and Schwartz, 1999, p.83; National Research Council, 1999)
Transfer occurs based on prior knowledge; (National Research Council, 1999)	Show specific skills, activities, and dispositions in context (without overemphasizing context) (Billing, 2007, p. 509)	Promote perspective taking (ask students to consciously imagine the perspectives and viewpoints of others) (Barber, 2012)	Collaboration among librarians and teachers, including discussing transfer across the institution (Herring and Bush, 2009)
Show underlying rules or principles (Billing, 2007p. 509); worked or partly worked examples reduce cognitive load, expose underlying principles (Billing, 2007p. 510)	Help students create their own systems/ models, helpful tools, and shortcuts (such as their own aids for math charts) (Bransford and Schwartz, 1999, p. 82)	Encourage students to set their own learning goals, encourage mastery goal orientation; sub-goals help students chunk and be less overwhelmed (Billing, 2007, p. 508)	Suggest students seek out others' opinions and feedback to challenge/improve models (Billing, 2007, p. 82-83)
Emphasize similar structures using bridging analogies (Billing, 2007, p. 510)	Use "schema-oriented questions to foster abstraction of a principle or problem schema from examples" (Billing, 2007, p. 509)	Feedback (different from advice) can allow students to "infer a general strategy themselves" (Billing, 2007, p. 511)	"Teaching knowledge transformation, rather than knowledge telling" (Billing, 2007, p. 511)

Teaching Recommendations

Over decades of teaching and learning scholarship on transfer (see table 3.1), scholars consistently identify several themes as promoting transfer. These include abstraction of ideas and concepts, metacognition, activation of prior knowledge, and active learning. Drawing on this literature and the authors' own teaching experiences, the following proposes three opportunities for IL instructors to experiment and encourage transfer of learning within the particular PCK of information literacy: cultivating dispositions that foster exploration and iteration, active learning, and stimulating metacognitive abilities. Table 3.2 lists specific examples linking transfer practices to pedagogical content knowledge for information literacy.

Table 3.2. Examples of Pedagogical Content Knowledge

Preparation for Learning	Active Learning	Metacognition & Reflection	Social Learning
Ask students to list ways information literacy skills can be or have been used in daily life or beyond their assignment: How do they find information for a significant purpose? How does someone become an authority on something they're passionate about, like trance music or snowboarding?	Problem-based or real-world scenarios, e.g., background research on community partner organization for leadership project; how to find information from stakeholders in an assessment of community environmental needs and concerns	Encourage students to consider voices missing from the conversation, such as perspectives and needs of African teachers during a discussion of solutions for education quality in African schools, or how a lack of attention to user experience could result in engineering failure.	Ask students to discuss strategies they used and places they got stuck the last time they had an assignment using outside sources. How might these strategies be useful to their peers in the current context?
Use case studies and real-world examples of IL problems (such as attribution of song samples in pop music, writing informational pamphlets for a protest event, or building something based on a design inspiration).	Encourage students to map or diagram their research process and current understandings of topics.	Incorporate metacognitive questions such as "What will your next step need to be for this project?" to encourage reflection and self-awareness.	Ask students to work in small groups to compare pros/cons of different search tools for a bilingual education project, then report to the larger group.
Boost student activation of prior knowledge of IL concepts and tools such as comparing database filters to online shopping sites.	Ask students to explore one or two tools and identify underlying principles.	Suggest that students choose a particular goal for the session or project, such as "Learn 3 strategies for narrowing search results effectively."	Ask students to trade their keyword or mind-mapping exercises with another student or group for additional ideas and troubleshooting.
Highlight similarities between structures, e.g., controlled vocabulary on many websites as well as library tools.		Attend final presentations or incorporate a reflection component into assignments asking students what went well, what could go better, and what they learned.	

Cultivating Dispositions that Foster Exploration and Iteration

Encouraging students to cultivate a sense of play, persistence, and curiosity can help engage and reinforce positive information searching schemas and strategies. For example, when Roberts discusses evaluating search results with students, she encourages students to look for patterns in highlighted or bolded search results as a way of understanding the underlying organization of information. This type of troubleshooting helps students learn to look more carefully at their search terms and learn to iterate based on what results show, encouraging shared problem-solving and a playful seeking mentality. Learning strategies to improve searches and receive more desirable results helps build a positive feedback loop for solving puzzles. Librarians can apply their PCK by developing the scaffolding and modeling that helps students recognize patterns and organizing structures they will later independently develop.[6]

A strategic approach to problem-solving and search strategies requires adaptability. For instance, both the authors encourage students to recognize discipline-specific vocabulary or source types prioritized in their discipline and to tailor their strategies to those specific norms. Over time, problem-solving abilities are more beneficial to students than procedural or fact-based knowledge.[7] As Project Information Literacy identified among recent college graduates, there was often a disconnect between students' perceptions of their search abilities and sources used in the field, compared to the strategies and sources employers wanted students to use.[8]

In early transfer research, teaching strategies to encourage transfer such as "hugging" and "bridging" were proposed, where hugging emphasizes similar situations to encourage low road transfer and bridging aims to teach for high road transfer by explicitly encouraging students to abstract the skills to other problems or situations.[9] These bridging examples can be especially productive and engaging when they activate prior knowledge. A library instructor might ask students to consider when, in their personal lives, they have searched strategically, knowing what they want and identifying key resources to get it, or when they have searched serendipitously, discovering an information source by chance and then building on it. This can be deployed in more academic contexts, as well. For example, Kuglitsch has explicitly discussed the difference between a workplace engineering environment and an academic engineering environment, asking students to identify similarities and differences in contextual pressures or expectations and consequently information seeking. Bridging the work world of engineering, which many students are familiar with from internships, with the academic world can help students understand not just the requirements in each but the reasons underlying them, increasing the ability to transfer assessment of information priorities in multiple contexts. As a point of motivation, research suggests that engineers who engage with the literature of their field most intensively tend to be recognized as experts and gatekeepers in their organizations.[10]

Additionally, helping students build schemas or deeper understandings of their fields' information practices and sources may assist students in critically synthesizing sources and viewpoints.[11] With graduate students, Roberts often teaches literature review matrices as a visual way of organizing information and building mental maps of viewpoints and methodologies within students' fields, effectively creating their own schemas. These visual organizers help students with the Scholarship as a Conversation frame as they summarize, contrast, identify gaps, and begin to participate through their own contribution to the conversation. Kuglitsch often uses mind mapping to help students contextualize their research questions, explore smaller branches of a topic, and bring questions together to form new research questions, visualizing the concepts of Research as Inquiry. This visualization can help students who may struggle to see how they can contribute new knowledge on the relatively small scale of a term paper.

Finally, a focus on play and process helps normalize challenges for students and balances the affective struggles of information-seeking. Lowering the stakes may reduce library anxiety and allow students to more effectively process large amounts of information.[12] When working with graduate students, Roberts uses PCK to talk openly about the highs and lows of Kuhlthau's Information Search Process and includes affective questions to help students reflect on their search processes and expectations.[13]

Within applied contexts, such as engineering, business, healthcare, and other fields, library research can be integrated with design to cultivate playful, flexible, and inquiry-based team environments. Through a group of researchers on campus, Roberts has seen an innovative way of creating this type of environment: high school students learn to construct infographics that communicate science concepts and consider credibility, reliability, and ethics in working with data sources. Their infographics may ultimately be shared publicly so that students get to participate in science journalism as they learn science concepts.[14] Fosmire and Radcliffe propose an Information Rich Design Model for engineering that interweaves the information-seeking process throughout the design experience quite explicitly, tying the model to concerns of engineering quality, creativity, and ethics.[15] Table 3.1 strategies for "Preparation for Learning" and "Social Learning" can help support the suggestions in this case study and give further IL-specific examples of PCK for these ideas.

Active Learning

Active learning opportunities, including problem-based learning, design thinking, and hands-on scenarios, are thought to help students connect abstract concepts with real-world application and context.[16] In terms of PCK for IL instructors, this might take the form of librarians embedding in practicum or capstone experiences or acting as consultants to project teams.[17] Roberts has developed a partnership with a capstone leadership class where students serve as consultants to community-based non-profits. Roberts works with classes to identify what they already know about their organizations and stimulate question posing that help identify gaps in their knowledge. Roberts then facilitates group work where students consider the context of their community organization and related groups with shared missions or similar practices at the local and national levels from whom they can learn. Next, teams spend time searching for information using advanced Google search techniques to find strategic planning documents or trends in their industry as well as trade publications and scholarly best practices through library databases. Because these sessions are grounded in real-world information needs, students see the relevance of searching for information and have specific contexts with which to apply search strategies and techniques.

Another active learning strategy that works well in the information literacy classroom is to demonstrate an example of concepts in one specific context, and then ask students to work through the problem in another. For example, the instructor might discuss assessing the trustworthiness of a news story and developing criteria for credibility, then ask students to develop and apply criteria for an analogous, yet different situation for far transfer. This might be evaluating children's nonfiction books for a second-grade reading buddy or assessing the evidence for an unsettled scientific question, like nutrition guidelines.

Learning by teaching is an approach that can be incorporated into both longer and shorter instruction sessions and can mirror the kind of on-the-job learning students will experience in internships or as entry-level employees.[18] Kuglitsch has asked students to form small teams, explore an information source, and then return to the larger group, with each team then teaching the rest of the class about the kinds of questions the source can help answer, how to use the source, and what aspects of the source are similar to or different from more familiar sources like Google or Wikipedia. This team learning and teaching approach has also worked well when asking students to analyze the way authors use citations in academic papers: a group might analyze who is cited and why in a methods section, an introduction, and a discussion section and then teach that out to the rest of the class. Students have been engaged and eager to compare their area of authority with others'. When these scenarios are performed fully in class, they typically take most of the session, but when a class is even shorter than the typical one-shot, the team learning could be assigned as preparatory work, perhaps taking place in an online learning environment.

In a one-shot, short problem-based learning "warm-up" scenarios that take advantage of librarian PCK can help students remember the real-world value of IL skills, even when their academic assignment may be more limited. For instance, Roberts has used problem-based scenarios around stakeholders in public education (teachers, parents, principals, policymakers) to help students consider authority and access to information in the education field, as well as to begin to differentiate between types of education sources and information needs. Kuglitsch has found the same approach to be effective in environmental science and engineering design contexts.

Librarian office hours held near a lab or work location can also help promote point-of-need assistance, as Roberts has seen with her liaison department by holding office hours inside the education building. Students, staff, and faculty often stop to say hello, then casually discuss specific projects or information needs. Proximity and low-stakes conversations both seem to facilitate these interactions. Kuglitsch has presented research consultations for students in engineering as consultations with a subject-matter expert, an approach familiar to the discipline, where the subject, in this case, is finding information. Table 3.1 suggestions for "Active Learning" can support the recommendations in this section.

Providing Opportunities for Metacognition and Reflection

Metacognitive reflection fosters transfer of IL skills, as seen in table 3.1. Metacognition, an umbrella term, describes the practice of reflection, self-monitoring, and awareness of opportunities for transfer, among other features.[19] Salomon and Perkins indicate that without metacognitive awareness and thoughtful abstraction, far or high road transfer may be impossible.[20]

Reframing earlier views of transfer, Bransford and Schwartz advocate for a "preparation for learning" view to adapt students' knowledge to new situations and build or discard mental schemas.[21] This view of transfer supports students' use of metacognitive strategies to monitor and reflect on their progress, with support from experts who can provide feedback and additional perspective on gaps in knowledge and growth.[22]

In terms of PCK within library instruction, this can be promoted in several ways. A library instructor might suggest that students choose a particular goal for the session or project, such as "Learn three strategies for narrowing search results effectively." Incorporating explicit reflection time, asking students to explain to others, or promoting "think aloud" during searching provide an opportunity to open the conversation. Kuglitsch models her search thought process, for example, taking particular care to highlight connections with other information seeking situations: e.g., noting that she is not finding as many results as hoped for, but that in other situations, modifying search terms and experimenting helped her find a productive search strategy. Or she might choose to highlight the idea that primary sources are those produced by a person experiencing a situation by comparing historical primary sources with scientific primary sources.

Though modeling metacognition is useful, it is also important to provide opportunities for students to draw genuine connections using their own frame of reference. Kuglitsch also uses think-pair-share activities in which students are asked to connect current experiences to past experiences, or explicitly to connect the session experience with their desired future experiences, as a way to derive general principles, and increase motivation. If faculty are amenable, embedding a reflection component into assignments can be a venue as well, as both Roberts and Kuglitsch have done.

In all of these situations, providing feedback is more useful than advice or criticism. Billing notes that feedback rather than criticism, in particular, can encourage students to construct guidelines and mental models for themselves rather than relying on the frameworks provided by instructors and leading to more authentic transfer.[23] Feedback also offers an opportunity to support positive transfer and realign unhelpful transfers.

Encouraging engagement over time, before, during, and after library instruction is a powerful strategy for promoting reflection, keeping libraries in the minds of students and faculty, and promoting transfer.[24] This extended engagement poses some unique challenges for librarians teaching primarily one-shot sessions, but several tactics can be used to overcome these challenges. Roberts and Kuglitsch frequently conduct pre-session surveys to elicit students' past information needs, behaviors, and experiences. This not only helps librarians prepare more relevant lessons, it also activates prior knowledge. Faculty commitment allows more intensive but still manageable approaches: embedding librarians into the course LMS, so they can continue to engage students around the research experience; returning to visit classes for short discussions around research experiences at different stages in the research process, as Roberts has done; engaging faculty to integrate IL reflections and prompts into their regular instructional practices after a one-shot, as both Roberts and Kuglitsch do regularly. All of these approaches encourage reflection before and after the session, consolidating and promoting transfer.

Another option for engagement over time is by attending final presentations, poster sessions, or simulations of professional presentations. Engaging with students as they present final projects provides an opportunity to ask students to reflect on their process, closing the loop from finding to using information. For students in applied fields, this can be an opportunity to connect the tools, processes, and concepts they have learned in class to potential future work situations.

Discussion and Conclusion

By encouraging reflection in the classroom, IL instructors are engaging in PCK, bringing IL full circle in students' experiences, and tying IL to past experience and future plans. An attention to future IL needs and potential experiences, such as workplace IL practices in students' chosen fields, can help students understand IL instruction as a meaningful experience and encourage habits of mind that will promote future growth, especially when taught using active learning methods that encourage reflection and iteration. As discussed in the teaching recommendations for cultivating dispositions that foster exploration and iteration, librarians engage in PCK by framing IL instruction in the language of the discipline, presenting abstract structures and patterns that simultaneously both catch and promote student interest. To position students to succeed at exploring their own interests in the workplace—and academically—it is necessary for students to develop an ability and willingness to recognize patterns and the structures that underlie information. Such abilities form a strategic approach as well as the disposition to flexibly explore and adapt to new information landscapes. Teaching to these underlying structures is more effective in promoting transfer—and more engaging for students as well as librarians.

Grounding these structures in lived experience and hoped-for futures can bring the affective side of IL into play as well. Intellectual transfer of IL is important to ground students' future lifelong learning, but addressing the affective side of IL is key to fostering the habits and choices that encourage students to not only be capable of learning but to actively seek it out, an aspect of PCK that can be addressed by providing opportunities for metacognition and reflection. What use is an extensive intellectual understanding of the idea that research is inquiry to create new knowledge—whether in an academic context a or a personal quest—if a student is deterred by the discomfort of seeking out, synthesizing, and creating that knowledge? When librarians teach their unique knowledge of the affective information search process, they help students understand that discomfort is part of the process rather than a personal flaw, fostering student persistence. Using active learning to explore affective and cognitive aspects of IL is a prime example of PCK within the scope of library instructors. By teaching to normalize the affective aspects of IL, research and learning, librarians can give students the tools they need to build their own futures creatively and wholeheartedly.

ENDNOTES

1. Mia O'Brien, "Navigating the SoTL Landscape: A Compass, Map and Some Tools for Getting Started," *International Journal for the Scholarship of Teaching and Learning* 2, no. 2 (July 1, 2008), https://doi.org/10.20429/ijsotl.2008.020215.
2. David Billing, "Teaching for Transfer of Core/Key Skills in Higher Education: Cognitive Skills," *Higher Education* 53, no. 4 (April 1, 2007): 483–516, https://doi.org/10.1007/s10734-005-5628-5.
3. David N. Perkins and Gavriel Salomon, "Teaching for Transfer," *Educational Leadership* 46, no. 1 (1988): 25.
4. Association of College & Research Libraries, *Framework for Information Literacy for Higher Education* (Chicago: American Library Association, 2016), http://www.ala.org/acrl/standards/ilframework.
5. Association of College & Research Libraries, *Framework*, 2–3.
6. James E. Herring and Stephanie J. Bush, "Information Literacy and Transfer in Schools: Implications for Teacher Librarians," *The Australian Library Journal* 60, no. 2 (May 1, 2011): 123–32, https://doi.org/10.1080/00049670.2011.10722584.
7. John D. Bransford and Daniel L. Schwartz, "Rethinking Transfer: A Simple Proposal with Multiple Implications," *Review of Research in Education* 24 (1999): 64, https://doi.org/10.2307/1167267.
8. Alison J. Head, "Learning Curve: How College Graduates Solve Information Problems Once They Join the Workplace," *Project Information Literacy Research Report*, 2012, 1–38, https://doi.org/10.2139/ssrn.2165031.
9. Perkins and Salomon, "Teaching for Transfer," 28.
10. Carol Tenopir and Donald Ward King, "Factors Affecting Information Seeking and Use," in *Communication Patterns of Engineers* (Hoboken, NJ: John Wiley, 2004), 79–80.
11. Bransford and Schwartz, "Rethinking Transfer," 82.
12. Qun G. Jiao, Anthony J. Onwuegbuzie, and Christine E. Daley, "Factors Associated with Library Anxiety," 1997, https://eric.ed.gov/?id=ED416895.
13. Carol Collier Kuhlthau, *Seeking Meaning: A Process Approach to Library and Information Services*, 2nd ed (Westport, CT: Libraries Unlimited, 2004).
14. Gary Rob Lamb et al., "Science News Infographics: Teaching Students to Gather, Interpret, and Present Information Graphically," *The Science Teacher* 81, no. 3 (March 1, 2014): 29.
15. Michael Fosmire and David F. Radcliffe, *Integrating Information into the Engineering Design Process* (West Lafayette, IN: Purdue University Press, 2014).
16. Bransford and Schwartz, "Rethinking Transfer," 64; James P. Barber, "Integration of Learning: A Grounded Theory Analysis of College Students' Learning," *American Educational Research Journal* 49, no. 3 (2012): 590–617, https://doi.org/10.3102/0002831212437854; National Research Council, *How People Learn: Brain, Mind, Experience, and School: Expanded Edition*, 1999, https://doi.org/10.17226/9853.
17. David Shumaker, *The Embedded Librarian: Innovative Strategies for Taking Knowledge Where It's Needed* (Medford, NJ: Information Today, Inc, 2012).

18. Rod Gerber and Charles Oaklief, "Transfer of Learning to Strengthen Workplace Training," in *Training for a Smart Workforce*, ed. Rodney Gerber and Colin Lankshear (London; New York: Routledge, 2000), 177–92.

19. Barry J. Zimmerman and Adam R. Moylan, "Self Regulation: Where Metacognition and Motivation Intersect," in *Handbook of Metacognition in Education*, ed. Douglas J. Hacker, John Dunlosky, and Arthur C. Graesser (New York: Routledge, 2009), 299.

20. Gavriel Salomon and David N. Perkins, "Rocky Roads to Transfer: Rethinking Mechanism of a Neglected Phenomenon," *Educational Psychologist* 24, no. 2 (Spring 1989): 126.

21. Bransford and Schwartz, "Rethinking Transfer," 68.

22. Ibid., 84.

23. Billing, "Teaching for Transfer of Core/Key Skills in Higher Education."

24. Char Booth, *Reflective Teaching, Effective Learning* (Chicago: American Library Association, 2011).

BIBLIOGRAPHY

Association of College & Research Libraries. *Framework for Information Literacy for Higher Education*. Chicago: American Library Association, 2016. http://www.ala.org/acrl/standards/ilframework

Barber, James P. "Integration of Learning: A Grounded Theory Analysis of College Students' Learning." *American Educational Research Journal* 49, no. 3 (2012): 590–617. https://doi.org/10.3102/0002831212437854.

Billing, David. "Teaching for Transfer of Core/Key Skills in Higher Education: Cognitive Skills." *Higher Education* 53, no. 4 (April 1, 2007): 483–516. https://doi.org/10.1007/s10734-005-5628-5.

Booth, Char. *Reflective Teaching, Effective Learning*. Chicago: American Library Association, 2011.

Bransford, John D., and Daniel L. Schwartz. "Rethinking Transfer: A Simple Proposal with Multiple Implications." *Review of Research in Education* 24 (1999): 61–100. https://doi.org/10.2307/1167267.

Fosmire, Michael, and David F. Radcliffe. *Integrating Information into the Engineering Design Process*. West Lafayette, IN: Purdue University Press, 2014.

Gerber, Rod, and Charles Oaklief. "Transfer of Learning to Strengthen Workplace Training." In *Training for a Smart Workforce*, edited by Rodney Gerber and Colin Lankshear, 177–92. London; New York: Routledge, 2000.

Head, Alison J. "Learning Curve: How College Graduates Solve Information Problems Once They Join the Workplace." *Project Information Literacy Research Report*, 2012, 1–38. https://doi.org/10.2139/ssrn.2165031.

Herring, James E., and Stephanie J. Bush. "Information Literacy and Transfer in Schools: Implications for Teacher Librarians." *The Australian Library Journal* 60, no. 2 (May 1, 2011): 123–32. https://doi.org/10.1080/00049670.2011.10722584.

Jiao, Qun G., Anthony J. Onwuegbuzie, and Christine E. Daley. "Factors Associated with Library Anxiety," 1997. https://eric.ed.gov/?id=ED416895.

Kuhlthau, Carol Collier. *Seeking Meaning: A Process Approach to Library and Information Services*. 2nd ed. Westport, CT: Libraries Unlimited, 2004.

National Research Council. *How People Learn: Brain, Mind, Experience, and School: Expanded Edition*, 1999. https://doi.org/10.17226/9853.

O'Brien, Mia. "Navigating the SoTL Landscape: A Compass, Map and Some Tools for Getting

Started." *International Journal for the Scholarship of Teaching and Learning* 2, no. 2 (July 1, 2008). https://doi.org/10.20429/ijsotl.2008.020215.

Perkins, David N., and Gavriel Salomon. "Teaching for Transfer." *Educational Leadership* 46, no. 1 (1988): 22–32.

Salomon, Gavriel, and David N. Perkins. "Rocky Roads to Transfer: Rethinking Mechanism of a Neglected Phenomenon." *Educational Psychologist* 24, no. 2 (Spring 1989): 113.

Shumaker, David. *The Embedded Librarian: Innovative Strategies for Taking Knowledge Where It's Needed*. Medford, NJ: Information Today, Inc, 2012.

Tenopir, Carol, and Donald Ward King. "Factors Affecting Information Seeking and Use." In *Communication Patterns of Engineers*. Hoboken, NJ: John Wiley, 2004.

Zimmerman, Barry J., and Adam R. Moylan. "Self Regulation: Where Metacognition and Motivation Intersect." In *Handbook of Metacognition in Education*, edited by Douglas J. Hacker, John Dunlosky, and Arthur C. Graesser, 299–315. New York: Routledge, 2009.

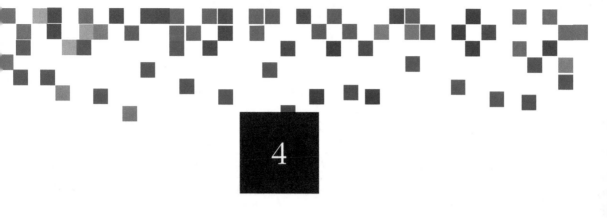

4

Crosswalking the Disciplines:

Reimagining Information Literacy Instruction for a History Methods Course

Bobby Smiley

Introduction

As experienced researchers, we often forget that we hold an almost invisible layer of disciplinary knowledge related to practice, whether it's determining which sources are best to use, how to use them, or how to ask questions of them. For students beginning to learn the canons of research unique to a discipline, just tackling the specialized vocabulary of a field can be a daunting or truly off-putting experience. The motivation behind the Scholarship of Teaching and Learning (SoTL) project discussed in this case study was to investigate ways to enable students learning the craft of research in their field to recognize the silent critical moves that scholars themselves make without usually realizing it. Enabled by the Lilly Fellows Teaching Program at Michigan State University, this research explored what will be termed in this case study as "disciplinary information literacy" (DIL), a signature pedagogy designed to help devise concrete teaching strategies for complementing both the need for general information literacy and the ability to source, consume, and analyze information within a disciplinary context.[1] By doing so for our students, librarians, armed with subject knowledge and research practices in the field we know so well, can, as Michel Foucault wrote in a different context, help "to render visible what precisely is visible, which is to say, to make appear what is so close, so immediate, so intimately linked to ourselves that, as a consequence, we do not perceive it."[2]

As information professionals, librarians are often called upon to acquaint students with information literacy (IL). For librarians, an investment in sound, effective pedagogy is necessarily embedded in IL, and instruction in that area is usually the locus of teaching in

the library. While definitions are manifold, in this context, IL can be understood through the Association of College and Research Libraries (ACRL) *Framework for Information Literacy for Higher Education*.[3] The ACRL *Framework* encompasses six "frames": Authority Is Constructed and Contextual, Information Creation as a Process, Information Has Value, Research as Inquiry, Scholarship as Conversation, and Searching as Strategic Exploration. Without unpacking each, what makes this approach to IL especially useful is its grounding in what Erik Meyer and Ray Land have called "threshold concepts." "A threshold concept can be considered as akin to a portal," Meyer and Land explain, "opening up a new and previously inaccessible way of thinking about something," and offer "a transformed way of understanding, or interpreting, or viewing something without which the learner cannot progress."[4] For instance, understanding that Scholarship as Conversation implies understanding the narrative nature of history, how it's sourced, and how the discipline itself is a product of scholarly discourse—in effect, how historians make history. Once recognized, students can begin to read historians' accounts as interpretive arrangements of evidence, in dialogue with both the period being chronicled and existing scholarship.

At the same time, librarians with subject specialties (such as history, literature, biological sciences) are frequently responsible for providing instruction specific to their collection area. For those familiar with the research practices in a given area of scholarship, library sessions can be an incredible boon. But for students new to a discipline, these sessions can be overwhelming or simply unhelpful, with too much information in an abbreviated amount of time (usually a single class session) and delivered in a manner that presupposes literacy in that field. The besetting problem, at least observed anecdotally, is that these sessions are divorced from the ACRL *Framework* principles and are treated more as "bibliographic instruction" and less as "information literacy"; that is, greater emphasis is placed on student mastery of subject-specific print and electronic resources and the library catalog rather than (or as a complement to) exploring information literacy threshold concepts through working with those resources. In practice, library instruction that explicitly addresses IL often resides in first-year experience or introductory composition courses and is not always (or perhaps less frequently) paired with content from a single discipline.[5] Proposed in this case study is an argument for working toward disciplinary information literacy (DIL), which places in conversation threshold concepts unique to a specific discipline and those that animate IL instruction. What follows is an elaboration of that idea explored through a SoTL project and novel ways to envision instruction informed by that research.

SoTL Project Background and Research

When the author conducted his research, he was the subject librarian for American history and library liaison to the History department at Michigan State University, a Research 1 Land Grant university, with around 51,000 students and 13,000 FTE. Founded as an agricultural college, Michigan State has historically focused on applied sciences, and while strong in areas such as digital humanities, the university is better known as STEM and School of Education institution and not for its humanities programs. In his work at the MSU Libraries, the author served as the principal library instructor for the introductory methods course, HST 201 (Historical Methods and Skills). A required course for history majors and minors, as well as for social studies education students, HST 201 is designed to introduce the fundamentals of historical scholarship using the context of a given historical topic (e.g., "Weimar Germany," "Revolutionary Mexico," "Slavery and New Media"). Traditionally, library sessions for these courses have been single classes that cover general history resources and are tailored to the historical context in which the course is set.

Despite the best efforts of librarians and professors, there are many students who appear to struggle in HST 201 to understand the nature of the resources themselves (e.g., primary versus secondary sources), make connections between those resources and how historians use them, as well as how to formulate historical questions to search effectively for resources. Moreover, they lack a sense of how histories are constructed by historians or how formal arguments are assembled in historical writing. As the author has observed in his teaching and in conversations with instructors, these issues cut across all sections of HST 201, irrespective of course topic or instructor effectiveness. What is lacking, the historian Lendol Calder explains, is "what beginning students in the professions [i.e., professional university programs, such as nursing and engineering] have but history beginners typically do not: ways of being taught that require them to do, think, and value what practitioners in the field are doing, thinking, and valuing."[6]

This SoTL project had two major components: first, field research with historians to discuss and determine thresholds concepts in their field; second, to create a library session (or sessions) curriculum for introductory historical methods courses. Reimagining the library session, the second part of the project provided a template for how subject librarians, collaborating with course instructors, could design student-centered lessons that both introduce students to the language and research practices of a scholarly community through subject-specific library resources relevant to their coursework. Understood as a signature pedagogy, these proposed DIL sessions would re-engineer all structures (surface, deep, and implicit) of a typical class meeting.[7] More than simply a demonstration of databases or how the catalog works, DIL sessions would seek in their deep structure to empower students by leveraging the vocabulary of the field to recognize and locate the best sources and to distinguish and understand the difference between the nature of sources (primary and secondary). In the implicit structure, students would explore why knowing source types and their differences matters and how those sources are used in argumentation, arrangement of evidence, and the structure of scholarly articles. These explorations can assist in the formulation of historical questions for research (questions that go beyond summary and critically index change over time), which is foundational for constructing histories. But while these concerns center around scholarly communication, the focus of disciplinary information literacy as a signature pedagogy—not only for designing effective classroom instruction at the surface structure to instill these literacies but lessons that continue to serve students as they themselves become beginning researchers in the field.

To determine the disciplinary elements of DILs, this case study interviewed eight tenure-track faculty members in the history department (from assistant to full professors), asking a series of questions ranging from faculty experience with library sessions and classroom teaching/assessment to student learning, and foundational threshold concepts in history. The questions were developed, in part, to address the threshold concepts from the ACRL *Framework*, as well as what Arlene Díaz, Joan Middendorf, David Pace, and Leah Shopkow term "bottlenecks": that is, uniquely disciplinary concepts that often challenge student learning.[8] Responses were grouped and coded (based on recurrent themes that could be abstracted from conversations and understood as threshold concepts) and placed into categories of knowledge, skills, and attitudes.[9]

Interviews revealed that faculty held similar views on what knowledge, skills, and attitudes students needed to develop literacy within the discipline. These findings are displayed in figure 4.1 and grouped into one of those three categories. In particular, the majority of faculty noted the difficulty students had in formulating historical questions (skill), the importance of knowing about primary and secondary sources and their reliability (knowledge), familiarity with a variety of resources (knowledge), and cultivating curiosity about the past (attitude). Additionally, in the course of these interviews, these professors also argued for an expanded role for librarians to help reinforce those literacies.

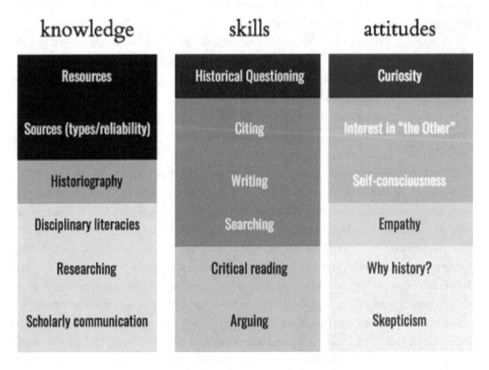

Figure 4.1. The historians' threshold concepts after coding the interview data. (The darker shading indicates the frequency with which a concept was raised in interviews.)

From Research to Instruction

To translate that coded data into a curriculum, the project borrowed an approach for establishing semantic interoperability from bibliographic control: the metadata schema crosswalk. For catalogers, a crosswalk is a "chart or table ... that represents the semantic mapping of fields or data elements in one data standard to fields or data elements in another standard that has a similar function or meaning."[10] (See figure 4.2.)

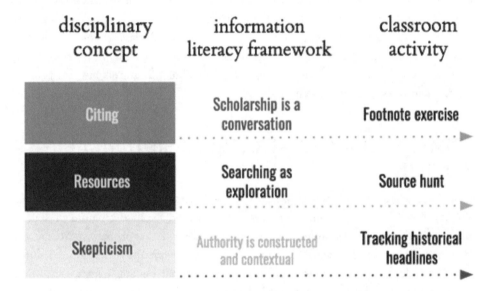

disciplinary concept	information literacy framework	classroom activity
Citing	Scholarship is a conversation	Footnote exercise
Resources	Searching as exploration	Source hunt
Skepticism	Authority is constructed and contextual	Tracking historical headlines

Figure 4.2. Threshold concept crosswalk paired with potential classroom activities.

Here, that mapping takes place between the threshold concepts divined from the historians interviewed and the ACRL *Framework*. For instance, the historians discussed the importance of citation as a foundational concept in the discipline, one that acknowledges the contributions of historical actors as well as contemporaries already engaged in a scholarly discussion. Their descriptions of citation echoed the knowledge practices outlined in the frame, Scholarship as Conversation. By identifying and encouraging skepticism as an historical threshold concept, the historians directly invoked language used to describe some of the learning dispositions for Authority is Constructed and Contextual (for instance, "develop awareness of the importance of assessing content with a skeptical stance").[11] For the purposes of designing and piloting a curriculum, a less elaborate or detailed crosswalk was undertaken, but the value of this approach could potentially be augmented and amplified by an even more extensive alignment across threshold concepts. Ultimately, this approach enables librarians to envision disciplinary information literacy as a complementary conversation between threshold concepts that are unique to both library instruction as well as subject-specific knowledge practices.

With the crosswalk furnishing the theoretical frame, the balance of the SoTL project concentrated on developing lessons and articulating learning outcomes for potential IL sessions. Working with one of the interviewed history faculty members, the author designed two in-class sessions around disciplinary information literacy for a section of the HST 201 (Historical Methods and Skills) course. For this section, the instructor framed course content around the history of underrepresented persons in the United States, focusing several themes and episodes from the nineteenth and twentieth centuries. In their discussions, the author and course instructor identified a principal student bottleneck to history learning around understanding the nature, purpose, and use of source material—whether primary or secondary. As such, the author led two full class sessions centered on DIL at the beginning of the semester, one dedicated to primary sources, the other exploring secondary sources. In the narrative that follows, the author will unpack how the primary source session was devised and delivered.

PRIMARY SOURCES—TRACKING HISTORICAL HEADLINES

For the first session, the author was asked to construct a lesson that would acquaint students with the library's online resources, reinforce information about the nature of sources already introduced, and communicate the plural perspectives that primary sources reveal. Referencing the research conducted and the ACRL *Framework*, the instructor and author identified a threshold concept from history, as well as information literacy, that would be crosswalked for the lesson: historical skepticism and Authority is Constructed and Contextual. Forming the basis of disciplinary information literacy, this crosswalking also served to help develop the learning outcomes developed for the session:

- Identify and explain why a source is a primary source for historians.
- Locate primary sources, and distinguish perspectives chronicled about a common event.
- Point out differences among selected sources (nature and content) and formulate an explanation using those sources as to why they might differ or contradict each other.

In preparation for the class, an online guide was designed that provided links to the library catalog, a brief explanation of different source types, and a deliberately small number of selected primary, secondary, and tertiary sources relevant to the course.[12]

A feature of disciplinary information literacy is an emphasis on leveraging threshold concepts to drive instruction and using library resources instrumentally to illustrate those concepts. For instance, in this class, demonstration of library resources was couched in terms of those threshold concepts; that is, facility with the library catalog or a particular database was necessary for teaching those concepts and not an end itself. This emphasis serves several purposes. First, DIL attempts to connect the library research activity not simply to finding material but also making it a part of the liminal learning experience embedded in the threshold concept idea.[13] Second, by reorienting instruction toward disciplinary information literacy, librarians can help activate, build upon, and reinforce knowledge already introduced by professors (in this case, the nature of source material). Finally, this approach helps to model a more authentic learning experience. Historians learn library research for scholarly investigation and not technical mastery of the catalog or online resources—that mastery is necessary for the research process, but that research is foundationally animated by threshold concepts originating in a discipline. By framing instruction as a crosswalk between threshold concepts, librarians can teach information literacy while using their own subject knowledge for mutual reinforcement.

This session began with a think-pair-share exercise aimed at stimulating discussion and focusing the class on the idea and substance of primary sources. Students were asked to recall everything about their previous class meeting and to spend two minutes writing down those recollections. After pairing up and sharing their recorded memories, students shared out with the class. In the short discussion that followed, students noted differences among the accounts, with some listing only the content of that class meeting, while others mentioning time, duration, and location, and others still referencing individual students, the professor, and assigning motivations for actions. After a few guiding questions, students eventually understood the reason for the exercise: they had created a primary source document. For those students who held onto their document, their accounts would constitute the historical record (and those lost removing voices from that record). By personally producing a primary source, students could begin the session both more focused on the topic and aware how historical narratives can vary, and professors could have those fundamental disciplinary concepts bolstered in an additional context.[14]

Framing the balance of the session around disciplinary information literacy (crosswalked threshold concepts), the class briefly surveyed the online guide, including the library catalog and selected electronic resources. After this survey, the author introduced an activity based on course content covered in their previous meeting. Having shown students how to search selected databases, they were asked to use two historical newspaper databases to find seven contemporaneous articles (from June 1921) covering a common event ("Tulsa race riots") from different newspapers. Students worked in pairs and read the accounts they found, noting their differences and the newspaper names and recorded the steps they took in finding those articles. In the discussion that followed, students began by explaining how they found their articles, such as using database faceting features to narrow their search. These actions were then linked to the articles themselves (for instance, when during June 1921 did reporting move from journalistic accounts to editorial musings?). The bulk of discussion centered around the sources themselves, and why the newspaper language differed among publications. For national newspapers, headlines, such as "TULSA DEAD TOTAL 85 NINE OF THEM WHITE" (*Boston Globe*), "BLAME RED PROPAGANDA FOR TULSA RACE RIOTS.: Efforts of Radicals Urging Negroes to Demand Equality Result in Death of Over 100 Persons" (*Los Angeles Times*), or "RACE WAR RENEWED, DEATH TOLL MOUNTS" (*Washington Post*) already suggest a particular reading of what unfolded. But in newspapers published for an African American audience, such as the *Baltimore Afro-American* and *Chicago Defender*, the students observed how the narrative accounts contrasted with national newspapers, whether by emphasis (placing stress on different causes) or by inclusion of information not mentioned (crowd sizes, individuals killed, extent of damage). Here the "authoritative" account was indeed contextual, requiring students to conduct further research to qualify or confirm the content in the articles they selected. In closing the session, students reflected on their research topics and how they might identify and locate primary sources, and then assess what those primary sources communicated.

Conclusions

While framing library sessions around disciplinary information literacy provides an additional way to envision instruction, the SoTL project on which this chapter is based relied on several conditions that enabled the teaching possibilities discussed. Perhaps most important, throughout the research and teaching process, the author had faculty buy-in, whether concerning the theoretical basis of the project (i.e., threshold concept conversations), designing sessions to dovetail with assignments, or professor interest in re-imagining the information literacy session. Without the enthusiastic support of the faculty, the project would have been much more difficult to realize. Moreover, instruction leaned heavily on the author's subject knowledge and required several pre-class meetings with teaching faculty to tailor sessions. The faculty involved also extended multiple, full-class sessions to the librarian for instruction. As such, preparation was more extensive and involved than the author's usual IL sessions. Additionally, despite wanting to reveal tacit disciplinary knowledge, the author did not explain why the DIL signature pedagogy was used or how it was connected to the ACRL *Framework*, nor did he highlight how this approach contrasted at various structures with more typical library class meetings. Making those elements and connections more manifest, as well as having students do the crosswalking themselves, could engage student learning in novel and beneficial ways. Finally, in the session discussed, students demonstrated comprehension through check-for-understanding questions and other forms of informal formative assessment. However, what needs development is a standardized assessment tool, one that gauges both formative and summative assessments. Like many other elements of DIL, assessment, too (especially summative assessment), requires faculty support as well as any further study longitudinally (semester, year, etc.).

While the foregoing suggests potential limitations or challenges, the idea of disciplinary information literacy is part of an effort reconceive the IL class session. When faced with a single chance to work with a class, librarians can be hemmed in by time constraints or professor expectations and feel there is limited pedagogical space to experiment. What makes the ACRL *Framework* a useful document is its accent on making *learning* the foundation of information literacy and not just skills acquisition. The SoTL project behind this case study helped open a deliberative space to explore how disciplinary and information literacy learning could be fruitfully mobilized for connecting what is unique to the library's instruction with those ideas particular to subject knowledge. For library instructors to move beyond simple demonstration, understanding the disciplinary bottlenecks and foundational concepts as determined by history faculty in the course of SoTL research and contextualizing those within the ACRL *Framework* could furnish librarians with a solid place to begin reimagining a signature pedagogy.

ENDNOTES

1. Lee S. Schulman, "Signature Pedagogies in the Professions," *Daedalus*, 134 (3) (2005), 52–59. By signature pedagogy, the author is thinking of "types of teaching that organize the fundamental ways in which future practitioners are educated for their new professions" (52). In this case study, that profession is understood as an academic historian.
2. Michel Foucault, "La philosophie analytique de la politique (1978)," in *Dits et écrits II, 1976-1988*, eds. D. Defert and F. Ewald, Id. (Paris: Gallimard, 2001), 540. Quoted from Daniele Lorenzini, "Foucault and the Analytic Philosophy of Politics," *Carceral Notebooks* 9 (2013), 99.
3. Association of College and Research Libraries (ACRL), *Framework for Information Literacy for Higher Education* (January 2016), accessed October 30, 2017, http://www.ala.org/acrl/standards/ilframework.
4. Jan H. F. Meyer and Raymond Land, "Threshold concepts and troublesome knowledge (2): epistemological considerations and a conceptual framework for teaching and learning," *Higher Education*, 49 (3) (2005), 373.
5. Rebecca Kuglitsch, "Teaching for Transfer: Reconciling the Framework with Disciplinary Information Literacy," *portal: Libraries and the Academy*, 15 (3) (July 2015), 457–70. Kuglitsch does an excellent job of examining the relationship between "information literacy (IL) as a generalizable skill versus IL as a discipline-based competence" (457). At the time this case study was drafted, the author was unaware of Kuglitsch's work but would like to acknowledge how her argument and my analysis, while differing in some instances, operate in a similar theoretical register and offer suggestions that are complementary but not identical. Moreover, her invocation of "disciplinary information literacy" is more descriptive of a larger project, whereas I am employing the "disciplinary information literacy" as a distinctive set of teaching practices and assumptions that define a signature pedagogy.
6. Lendol Calder, "Uncoverage: Toward a Signature Pedagogy for the History Survey," *Journal of American History*, 33 (March 2006), 1361.
7. Schulman, "Signature Pedagogies in the Professions," 54–55.
8. Arlene Díaz, Joan Middendorf, David Pace, and Leah Shopkow, "The History Learning Project: A Department 'Decodes' Its Students," *Journal of American History*, (94) 4 (March 2008), 1211–24.
9. Kurt Kraiger, J. Kevin Ford, Eduardo Salas, "Application of Cognitive, Skill-Based, and Affective Theories of Learning Outcomes to New Methods of Training Evaluation," *Journal of Applied Psychology*, 78 (1993), 311–28. Coding was necessary, inasmuch as the historians interviewed were unfamiliar with "threshold concepts" and had different vocabulary for explaining the same idea.
10. "Crosswalk," *s.v.*, *Introduction to Metadata*, 3rd ed., ed. Murtha Baca (Los Angeles: Getty Institute, 2016), accessed October 30, 2017, http://www.getty.edu/publications/intrometadata/glossary/.
11. "Scholarship as Conversation: Knowledge Practices," Association of College and Research Libraries, *Framework for Information Literacy for Higher Education*, accessed October 30, 2017, http://www.ala.org/acrl/standards/ilframework.
12. Qualifying "small" with "deliberately" is intended to emphasize the careful curation of selected sources for the course over against an exhaustive exposure of all library resources potential

germane to the disciplinary. For the purposes of pedagogy, the author feels (based on anecdotal and experiential evidence) a far more limited set of resources is most appropriate and effective for an introductory course guide.

13. Threshold concepts are described as possessing six attributes: transformative, troublesome, irreversible, integrative, bounded, and liminal. Meyer and Land have likened the crossing of the pedagogic threshold to a "rite of passage" (drawing on the ethnographic studies of Arnold Gennep and Victor Turner) in which a transitional or liminal space has to be traversed. See "Editors' Preface: Threshold Concepts and Transformational Learning," in Ray Land, Jan H. F. Meyer, Caroline Baillie, eds., *Threshold Concepts and Transformational Learning* (Rotterdam: Sense Publishers, 2010), ix–xlii.

14. The activity took approximately ten minutes from start to finish, but the author had a total of ninety minutes within which to teach.

BIBLIOGRAPHY

Association of College and Research Libraries (ACRL). *Framework for Information Literacy for Higher Education* (January 2016). Accessed October 30, 2017. http://www.ala.org/acrl/standards/ilframework.

Baca, Murtha, ed. *Introduction to Metadata*. 3rd ed. Los Angeles: Getty Institute, 2016. Accessed October 30, 2017. http://www.getty.edu/publications/intrometadata/glossary/.

Calder, Lendaol. "Uncoverage: Toward a Signature Pedagogy for the History Survey." *Journal of American History*, 33 (March 2006): 1358–71. http://doi.org/10.2307/4485896.

Díaz, Arlene, Joan Middendorf, David Pace, and Leah Shopkow. "The History Learning Project: A Department 'Decodes' Its Students." *Journal of American History* (94) 4 (March 2008): 1211–24. https://doi.org/10.2307/25095328.

Kraiger, Kurt, J. Kevin Ford, and Eduardo Salas. "Application of Cognitive, Skill-Based, and Affective Theories of Learning Outcomes to New Methods of Training Evaluation." *Journal of Applied Psychology*, 78 (1993): 311–28. https://doi.org/10.1037/0021-9010.78.2.311.

Kuglitsch, Rebecca. "Teaching for Transfer: Reconciling the Framework with Disciplinary Information Literacy." *portal: Libraries and the Academy*, 15 (3) (July 2015), 457–70.

Land, Ray, Jan H. F. Meyer, and Caroline Baillie, eds. *Threshold Concepts and Transformational Learning*. Rotterdam: Sense Publishers, 2010.

Lorenzini, Daniele. "Foucault and the Analytic Philosophy of Politics." *Carceral Notebooks* 9 (2013): 98–102.

Meyer, Jan H. F., and Raymond Land. "Threshold concepts and troublesome knowledge (2): epistemological considerations and a conceptual framework for teaching and learning." *Higher Education*, 49 (3) (2005): 373–88.

Schulman, Lee S. "Signature Pedagogies in the Professions." *Daedalus*, 134 (3) (2005): 52–59.

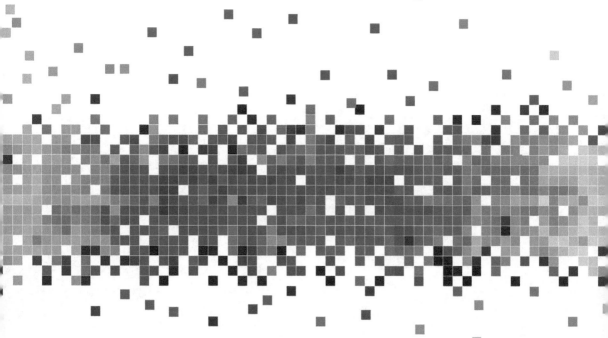

Section II
SoTL Theory

Theory and the Scholarship of Teaching and Learning:

Inquiry and Practice with Intention

Nancy L. Chick

The question of theory in the scholarship of teaching and learning (SoTL) is a contentious and confused one. The field has been criticized for allegedly being atheoretical and undertheorized, and practitioners have been criticized for not identifying the theoretical frameworks that influence their specific projects.[1] Hutchings troubles these claims by asking, "Which (and whose) theories [are we] talking about?"[2] This tension invokes the "conservative" nature of many discussions of SoTL, which "promote a narrow definition of SoTL (including its questions, methods, evidence, and genre) as the norm, suggesting that variations lack important qualities of SoTL."[3]

This background begs the question: What *is* theory? A narrow, field-specific definition suggests that much SoTL is indeed lacking, while a broader definition allows for both the presence and growth of theory in SoTL. The *Oxford English Dictionary* defines theory as "the conceptual basis of a subject or area of study. Contrasted with *practice*."[4] It then breaks down the specific meanings within different disciplines, such as mathematical theorems or bodies of knowledge about specific mathematical concepts, literary and artistic critical methods arising from ideological assumptions, and scientific hypotheses or explanations of phenomena resulting from examinations of facts. This fuller recognition of meanings drawn from across disciplines honors the multidisciplinary nature of SoTL.

Theory in SoTL is, then, the conceptual basis for the practice of SoTL—or, more precisely, the conceptual *bases* for the *practices* of SoTL—as well as the bodies of knowledge, methodological assumptions, and explanations of phenomena that are deployed (explicitly or implicitly) from a range of contexts within SoTL. Put another way, theory is thinking on a meta level, a metacognitive move in which practitioners become aware, critical, and intentional of how and why they are doing their practice. It involves taking stock of

the existing conversations to move beyond definitions,[5] to critically evaluate gaps and limitations, and to maintain forward momentum in the field. As Chick and Poole have noted, such "meta-SoTL" (or work *about* SoTL, which includes theory and theorizing) "chronicles and even celebrates its ongoing sense of becoming and its confluence of diverse and serious inquiries from specific contexts."[6] This work is essential for SoTL to continue to grow as a practice (e.g., a research-based approach to teaching, or a teaching/learning-focused area of research), as way of thinking (e.g., teaching is best informed by evidence from the learners), and as a field (i.e., an emerging, pluralistic body of knowledge, values, and practices about postsecondary teaching and learning). What these criticisms suggest, however, is that SoTL practitioners need to name their theories. With this naming, SoTL will be (and will be better understood as) *explicitly* intentional, self-reflective, and self-critical.

SoTL as Theory

SoTL is predicated on some conceptual bases that can and should be articulated. First, as Hutchings and Shulman imply in their description of SoTL as an act of "going meta,"[7] the lens of SoTL can in itself be a kind of theory. Their taxonomy of SoTL inquiries has become a touchstone for the field, organizing the work of SoTL by the questions it asks. One type explicitly aligns with theory in its focus on "formulating a new conceptual framework for shaping thought about practice."[8] The three other types of SoTL inquiries named in the taxonomy seem very practical: "what works" questions "seeking evidence about the relative effectiveness of different approaches," "what is" questions "describing *what it looks like*," and "visions of the possible" questions framing learning experiences in a new way. However, even the seemingly practical inquiries of SoTL are undergirded by some important and often unarticulated assumptions about teaching, learning, and the connections between the two.

SoTL inquiry rests on complex assumptions about the relationship between teaching and learning. Scott Kim's ambigram of "learn" as an inversion of "teach" illustrates *the first part* of a powerful conceptual basis for SoTL.[9] It is the hope and aspiration of SoTL that learning will be a reflection of teaching: it's not "does it work?" but "what works?" Trigwell and Shale have called this connection "pedagogic resonance."[10] O'Brien's SoTL compass identifies the teacher as "the designer of learning," one who "can ... do" something "to enable learning."[11] SoTL aims to build "pedagogical content knowledge,"[12] or teaching one's subject matter in ways that are informed by how students learn it. Shulman's notion of signature pedagogies is predicated on the assumption that they "form habits of the mind, habits of the heart, and habits of the hand" in the students who are future professionals, and that "the way we teach will shape how professionals behave."[13] And so on.

Significantly, though, much of SoTL identifies the absence of, or barriers in, this teaching-learning connection, problematizing a simple cause-and-effect relationship. Before describing such successes, many "what works?" projects identify particular teaching activities with a negative effect on student learning (e.g., multiple-choice tests, traditional lectures), and rich "what is?" projects chronicle what moments of unmoored learning look like.[14] The reasons are many. Foundational works on how students learn[15] challenge the simplicity of learning and its processes, identifying these and many other ways learning can be muddled. Shulman describes the "pedago-pathologies" of "*amnesia*," "*fantasia*," and "*inertia*"—disconnections between teaching and learning resulting from learners forgetting, misunderstanding, or leaving behind what was taught.[16] Pace and Middendorf's renowned model of "decoding the disciplines" asks teachers to identify obstacles or "bottlenecks" in the learning process, as does Meyer and Land's notion of threshold concepts.

In this way, SoTL is grounded in the need to "represent complexity well,"[17] and the tenuous relationship between teaching and learning. With theory as a guide, SoTL work demonstrates that "learning is not *determined* by teaching" but is instead "*dependent* on teaching."[18] Undergirded by a sense of optimism, though, SoTL is an act toward greater alignment between learning and teaching, which is the subject of the majority of its projects and many of its key concepts—and forms part of its conceptual basis for how the work is done.

Disciplinary Theories in SoTL

From its origins, SoTL has been recognized as "grounded in the disciplines,"[19] by definition informed by the epistemologies, understandings, assumptions, and practices of disciplinary experts. As Poole notes, the work of SoTL is inherently shaped by what its practitioners and those who influence those practitioners consider "research."[20] It affects choices in research question, project design, what counts as evidence, and even what its publications look like. It also affects the choices in theories applied in the work, resulting in "a more situated view of 'theory,' as emerging from, engaging with, connecting to, and underwriting wide-rangingly different disciplinary styles of inquiry and interpretation."[21]

For obvious reasons, there is a strong call for the use of educational theories in SoTL. Gibbs has criticized SoTL practitioners for "conduct[ing] pedagogical inquiry without sufficient knowledge of or reference to the theoretical armature of education and other learning science fields."[22] Miller-Young and Yeo more generously note that members of the multidisciplinary field of SoTL could benefit from a better understanding of the range of lenses and methodologies used in educational research. SoTL researchers can benefit from being aware of their philosophical approach and theoretical assumptions about learning because it will help them ask new questions, design better studies, and more strongly articulate their findings, especially to colleagues with different world views. This will also benefit the field, not only by improving communication and understanding across disciplines, but also because theoretically grounded work is one way for SoTL to achieve broader impact across studies and make new contributions to knowledge about teaching and learning beyond single classrooms.[23]

Others have also brought in theoretical frameworks from their home disciplines as significant foundations for SoTL. Hutchings cites, for example, Salvatori and Donahue's scholarship on moments of difficulty in learning, which is grounded in theories from

English studies, including "the hermeneutics of Hans-Georg Gadamer, literary theory by George Steiner, Helen Elam, Wolfgang Iser, and others."[24] She also notes another's focus on semantic theory and "the power of signs and symbols," and others who draw from the "highly relevant theoretical frameworks and foundations" in "sociology, anthropology, and management (to name a few)." Social network theory, for instance, has found traction in the field,[25] and Chick uses multicultural theory to make sense of some of the disciplinary debates in and about SoTL.[26] Clearly, theories relevant to SoTL come from all fields, but identifying the myriad frameworks associated with specific theorists, schools of thought, and disciplines relevant to SoTL falls well outside of the scope of this chapter.

More generally, Berenson encourages SoTL practitioners to identify "their tradition of inquiry" *vis-à-vis* positivism and constructivism (put simply, knowledge as objectively observable and measurable, or knowledge as socially constructed).[27] A sociologist and educational developer, Berenson offers a good reminder that many theories don't simply fall within a single discipline, and they need not stay within any single discipline. They become part of the "commons," the trading zone in which SoTL practitioners share their approaches, practices, and findings. Hutchings and Huber have cited SoTL's "methodological and theoretical pluralism" as one of its strengths.[28] This need to name the components of SoTL work is not new. Many have been encouraging SoTL practitioners to name their methodologies and methods,[29] their contexts,[30] even their ethics approvals—often in the face of claims that these components are faulty, absent, or ignored in the work. But, as Berenson reminds, these components of the work need to be intentional, visible, and named.

From Theory-Informed Teaching to Theory-Informed SoTL

The case studies that follow suggest another way of thinking about theory and SoTL. They offer examples in which the authors explore how broader frameworks, theoretical approaches, and ways of thinking can inform teaching and learning, grounding teaching design and practice with significant intentions—and naming them.

This attention to theoretically informed teaching in the context of a SoTL book resonates with research showing that the quality of students' learning is affected by the teacher's conceptions of *what teaching and learning mean*—or the teacher's theoretical framework.[31] Trigwell, Prosser, and Waterhouse have found that students use deeper approaches to learning when their teacher has a specific intention or understanding of teaching, described as a "Conceptual Change/Student-Focused Approach":

> This approach is one in which teachers adopt a student-focused strategy to help their students change their world views or conceptions of the phenomena they are studying. Students are seen to have to construct their own knowledge, and so the teacher has to focus on what the students are doing in the teaching-

learning situation. A student-focused strategy is assumed to be necessary because it is the students who have to re-construct their knowledge to produce a new world view or conception. The teacher understands that he/she cannot transmit a new world view or conception to the students.[32]

This theoretically informed approach to teaching, then, has a greater effect on students' depth of learning than specific class activities. With this "chain of relations from teacher thinking to the outcomes of student learning"[33] in mind, the case studies in this section of *The Grounded Instruction Librarian* set up SoTL projects that explicitly trace the theoretical intentions in the teaching to the students' learning by investigating their impact and effectiveness according to these frameworks.

Seale's case study on "historicizing the library," for example, illustrates the cross-pollination that is possible both in librarian partnerships with disciplinary faculty and in SoTL. She "goes meta" in thinking about her teaching, her students' learning, and her discipline of librarianship in a variety of ways, including the decoding the disciplines framework and the notion of historical thinking:

> Rather than teaching the "facts" of *what* of library systems, historicizing the library seeks to get at the *how* by uncovering their historical constructedness … and to get students and other users to question library resources, to understand them as always incomplete and inflected by the social world.

This approach to library instruction helped her identify key bottlenecks in how students learn information literacy. A SoTL project on Seale's historicized library might then explore *how* students "question [library systems] instead of assuming their transparency," what their questioning looks like, how they respond to this new way of looking at their relationship to library research, and how it affects their actual research practices and products. If what they gain from the library is "always incomplete and inflected by the social world," what do the processes and products of students' research look like?

Moeller and Arteaga challenge readers to re-envision the common one-shot, skills-based library instruction through the lens of critical pedagogy and critical information literacy, asking what library instruction would look like if the learner and the learning are placed at the center, empowered, and understood within their social, cultural, political, and economic contexts. Such a learner-centered, reflective pedagogy would be "transformational" for students. Moeller and Arteaga leave open what these pedagogies might look like, as well as their subsequent SoTL inquiries, which would presumably be inquiries that demonstrate the nature of these transformations and the ways in which students understood the significance of information literacy within their own lives and their own communities.

Shields, Denlinger, and Webb describe information literacy classes that use specifications grading, a strategy based partly on educational research on student motivation for learning, namely that students are more intrinsically motivated when they are working to master specific standards to pass their assignments, rather than working to earn specific points to achieve specific grades. While multiple library courses at their institution have been redesigned with specifications grading, Shields and colleagues note that none has "yet been formally studied," and "instructors using SG need to conduct evidence-based research." Although their proposed SoTL questions address the practice of specifications grading, they also explicitly reach back to its basis in student motivation, significantly proposing a theoretically informed SoTL that extends beyond specifications grading:

> To what extent are students more/less motivated in a SG class than non-SG? How does student agency/choice affect motivation? How do transparency and clarity of expectations affect motivation? For the instructor, to what extent does SG actually save time, or is the time spent grading simply exchanged for time spent developing specifications, providing feedback, engaging with students, and related tasks? What value do students and instructors place on feedback, and how does that differ by group? How does an SG course compare to a pure rubric-based course? Do students aim for a higher or lower grade in an SG course than what they might achieve in a traditionally graded course? How effective might SG be for teaching at-risk students, international students, or first-generation college students?

To be clear, while there is attention to the specifications grading here, their emphasis is less on any mechanics of the activity and more on larger issues of student motivation, including their sense of agency, what they value, and what they "aim for."

Tysick, Maloney, Sajecki, and Thomas describe a one-credit library lab taught in two different ways. In one semester, the activities in the lab were based on constructivist theories of learning, particularly the expectation that students would draw on their pre-existing information literacy skills as they continued to learn and build on these skills in the lab course. The next semester, the library lab was redesigned according to the social constructivist notion that students learn in community and conversation with each other. Initial assessments using course evaluations, student feedback, and instructor/librarian reflections suggest some successes, and Tysick, Maloney, Sajecki, and Thomas propose this course design "be used as a theoretical model" for information literacy instruction. What's most interesting here, though, is that they don't frame their course revision simply as adding group or collaborative learning; instead, they draw on the conceptual deliberateness of shifting from constructivism to social constructivism—different theories for how learning happens. A SoTL project aligned with this course would then begin with questions grounded in social constructivism, rather than asking simply if group-based infographics and outline assignments were more effective.

McKinney and Webber draw on Entwistle, Nisbet, and Bromage's model of increasingly broad spheres of a teaching-learning environment, including a course's learners, the educator's beliefs, the institutional context, a discipline's expectations, and the broader sector of higher education. The authors use this model as a tool for reflection and learning design within a graduate library course in which the students prepare for their future roles as teachers. Introducing this more complex model for understanding learning reportedly shifted their teaching approaches from "transmissive to more constructivist"—again, pointing to the importance of theoretically informed teaching, which could then result in theoretically explicit SoTL.

Librarians, Theory, and SoTL

In addition to investigating theoretically informed library instruction, readers of this book may also advance the conversation of theory in SoTL by articulating the theoretical frameworks librarians offer. For instance, fundamental to teaching, learning, and SoTL is the notion of "knowing." So what does this mean to librarians? What is "knowing" and "knowledge"? "Information" may translate to other disciplines as something more basic, more static than librarians intend, so what is the knowledge librarians understand in the idea of "information" and why is it important? What does it look like? What is its purpose? Who can have it? How do they get it? What do they do with it? How do librarians know when someone has it? What happens when it is missing? What are the implications then for librarians' teaching and learning? What are the implications for other contexts for teaching and learning? What questions does it raise about teaching and learning? And what are the implications for SoTL? In this way, librarians will help grow the field of the scholarship of teaching and learning.

ENDNOTES

1. Mary Taylor Huber and Pat Hutchings, "The Place—and Problem—of Theory," *Arts and Humanities in Higher Education* 7, no. 3 (2008): 227. See also Mary Taylor Huber, "Disciplines, Pedagogy, and Inquiry-Based Learning about Teaching," in *Exploring Research-Based Teaching*, ed. C. Kreber (San Francisco: Jossey-Bass, 2006), 63–72; Pat Hutchings, "Theory: The Elephant in the Scholarship of Teaching and Learning Room," *International Journal for the Scholarship of Teaching and Learning* 1, no. 1 (January 2007): 1–4.
2. Hutchings, "Theory," 1.
3. Nancy L. Chick, "Difference, Power, and Privilege in the Scholarship of Teaching and Learning: The Value of Humanities SoTL," in *The Scholarship of Teaching and Learning In and Across the Disciplines*, ed. Kathleen McKinney (Bloomington, IN: Indiana UP, 2013), 18.
4. *Oxford English Dictionary*, s.v. "theory," accessed May 1, 2018, http://www.oed.com.
5. S. Booth and L. C. Woollacott, "On the Constitution of SoTL: Its Domains and Contexts," *Higher Education* 75, no. 3 (March 2018): 537–51.
6. Nancy Chick and Gary Poole, "The Necessary and Dual Conversations in a Vibrant SoTL," *Teaching & Learning Inquiry* 1, no. 1 (March 2014): 1.
7. Pat Hutchings and L. S. Shulman, "The Scholarship of Teaching: New Elaborations, New Developments," *Change* 31, no. 5 (1999): 10–15.

8. Pat Hutchings, introduction to *Opening Lines: Approaches to the Scholarship of Teaching and Learning* (Menlo Park, CA: Carnegie Foundation for the Advancement of Teaching, 2000), 5.

9. Scott Kim, "An Optical Illusion: The Inversions of Scott Kim," accessed May 1, 2018, http://www.anopticalillusion.com/2012/04/the-inversions-of-scott-kim.

10. Keith Trigwell and Suzanne Shale, "Student Learning and the Scholarship of University Teaching," *Studies in Higher Education* 29, no. 4 (2004): 523–36.

11. Mia O'Brien, "Navigating the SoTL Landscape: A Compass, Map, and Some Tools for Getting Started," *International Journal for the Scholarship of Teaching and Learning* 2, no. (2008): 2.

12. Lee S. Shulman, "Those Who Understand: Knowledge Growth in Teaching," *Educational Researcher* 15, no. 2 (February 1986): 4–14.

13. Lee S. Shulman, "Signature Pedagogies in the Professions," *Daedalus* 134, no 2 (Summer 2005): 59. See also Regan A. R. Gurung, Nancy L. Chick, and Aeron Haynie, *Exploring Signature Pedagogies: Approaches to Teaching Disciplinary Habits of Mind* (Sterling, VA: Stylus, 2009); Nancy L. Chick, Regan A. R. Gurung, and Aeron Haynie, *Exploring More Signature Pedagogies: Approaches to Teaching Disciplinary Habits of Mind* (Sterling, VA: Stylus, 2012).

14. Kathrin F. Stanger-Hall, "Multiple-Choice Exams: An Obstacle for Higher-Level Thinking in Introductory Science Classes," *CBE—Life Sciences Education* 11, no. 3 (2012): 294–306.

15. John D. Bransford, Ann L. Brown, and Rodney R. Cocking, *How People Learn: Brain, Mind, Experience, and School* (Washington DC: National Academy Press, 2000); Susan A. Ambrose, Michael W. Bridges, Michele DiPietro, Marsha C. Lovett, and Marie K. Norman, *How Learning Works: 7 Research-Based Principles for Smart Teaching* (San Francisco: Jossey-Bass, 2010).

16. Lee S. Shulman, "Taking Learning Seriously," *Change: The Magazine of Higher Education* 31, no. 4 (1999): 10–17.

17. Gary Poole, "Square One: What Is Research?," in *The Scholarship of Teaching and Learning In and Across the Disciplines*, ed. Kathleen McKinney (Bloomington, IN: Indiana UP, 2013), 135–51.

18. Brent Davis, Dennis Sumara, and Rebecca Luce-Kapler, *Engaging Minds: Cultures of Education and Practices of Teaching* (New York, Routledge, 2015), 75.

19. Mary Taylor Huber and Sherwyn P. Morreale, *Disciplinary Styles in the Scholarship of Teaching and Learning: Exploring Common Ground* (Washington DC: American Association of Higher Education, 2002).

20. Poole, "Square One." Faculty developers, institutional ethics boards, granting bodies, tenure and promotion committees, and many others aside from the actual practitioners affect the practices of SoTL, an issue that needs greater exploration.

21. Huber and Hutchings, "The Place," 227.

22. Ibid.

23. Janice Miller-Young and Michelle Yeo, "Conceptualizing and Communicating SoTL: A Framework for the Field," *Teaching & Learning Inquiry* 3, no 2. (2015): 40.

24. Hutchings, "Theory," 1–2.

25. For example, see Torgny Roxå and Katarina Mårtensson, "Significant Conversations and Significant Networks–Exploring the Backstage of the Teaching Arena," *Studies in Higher Education* 34, no. 5 (2009): 547–59; and Jeff Webb and Ann Engar, "Exploring Classroom Community: A Social Network Study of Reacting to the Past," *Teaching & Learning Inquiry* 4, no. 1 (March 2016): 1–17.

26. Chick, "Difference," 15–33.

27. Carol Berenson, "Identifying a Tradition of Inquiry: Articulating Research Assumptions," in *SoTL in Action: Illuminating Critical Moments of Practice*, ed. Nancy L. Chick (Sterling, VA: Stylus, 2018), 42–52.

28. Pat Hutchings and Mary Taylor Huber, "Placing Theory in the Scholarship of Teaching and Learning," *Arts and Humanities in Higher Education* 7, no. 3 (2008), 233.

29. See for example Chick "Difference," Nancy L. Chick, "'Methodologically Sound' Under the 'Big Tent': An Ongoing Conversation," *International Journal for the Scholarship of Teaching and Learning* 8, no. 2 (2014): 1–15; and Regan Gurung, "Getting Foxy: Invoking Different Magesteria in the Scholarship of Teaching and Learning," *Teaching & Learning Inquiry* 2, no. 2 (March 2014): 109–14.

30. See Erik Blair, "The Challenge of Contextualising the Scholarship of Teaching and Learning," *Teaching & Learning Inquiry* 1, no. 1 (March 2013): 127–30; and Lee Shulman, "Situated Studies of Teaching and Learning: The New Mainstream," filmed October 2013, ISSOTL 2013 Conference, Raleigh, NC, 1:02, posted October 11, 2013, https://youtu.be/bhvwLW-5zMM.

31. Keith Trigwell, Michael Prosser, and Fiona Waterhouse, "Relations Between Teachers' Approaches to Teaching and Students' Approaches to Learning," *Higher Education* 37 (1999): 57.

32. Trigwell, Prosser, and Waterhouse, "Relations Between Teachers," 62.

33. Ibid., 57.

BIBLIOGRAPHY

Ambrose, Susan A., Michael W. Bridges, Michele DiPietro, Marsha C. Lovett, and Marie K. Norman. *How Learning Works: 7 Research-Based Principles for Smart Teaching*. San Francisco: Jossey-Bass, 2010.

Berenson, Carol. "Identifying a Tradition of Inquiry: Articulating Research Assumptions." In *SoTL in Action: Illuminating Critical Moments of Practice*, edited by Nancy L. Chick, 42–52. Sterling, VA: Stylus 2018.

Blair, Erik. "The Challenge of Contextualising the Scholarship of Teaching and Learning." *Teaching & Learning Inquiry* 1, no. 1 (March 2013): 127–30.

Booth, S., and L. C. Woollacott. "On the Constitution of SoTL: Its Domains and Contexts." *Higher Education* 75, no. 3 (March 2018): 537–51.

Bransford, John D., Ann L. Brown, and Rodney R. Cocking. *How People Learn: Brain, Mind, Experience, and School*. Washington DC: National Academy Press, 2000.

Chick, Nancy L. "Difference, Power, and Privilege in the Scholarship of Teaching and Learning: The Value of Humanities SoTL." In *The Scholarship of Teaching and Learning In and Across the Disciplines*, edited by Kathleen McKinney, 15–33. Bloomington, IN: Indiana UP, 2013.

———. "'Methodologically Sound' Under the 'Big Tent': An Ongoing Conversation." *International Journal for the Scholarship of Teaching and Learning* 8, no. 2 (2014): 1–15.

Chick, Nancy L., Regan A. R. Gurung, and Aeron Haynie. *Exploring More Signature Pedagogies: Approaches to Teaching Disciplinary Habits of Mind*. Sterling, VA: Stylus, 2012.

Chick, Nancy, and Gary Poole. "The Necessary and Dual Conversations in a Vibrant SoTL." *Teaching & Learning Inquiry* 1, no. 1 (March 2014): 1–2. https://doi.org/10.20343/teachlearninqu.2.1.1.

Davis, Brent, Dennis Sumara, and Rebecca Luce-Kapler. *Engaging Minds: Cultures of Education and Practices of Teaching*. New York, Routledge, 2015.

Gurung, Regan A. R. "Getting Foxy: Invoking Different Magesteria in the Scholarship of Teaching and Learning." *Teaching & Learning Inquiry* 2, no. 2 (March 2014): 109–14.

Gurung, Regan A. R., Nancy L. Chick, and Aeron Haynie. *Exploring Signature Pedagogies: Approaches to Teaching Disciplinary Habits of Mind*. Sterling, VA: Stylus, 2009.

Huber, Mary Taylor. "Disciplines, Pedagogy, and Inquiry-Based Learning about Teaching." In *Exploring Research-Based Teaching*, edited by C. Kreber, 63–72. San Francisco: Jossey-

Bass, 2006.

Huber, Mary Taylor, and Pat Hutchings. "The Place–and Problem–of Theory." *Arts and Humanities in Higher Education* 7, no. 3 (2008): 227–28.

Huber, Mary Taylor, and Sherwyn P. Morreale. *Disciplinary Styles in the Scholarship of Teaching and Learning: Exploring Common Ground.* Washington DC: American Association of Higher Education 2002.

Hutchings, Pat. Introduction to *Opening Lines: Approaches to the Scholarship of Teaching and Learning.* Menlo Park, CA: Carnegie Foundation for the Advancement of Teaching, 2000, 1–10.

———. "Theory: The Elephant in the Scholarship of Teaching and Learning Room." *International Journal for the Scholarship of Teaching and Learning* 1, no. 1 (January 2007): 1–4.

Hutchings, Pat, and Mary Taylor Huber. "Placing Theory in the Scholarship of Teaching and Learning." *Arts and Humanities in Higher Education* 7, no. 3 (2008): 229–44.

Hutchings, Pat, and L. S. Shulman. "The Scholarship of Teaching: New Elaborations, New Developments." *Change* 31, no. 5 (1999): 10–15.

Kim, Scott. "An Optical Illusion: The Inversions of Scott Kim." Accessed May 1, 2018, http://www.anopticalillusion.com/2012/04/the-inversions-of-scott-kim.

Miller-Young, Janice, and Michelle Yeo. "Conceptualizing and Communicating SoTL: A Framework for the Field." *Teaching & Learning Inquiry* 3, no 2. (2015): 37–53.

O'Brien, Mia. "Navigating the SoTL Landscape: A Compass, Map, and Some Tools for Getting Started." *International Journal for the Scholarship of Teaching and Learning* 2, no. (2008): 1–20.

Oxford English Dictionary, s.v. "theory." Accessed May 1, 2018. http://www.oed.com.

Poole, Gary. "Square One: What Is Research?" In *The Scholarship of Teaching and Learning In and Across the Disciplines*, edited by Kathleen McKinney, 135–51. Bloomington, IN: Indiana UP, 2013.

Roxå, Torgny, and Katarina Mårtensson. "Significant Conversations and Significant Networks—Exploring the Backstage of the Teaching Arena." *Studies in Higher Education* 34, no. 5 (2009): 547–59.

Shulman, Lee S. "Signature Pedagogies in the Professions." *Daedalus* 134, no 2 (Summer 2005): 52–59.

———. "Situated Studies of Teaching and Learning: The New Mainstream." Filmed October 2013. ISSOTL 2013 Conference, Raleigh, NC, 1:02. Posted October 11, 2013. https://youtu.be/bhvwLW-5zMM.

———. "Taking Learning Seriously." *Change: The Magazine of Higher Education* 31, no. 4 (1999): 10–17.

———. "Those Who Understand: Knowledge Growth in Teaching." *Educational Researcher* 15, no. 2 (February 1986): 4–14.

Stanger-Hall, Kathrin F. "Multiple-Choice Exams: An Obstacle for Higher-Level Thinking in Introductory Science Classes." *CBE—Life Sciences Education* 11, no. 3 (2012): 294–306.

Trigwell, Keith, Michael Prosser, and Fiona Waterhouse. "Relations Between Teachers' Approaches to Teaching and Students' Approaches to Learning." *Higher Education* 37 (1999): 57–70.

Trigwell, Keith, and Suzanne Shale. "Student Learning and the Scholarship of University Teaching." *Studies in Higher Education* 29, no. 4 (2004): 523–36.

Webb, Jeff, and Ann Engar. "Exploring Classroom Community: A Social Network Study of Reacting to the Past." *Teaching & Learning Inquiry* 4, no. 1 (March 2016): 1–17.

6

Visions of the Possible:

A Critical Pedagogical Praxis for Information Literacy Instruction

Christine M. Moeller and Roberto A. Arteaga

Introduction: Hutchings' Questions and Library Instruction

Hutchings suggests that teachers should look at moments of difficulty and treat them as learning moments from which to develop a greater understanding of their teaching and learning practices. Looking at information literacy instruction broadly, the authors framed their investigation around Hutchings' taxonomy of questions for the Scholarship of Teaching and Learning (SoTL), asking, "What is the current state of information literacy instruction and crafting 'visions of the possible' that could inform librarians' teaching practices?"[1] What, then, are those moments of difficulty that librarians are facing, what are the visions of the possible for information literacy instruction, and how can those visions contribute further to student learning?

With the introduction of the Association of College & Research Libraries (ACRL) *Framework for Information Literacy for Higher Education* in 2014, library instruction began an official shift away from skill-based training into teaching that focused on dispositions and knowledge practices. However, even after the ACRL *Framework* was ratified in 2016, and despite its call for information literacy to be "systematically integrated" into the academic curriculum, one-shot sessions remain ubiquitous in library instruction.[2] From a pedagogical perspective, this model for providing instruction is largely ineffective because it is not scalable, makes learning difficult to assess, and prevents librarians and their work from being fully integrated into the curriculum by presenting them as guest lecturers.[3] Contributing to the complexity of this problem is the nature of information literacy practice, which is both inward- and outward-facing.[4] Looking inward, librarians do not always perceive themselves as teachers or may not feel they have the necessary experience to take

on the role of a teacher.[5] Looking outward, students, faculty, and other campus partners do not have a thorough understanding of information literacy or how librarians can contribute to student learning.[6] As Downey observes, "librarians and other educators have been largely unsuccessful with teaching information literacy because of how they teach it, due to a lack of teaching skill and training, poorly devised curriculum, inability to embed information literacy in the overall curriculum, and limitations of common instructional models."[7]

In an attempt to address these issues, librarians are increasingly looking to critical pedagogy and critical information literacy. Critical information literacy is "an expanded version of information literacy that places the learner at the center in a more empowered role and focuses on the sociopolitical, economic, and cultural aspects of all types and stages of information and the research process."[8] In this approach to information literacy, students become active agents in learning that matters to them. As Elmborg explains, "rather than focus on knowledge acquisition, students [must] identify and engage significant problems in the world."[9] Taking student engagement as the starting point, librarians can then focus on helping students develop a critical consciousness[10] that enables them to "take control of their lives and their own learning."[11] With this vision of information literacy and student learning in mind, the authors wanted to know what pedagogical approach could help make this vision possible. This led to the formulation of a "conceptual framework for shaping thought about practice" as a way of discussing a pedagogy that will support critical information literacy and transformative learning.[12]

If librarians hope to increase their contributions to student learning and change how their work is perceived, they must reexamine and reconsider library instruction and what it ultimately aims to achieve in order to develop a teaching practice that actively empowers students and their learning. To successfully enact critical information literacy, librarians need to develop a critical pedagogical praxis, a method of teaching based on the interplay of theory and practice, which arises from the need to reshape library instruction through a critical analysis of a librarian's practice, their approach to teaching, and their attitudes about learning. This critical pedagogical praxis, which includes the drafting of a teaching statement, the intentional design of instruction, the adoption of a learner-centered approach to teaching, and a critical reflective stance, constitutes a pedagogical foundation that aims to transform teaching practices beginning with the teachers themselves.

Crafting a Teaching Statement

In a study of librarians' teaching identity, Walter explains that librarians need to develop a teaching identity that more closely resembles research in teacher education. By shifting the discussion to this matter, Walter argues, teaching librarians may be able to "present a well-defined professional identity to campus colleagues who have historically misunderstood their work."[13] A teaching statement (also called a teaching philosophy), which has been a critical piece of teacher education portfolios and dossiers for decades, has gone largely unexplored in library literature and can serve as a first step in the development of that identity.[14]

Goodyear and Allchin, in their discussion of statements of teaching philosophy, state that "articulating an individual teaching philosophy provides the foundation by which to clarify goals, to guide behavior, to see scholarly dialogue on teaching, and to organize evaluation."[15] For this reason, a teaching philosophy serves as the foundation of a critical pedagogical praxis. A teaching statement should address a librarian's approach in the classroom and "make explicit [their] commitment to quality teaching and learning, establish definitions of what those look like, and map out how they are implemented in [their] classroom."[16] However, the format, length, and purpose of a teaching statement will vary by the context in which the statement is used. In fact, Schonwetter et al. suggest that teachers should keep their teaching statements in two formats: one for personal reflection and another to provide to students and managers for evaluation.[17]

At its core, a teaching statement is an exploration of the assumptions that a teacher makes about teaching and learning. At the same time, it also provides an outline of the principles that justify the teaching choices a teacher makes in designing instruction aimed at meeting the needs of their students. This exploration, which asks librarians to "compare their theoretical self with their actual self," brings reflectivity to their practice.[18] The process of reflection is meant to be an ongoing process, one that engages the librarian before, during, and after each teaching interaction and pushes them to reflect on what needs to be accomplished, what has worked and what has not, and how to best shape their own perceptions and approaches to teaching. This will set the groundwork needed to guide librarians through the development of a critical pedagogical praxis.

Designing Instruction Intentionally

Using the teaching statement as a foundation, librarians can begin to intentionally design their instruction, whether for a credit course or a one-shot instruction session. Many methods for designing instruction, such as backward design or the ADDIE model, take a systematic approach, requiring the instructor to walk through a specific series of steps to determine what instruction is appropriate for a given situation. Furthermore, models like ADDIE, which are rooted in the instructional systems development model created for the armed forces in the 1970s, focus on training people quickly, efficiently, and consistently.[19] In doing so, however, these models reduce learners and learning to a series of bullet points, ordered steps, or lists of characteristics. These formulaic instructional design models also place the power in the hands of the teacher and situate the learners as the direct objects of the teacher's actions, instead of including them as co-participants in the design process. Critical instructional design, by contrast, focuses on neither efficiency nor standardization, but instead "prioritizes collaboration, participation, social justice, learner agency, emergence, narrative, and relationships of nurture between students and between teachers and students."[20] This approach attempts to move instructional design away from teacher-centered, "see, do, repeat" teaching strategies that resemble a banking model of instruction.[21] Rather, critical instructional design focuses on developing opportunities for student engagement within the "messy work" of teaching and learning.[22]

Like the other components of critical pedagogical praxis, the intentional design of instruction requires a reflective practice. Instruction does not occur in a vacuum but rather has a time, place, and a context replete with various "situational factors."[23] Reflecting on these factors, which include the learner characteristics, student motivations, and the context for learning, will help librarians define their particular context and the circumstances for their instruction. In addition to considering situational factors, librarians need to ask questions such as, what is the goal of the instruction, who are the students, what might students learn from this experience, how can this experience build on students' previous experiences, what do the students themselves want from this experience, and how can this instruction provide opportunities for learning, exploration, and curiosity for all learners? Thinking through these questions will help librarians make intentional choices about what to teach explicitly, how the instruction fits into a course or curriculum as a whole, and why specific teaching and learning activities are appropriate for the given context. Through the articulation of this decision-making process, librarians can in turn be transparent with students about the goals and purposes of instruction and related teaching and learning activities. To improve student learning, librarians should help students understand "how and why instructors [have] structured their learning experiences in particular ways."[24] In order to empower students to be active agents in their own learning process, librarians must be able to articulate their own reflective decision-making process as related to the design of instruction.

Fostering Learner-Centered Teaching

When librarians design their instruction intentionally, they are already moving toward a learner-centered approach to teaching (also referred to as student-centered teaching). This approach situates the student at the center of the learning process and places emphasis on transforming student beliefs about learning. However, as Weimer explains, this approach to teaching not only transforms students but it can also transform what teachers believe about learning and, more important, their role as teachers.[25]

Student-centered learning* can be traced back to the works of Dewey and Vygotsky, but the term learner-centered teaching (LCT) traces its origins to the shifts in curriculum planning and pedagogy that occurred in the 1970s and 1980s.[26] In the field of education, which is of particular relevance to teaching librarians, the works of Weimer, Blumberg, and Doyle have promoted the use of LCT approaches to create learning environments that optimize students' opportunities to learn while challenging teachers to transform their teaching methods through a gradual process of negotiation of power that also includes the student.[27]

Weimer articulates five core aspects of LCT:[28] the role of the teacher, the balance of power, the function of content, the responsibility for learning, and the purposes and processes of evaluation.[29] These components, and LCT itself, adhere to a constructivist

---

* Since the 1930s, educators have distinguished between *teacher-centered learning*, where the teacher exerts control over the students and is the most active person in the classroom, and *student-centered learning*, where students take a more active role in the classroom.

approach to teaching[30] and allow teachers to implement LCT practices in incremental ways, creating more flexibility and lessening the burden that a complete overhaul in teaching methods and activities may have in the classroom.[31] For both the teacher and the student, the transition to a learner-centered approach requires more time and involves more work. Undoubtedly, resistance will be a part of this transition, but the best way to respond to any such resistance will be through open communication. For students, this will require the teacher to be explicit about the rationale for the changes, to provide encouragement and motivation, and to solicit regular feedback on their teaching and student learning.[32]

The rate at which changes in teaching methods are accepted will vary by context, and any changes that occur, along with their chances of success, hinge on the relationships a teacher is able to establish. Doyle claims that "the likelihood of our criticism being accepted and valued by our students is tied directly to the relationship we have with them," and that teachers need to foster a relationship-driven classroom where students feel safe to communicate with the teacher and do work that they value.[33] Thus, in order to develop classrooms that are relationship-driven, librarians must first seek to understand their students and their motivations for learning and then learn about the context for teaching in order to establish an environment that fosters student motivation and commitment, instead of seeking to control them.[34] As part of a critical pedagogical praxis, the development of a learner-centered practice will play an important part in building a classroom environment that fosters student learning through the sharing of power in the classroom. As with the other components, reflection will also play a role in this process of development, especially as the teacher transitions from "instructor-centered teaching [focused] on knowledge dissemination to using learner-centered approaches that help students construct and use content in meaningful ways."[35] In this way, then, librarians become facilitators for the students' process of meaning-making.

Establishing a Reflective Practice

Reflection as an important part of any pedagogical practice has been discussed broadly across education,[36] and more specifically within the context of library instruction.[37] These authors, among others, argue that reflection serves multiple purposes but first and foremost provides a basis for continuous pedagogical improvement. Larrivee contends that without critical reflection, teachers will "stay trapped in unexamined judgments, interpretations, assumptions, and expectations."[38] Being able to explain one's teacher identity, approaches to teaching, and pedagogical goals enables instruction librarians to develop a practice that is constantly adapting to best meet the needs of their community. While critical reflection underlies each of the parts of a critical pedagogical praxis, so too does it stand on its own, working in conjunction with the other components as an intentional process in and of itself. By adopting a habit of reflection, librarians can remain aware of their goals, expectations, and attitudes toward teaching.

As teaching librarians work to challenge students to transform their beliefs, values, and ways of knowing, so too must they themselves do the same by engaging in a reflective practice. Larrivee identifies three essential practices of reflection: making time for intentional reflection, becoming a problem-solver, and questioning the status quo.[39] Making time for reflection may mean writing regularly in a journal or it could mean spending fifteen minutes after an instruction session responding to questions such as "What did I do well? What could I do differently? What brought me joy?"[40] Teaching librarians may often reflect on such questions mentally, but by making a record of their thoughts and experiences immediately after teaching, they can "look more objectively at their behaviors in the classroom."[41] In asking such questions, librarians can begin to become problem-solvers, learn from their experiences, address feedback, and work to improve instruction. Throughout this process of problem-solving, librarians must also continue to question the status quo and the assumptions that often underpin their teaching practices. This process of reflection requires questioning beliefs about teaching and learning and evaluating responses to those beliefs. Although this process is complicated and may create moments of additional uncertainty, anxiety, and discomfort, reflective practice provides opportunities for personal growth as an educator, which is an essential element for improving student learning.

Pedagogical improvement may be one of the main goals of reflective practice but it is not the only benefit. A reflective practice does not focus solely on the negative aspects of instruction, such as the problems that need to be addressed, but it is also a positive activity that can reveal or reaffirm effective teaching practices.[42] When librarians incorporate reflection into their instruction and adopt it as a pedagogical habit, they can also identify the ways in which their teaching and student learning have improved over time. In this way, librarians can strengthen their own teaching, identify effective practices, and develop new visions for what is possible in the information literacy classroom.

Concluding Thoughts

Given the current state of information literacy instruction, librarians seeking to adopt critical pedagogical praxis will face "philosophical and practical tensions" within the context of both higher education and librarianship.[43] One-shot instruction sessions, even those that are scaffolded across a student's academic experience, are inadequate for instruction that aims to be transformational in nature. Deep learning and developing habits of mind require a comprehensive approach to instruction that moves beyond a quick injection. As Eisenhower and Smith observe, "As librarians, our engagement [with pedagogy] is not given but must be wrested from situations that would reduce such engagement to the motives of efficiency."[44] To adopt a critical pedagogical praxis may mean changing what the profession has been doing in the past, but that change will be necessary if librarians want to facilitate significant learning beyond their classroom.

Similarly, if librarians truly value lifelong learning, then information literacy instruction ought to focus on the habits of mind that support lifelong learning abilities, instead of focusing on skills-based approaches to research.[45] Such change requires librarians to shift their pedagogical focus toward a transformative education that empowers students to become engaged participants in their lives, society, and the problems and issues that matter to them. By embracing a critical pedagogical praxis, librarians can begin to engage with their own teaching in a way that moves beyond efficiency and standardization to instead focus on the student and in creating learning environments that holistically empower and transform them. In doing so, librarians can begin to expand the reach of their work as educators and, in turn, contribute meaningfully to their educational missions, thus bringing new visions of the possible to life.

ENDNOTES

1. Pat Hutchings, *Opening Lines: Approaches to the Scholarship of Teaching and Learning* (Menlo Park, CA: Carnegie Foundation, 2000), 4.
2. Association of College & Research Libraries, *Framework for Information Literacy for Higher Education* (Chicago: Association of College & Research Libraries (ACRL), 2016), http://www.ala.org/acrl/standards/ilframework.
3. Melissa Bowles-Terry and Carrie Donovan, "Serving Notice on the One-Shot: Changing Roles for Instruction Librarians," *International Information & Library Review* 48, no. 2 (2016): 137–41.
4. Veronica Arellano Douglas and Joanna Gadsby, "Gendered Labor and Library Instruction Coordinators: The Undervaluing of Feminized Work," in *ACRL 2017 Proceedings* (Chicago: American Library Association, 2017), http://www.ala.org/acrl/conferences/acrl2017/papers.
5. Scott Walter, "Librarians as Teachers: A Qualitative Inquiry into Professional Identity," *College & Research Libraries* 69, no. 1 (2008): 51–71; Jacalyn E. Bryan, "The Preparation of Academic Librarians Who Provide Instruction: A Comparison of First and Second Career Librarians," *Journal of Academic Librarianship* 42, no. 4 (2016): 340–54; Emily Wheeler and Pamela McKinney, "Are Librarians Teachers? Investigating Academic Librarians' Perceptions of Their Own Teaching Skills," *Journal of Information Literacy* 9, no. 2 (2015): 111.
6. Carolyn Caffrey Gardner and Jamie White-Farnham, "'She Has a Vocabulary I Just Don't Have': Faculty Culture and Information Literacy Collaboration," *Collaborative Librarianship* 5, no. 4 (2013): 235–42; Jonathan Cope and Jesús E. Sanabria, "Do We Speak the Same Language?: A Study of Faculty Perceptions of Information Literacy," *portal: Libraries and the Academy* 14, no. 4 (2014): 475–501; Yvonne Nalani Meulemans and Allison Carr, "Not at Your Service: Building Genuine Faculty-Librarian Partnerships," *Reference Services Review* 41, no. 1 (2013): 80–90.
7. Annie Downey, *Critical Information Literacy: Foundations, Inspiration, and Ideas* (Sacramento, CA: Library Juice Press, 2016), 16–17.
8. Downey, *Critical Information Literacy*, 173.
9. James Elmborg, "Critical Information Literacy: Implications for Instructional Practice," *Journal of Academic Librarianship* 32, no. 2 (2006): 193.
10. Critical consciousness "refers to learning to perceive social, political, and economic contradictions, and to take action against the oppressive elements of reality." Paulo Freire, *Pedagogy of the Oppressed*, trans. Myra Bergman Ramos (New York: Continuum, 1970), 35.
11. Elmborg, "Critical Information Literacy," 193.
12. Hutchings, *Opening Lines*, 5.
13. Walter, "Librarians as Teachers," 60.
14. For detailed information about how to write a teaching statement, the following publications are a great start: Janelle Zauha, "The Importance of a Philosophy of Teaching Statement to the Teacher/Librarian," *Communications in Information Literacy* 2, no. 2 (2008): 64–66; Dieter J. Schönwetter et al., "Teaching Philosophies Reconsidered: A Conceptual Model for the Development and Evaluation of Teaching Philosophy Statements," *International Journal for*

Academic Development 7, no. 1 (2002): 83–97; Gail Goodyear and Douglas Allchin, "Statements of Teaching Philosophy," in *To Improve the Academy. Resources for Student, Faculty, & Institutional Development*, vol 17, ed. Matthew Kaplan and Deborah Lieberman (Stillwater, OK: New Forums Press, 1998), 103–22.

15. Goodyear and Allchin, "Statements of Teaching Philosophy," 103.
16. Zauha, "The Importance of a Philosophy of Teaching Statement," 64.
17. Schönwetter et al., "Teaching Philosophies Reconsidered," 90.
18. Goodyear and Allchin, "Statements of Teaching Philosophy," 117.
19. Gary R. Morrison et al., *Designing Effective Instruction* (Hoboken, NJ: Wiley, 2013), 13.
20. "Critical Instructional Design—Digital Learning from a Critical Pedagogical Perspective," accessed August 1, 2017, http://criticalinstructionaldesign.com/.
21. As Freire explains, "In the banking concept of education, knowledge is a gift bestowed by those who consider themselves knowledgeable upon those whom they consider to know nothing." Freire, *Pedagogy of the Oppressed*, 72.
22. Maryellen Weimer, "Five Characteristics of Learner-Centered Teaching," *The Teaching Professor* (blog), August 8, 2012, https://www.teachingprofessor.com/topics/teaching-strategies/active-learning/five-characteristics-of-learner-centered-teaching/.
23. L. Dee Fink, *Creating Significant Learning Experiences: An Integrated Approach to Designing College Courses* (San Francisco, CA: Jossey-Bass, 2003).
24. Mary-Ann Winkelmes, "Transparency in Teaching Faculty Share Data and Improve Students' Learning," *Liberal Education* 99, no. 2 (2013): 48.
25. Maryellen Weimer, *Learner-Centered Teaching: Five Key Changes to Practice*, 2nd ed., (San Francisco, CA: Jossey-Bass, 2013), 26.
26. Phil Benson, "Learner-Centered Teaching," in *The Cambridge Guide to Pedagogy and Practice in Second Language Teaching*, ed. A. Burns and J. C. Richards (New York: Cambridge University Press, 2012), 30.
27. Weimer, *Learner-Centered Teaching*; Phyllis Blumberg, *Developing Learner-Centered Teaching: A Practical Guide for Faculty* (San Francisco: Jossey-Bass, 2009); Terry Doyle, *Learner-Centered Teaching: Putting the Research on Learning into Practice* (Sterling, VA: Stylus, 2011).
28. Also discussed in Blumberg, *Developing Learner-Centered Teaching*.
29. Weimer, *Learner-Centered Teaching*, 10–11.
30. Constructivist learning theory claims that students use prior knowledge to, individually or socially, construct new knowledge and meaning. Thus, a constructivist approach to teaching is one where the instructor is no longer the "single conduit of knowledge between the learners and the learning experience." David C. Leonard, "Constructivism," *Learning Theories, A to Z* (Westport, CT: Oryx Press, 2002).
31. Phyllis Blumberg, "How Critical Reflection Benefits Faculty as They Implement Learner-Centered Teaching," *New Directions for Teaching and Learning* 2015, no. 144 (2015): 89.
32. Weimer, *Learner-Centered Teaching*, 208–11.
33. Doyle, *Learner-Centered Teaching*, 71.
34. Ibid., 75.
35. Blumberg, "How Critical Reflection Benefits Faculty," 87.
36. Stephen D. Brookfield, *Becoming a Critically Reflective Teacher* (San Francisco, CA: John Wiley & Sons, 2017); John Dewey, *How We Think: A Restatement of the Relation of Reflective Thinking to the Educative Process* (Boston: Heath and Co., 1933); Barbara Larrivee, "Transforming Teaching Practice: Becoming the Critically Reflective Teacher," *Reflective Practice* 1, no. 3 (2000): 293–307; Jack Mezirow, *Fostering Critical Reflection in Adulthood: A Guide to Transformative and Emancipatory Learning* (San Francisco: Jossey-Bass, 1991); Donald A. Schön, *The Reflective Practitioner: How Professionals Think in Action* (New York: Basic Books, 1983).

37. Margaret E. S. Forrest, "On Becoming a Critically Reflective Practitioner," *Health Information & Libraries Journal* 25, no. 3 (2008): 229–32; Heidi Jacobs, "Falling out of Praxis: Reflection as a Pedagogical Habit of Mind," in *Critical Library Pedagogy Handbook, Volume One: Essays and Workbook Activities*, vol. 1, 2 vols., ed. Nicole Pagowsky and Kelly McElroy (Chicago: American Library Association, 2016), 1–7; Michelle Reale, *Becoming a Reflective Librarian and Teacher: Strategies for Mindful Academic Practice* (Chicago: ALA Editions, 2017); Jean Sheridan, "The Reflective Librarian: Some Observations On…," *Journal of Academic Librarianship* 16, no. 1 (1990): 22; Elizabeth K. Tompkins, "A Reflective Teaching Journal: An Instructional Improvement Tool for Academic Librarians," *College & Undergraduate Libraries* 16, no. 4 (2009): 221–38.
38. Larrivee, "Transforming Teaching Practice," 294.
39. Ibid.
40. Maria T. Accardi and Michelle Reale, "Critical Reflection to Improve and Grow as Librarians Who Teach," June 2, 2017.
41. Larrivee, "Transforming Teaching Practice," 297.
42. Mandi Goodsett, "Reflective Teaching: Improving Library Instruction Through Self-Reflection," *The Southeastern Librarian* 62, no. 3 (2014): 15.
43. Gr Keer, "Barriers to Critical Pedagogy in Information Literacy Teaching," in *Critical Library Pedagogy Handbook*, ed. Nicole Pagowsky and Kelly McElroy, vol. 1 (Chicago: American Library Association, 2016), 71.
44. Cathy Eisenhower and Dolsy Smith, "The Library as 'Stuck Place': Critical Pedagogy in the Corporate University," in *Critical Library Instruction: Theories and Methods*, ed. Maria T. Accardi and Emily Drabinski (Duluth, MN: Library Juice Press, 2010), 316.
45. For more on lifelong learning and its place among ALA's Core Values of Librarianship, see also James Elmborg, "Tending the Garden of Learning: Lifelong Learning as Core Library Value," *Library Trends* 64, no. 3 (2016): 533–55.

BIBLIOGRAPHY

Accardi, Maria T., and Michelle Reale. "Critical Reflection to Improve and Grow As Librarians Who Teach." Paper presented at the ACRL Instruction Section Management & Leadership Committee Discussion Series, June 2, 2017. https://www.youtube.com/watch?v=8rzfl6qbFh0&feature=youtu.be.

Association of College & Research Libraries. *Framework for Information Literacy for Higher Education*. Chicago: Association of College & Research Libraries (ACRL), 2016. http://www.ala.org/acrl/standards/ilframework.

Arellano Douglas, Veronica, and Joanna Gadsby. "Gendered Labor and Library Instruction Coordinators: The Undervaluing of Feminized Work." In *ACRL 2017 Proceedings*. Chicago: American Library Association, 2017. http://www.ala.org/acrl/conferences/acrl2017/papers.

Benson, Phil. "Learner-Centered Teaching." In *The Cambridge Guide to Pedagogy and Practice in Second Language Teaching*, edited by A. Burns and J. C. Richards, 30–37. New York: Cambridge University Press, 2012.

Blumberg, Phyllis. *Developing Learner-Centered Teaching: A Practical Guide for Faculty*. San Francisco: Jossey-Bass, 2009.

———. "How Critical Reflection Benefits Faculty as They Implement Learner-Centered Teaching." *New Directions for Teaching and Learning* 2015, no. 144 (2015): 87–97.

Bowles-Terry, Melissa, and Carrie Donovan. "Serving Notice on the One-Shot: Changing Roles for Instruction Librarians." *International Information & Library Review* 48, no. 2 (2016): 137–42.

Brookfield, Stephen D. *Becoming a Critically Reflective Teacher.* San Francisco, CA: John Wiley & Sons, 2017.

Bryan, Jacalyn E. "The Preparation of Academic Librarians Who Provide Instruction: A Comparison of First and Second Career Librarians." *Journal of Academic Librarianship* 42, no. 4 (2016): 340–54.

Cope, Jonathan, and Jesús E. Sanabria. "Do We Speak the Same Language?: A Study of Faculty Perceptions of Information Literacy." *Portal: Libraries and the Academy* 14, no. 4 (2014): 475–501.

"Critical Instructional Design—Digital Learning from a Critical Pedagogical Perspective." Accessed August 1, 2017. http://criticalinstructionaldesign.com/.

Dewey, John. *How We Think: A Restatement of the Relation of Reflective Thinking to the Educative Process.* Boston: Heath and Co., 1933.

Downey, Annie. *Critical Information Literacy: Foundations, Inspiration, and Ideas.* Sacramento, CA: Library Juice Press, 2016.

Doyle, Terry. *Learner-Centered Teaching: Putting the Research on Learning into Practice.* Sterling, VA: Stylus, 2011.

Eisenhower, Cathy, and Dolsy Smith. "The Library as 'Stuck Place': Critical Pedagogy in the Corporate University." In *Critical Library Instruction: Theories and Methods*, edited by Maria T. Accardi and Emily Drabinski, 305–17. Duluth, MN: Library Juice Press, 2010.

Elmborg, James. "Critical Information Literacy: Implications for Instructional Practice." *Journal of Academic Librarianship* 32, no. 2 (2006): 192–99.

———. "Tending the Garden of Learning: Lifelong Learning as Core Library Value." *Library Trends* 64, no. 3 (2016): 533–55.

Fink, L. Dee. *Creating Significant Learning Experiences: An Integrated Approach to Designing College Courses.* San Francisco, CA: Jossey-Bass, 2003.

Forrest, Margaret E. S. "On Becoming a Critically Reflective Practitioner." *Health Information & Libraries Journal* 25, no. 3 (2008): 229–32.

Freire, Paulo. *Pedagogy of the Oppressed.* Translated by Myra Bergman Ramos. New York: Continuum, 1970.

Gardner, Carolyn Caffrey, and Jamie White-Farnham. "'She Has a Vocabulary I Just Don't Have': Faculty Culture and Information Literacy Collaboration." *Collaborative Librarianship* 5, no. 4 (2013): 235–42.

Goodsett, Mandi. "Reflective Teaching: Improving Library Instruction Through Self-Reflection." *The Southeastern Librarian* 62, no. 3 (2014).

Goodyear, Gail, and Douglas Allchin. "Statements of Teaching Philosophy." In *To Improve the Academy. Resources for Student, Faculty, & Institutional Development*, edited by Matthew Kaplan and Deborah Lieberman, 17:103–22. Stillwater, OK: New Forums Press, 1998.

Hutchings, Pat. *Opening Lines: Approaches to the Scholarship of Teaching and Learning.* Menlo Park, CA: Carnegie Foundation, 2000.

Jacobs, Heidi. "Falling out of Praxis: Reflection as a Pedagogical Habit of Mind." In *Critical Library Pedagogy Handbook, Volume One: Essays and Workbook Activities*, edited by Nicole Pagowsky and Kelly McElroy 1:1–7. Chicago: American Library Association, 2016.

Keer, Gr. "Barriers to Critical Pedagogy in Information Literacy Teaching." In *Critical Library Pedagogy Handbook*, edited by Nicole Pagowsky and Kelly McElroy, 1:65–74. Chicago:

American Library Association, 2016.

Larrivee, Barbara. "Transforming Teaching Practice: Becoming the Critically Reflective Teacher." *Reflective Practice* 1, no. 3 (2000): 293–307.

Leonard, David C. "Constructivism." *Learning Theories, A to Z.* Westport, CT: Oryx Press, 2002.

Meulemans, Yvonne Nalani, and Allison Carr. "Not at Your Service: Building Genuine Faculty-Librarian Partnerships." *Reference Services Review* 41, no. 1 (2013): 80–90.

Mezirow, Jack. *Fostering Critical Reflection in Adulthood: A Guide to Transformative and Emancipatory Learning.* San Francisco: Jossey-Bass, 1991.

Morrison, Gary R., Steven M. Ross, Howard K. Kalman, and Jerrold E. Kemp. *Designing Effective Instruction.* Hoboken, NJ: Wiley, 2013.

Reale, Michelle. *Becoming a Reflective Librarian and Teacher: Strategies for Mindful Academic Practice.* Chicago: ALA Editions, 2017.

Schön, Donald A. *The Reflective Practitioner: How Professionals Think in Action.* New York: Basic Books, 1983.

Schönwetter, Dieter J., Laura Sokal, Marcia Friesen, and K. Lynn Taylor. "Teaching Philosophies Reconsidered: A Conceptual Model for the Development and Evaluation of Teaching Philosophy Statements." *International Journal for Academic Development* 7, no. 1 (2002): 83–97.

Sheridan, Jean. "The Reflective Librarian: Some Observations On…" *Journal of Academic Librarianship* 16, no. 1 (1990): 22.

Tompkins, Elizabeth K. "A Reflective Teaching Journal: An Instructional Improvement Tool for Academic Librarians." *College & Undergraduate Libraries* 16, no. 4 (2009): 221–38.

Walter, Scott. "Librarians as Teachers: A Qualitative Inquiry into Professional Identity." *College & Research Libraries* 69, no. 1 (2008): 51–71.

Weimer, Maryellen. "Five Characteristics of Learner-Centered Teaching." *The Teaching Professor* (blog), August 8, 2012. https://www.teachingprofessor.com/topics/teaching-strategies/active-learning/five-characteristics-of-learner-centered-teaching/.

———. *Learner-Centered Teaching: Five Key Changes to Practice.* 2nd ed., San Francisco, CA: Jossey-Bass, 2013.

Wheeler, Emily, and Pamela McKinney. "Are Librarians Teachers? Investigating Academic Librarians' Perceptions of Their Own Teaching Skills." *Journal of Information Literacy* 9, no. 2 (2015): 111.

Winkelmes, Mary-Ann. "Transparency in Teaching Faculty Share Data and Improve Students' Learning." *Liberal Education* 99, no. 2 (2013): 48–55.

Zauha, Janelle. "The Importance of a Philosophy of Teaching Statement to the Teacher/Librarian." *Communications in Information Literacy* 2, no. 2 (2008): 64–66.

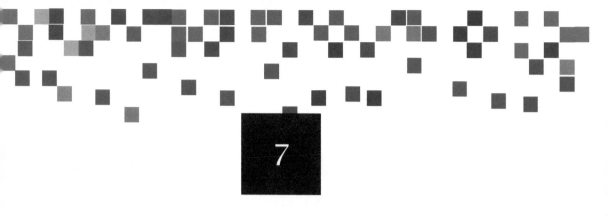

7

Historicizing the Library:

Information Literacy Instruction in the History Classroom

Maura Seale

Introduction

In 2013, Georgetown University's Center for New Designs in Learning and Scholarship invited historian David Pace to work with the History department on redesigning its general education courses. Pace is best known for his Decoding the Disciplines Project, which focuses on disciplinary bottlenecks to learning, and emerged from his work on the History Learning Project.[1] The librarian for American and European history was invited to participate in the redesign workshops and offer the library's perspective.

As a result of the workshops, a subset of the general education (History 099) courses at Georgetown, a large doctoral university with approximately 7,500 undergraduate and 11,000 graduate students,[2] now include "History Lab." In History Lab, students are asked to essentially "do" history, which entails finding and engaging with both primary and secondary sources in ways that parallel how historians work with sources. The library instruction for these courses draws on the Scholarship of Teaching and Learning (SoTL) in history as well as critical information literacy; its goal is to get students to think about library resources as historical rather than natural.

This is a crucial component of historical thinking and an essential element in empowering students to critically use library resources. Denaturalizing and historicizing library resources introduce distance into students' understanding of library resources and allows them to see how collections developed historically, how some primary sources were preserved while others were not, as well as how some primary sources that they are able to imagine might never have existed. It empowers students and allows them to use these

resources more effectively, to recognize that controlled vocabularies are constructed, that article indexes carry traces of their print predecessors, and that the information landscape is subject to the same sort of power dynamics as the social world.

This case study outlines several prominent theories in the SoTL in history and then traces how that scholarship was integrated with critical information literacy in Georgetown University's History 099 library instruction sessions.

Decoding the Disciplines

Decoding the Disciplines is a framework for teaching students how to engage in higher-order, disciplinary thinking. The reasons underlying this approach are that

> the mental operations required of undergraduates differ enormously from discipline to discipline, that these ways of thinking are rarely presented to students explicitly, that students generally lack an opportunity to practice and receive feedback on particular skills in isolation from others, and that there is rarely a systematic assessment of the extent to which students have mastered each of the ways of thinking that are essential to particular disciplines.[3]

The seven-step process of decoding begins by identifying the integral moments where students get stuck and are unable to progress in the discipline. These "bottlenecks" can be both cognitive and affective. The second step is where the decoding happens: the goal of this step is to "make explicit the mental operations that students must master in order to overcome specific bottlenecks in a course. Since many of these are so automatic to instructors that they have become invisible, a systematic process of deconstructing disciplinary practice is necessary."[4] Once these implicit mental moves are articulated, they can be modeled and students can practice with them. Although there are additional steps in the framework, this case study focuses on the first two steps.

Procedural Knowledge

Decoding the Disciplines, although meant to be applicable to all disciplines, echoes recent work on SoTL in history. In *Thinking Historically: Educating Students for the Twenty-First Century*, Stephane Lévesque seeks to "devise a conceptualization of history and identify procedural concepts of the discipline relevant to twenty-first-century students, to give students the means to a more critical and disciplinary study of the past."[5] Crucial to Lévesque's understanding of history is the distinction between substantive and procedural knowledge. Substantive knowledge is knowledge of the content of history—the events, people, and other elements that constitute the past. It is the *what* of history. In contrast, procedural concepts are about "structuring or giving sense and coherence to events in history (concepts giving shape to historical practice and thinking about the past)."[6] Procedural knowledge is the *how* of history. Lévesque focuses on procedural knowledge because it is core to disciplinary thinking in history and because it is what enables students to adopt a critical stance towards history, as well as heritage and myth, which are common-sense, uncritical uses of history: "Without procedural thinking, students are left passively absorbing the narratives and viewpoints of authorities, too puzzled or indifferent to use the tools and mechanisms for making sense of the past. Thus, students *cannot* practice history or even think critically about its content if they have no understanding of how one constructs and shares historical knowledge."[7] When students grasp the *how* of history, they are able to unpack truth claims about the *what*. To Lévesque, "to think historically is thus to understand how knowledge has been constructed and what it means."[8]

Lévesque identifies five procedural concepts, which are tied to "essential questions": historical significance, continuity and change, progress and decline, evidence, and historical empathy.[9] As with the bottlenecks of Decoding the Disciplines, these ideas are central to history and students cannot progress without comprehending them, but they are not often articulated or taught.[10] Lévesque is careful to note that although he and other scholars such as Peter Seixas suggest these procedural elements of history are central to the practice of history, the elements themselves "should not be viewed as fixed or given but as developing, always problematic and incomplete, contingent on and limited by people's own historiographical culture."[11] As with other disciplines, history is produced and exists within historically specific social, political, and economic formations. The procedural concepts of history, or the rules of any discipline, then, are not eternal and unchanging, but instead constantly produced and reproduced.

Historical Thinking

Sam Wineburg's pedagogical theory is rooted in what he terms "historical thinking." Similar to Lévesque's procedural knowledge, historical thinking is a method, approach, or epistemology, rather than the specific content of history. For Wineburg, historical thinking resides in the tension between familiarity and strangeness, "between feelings of proximity to and feelings of distance from the people we seek to understand. Neither of these poles does full justice to history's complexity, and veering to one side or the other only dulls history's jagged edges and leaves us with cliché and caricature."[12] The familiarity and strangeness that constitute historical thinking cannot be resolved, as both are irreducible and essential; it is instead working within "two contradictory positions: first, that our established modes of thinking are an inheritance that cannot be sloughed off; second, that if we make no attempt to slough them off, we are doomed to a mind-numbing presentism that reads the present onto the past."[13] Although Wineburg does not outline a framework as Lévesque does, his notion of historical thinking is fundamentally connected to asking questions, analyzing and synthesizing evidence, and practicing empathy. Wineburg also emphasizes approaching the past with "a kind of caution" and "humility before the narrowness of our contemporary experience"[14] to avoid presentism in efforts to make sense of history.

Uncoverage

In contrast to Wineburg and Lévesque, Lendol Calder specifically focuses on the traditional survey course, which rather than "covering" topics should "uncover" the processes by which history comes into being: "Survey instructors should aim to uncover history. We should be designing classroom environments that expose the very things hidden away by traditional survey instruction: the linchpin ideas of historical inquiry that are not obvious or easily comprehended; the inquiries, arguments, assumptions, and points of view that make knowledge what it is for practitioners of our discipline; the cognitive contours of history as an epistemological domain."[15] Similar to Decoding the Disciplines, the procedural knowledge of Lévesque and the historical thinking of Wineburg, Calder seeks to articulate how historians approach the past, rather than recounting the "facts." He identifies six elements of what he calls "historical mindedness": questioning, connecting, sourcing, making inferences, considering alternate perspectives, and recognizing limits to one's knowledge.[16] There are clear continuities with both Wineburg and Lévesque: the importance of questions, empathy and understanding the limitations of what can be known, and synthesis and analysis of evidence.

Calder, like Lévesque, notes that the ultimate goal is not just for students to do history but to learn to critically assess truth claims made about history. He calls this the "moral" dimension of history: "What the past means for our ethics and self-knowledge and how knowledge of the past shapes our general understanding of the world (and vice versa)."[17] Wineburg, too, emphasizes the political, moral, or ethical element of historical thinking: "Mature historical knowing teaches us to do the opposite: to go beyond our own image, to go beyond our brief life, and to go beyond the fleeting moment in human history into which we've been born."[18] For each of these scholars, doing history is rooted in perceiving and understanding the constructedness of narratives about the past and grappling with both the ongoing relevance of the past to the present and also its ultimate unknowability.[19] Doing history requires students to sit with irresolvable ideas of politics, power, and ambiguity.

Critical Information Literacy

In her recent book, *Critical Information Literacy: Foundations, Inspiration, and Ideas*, Annie Downey presents a working definition of critical information literacy (CIL) while acknowledging that there is no "fully developed and agreed upon definition."[20] CIL is grounded in a critical approach to information sources that seeks to unpack and understand the power dynamics and social, economic, and political contexts in which information is produced and used. It also recognizes the affective dimensions of research,[21] questions notions of neutrality and "skills,"[22] and promotes agency, empowerment, and sometimes liberation.[23]

In its emphasis on context, CIL might also be understood as historicizing or thinking historically about the library. CIL brings larger questions of power dynamics and political, economic, and social contexts of information to library instruction. Some library users might think about using library systems through the prism of presentism and assume their workings are transparent and obvious to users.[24] Many might not pay attention to the histories that have led to current library systems, but these systems are the products of specific decisions and choices made by particular actors. Rather than teaching the "facts" or *what* of library systems, historicizing the library seeks to get at the *how* by uncovering their historical constructedness. Historicizing library systems and, by extension, the library research process is a key element in locating them within larger social formations; to historicize is to denaturalize and make obvious the constructedness. The project of historicizing the library seeks to uncover the "jagged edges" of libraries and to get students and other users to question the library, to understand it as always incomplete and inflected by the social world, rather than taking it at face value. This project also seeks to empower those who conduct library research and use library systems. When the constructedness of the library is uncovered and revealed, it is no longer mysterious, and users are able to employ it to their own ends; they are able to question it and approach it critically, rather than simply adapting to its limitations and drawbacks. These moves work to introduce a critical distance between users of library systems and those systems themselves. That distance is necessary for questioning, challenging, and, ultimately, effectively using those systems to conduct library research. As such, historicizing the library resonates with the broad ethos and goals of CIL.

Historicizing the Library in Practice

The Georgetown History faculty very much wanted students in general education courses to practice doing history and included it in the learning goals: "Students will be introduced to the rudiments of historical research, including the use of library and online resources, basic notions of historiography, and the purpose and practice of proper citation methods."[25] The workshops, using the Decoding the Disciplines framework and History Learning Project, thought through the bottlenecks in historical research and writing, and tried to articulate the tacit knowledge, thought processes, and practices that experts bring to historical research and writing. The workshops also looked at ways to model and have students practice working through these bottlenecks during History Lab. The bottlenecks included reading and comprehending a scholarly article, finding both primary and secondary sources, working with primary sources as evidence, analyzing textual and non-textual primary sources (images, music, maps, data, material culture), and citation.[26] Each of these bottlenecks would eventually become the subject of a History Lab. Identifying and explicitly teaching these practices speaks not just to Calder's call for uncovering what historians do, but also touches on Lévesque's procedural knowledge and its emphasis on evidence.

These specific bottlenecks were contextualized by broader bottlenecks of historical practice: understanding that history is not a series of facts, but analysis and interpretation based on evidence; the importance of contingency; and that as interpreters of history, individuals are situated historically, and their viewpoints are not neutral, objective, or transparent. These bottlenecks resonate with Wineburg's notion of historical thinking and the approach and goals of critical information literacy. With both history and the library, students tend toward presentism or interpreting the unfamiliar in terms of what they already know. This works against the questioning and analysis of evidence emphasized by both SoTL in history and CIL and, ultimately, against students effectively using library systems to conduct research. Students need to recognize the strangeness of library systems without being put off by it, to paraphrase T. Mills Kelly, and work between familiarity and strangeness.[27]

Library systems and research practices, too, are situated historically, and library instruction that foregrounds this concept can counter the bottleneck of presentism. Information is always produced, organized, and consumed within specific historical contexts, and expert library research is grounded in and draws on historical thinking. The library instruction sessions for History Lab focused on two broad concepts that work to historicize the library. The first is an understanding of the overarching history of library systems and how that history can be seen in the ways systems are currently structured. For example, online library catalogs still rely on metadata and controlled vocabulary as access points, just as physical card catalogs did, while article indexes duplicate indexes that once appeared in print format, like *Historical Abstracts*. The second concept is library system architecture, which is also often tied to the individual histories of systems. This includes distinctions between different forms of searching (full-text, record, specific field) and more abstract concepts like metadata and controlled vocabulary. Instruction that focuses on these concepts uncovers what libraries and librarians do, just as Calder seeks to uncover what historians do, and reveals library systems to be historical and constructed. Understanding how library systems work and then practicing research with that new knowledge gets students closer to the *how* of library systems and research. This approach articulates, models, and then asks students to practice Lévesque's procedural knowledge of the library.

Other concepts can be used to further point to the history and constructedness of library systems and research. Controlled vocabulary is not just a useful way to refine a search, it is also often inaccurate, dated, and makes assumptions about the social world—for example, that whiteness, maleness, and cis-ness do not need to be named, presumably because they are normal. Databases such as of *America: History & Life* and *Historical Abstracts* began as print indexes and now, as article databases, they cover different sets of journals due to their origins as print indexes. Journal articles are also commodities, though, and so the form of these databases is unlikely to change given the economics of scholarly publishing. Primary source databases require huge amounts of labor to produce and, as such, students only have access to these materials because libraries purchase them. This directly affects which primary sources are accessible at any given institution. Readex's *America's Historical Imprints* and Gale's *Sabin Americana* are based on bibliographies compiled by white Anglo-American men during the late nineteenth and early twentieth centuries.[28] The sources in these databases, the sources students have easy access to because they were compiled, digitized, and then purchased by Georgetown, are necessarily subject to contemporary notions of value, importance, and authority at play in the creation of the bibliographies and their digital counterparts and in Georgetown's purchasing of the databases.

The goal is not that students retain all of this information but rather to openly articulate and uncover aspects of library systems and research that they might not have considered before, so that they might question them instead of assuming their transparency. Learning about the library in these terms works against presentism by denaturalizing the present and tracing its connections with the past. Questioning is at the heart of doing history because it indicates engagement with rather than rejection of history's unfamiliarity and ambiguity, an engagement that seeks to make sense of and understand. As Lévesque, Wineburg, Calder, and Kelly suggest from the perspective of the SoTL in history, and as CIL theorists, scholars, and practitioners describe, the ability to question is ultimately empowering for students. Uncovering the library opens a critical distance between users and library systems and research; it creates a space in which questioning can occur and the realization that these systems can, and should be, questioned.

The Decoding the Disciplines framework uncovers the how and why of what librarians and historians do. To uncover is to make legible. Once something is legible, it can be understood and used by others. Being able to explain disciplinary practices to students so that they may do them themselves ultimately empowers students to participate in disciplinary conversations and learn on their own and destabilizes notions of disciplinary power and authority. Disciplinary research and practice become something anyone can engage in to some extent and less of an exclusive club with limited membership. Integrating Decoding the Disciplines and the SoTL in history can help library instruction move toward critical information literacy, toward empowering students, even when discussing ideas as mundane as controlled vocabulary and article indexes. Empowering students to become thoughtful and critical actors in the world is, ultimately, what Lévesque, Wineburg, and Calder argue historical thinking fosters and what critical information literacy instruction rooted in historical thinking can promote.

Conclusion

Decoding the Disciplines offers a framework for reflecting on and revising instructional practice by drawing on classroom experience and disciplinary expertise. As such, it offers a way for faculty and librarians to speak across various boundaries, whether of semester-long courses as opposed to one-shot workshops or subject-specific rather than generalist expertise—and for librarians to understand and articulate information literacy or library instruction as of a piece with disciplinary thinking, and thus vital. The SoTL in history largely follows Decoding the Disciplines in its attempts to unpack expert practice in history and then have students work through it. Lévesque's procedural knowledge, Wineburg's historical thinking, and Calder's uncoverage represent varying but overlapping ways of grappling with and articulating historical practice; the overarching goal to empower students to engage thoughtfully with the past and present. CIL likewise seeks to empower students to participate critically in library systems and research. The project of historicizing the library draws together these approaches to develop a library pedagogy that focuses on helping students think historically about library systems and research.

ENDNOTES

1. "Decoding the Disciplines," *Decoding the Disciplines*, accessed February 6, 2018, http://decodingthedisciplines.org/; Arlene Diaz, Joan Middendorf, David Pace, and Leah Shopkow, "The History Learning Project: A Department 'Decodes' Its Students," *Journal of American History* 94, no. 4 (2008): 1211–24.

2. Georgetown University Office of Assessment and Decision Support, "2016–2017 Common Data Set," Georgetown Office of Assessment and Decision Support, accessed February 6, 2018, https://oads.georgetown.edu/commondataset.

3. Joan Middendorf and David Pace, "Decoding the Disciplines: A Model for Helping Students Learn Disciplinary Ways of Thinking," *New Directions for Teaching and Learning* 2004, no. 98 (2004): 3.

4. "Step 2: Uncover the Mental Operations that Students Must Master to Get Past the Bottleneck," *Decoding the Disciplines*, accessed October 27, 2017, http://decodingthedisciplines.org/step-2-uncover-the-mental-task/.

5. Stéphane Lévesque, *Thinking Historically: Educating Students for the Twenty-First Century* (Toronto: University of Toronto Press, 2008), 8.

6. Lévesque, *Thinking Historically*, 16.

7. Ibid., 17.

8. Ibid., 27.

9. Ibid., 37.

10. Ibid., 32.

11. Ibid., 33.

12. Sam Wineburg, "Historical Thinking and Other Unnatural Acts," *The Phi Delta Kappan* 80, no. 7 (1999): 490.

13. Wineburg, "Historical Thinking," 493.

14. Ibid., 497; Donald A. Yerxa, ed., *Recent Themes in Historical Thinking: Historians in Conversation* (Columbia, SC: University of South Carolina Press, 2008), 37.

15. Lendol Calder, "Uncoverage: Toward a Signature Pedagogy for the History Survey," *The Journal of American History* 92, no. 4 (2006): 1363.

16. Calder, "Uncoverage," 1364.

17. Ibid., 1366.

18. Wineburg, "Historical Thinking," 498.

19. T. Mills Kelly, *Teaching History in the Digital Age* (Ann Arbor, MI: University of Michigan Press, 2013), 22–23, itemizes commonalities in the theorizing of historical thinking: "The ability to tell the difference between a primary and a secondary source. The ability to "source the source"; that is, figure out who created the source, when it was created, and so on. The ability to obtain information about the authority of the source and to assess that authority in light of other evidence. The ability to set sources in their proper chronological order and to understand why that ordering is important. The ability to construct an original argument based upon evidence from various sources. The ability to recognize the strangeness of the past without being put off by that strangeness. The ability to make comparative judgments about evidence. The ability to recognize what one does not or cannot know from the evidence at hand. The ability to understand that events are understood differently by different people. The ability to triangulate between and among sources. The ability to ask probing questions—not just what happened, but why did it happen this way and why didn't it happen that way? The ability to recognize the role of causality. The ability to critique evidence both on its own terms and in terms of its value to a larger analytical project. The ability to recognize lines of argument in historical thought. The ability to present the past in clear ways, whether in writing or in other media, saying what can be said and not saying what cannot."

20. Annie Downey, *Critical Information Literacy: Foundations, Inspiration, and Ideas* (Sacramento, CA: Library Juice Press, 2016), 41.

21. Maria T. Accardi, Emily Drabinski, and Alana Kumbier, *Critical Library Instruction: Theories and Methods* (Duluth, MN: Library Juice Press, 2010), xiii.

22. Eamon Tewell, "A Decade of Critical Information Literacy: A Review of the Literature," *Communications in Information Literacy* 9, no. 1 (2015): 25.

23. Tewell, "A Decade of Critical Information Literacy"; Accardi, Drabinski, and Kumbier, *Critical Library Instruction*.

24. This is a broad generalization, but as Wineburg points out, this is "our psychological condition at rest," "Historical Thinking," 496.

25. Georgetown University History Department, "Learning Goals for all Academic Programs," Georgetown Department of History, accessed October 27, 2017, https://history.georgetown.edu/about/learning-goals#.

26. These are similar to the bottlenecks identified in the History Learning Project. Diaz, Middendorf, Pace, and Shopkow, "History Learning Project," 1223.

27. Kelly, *Teaching History in the Digital Age*, 22.

28. Readex's *America's Historical Imprints* is based on Charles Evans's *The American Bibliography: A Chronological Dictionary of All Books, Pamphlets and Periodical Publications Printed in the United States of America from the Genesis of Printing in 1639 Down to and Including the Year 1820, with Bibliographical and Biographical Notes*, which he began compiling in 1902. Clifford Shipton continued the work after Evans's death in 1935. Ralph Shaw and Richard H. Shoemaker extended the bibliography's coverage through 1829. Evans was affiliated with the American Antiquarian Society and co-founded the American Library Association. Shipton was the head librarian of the American Antiquarian Association. Shaw and Shoemaker also worked in libraries. Shipton's influence on the *Bibliography*, and the resulting digital collection, can be seen in its geographic focus on areas that would become the United States and concomitant exclusion of other parts of British America and exclusion of non-English language material. The Bibliography was a site for arguments by Shipton and his contemporaries about "what constituted the print heritage of America" and, hence, America itself. David S. Shields, "On the Circumstances Surrounding the Creation of *Early American Literature*," *Early American Literature* 50, no. 1 (2015): 24; Brendan Rapple, "Evans, Charles (1850–1935), Librarian and Bibliographer," *American National Biography*, accessed February 25, 2018, https://doi.org/10.1093/anb/9780198606697.article.2000327. *Sabin Americana* is based on Joseph Sabin's *A Dictionary of Books Relating to America, from Its Discovery to the Present Time*, also known as *Biblioteca Americana*. Sabin was an Anglo-American bookseller. After his death, the *Biblioteca* was completed with funding from the Carnegie Corporation under the direction of librarians Wilberforce Eames and R. W. G. Vail. John Mark Tucker, "Sabin, Joseph (1821–1881), Bibliographer and Bookseller," *American National Biography*, accessed February 25, 2018, https://doi.org/10.1093/anb/9780198606697.article.2000309. These are very brief overviews of the histories of two digital primary source databases, but all library resources have similar histories. For in-depth examples of "doing history" with library resources, see Ian Gadd, "The Use and Misuse of *Early English Books Online*," *Literature Compass* 6, no. 3 (2009): 680–92 and Bonnie Mak, "Archaeology of a Digitization," *Journal of the Association for Information Science and Technology* 65, no. 8 (2014): 1515–26.

Bibliography

Accardi, Maria T., Emily Drabinski, and Alana Kumbier, eds. *Critical Library Instruction: Theories and Methods*. Duluth, MN: Library Juice Press, 2010.

Calder, Lendol. "Uncoverage: Toward a Signature Pedagogy for the History Survey." *The Journal of American History* 92, no. 4 (2006): 1358–70.

"Decoding the Disciplines." *Decoding the Disciplines.* Accessed February 6, 2018. http://decodingthedisciplines.org/.

Diaz, Arlene, Joan Middendorf, David Pace, and Leah Shopkow. "The History Learning Project: A Department 'Decodes' Its Students." *Journal of American History* 94, no. 4 (2008): 1211–24.

Downey, Annie. *Critical Information Literacy: Foundations, Inspiration, and Ideas.* Sacramento, CA: Library Juice Press, 2016.

Gadd, Ian. "The Use and Misuse of *Early English Books Online.*" *Literature Compass* 6, no. 3 (2009): 680–92.

Georgetown University Department of History. "Learning Goals for all Academic Programs." *Georgetown University Department of History.* Accessed October 27, 2017. https://history.georgetown.edu/about/learning-goals#.

Georgetown University Office of Assessment and Decision Support. "2016–2017 Common Data Set." Georgetown University Office of Assessment and Decision Support. Accessed February 6, 2018. https://oads.georgetown.edu/commondataset.

Kelly, T. Mills. *Teaching History in the Digital Age.* Ann Arbor, MI: University of Michigan Press, 2013.

Lévesque, Stéphane. *Thinking Historically: Educating Students for the Twenty-First Century.* Toronto: University of Toronto Press, 2008.

Mak, Bonnie. "Archaeology of a Digitization." *Journal of the Association for Information Science and Technology* 65, no. 8 (2014): 1515–26.

Middendorf, Joan, and David Pace. "Decoding the Disciplines: A Model for Helping Students Learn Disciplinary Ways of Thinking." *New Directions for Teaching and Learning* no. 98 (2004): 1–12.

Rapple, Brendan. "Evans, Charles (1850–1935), Librarian and Bibliographer." *American National Biography.* Accessed February 25, 2018. https://doi.org/10.1093/anb/9780198606697.article.2000327.

Shields, David S. "On the Circumstances Surrounding the Creation of *Early American Literature.*" *Early American Literature* 50, no. 1 (2015): 21–40.

"Step 2: Uncover the Mental Operations that Students Must Master to Get Past the Bottleneck." *Decoding the Disciplines.* Accessed October 27, 2017. http://decodingthedisciplines.org/step-2-uncover-the-mental-task/.

Tewell, Eamon. "A Decade of Critical Information Literacy: A Review of the Literature." *Communications in Information Literacy* 9, no. 1 (2015): 24–43.

Tucker, John Mark. "Sabin, Joseph (1821–1881), Bibliographer and Bookseller." *American National Biography.* Accessed February 25, 2018. https://doi.org/10.1093/anb/9780198606697.article.2000309.

Wineburg, Sam. "Historical Thinking and Other Unnatural Acts." *The Phi Delta Kappan* 80, no. 7 (1999): 488–99.

Yerxa, Donald A., ed. *Recent Themes in Historical Thinking: Historians in Conversation.* Columbia, SC: University of South Carolina Press, 2008.

8

Not Missing the Point(s):

Applying Specifications Grading to Credit-Bearing Information Literacy Classes

Kathy Shields, Kyle Denlinger, and Meghan Webb

Introduction

Librarians at the Z. Smith Reynolds Library (ZSR) have been involved in teaching credit-bearing information literacy courses since 2002.[1] Recently, a group of instruction librarians at ZSR began implementing the ideas outlined in Linda Nilson's 2015 book, *Specifications Grading: Restoring Rigor, Motivating Students, and Saving Faculty Time,* to address some of the challenges they all shared, including motivating students, providing meaningful feedback, and conveying appropriate course expectations.[2] As a new grading model, specifications grading (SG) has not yet been explored as it applies to credit-bearing information literacy instruction. Its emphasis on competency-based learning has the potential to profoundly influence the way we teach and assess our students and it directly aligns with our values as instructors.

In this case study, the authors share the connection between Scholarship of Teaching and Learning (SoTL) theory and SG, an overview of SG, their experience so far of using SG to design and teach courses, and suggestions for further research.

Overview of Specifications Grading (SG)

Mia O'Brien challenges SoTL practitioners to take a more student-centered, reflective, evidence-based approach to the design of teaching and learning activities.[3] After reflecting on O'Brien's SoTL Compass, it becomes apparent that Nilson's proposed specifications grading system sits squarely within the kinds of deliberately designed activities for which

O'Brien advocates, particularly in the way SG asks, "What will my students learn and why is it significant?"[4] and "What can I do to support students to learn effectively?"[5] This section explores what SG is and how it answers both of these questions.

In her book, Nilson presents a somewhat radical alternative to traditional points-based grading systems, which she sees as being inherently flawed.[6] Points-based systems, Nilson argues, are ineffective at assessing outcomes and do not motivate students to do any more work than the minimum required to earn a passing grade. In fact, Nilson claims that they may actually incentivize students to produce sloppy work and enter into the kinds of negotiations instructors find so tiring: asking for extensions, arguing for points, and settling for partial credit. Nilson also says that the wide discretion afforded to instructors in their evaluations of students, coupled with the tremendous pressure put on instructors to "pass" students, means that often it is *only* those students who earn an A who even approach achieving the learning outcomes (LOs), to say nothing of those who earn lower grades. "A grade of C," Nilson writes, "does not communicate competency in any particular skill or ability; students routinely pass courses even though their graded work falls considerably below our objectives for them."[7] Traditional, points-based grading, in other words, is a fine mechanism for "passing" students but it says very little about what that "pass" actually means. Clearly, if students are earning credit for a course but cannot demonstrate achievement of the learning outcomes, there is a serious disconnect between the grade and the assessment of learning.

Nilson's proposed specifications grading system encourages doing away with points-based grading entirely. In an attempt to increase rigor, align grades to outcomes, support and motivate students to achieve higher learning, and eliminate some of the drudgery of grading, Nilson outlines a system in which all (or most) assignments are graded on a pass/fail basis. In SG, instructors hold students to very high standards that must be met in order to earn a passing grade. These standards, or *specifications*, are closely aligned with the learning outcomes for each assignment and are presented to students in the form of a checklist or a single-level rubric. If a student fails to meet even a single specification, Nilson reasons that the student has not successfully demonstrated achievement of the outcomes. She suggests that the student receive a non-passing grade for the assignment, at which point the instructor may provide the student an opportunity to revise to prove mastery of the content. Compared to most multi-level rubric assessment, which could award students points for things like "grammar and mechanics" while the core objectives remain unmet, with SG, it is all or nothing—everything is weighted with equal importance. Arriving at the set of specifications for each assignment becomes an exercise in "teaching-as-design,"[8] in which the instructor must carefully reflect on what is essential to demonstrate the outcome. Such concern for alignment, design, and assessment of learning is a hallmark of the kinds of SoTL activities for which O'Brien advocates.

However, SG does not call for abolishing letter grades altogether. Rather, like traditional grading, Nilson suggests that the final letter grade be representative of the extent to which the student has demonstrated achievement of the outcomes. The difference, however, is that higher letter grades in SG correspond to "bundles" of *more* or *more difficult* assignments, not simple accumulation of more points. Students then select their desired grade and corresponding workload. For example, a student attempting to earn an A would complete more or more difficult work than a student attempting to earn a B, but both students would be expected to meet the specifications for each required assignment. A high final grade, then, would indicate that a student has demonstrated achievement of the LOs at a higher level than would otherwise be required for a lower grade. This approach has numerous benefits, which Nilson supports by linking to abundant research on student motivation.[9] SG raises student confidence by presenting the student with clear expectations, increases student autonomy by giving students meaningful choice in the activities they complete, motivates students to perform at a high level, and makes student work much more authentic by shifting the locus of control to the student and giving students complete ownership over their grade.[10]

Although Nilson does not explicitly say it, SG should be thought of as much more than a grading mechanism—it is a framework for "teaching-as-design" that requires careful reflection on the part of the instructor. Before implementing SG, an instructor must first determine what is essential to the course; that is, "what must be learned"[11] and how the instructor's design can support students in that learning. SG is borne out of a concern for student learning and demands the kind of deliberate design and systematic implementation required of all SoTL activities.[12]

Literature Review

In developing SG, Nilson draws from research and practice on various grading methodologies and student motivation. She criticizes traditional grading, which she argues places an unnecessary focus on points, an extrinsic motivator. One of the problems with such traditional grading systems is that this performance-orientation might influence strategies on the part of students that have little to do with learning or mastery of course content.[13] For example, students often lack the motivation to meaningfully engage with instructor feedback, as it is generally received after the opportunity to incorporate it into their work has passed.[14] However, steering assessment to the course learning objectives and promoting mastery orientation has demonstrated an increase in students' intrinsic motivation.[15]

Student motivation is layered in complexity; however, studies suggest that motivation is changeable and responsive to course design and classroom experiences.[16] Traditional approaches to measuring student motivation in the classroom have considered psychological motives and need achievement theory, addressing how both opportunities for success and a fear of failure can motivate students.[17]

In terms of grading and library instruction, credit-bearing library instruction is still relatively new to the university campus. Most librarians have not received instructional training and may find developing assessment tools daunting.[18] In addressing student motivation specifically within credit-bearing library instruction courses, Jacobson and Xu studied the personal characteristics most highly associated with ideal or best library instructors and found four aspects of instruction that have an influence on motivation: "course design, teaching behaviors, active engagement and student autonomy."[19] The authors note that "clarity, along with other teaching factors such as enthusiasm and interaction, has positive effects on teacher effectiveness, student performance, and student motivation levels."[20] Both clarity and agency are central components of SG.

While little research has been done to support SG, much research has been done to support the alternative grading systems that inspired SG—for example, pass/fail grading systems and contract grading. SG also draws from the concepts of competency-based education—a much more recent development.[21]

Much of the research on pass/fail grading was conducted in the late 1960s and early 1970s, and at that time, many of the findings were negative, as it was found to inhibit student motivation.[22] More recent research, however, has shown some value in this method. In a recent study, some students actually chose to be graded pass/fail because they perceived it would be less stressful than being traditionally graded, which has potential implications for students' overall well-being.[23] However, SG is not completely pass/fail. Although individual assignments are graded as pass/fail in SG, students are still working toward an overall letter grade.

Contract grading, or the "learning contracts" system, is another predecessor of SG. The original contract grading system involves two-way agreements between the supervising faculty member and each individual student about what the student would produce to earn the preferred grade in the course. The contract grading system also includes a design for a single contract developed solely by the instructor (with or without student feedback) that students must follow to earn their desired grade.[24]

Studies have demonstrated multiple benefits associated with the contract grading system, such as developing a trusting learning environment, engaging multiple learning styles, increasing the effectiveness of evaluative feedback, and increasing student motivation and satisfaction.[25] Additionally, contract grading allows for greater student accountability and sense of ownership in the evaluation process, as "the contract removes, or at least diminishes their helpless feeling since fulfilling the contract is wholly a matter of concrete activities over which they can keep control."[26] However, only a few instances of contract grading have been found to advocate tying course grades to learning outcomes, an essential component of SG.[27]

Case Study: Applying Specifications Grading to LIB classes at WFU

CONTEXT

Wake Forest University is a mid-sized private institution with an undergraduate enrollment of just under 5,000 students. Instruction librarians at the Z. Smith Reynolds Library, the main library on campus, teach more than forty sections of the popular series of 1.5-credit information literacy courses each year, including thirty sections of the introductory-level LIB 100 "Academic Research and Information Issues," as well as ten sections at the 200 level, including LIB 210 for social science majors, LIB 220 for science majors, and various special topics courses. These courses are traditionally offered face-to-face, but LIB 100 is also offered in a fully-online version once or twice a year. In 2016, the librarian teaching the fully online section of LIB 100 was the first to make the transition to specifications grading, and based on this librarian's positive experiences, other librarians have since expressed interest. At the time of this writing, two ZSR librarians have taught a total of three sections using SG and an additional two librarians are currently in the process of implementing SG in their own courses.

INITIAL IMPRESSIONS

For the instructors, the transition to SG had profound effects on how they designed their courses. Transitioning to SG required significant amounts of reflection on what constitutes basic achievement of the learning outcomes for each class—that is, what constitutes a C— and allowed for each instructor to build upon that basic mastery and introduce more rigor into the higher-level "tracks" or "bundles." By designing for mastery rather than point accumulation, each instructor could be confident that a student earning an A would be able to demonstrate significantly greater mastery of the concepts than a student earning a C.

In all sections in which SG has been implemented, the removal of the points system had a number of effects on both the instructors and the students. For instructors, grading was no longer a subjective exercise in how many points a particular component was worth or in deciding how many points to deduct when a student's work was found lacking. Rather, students either met or did not meet all of the specifications, and instructors provided detailed feedback accordingly. Feedback became a crucial element for the students in order to understand why they did not pass a particular assignment. Both instructors have noticed a marked difference in the number of students lobbying for a higher grade; when students did challenge a "no pass," they had to look closely at the specifications and the instructor comments to understand why they did not pass, not just ask for a few extra points to be awarded back. Instances of "No Pass," while somewhat rare, were opportunities for conversations about how the work might be improved to meet the specifications. Although it still took a significant portion of instructor time to grade and provide feedback to students (especially because of the writing-intensive nature of assignments), this time was spent reading and providing targeted feedback, which led to "less mental exertion required to deliberate over small differences in points."[28] When SG was implemented in LIB 210 in the second half of the spring semester, the majority of students enrolled were graduating seniors. SG enabled students to choose to pursue an A or, in some instances, to pursue a lesser grade if they were more interested in earning a credit than earning a high grade. Either way, because of how the assignments were structured, instructors could rest assured that students still gained mastery of the core learning outcomes, and students largely felt empowered to choose their grade and the corresponding amount of work. The final grade, therefore, never felt punitive as it might feel in a points-based system; grades truly reflected each student's level of mastery of the course learning outcomes.

In both courses, students had a generally positive response to SG, particularly the transparency and the agency that it provided them. This was especially important in the online sections of LIB 100, as almost every student was entirely new to online learning and many were understandably anxious; for these students, SG provided much-needed transparency. The few students who expressed uncertainty about SG cited discomfort with the inability to earn partial credit on assignments or the requirement to complete consistently high-level work, despite being able to choose their workload.

CHALLENGES

SG does have several challenges, the first of which is conveying to students how this new grading system will work. The system needs to be thoroughly explained early in the course so that students feel equipped to be successful. One way of ensuring comprehension is to have students take a required syllabus quiz before or after the first class, or as an interactive activity in class that asks them about some of the most important aspects of this grading system. It can also be a challenge to get students, especially high-achieving students, to buy into an SG system, but it is the instructors' experience that the kind of autonomy afforded them by SG and the kind of transparency SG requires quickly override any initial anxiety.

There is also an up-front cost on the instructor side, as it takes significant time to set up a course according to SG. This includes the time needed to create detailed, thoughtful descriptions and checklists/rubrics for each assignment as well as time to create the "tracks" or "bundles" that correspond to each letter grade. The instructor must decide which of the assignments are essential to mastery at the C-level and how to increase rigor for those students at the A- and B-levels. An additional challenge involves the grade book, as most traditional learning management systems (LMS) are not set up to accommodate the "bundled" nature of the assignments in SG. Instructors must decide whether they want to create a workaround in the LMS or use an external product to manage their grades, which can introduce privacy concerns as well as technological issues.

Criticisms of Specifications Grading

While many of the concepts grounding SG, including contract-based grading, are supported by a strong body of research, SG itself has not yet been formally studied. Nilson's sources are primarily personal communications and anecdotes, rather than published research studies.[29] This is Prescott's main critique of SG in her review of Nilson's book: "I would seriously consider adopting this scheme if published evidence of student gains were available."[30] Prescott does, however, remark on the potential value of SG: "The method does allow for linking specific learning outcomes more transparently and is worth consideration."[31] In order to be taken seriously, therefore, instructors using SG need to conduct evidence-based research.

However, it is important to note that traditional grading is not grounded in research, either.[32] Traditional methods based on arbitrary points and letter grades are much more susceptible to idiosyncrasies in instructor grading practices and less transparent than a standards-based, mastery learning, or SG method. Unless instructors are critical and reflective of their own expectations and how these expectations are linked to learning outcomes, then grades are being based largely on subjective criteria.

SG may also fall subject to criticisms of the pass/fail grading system, as noted earlier. SG is not, however, a true pass/fail system, as students are working toward an overall letter grade that is aligned with learning outcomes. Because these final grades have an associated workload that is student-selected, and because Nilson emphasizes revision for mastery, SG manages to avoid many of the shortcomings of true pass/fail grading.

SG may also be criticized for the commitment it requires on the part of the instructor. Not only does SG require significant investments in time to develop assignment checklists and align assignments to outcomes, but it may also require additional effort to get students to understand and buy into a SG course. Some instructors may see this effort as too great a burden.

Another criticism of SG is that it is too prescriptive. Most would agree that learning is a messy process and cannot be reduced to a list of requirements. In addition, it doesn't translate to the real world, as employees are not typically given detailed specifications to complete a given task successfully on the job.

Future Research

Since SG currently lacks a large body of evidence, there are rich possibilities to contribute to further SoTL research on this topic. Aside from a few recent articles in academic journals,[33] much of the current discussion around SG is taking place through blog posts and online forums by faculty who are implementing SG in their courses.[34] Some of the questions that remain to be explored include: To what extent are students more/less motivated in a SG class than non-SG? How does student agency/choice affect motivation? How do transparency and clarity of expectations affect motivation? For the instructor, to what extent does SG actually save time, or is the time spent grading simply exchanged for time spent developing specifications, providing feedback, engaging with students, and related tasks? What value do students and instructors place on feedback, and how does that differ by group? How does an SG course compare to a pure rubric-based course? Do students aim for a higher or lower grade in an SG course than what they might achieve in a traditionally graded course? How effective might SG be for teaching at-risk students, international students, or first-generation college students?

Studies addressing these questions should be carried out at a variety of institutions and in different contexts (including library instruction) to determine whether SG can be applied effectively. For the purposes of this project, the librarians who teach LIB 100 and LIB 210 plan to implement SG-designed courses in the 2017–2018 school year and investigate some of the questions identified earlier, at least in terms of the credit-bearing library courses at WFU.

ENDNOTES

1. Rosalind Tedford and Lauren Pressley, "Administrative Support for Librarians Teaching For-Credit Information Literacy," in *Best Practices for Credit-Bearing Information Literacy Courses*, ed. Christopher Vance Hollister (Chicago: Association of College and Research Libraries, 2010), 42–52.
2. Linda Nilson, *Specifications Grading: Restoring Rigor, Motivating Students, and Saving Faculty Time* (Sterling, VA: Stylus Publishing, 2015).
3. Mia O'Brien, "Navigating the SoTL Landscape: A Compass, Map and Some Tools for Getting Started," *International Journal for the Scholarship of Teaching and Learning* 2, no. 2 (July 2008), https://doi.org/10.20429/ijsotl.2008.020215.
4. O'Brien, "Navigating the SoTL Landscape," 6.
5. Ibid., 11.
6. Nilson, *Specifications Grading*.
7. Ibid., 24.
8. O'Brien, "Navigating the SoTL Landscape," 12.
9. Nilson, *Specifications Grading*, chap. 8.
10. Ibid., 108–9.
11. O'Brien, "Navigating the SoTL Landscape."
12. Ibid., 1–2.
13. Ramarao Desiraju and C. Gopinath, "Encouraging Participation in Case Discussions: A Comparison of the Mica and the Harvard Case Methods," *Journal of Management Education* 25, no. 4 (August 2001): 397, https://doi.org/10.1177/105256290102500404.
14. Donna M. Elkins, "Grading to Learn: An Analysis of the Importance and Application of Specifications Grading in a Communication Course," *Kentucky Journal of Communication* 35, no. 2 (Fall 2016): 26–48.
15. Barbara E. Fassler Walvoord and Virginia Johnson Anderson, *Effective Grading: A Tool for Learning and Assessment in College*, 2nd ed., The Jossey-Bass Higher and Adult Education Series (San Francisco: Jossey-Bass, 2010); Jessica Lahey, "Letter Grades Deserve an 'F,'" *The Atlantic*, March 12, 2014, https://www.theatlantic.com/education/archive/2014/03/letter-grades-deserve-an-f/284372/.
16. Martin V. Covington, "A Motivational Analysis of Academic Life in College," in *The Scholarship of Teaching and Learning in Higher Education: An Evidence-Based Perspective*, ed. Raymond P. Perry and John C. Smart (Dordrecht, Netherlands: Springer, 2007), 661–712; Walvoord and Anderson, *Effective Grading*.
17. Walvoord and Anderson, *Effective Grading*.
18. Margaret Burke, "Academic Libraries and the Credit-Bearing Class," *Communications in Information Literacy* 5, no. 2 (September 2011): 169.
19. Trudi Jacobson and Lijuan Xu, "Motivating Students in Credit-Based Information Literacy Courses: Theories and Practice," *portal: Libraries and the Academy* 2, no. 3 (July 2002): 424, https://doi.org/10.1353/pla.2002.0055.
20. Jacobson and Lijuan Xu, "Motivating Students," 429.
21. Nilson, *Specifications Grading*; Paul LeBlanc, "Competency-Based Education and Regional Accreditation," *Inside Higher Ed*, January 31, 2013, https://www.insidehighered.com/views/2013/01/31/competency-based-education-and-regional-accreditation.
22. David J. Otto, "A Study of the Pass/Fail Grading System" (Edmonton, AB: University of Alberta, 1972), https://eric.ed.gov/?id=ED077472.
23. Kristina Nyström, "When Students Are Allowed to Choose: Grading Scale Choices for Degree Projects," *Studies in Higher Education*, 2017, 1–10, https://doi.org/10.1080/03075079.2017.1290062.

24. Nilson, *Specifications Grading*, 74.

25. Tammy Bunn Hiller and Amy B. Hietapelto, "Contract Grading: Encouraging Commitment to the Learning Process through Voice in the Evaluation Process," *Journal of Management Education* 25, no. 6 (December 2001): 660–84, https://doi.org/10.1177/105256290102500605; Jane Danielewicz and Peter Elbow, "A Unilateral Grading Contract to Improve Learning and Teaching," *College Composition and Communication* 61, no. 2 (2009): 244–68.

26. Danielewicz and Elbow, "A Unilateral Grading Contract to Improve Learning and Teaching," 255.

27. Bernard W. Andrews, "Musical Contracts: Fostering Student Participation in the Instructional Process," *International Journal of Music Education* 22, no. 3 (December 2004): 219–29, https://doi.org/10.1177/0255761404047398; Malcolm Shepherd Knowles, *Self-Directed Learning: A Guide for Learners and Teachers* (New York: Association Press, 1975); Malcolm S. Knowles, *The Modern Practice of Adult Education: From Pedagogy to Andragogy* (Englewood Cliffs, NJ: Cambridge Adult Education, 1980); Malcolm S. Knowles, *Using Learning Contracts*, The Jossey-Bass Higher Education Series (San Francisco: Jossey-Bass, 1986).

28. Elkins, "Grading to Learn," 39.

29. Nilson, *Specifications Grading*.

30. Sarah G. Prescott, "Will Instructors Save Time Using a Specifications Grading System?," *Journal of Microbiology & Biology Education* 16, no. 2 (July 2015): 298, https://doi.org/10.1128/jmbe.v16i2.1027.

31. Prescott, "Will Instructors Save Time."

32. Robert J. Marzano, *Transforming Classroom Grading* (Alexandria, VA: Association for Supervision and Curriculum Development, 2000).

33. Matthew W. Bonner, "Grading Rigor in Counselor Education: A Specifications Grading Framework," *Educational Research Quarterly* 39, no. 4 (June 2016): 21–42; Elkins, "Grading to Learn."

34. Kate Owens, "An Adventure in Standards Based Algebra," *Kate S. Owens*, February 2, 2016, http://blogs.cofc.edu/owensks/2016/02/02/an-adventure-in-standards-based-algebra/; Robert Talbert, "Specifications Grading with the EMRF Rubric," *Casting Out Nines*, n.d., /blog/2016/specs-grading-emrf; Amanda Rosen, "Specifications Grading, Attempt 1, Day 0," *Active Learning in Political Science*, August 24, 2016, http://activelearningps.com/2016/08/24/specifications-grading-attempt-1-day-0/; Jason Mittell, "First Update on My Specifications Grading Experiment," *Just TV*, March 21, 2016, https://justtv.wordpress.com/2016/03/21/first-update-on-my-specifications-grading-experiment/.

BIBLIOGRAPHY

Andrews, Bernard W. "Musical Contracts: Fostering Student Participation in the Instructional Process." *International Journal of Music Education* 22, no. 3 (December 2004): 219–29. https://doi.org/10.1177/0255761404047398.

Bonner, Matthew W. "Grading Rigor in Counselor Education: A Specifications Grading Framework." *Educational Research Quarterly* 39, no. 4 (June 2016): 21–42.

Burke, Margaret. "Academic Libraries and the Credit-Bearing Class." *Communications in Information Literacy* 5, no. 2 (September 2011): 156–73.

Covington, Martin V. "A Motivational Analysis of Academic Life in College." In *The Scholarship of Teaching and Learning in Higher Education: An Evidence-Based Perspective*, edited by Raymond P. Perry and John C. Smart, 661–712. Dordrecht, Netherlands: Springer, 2007.

Danielewicz, Jane, and Peter Elbow. "A Unilateral Grading Contract to Improve Learning and Teaching." *College Composition and Communication* 61, no. 2 (2009): 244–68.

Desiraju, Ramarao, and C. Gopinath. "Encouraging Participation in Case Discussions: A Comparison of the Mica and the Harvard Case Methods." *Journal of Management Education* 25, no. 4 (August 2001): 394–408. https://doi.org/10.1177/105256290102500404.

Elkins, Donna M. "Grading to Learn: An Analysis of the Importance and Application of Specifications Grading in a Communication Course." *Kentucky Journal of Communication* 35, no. 2 (Fall 2016): 26–48.

Hiller, Tammy Bunn, and Amy B. Hietapelto. "Contract Grading: Encouraging Commitment to the Learning Process through Voice in the Evaluation Process." *Journal of Management Education* 25, no. 6 (December 2001): 660–84. https://doi.org/10.1177/105256290102500605.

Jacobson, Trudi, and Lijuan Xu. "Motivating Students in Credit-Based Information Literacy Courses: Theories and Practice." *portal: Libraries and the Academy* 2, no. 3 (July 2002): 423–41. https://doi.org/10.1353/pla.2002.0055.

Knowles, Malcolm S. *The Modern Practice of Adult Education: From Pedagogy to Andragogy.* Englewood Cliffs, NJ: Cambridge Adult Education, 1980.

———. *Using Learning Contracts.* The Jossey-Bass Higher Education Series. San Francisco: Jossey-Bass, 1986.

Knowles, Malcolm Shepherd. *Self-Directed Learning: A Guide for Learners and Teachers.* New York: Association Press, 1975.

Lahey, Jessica. "Letter Grades Deserve an 'F.'" *The Atlantic*, March 12, 2014. https://www.theatlantic.com/education/archive/2014/03/letter-grades-deserve-an-f/284372/.

LeBlanc, Paul. "Competency-Based Education and Regional Accreditation." *Inside Higher Ed*, January 31, 2013. https://www.insidehighered.com/views/2013/01/31/competency-based-education-and-regional-accreditation.

Marzano, Robert J. *Transforming Classroom Grading.* Alexandria, VA: Association for Supervision and Curriculum Development, 2000.

Mittell, Jason. "First Update on My Specifications Grading Experiment." *Just TV*, March 21, 2016. https://justtv.wordpress.com/2016/03/21/first-update-on-my-specifications-grading-experiment/.

Nilson, Linda. *Specifications Grading: Restoring Rigor, Motivating Students, and Saving Faculty Time.* Sterling, VA: Stylus Publishing, 2015.

Nyström, Kristina. "When Students Are Allowed to Choose: Grading Scale Choices for Degree Projects." *Studies in Higher Education*, 2017, 1–10. https://doi.org/10.1080/03075079.2017.1290062.

O'Brien, Mia. "Navigating the SoTL Landscape: A Compass, Map and Some Tools for Getting Started." *International Journal for the Scholarship of Teaching and Learning* 2, no. 2 (July 2008). https://doi.org/10.20429/ijsotl.2008.020215.

Otto, David J. "A Study of the Pass/Fail Grading System." Edmonton, AB: University of Alberta, 1972. https://eric.ed.gov/?id=ED077472.

Owens, Kate. "An Adventure in Standards Based Algebra." *Kate S. Owens*, February 2, 2016. http://blogs.cofc.edu/owensks/2016/02/02/an-adventure-in-standards-based-algebra/.

Prescott, Sarah G. "Will Instructors Save Time Using a Specifications Grading System?" *Journal of Microbiology & Biology Education* 16, no. 2 (July 2015): 298. https://doi.org/10.1128/jmbe.v16i2.1027.

Rosen, Amanda. "Specifications Grading, Attempt 1, Day 0." *Active Learning in Political Science*, August 24, 2016. http://activelearningps.com/2016/08/24/specifications-grading-attempt-1-day-0/.

Talbert, Robert. "Specifications Grading with the EMRF Rubric." *Casting Out Nines*, n.d. /blog/2016/specs-grading-emrf.

Tedford, Rosalind, and Lauren Pressley. "Administrative Support for Librarians Teaching For-Credit Information Literacy." In *Best Practices for Credit-Bearing Information Literacy Courses*, edited by Christopher Vance Hollister, 42–52. Chicago: Association of College and Research Libraries, 2010.

Walvoord, Barbara E. Fassler, and Virginia Johnson Anderson. *Effective Grading: A Tool for Learning and Assessment in College*. 2nd ed. The Jossey-Bass Higher and Adult Education Series. San Francisco: Jossey-Bass, 2010.

9

Teaching the Creation of New Knowledge:

Applying the Constructivist and Social Constructivist Theories of Learning

Cynthia A. Tysick, Molly K. Maloney, Bryan J. Sajecki, and Nicole Thomas

The Association of College and Research Libraries (ACRL) *Framework for Information Literacy for Higher Education* "grows out of a belief that information literacy as an educational reform movement will realize its potential only through a richer, more complex set of core ideas."[1] The interconnected core concepts that comprise the ACRL *Framework* are rich with participatory, social, and creator notions, such as constructed authority, scholarly conversations, and curious exploration. Through a learning process that involves experiences at both the individual and group levels, students cross a threshold of understanding and begin practicing information literacy concepts, working toward information fluency.

The University at Buffalo is a Tier 1 public research institution with a full-time undergraduate student population of 18,036.[2] This case study describes the University at Buffalo's one-credit library lab (iLab) embedded within a freshman writing and rhetoric course, ENG105. iLab has been taught since fall 2016 to approximately 1,400 freshmen each semester. During its first iteration, the six librarians teaching iLab employed a constructivist model of information literacy instruction; however, following evaluation of the learning outcomes, they changed course and thereafter followed a social constructivist model. The goal of this paper is to compare and contrast the constructivist and social constructivist theories of learning within the context of this undergraduate freshman case study, thus allowing other librarians to determine which model would best serve as the theoretical base for *their* pedagogical approach.

Constructing Models for Information Literacy Instruction

As students progress through the learning process, they build on their pre-existing knowledge base. Along the way, they will use parts of what they already know to interpret and add to the new material they encounter with the goal of "constructing" new knowledge. Education theorists have long debated whether or not this construction was best approached on an individual or group (social) basis.

According to the literature,[3] two models for student learning applicable to library instruction are the constructivist and social constructivist models. At the individual level, students construct their own knowledge through experiences and reflection; this is known as the constructivist theory of learning. Constructivists such as John Dewey affirm that "although the individual interacts with context and is affected by it, the individual's meaning still exists in his or her head regardless of the particular context."[4] However, social constructivist theorists such as Lev Vygotsky posit, "It is *impossible* for an individual to acquire knowledge of the external world without social interaction."[5] Learning happens at the group level as students construct knowledge through the creation of group artifacts and individual learning happens because of their work within the group.

Developing an information literacy curriculum is no different in its pedagogical approach to teaching and learning across disciplines. Questions arise, such as, In what context is the individual preferable over the group? Can these two learning theories be applied to information literacy curriculum that utilizes the ACRL *Framework*? Or is one theory more effective than the other? The Scholarship of Teaching and Learning (SoTL) provides an opportunity for librarians to explore both the constructivist and social constructivist models of teaching and learning in order to answer these questions. This information literacy curriculum case study of the University at Buffalo Libraries' iLab started with a constructivist model; however, after assessment and iteration, it was determined that the social constructivist model was more appropriate for a number of reasons.

iLab Adopts the Constructivist Model

According to Allen, "constructivist theory contends that the learner brings to the learning environment knowledge from past experience, and that knowledge has a strong influence upon how the learner constructs meaning and acquires new knowledge from new experiences."[6] In the first iteration of iLab, the syllabus and curriculum relied on this model. Students were expected to draw on their understanding of information literacy skills in order to complete assignments while ultimately improving upon this knowledge base by actively learning through their individual assignments. To organize and construct their final individual projects in iLab, the students were given an outline to complete. The outline walked them through the research process to create visual representations of their final individual topics in the writing and rhetoric portion of the course. Students were expected to create an infographic citing three high-quality sources and one image. The iLab outline was assessed to determine whether or not a student was able to construct new knowledge appropriate to a freshman level of understanding.

Kay and Kibble contend that "before the constructivist movement, theorists assumed that there was a single external reality, a privileged point of view. The mind was viewed as a blank slate that passively copied what was presented."[7] Through prompting by the iLab librarians, students proved that their minds were not blank slates at all. In essence, the librarian served as an instructional designer guiding student learning rather than as a content delivery mechanism. Snyder Broussard explicitly discusses this role, stating, "Cognitive constructivist approaches to teaching and learning typically have an instructor as a facilitator of the learning experience: one who designs the experience and helps ensure the encounter with the content is impactful."[8] In the position of "designer," the librarian role was one and the same with Broussard's "facilitator," providing "hands-on activity-based teaching and learning during which students develop their own frames of thought."[9] In sum, "constructivist learning environments can offer students the kinds of learning experiences that will foster the development of critical thinking skills, possibly leading to higher levels of achievement."[10] However, this approach relies on active learners at the individual level, as knowledge is created by the "process, rather than content."[11]

Problems with the Constructivist Model

With a focus on this constructivist model, the librarians developed the course to promote active learning. iLab fall 2016 was structured as multimodal with every other week as a seated class, and students controlled their own learning during the online weeks. When students completed the final project, the infographic with works cited, in week thirteen, results were below satisfactory due to several factors. Students were not required by their writing and rhetoric instructors to produce a final project that relied on specific, academic source types. Instead, librarians were advised *not* to emphasize scholarly resources and so chose to introduce students to sources like *Opposing Viewpoints in Context* to give them two sides of an argument in hopes that they would weave an informed conclusion into their topics. Other issues stemmed from the individualized nature of the project and the students' freedom to select any topic of their choosing. Minimal guidance with topic and source selection from writing and rhetoric instructors combined with little peer support resulted in reduced motivation to demonstrate their learning.

At the end of fall 2016, each librarian analyzed twenty infographics and reported their impressions. The analysis found that as far as digital literacy competencies were concerned, students' average grade was 70 percent. Grades of 85 percent or above, which is considered proficient, were achieved by 55 percent of students. They used images that did not adhere to copyright, failed to cite the images on the infographic, or chose images that did not relate to the topic chosen. The accompanying works cited fared slightly better with an average grade of 78 percent. Eighty percent of the students demonstrated minimal ability by citing at least one scholarly source, two supporting sources that were authoritative, and dates of publication averaging within the last ten years. Results highlighted that students struggled to apply research methods practiced in class, showing a disconnect between constructed knowledge and meaning. In addition, students were unable to effectively engage course material to the level required for competency.

iLab Changes Course

Due to these results, the librarians determined that iLab needed to be re-evaluated and a new approach was necessary. The librarians realized that they were employing the traditional guest lecture, one-shot librarian approach to teaching, rather than embracing the opportunities available to an embedded librarian with responsibilities for a credit-bearing course. Information literacy instruction within a one-shot environment lends itself to the constructivist model because students are working on individual research projects. Semester-long information literacy instruction allows librarians to utilize peer instruction and the social aspect of a classroom to employ the social constructivist model of teaching and learning. As embedded librarians in a credit-bearing course, the librarians could build a community of learners who could "be encouraged to feel comfortable with each other."[12]

The librarians realized that so much of the ACRL *Framework,* like understanding authority in context, creating new knowledge, and taking part in the scholarly conversation, was best approached from a social context, and decided to convert the individual infographic assignment into a group infographic assignment. The groups would also complete a research outline, called the Point/Reason/Example (PRE)-formula, requiring a clear point, reason, and example from each member (see Appendix 9A). The librarians believed that peer collaboration would increase participation, providing a platform for meaningful interaction and fostering the exchange of information. By changing the format to group work, the librarians felt confident the peer aspect would improve the overall experience of the course for the students. Several pieces of literature support this point. For example, Farkas talked about the valuable roles of peers in learning in regard to utilizing participatory technologies in the classroom. She stated, "Rather than seeing teaching as being focused on the instructor, students can learn from their peers."[13] And Stigmar remarked that "an increase in students [sic] social and self-awareness through collaboration and effective team-building in an interactive and warm classroom environment, lead to reduced student anxiety."[14] This warmth and cooperative learning empowers students.[15] Kay and Kibble strongly conclude that "to an extent, social constructivism subsumed earlier theories, and we regard it as the prevailing learning theory at the present time."[16] There is a long-lasting participatory culture created through social constructivist approaches to learning.

iLab Adopts the Social Constructivist Model

Social constructivist theory is based on the thought that "all learning is socially mediated, is a result of interactions with cultural tools, and is shaped through guidance of more knowledgeable others."[17] Havenga builds on this belief, stating, "The nature of social constructivism requires that teaching practices focus mainly on students' facilitation and responsibility to construct the learning content."[18] In spring 2017, the iLab syllabus no longer included online-only modules. It was taught face-to-face over thirteen weeks and was delivered as a "flipped" model (see Appendix 9B). Students were required to watch videos or read articles, complete a weekly assignment, and come to iLab prepared and ultimately work toward completing a group infographic project.

Students worked in groups of four to five students on a broad topic that they further narrowed and located credible sources using a number of library databases, Google Scholar, and the internet. The group infographic, similar to the individual one from the fall, now required students to first craft a PRE-formula group outline that included three points to their argument and supporting scholarly sources with direct quotations or statistics to be included in their infographics. By week ten, students had completed their group infographics and were ready to work on individual research projects for the writing and rhetoric portion of the course. They were required to use the same PRE-formula outline to model what they had learned in groups. iLab librarians assessed the individual outlines using the same criteria as the group outlines.

The pedagogical combination of modeling, repetition, and active group participation seemed to be the instructional formula that produced the type of movement needed for the majority of students to break through information literacy threshold concepts of authority, knowledge creation, and information has value. Ahn and Class remark that

> the person-to-person interaction via external dialogue inherent in the social constructivist approach lends itself to encouraging higher order thinking under the guidance of the facilitating professor. It also provides a type of practice or primer that engenders cognitive maturation and, ultimately, metacognitive abilities.[19]

Success with the Social Constructivist Model

Analysis of students' group infographics and both group and individual PRE-formula outlines showed a marked improvement from the previous semester. Students were able to effectively construct knowledge with one another and create a classroom culture of shared meaning and collaboration.

The infographics, now group-based, could not be directly compared to the individual student fall 2016 infographics but did show improvement. Students scored higher on their projects, 74 percent and 85 percent respectively, and the overall quality had significantly improved. One major revision that seems to have helped students stay focused on the project was the research outline (see Appendix 9A). The librarians developed the outline after instructors had expressed concern that their students could not weave the sources effectively into their written projects. The goal was to provide students with some prompts related to citing aspects of their arguments to better equip them for the writing process. The most significant change was the shift to group projects, which draws on the benefits of social dynamics absent from previous, individual iterations of the course. Farkas observes that "increased dialogue leads to a greater feeling of community amongst students, which reduces isolation and increased engagement."[20] Churcher, Downs, and Tewksbury found that within their understanding of running a course with a high interest in digital media and information skills, "the ability to learn through dialogue and interaction with others is central to knowledge generation."[21] Stigmar asserts the continuing positives of dialogue and collaboration, as he claims, "When students are engaged as partners working with others, student leadership skills are promoted and [they] learn to respect other perspectives, reaching a more nuanced understanding."[22] Being in a group gave the students more accountability and the peer support strengthened the mutual construction of knowledge. At the end of spring 2017, iLab students were asked to complete a post-assessment as a way to quantify information literacy competencies as outlined by the ACRL *Framework for Information Literacy for Higher Education*. The questions were mapped to each "frame" and tested students' knowledge and experience with threshold concepts within each frame. An analysis of fifteen sections of ENG105 iLab (22 percent of all sections taught) showed an average score of 83 percent. The librarians found that in those sections 85 percent of students scored at the proficient level. The improvement of information literacy proficiency directly correlates with student application and internalization of the research process through the group experience.

Why the Social Constructivist Model Works

In fall 2017, the librarians further revised the iLab syllabus. Learning objectives were added to each weekly lesson that would allow the librarians to incorporate pedagogy proven through their experience with information literacy instruction. iLab will continue to be delivered as a flipped model; however, each week students will complete an online assessment of the concepts being taught, come to iLab and go through a hands-on demonstration of the concepts, and finish an in-class "building block" exercise based on the weekly concept being covered. The first research project will still be a group infographic but with smaller groups of three to four members. This will allow more instruction both at the peer and librarian levels. Each group member will be required to find one scholarly source for their group project and they will then complete a research outline together before creating their group infographic. Pedagogically, the practice of modeling and repetition has been shown to be sound practice and has so far resulted in more student engagement and group collaboration. A major revision has been the number of weeks iLab runs from the original iteration of fifteen weeks. In order to give struggling students more individualized attention in both the writing and/or research process, iLab will now be taught over ten weeks. The first three weeks will be devoted to creating electronic portfolios and digital literacy while the remaining seven weeks model the research process two separate times, once as a group and once individually. The remaining weeks of the semester after iLab afford students and instructors the opportunity to dedicate more time to the writing process in the form of a five-week writing lab. Our student assessments, which involved a ten question pre- and post-test, have confirmed that students have grown and developed stronger information literacy skills through the course. There is a growing body of evidence to indicate students' information literacy skills developed during iLab are positively reflected in their individual research assignments within the writing and rhetoric portion of the course as well as in students' other coursework.

Conclusion

Embedding information literacy instruction into a writing course as a lab provides students with a safe space in which to experiment with ACRL *Framework* threshold concepts through low-stakes, media-rich group projects, allowing them to construct new knowledge in a social sandbox. iLab provides a unique venue for librarians to embrace the role of social facilitators, "exposing students to new ideas and creating a nurturing environment for learning—allow[ing] students to be more responsible for their own learning. Bringing students together to discuss ideas and solve problems collaboratively helps them to co-create an understanding of information literacy that is greater than what any one of them could have developed alone."[23] Moving forward, iLab will continue to embrace the social constructivist model, providing embedded instruction that will amplify information literacy skills for undergraduates in an innovative way.

Appendix 9A

PRE FORMULA OUTLINE

Use this outline for both your research projects in the iLab

Basic Outline
What is the title of your research topic? Make it catchy, be creative!

Give a one-sentence description of what you are adding to the conversation.

List the three or four (depending on your project requirements) key points you are adding to the conversation.

1.
2.
3.
4.

PRE Formula
Next, expand on your key points using the PRE formula. You must also include the full citation in MLA 8th and database or website for each of your examples' sources.

P. Point: state your point.

R. Reason: state the reason you believe or support your point.

E. Example: support your reason with a direct quote, summarized idea or data from one of your cited sources.

Example
Point: Data collection required for the development of traffic control and safety systems for self-driving cars presents ethical conflicts in personal privacy.

Reason: The possible use or misuse of collected personal data goes beyond the beneficial analysis for improved control and safety systems toward commercial uses by third parties without the informed consent of the driver.

Example: "However, if the instance-level data is in the hands of an insurer, auto manufacturer, or other entity, the driver might have little or no control over its 'secondary use' or sale to third parties, which could have undesirable consequences" (Dhar 82).

Citation in MLA 8th:
Dhar, Vasant. "Equity, Safety, and Privacy in the Autonomous Vehicle Era." *Computer*, vol. 49, no. 11, 2016, pp. 80-83. *IEEE Xplore*, https://doi.org/10.1109/MC.2016.326. Accessed January 9, 2016.
Database Name or Website URL: *IEEE Xplore*

Develop three to four key points using the PRE Formula.

Point #1:
Reason:

        Example:
        Citation in MLA 8th:
        Database Name or Website URL:

        Point #2:
        Reason:
        Example:
        Citation in MLA 8th:
        Database Name or Website URL:

        Point #3:
        Reason:
        Example:
        Citation in MLA 8th:
        Database Name or Website URL:

        Point #4:
        Reason:
        Example:
        Citation in MLA 8th:
        Database Name or Website URL:

Appendix 9B

ILAB SPRING 2017 SCHEDULE

Week Number	Before Class	In-class	After Class
1	View items in "Start Here" folder: • ePortfolio/Digication video • ePortfolio handout • iLab syllabus	Create ePortfolio for the course • Understand iLab expectations	

2	Watch week 2 videos:
	
	• The Cycle of Information
	• The Scholarly vs. Popular Sources
	• CRAAP Method
	• How Library Stuff Works: How to Evaluate Resources (the CRAAP Test)
	
	CPA: Complete CRAAP Test & Known Item Search Worksheet and bring 2 print copies to class.
		• Review CPA in pairs
		• What is a scholarly source?
		  1. Information Cycle & Scholarly Conversation
		  2. Experts in Context
		  3. "Abbreviated Scholarship" (blogs, tweets, interviews, etc.)
		• How do you know if an online source is scholarly from demo Wikipedia entry?
		  1. CRAAP Test
		• How do you find a journal article and a book from demo Wikipedia entry?
		  1. Run known item catalog and e-journals searches from demo Wikipedia entry	

3	Watch Week 3 videos: • Working in Groups • Narrowing a Topic Using Mind Mapping • Narrowing Your Topic **CPA: Complete Mind Map on Wikipedia example and bring 2 print copies to class.**	• Review CPA in pairs. • Work in groups to expand or narrow on group Wikipedia topic using mind mapping. • Demo of "Everything" (introduction of "controlled vocab" with subjects) • Work in groups to find overviews on expanded or narrowed Wikipedia topic. • Group Infographic Project Overview	
4	Watch Week 4 videos: • Creating a Basic Search Strategy **CPA: Complete the Basic Search Worksheet based on Wikipedia example and bring 2 print copies to class.**	• Review CPA in pairs. • Work in groups to revise search terms. • Demo on "Everything" using advanced options and limiters • Work in groups searching for four high-quality items on expanded Wikipedia topic.	

Week Number	Before Class	In-class	After Class
5	Watch Week 5 videos: • Copyright, Fair Use, and Plagiarism • Finding Data • Finding Images **CPA: Complete the Plagiarism Worksheet and bring 2 print copies to class.**	• Review CPA in pairs. • Introduction of Copyright and Intellectual Property • Work in groups to find an image, graph, or chart on your expanded Wikipedia topic. 1. Using Creative Commons Image Search for images 2. Finding data through articles or a Google search then apply the CRAAP test	**Finding Media Quiz due**
6	Watch Week 6 videos: • What are In-Text Citations? • MLA 8th Edition Citations **CPA: Complete the Framing the Conversation and Citing Sources worksheet based on Wikipedia demo entry and bring 2 print copies to class.**	• Review CPA in pairs and run comparisons of various citation generators. • Create a Works Cited list in MLA 8th based on research found on expanded Wikipedia topic using Purdue OWL. • Groups outline Infographic	**Group Infographic Outline due in UBLearns**
7 (attendance required)	Watch Week 7 videos: • Getting Started with Canva • How to Save an Infographic into a PDF • How to Create Hanging Indents for Works Cited **Choose a Canva template and share with your group.**	• Review Group Infographic Outline with Feedback. • Infographic creation on your group Wikipedia topic	**Research Vocabulary Quiz due**
8		Spring Break—no class	
9	Watch Week 9 videos: • Getting Started with Canva • Create PDF of Infographic. • Create PDF of Works Cited.	• Review course concepts through group mapping. • Seek! Card Game • Research Outline introduced • Infographic feedback (if needed)	**Group Infographic Project due in UBLearns AND ePortfolio**

Week Number	Before Class	In-class	After Class
10	Watch Week 10 videos: • Concept Mapping of Key Ideas **CPA: Complete Research Topic Mind Map & Best Basic Resources Worksheet and bring 2 print copies to class**.	• Work in pairs, use mind maps to narrow your arguments further. • Discussion of how adding something new to the conversation is what researchers do • Review resources found on the Best Basic Resources Research Guide using the Wikipedia demo entry. • Use *Best Basic Resources Research Guide* to find one entry that supports an aspect of the research topic.	
11	Watch Week 11 videos: • Advanced Article Searching • MLA 8th Citations (8th Edition) **CPA: Complete the Basic Database Search Worksheet and bring 2 print copies to class.**	• Work in pairs finding cited items in corresponding databases. • Identify disciplines that will cover your research. • How to read an item record (article and book) using demo Wikipedia entry examples. • Find articles on your research by revising your search terms based on item records.	**MLA 8th Citation Quiz due**
12	Watch Week 12 videos: • How to Spot Fake News • Academic Search Complete • Read "10 Ways to Spot a Fake News Article" **CPA: Complete the Fake News Worksheet and bring 2 print copies to class.**	• Fake News/Sneaky CRAAP • Finding alternative perspectives to your research topic through books or journal articles	**Progress Review Quiz due**
13		• Progress review based on quiz • Work on Research Outline	**Research Outline due in UBLearns**
14 & 15	No iLab Classes	Individual Conferences (optional)	

ENDNOTES

1. Association of College & Research Libraries, *Framework for Information Literacy for Higher Education* (Chicago: Association of College & Research Libraries (ACRL), 2016), http://www.ala.org/acrl/standards/ilframework.
2. Office of the Provost, "Enrollment," *University at Buffalo*, last modified February 28, 2018, https://www.buffalo.edu/provost/oia/facts-publications/factbook/student/enrollment.html.
3. Mary Snyder Broussard, *Reading, Research, and Writing* (Chicago: Association of College and Research Libraries, 2017), 25–26.
4. "Learning," in *International Encyclopedia of Organizational Studies*, ed. Stewart R. Clegg and James R. Bailey (Thousand Oaks, CA: SAGE Publications, 2008), 801–05.
5. Bharath Sriraman, "Collaborative Learning," in *Encyclopedia of Giftedness, Creativity, and Talent*, ed. Barbara Kerr (Thousand Oaks, CA: SAGE Publications, 2009), 158–60.
6. Maryellen Allen, "Promoting Critical Thinking Skills in Online Information Literacy Instruction Using a Constructivist Approach," *College & Undergraduate Libraries* 15, no. 1/2 (2008): 31.
7. Denise Kay and Jonathan Kibble, "Learning Theories 101: Application to Everyday Teaching and Scholarship," *Advances in Physiology Education* 40, no. 1 (2016): 21.
8. Snyder Broussard, *Reading, Research, and Writing*, 25.
9. John Chelliah and Elizabeth Clarke, "Collaborative Teaching and Learning: Overcoming the Digital Divide?," *On the Horizon* 19, no. 4 (2011): 279.
10. Allen, "Promoting Critical," 23.
11. Chelliah and Clarke, "Collaborative Teaching," 280.
12. Leslie Robinson, Ann Harris, and Rob Burton, "Saving Face: Managing Rapport in a Problem-Based Learning Group," *Active Learning in Higher Education* 16, no. 1 (2015): 22.
13. Meredith Farkas, "Participatory Technologies, Pedagogy 2.0 and Information Literacy," *Library Hi Tech* 30, no. 1 (2012): 85.
14. Martin Stigmar, "Peer-to-Peer Teaching in Higher Education: A Critical Literature Review," *Mentoring & Tutoring: Partnership in Learning* 24, no. 2 (2016): 133.
15. Ruth Ahn and Mary Class, "Student-Centered Pedagogy: Co-Construction of Knowledge through Student-Generated Midterm Exams," *International Journal of Teaching & Learning in Higher Education* 23, no. 2 (2011): 277.
16. Kay and Kibble, "Learning Theories," 24.
17. Ibid.
18. H. M. Havenga, "Project-Based Learning in Higher Education: Exploring Programming Students' Development towards Self-Directedness," *South African Journal of Higher Education* 29, no. 4 (2015): 137.
19. Ahn and Class, "Student-Centered Pedagogy," 277.
20. Farkas, "Participatory Technologies," 85.
21. Kalen Churcher, Edward Downs, and Doug Tewksbury, "'Friending' Vygotsky: A Social Constructivist Pedagogy of Knowledge Building through Classroom Social Media Use," *Journal of Effective Teaching* 14, no 1 (2014): 35.
22. Stigmar, "Peer-to-Peer Teaching in Higher Education," 133.
23. Farkas, "Participatory Technologies," 92.

BIBLIOGRAPHY

Ahn, Ruth, and Mary Class. "Student-Centered Pedagogy: Co-Construction of Knowledge through Student-Generated Midterm Exams." *International Journal of Teaching & Learning in*

Higher Education 23, no. 2 (2011): 269–81. http://files.eric.ed.gov/fulltext/EJ946152.pdf.

Allen, Maryellen. "Promoting Critical Thinking Skills in Online Information Literacy Instruction Using a Constructivist Approach." *College & Undergraduate Libraries* 15, no. 1/2 (2008): 21–38. https://doi.org/10.1080/10691310802176780.

Association of College & Research Libraries. *Framework for Information Literacy for Higher Education*. Chicago: Association of College & Research Libraries (ACRL), 2016. http://www.ala.org/acrl/standards/ilframework.

Chelliah, John, and Elizabeth Clarke. "Collaborative Teaching and Learning: Overcoming the Digital Divide?" *On the Horizon* 19, no. 4 (2011): 276–85. https://doi.org/10.1108/10748121111179402.

Churcher, Kalen M. A., Edward Downs, and Doug Tewksbury. "'Friending' Vygotsky: A Social Constructivist Pedagogy of Knowledge Building through Classroom Social Media Use." *Journal of Effective Teaching* 14, no. 1 (2014): 33–50. https://www.uncw.edu/jet/articles/Vol14_1/Churcher.pdf.

Farkas, Meredith. "Participatory Technologies, Pedagogy 2.0 and Information Literacy." *Library Hi Tech* 30, no. 1 (2012): 82–94. https://doi.org/10.1108/07378831211213229.

Havenga, H. M. "Project-Based Learning in Higher Education: Exploring Programming Students' Development towards Self-Directedness." *South African Journal of Higher Education* 29, no. 4 (2015): 135–57. http://dx.doi.org/10.20853/29-4-515.

Kay, Denise, and Jonathan Kibble. "Learning Theories 101: Application to Everyday Teaching and Scholarship." *Advances in Physiology Education* 40, no. 1 (2016): 17–25. https://doi.org/10.1152/advan.00132.2015.

"Learning." In *International Encyclopedia of Organizational Studies*, edited by Stewart R. Clegg and James R. Bailey, 801–05. Thousand Oaks, CA: SAGE Publications, 2008.

Office of the Provost. "Enrollment." *University at Buffalo*, last modified February 28, 2018. https://www.buffalo.edu/provost/oia/facts-publications/factbook/student/enrollment.html.

Robinson, Leslie, Ann Harris, and Rob Burton. "Saving Face: Managing Rapport in a Problem-Based Learning Group." *Active Learning in Higher Education* 16, no. 1 (2015): 11–24. http://dx.doi.org/10.1177/1469787415573355.

Snyder Broussard, Mary. *Reading, Research, and Writing*. Chicago: Association of College and Research Libraries, 2017.

Sriraman, Bharath. "Collaborative Learning." In *Encyclopedia of Giftedness, Creativity, and Talent*, edited by Barbara Kerr, 158–60. Thousand Oaks, CA: SAGE Publications, 2009.

Stigmar, Martin. "Peer-to-Peer Teaching in Higher Education: A Critical Literature Review." *Mentoring & Tutoring: Partnership in Learning* 24, no. 2 (2016): 124–36. http://dx.doi.org/10.1080/13611267.2016.1178963.

10

Using a Model of the Teaching-Learning Environment as Part of Reflective Practice

Pamela McKinney and Sheila Webber

Introduction

This case study focuses on the authors' use of Entwistle et al.'s[1] model of the Teaching-Learning Environment (TLE) in relation to two graduate-level information literacy (IL) classes. The authors start by briefly characterizing the classes and describing the TLE model. They note how it relates to their educational context in the United Kingdom (UK). They go on to discuss three ways in which they have used this model in teaching: as an aid to reflecting on and evaluating their teaching, as part of learning design, and as an object of learning for the students.

The IL classes are delivered in the Information School at the University of Sheffield (UoS), UK, as part of two masters-level librarianship programs (one on-campus and one distance learning). The classes aim to develop learners' understanding of themselves as information-literate citizens and teachers and introduce them to theories and models in the fields of IL, information behavior, teaching, and learning. Both classes are compulsory and earn one-quarter of the credits required in a full-time semester.

The Teaching and Learning Environment Model as a Framework for Reflection

Entwistle et al.'s model resulted from a large-scale educational research project (Enhancing Teaching-Learning Environments: ETL), investigating the teaching-learning environment of undergraduate students in the UK in five different disciplines. The project took a case study approach, using interviews, focus groups, document analysis, and observation. Threshold concepts,[2] which informed development of the Association of College and Research Libraries' *Framework for IL for Higher Education,*[3] also emerged from this project.

The TLE model (see figure 10.1) maps key elements which affect the quality of learning (for example, learner characteristics, teachers' pedagogic beliefs, course design, institutional policies, and organizations which provide course accreditation). The model encourages the educator to reflect not just on the learners and learning outcomes, but also on the educator's own beliefs and on factors within the institution, and in the wider world, which affect what is taught and how it can be taught. These wider influences include the ways of thinking and practicing in the discipline and the broader higher education environment.[4]

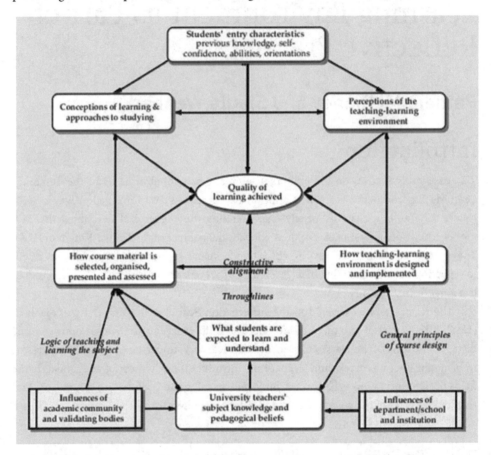

Figure 10.1. The Teaching and Learning Environment model (reproduced with permission from Entwistle, et al.)

For the ETL project, as for the authors of this case study, the educational environment is that of the UK. Tight[5] has carried out a series of investigations into the nature of research in higher education. In his analysis of English-language articles published in 2000, Tight[6] identified that the North American (NA) and non-NA research communities were largely separate. In particular, there were differences in authorship and research approach.

The predominantly British, Australian, and Nordic authors who emerged from a co-citation analysis[7] of non-NA journals were immediately recognizable to the authors of this paper as being key influences (and included researchers Ramsden, Biggs, and Entwistle cited in this case study). Entwistle and Hounsell were both investigators in the ETL project and part of the original group that developed what Tight[8] characterizes as the only distinctive research approach in higher education research, phenomenography. As is described later in this case study, studies using this qualitative research approach (which aims to discover variation in people's conception or experience of a phenomenon) were used in the classes described here; when selecting material to teach librarians about teaching, the authors drew on approaches which they have found valuable in their own pedagogic development.

Despite the UK origin of the TLE model, it can be used within many different cultural contexts. In this case study, the authors concentrate on showing how they have used it for reflection (rather than concentrating primarily on the actions arising from reflection). As well as providing an example, this could provide an opportunity for readers to reflect on how it compares with their own context and on the implications of the similarities and differences.

The TLE Model as a Tool for Educators' Reflection

As an educator, it is important to reflect on one's development as a teacher and how one's fundamental beliefs about "how people learn" change over time. The TLE model facilitates this process and encourages the educator to identify and question the forces that impact learning design. In this section, the authors start by considering the external forces that influence *what* they teach (the subject content) and *how* they teach it.[9] They go on to identify things which have helped to shape their own pedagogical beliefs. The section ends by briefly describing the authors' action research approach to teaching the IL classes.

The programs in which the authors' IL classes reside are accredited by CILIP (Chartered Institute of Library and Information Professionals), the UK's association for librarians. The CILIP Professional Knowledge and Skills Base (PKSB),[10] which sets out core knowledge and skills, is used as a framework to assess the programs, but CILIP is also interested in matters such as the quality of students' learning experience and evidence of faculty's engagement with the profession.

The vast majority of UK universities (including the most prestigious) are government funded and are subject to regular audits of teaching quality via an official body, the Quality Assurance Agency (QAA). The QAA also works with accreditation bodies such as CILIP to summarize required knowledge and competencies in every discipline in subject benchmarks. The benchmark for librarianship, information, knowledge, records, and archives management[11] states that graduates should understand the concept of IL and its application in education, the workplace, and society. Additionally, there is an emphasis on "inquiry and evidence-based practice" as a means of developing research abilities.

This emphasis is welcomed by the authors since it provides support for their use of inquiry-based learning (IBL) in teaching practice and their decision to teach students about IBL. In 2005, the Higher Education Funding Council for England made a substantial investment in its Centres for Excellence in Teaching and Learning program. This program led to the creation of CILASS, the Centre for Inquiry-based Learning in the Arts and Social Sciences, indicative of a national and institutional focus on IBL. Both authors were heavily involved in CILASS, McKinney as the educational developer responsible for an IL strand of development, evaluation and research, and Webber as an academic fellow. The experience had a profound effect on the conceptions and approaches to teaching of both authors. Furthermore, the role of IL in IBL has been a subject of research[12] and features in resources created to support IBL educational development.[13] This body of knowledge forms part of the learning resources and activities for students in the IL modules.

Institutional strategies, such as the University of Sheffield's Teaching, Learning, and Assessment strategy,[14] also shape the way teaching happens. For example, one institutional policy that has constrained the assessment approach is the strong guidance on how many words can be set for assessed work. This means that longer reflective portfolios, where students might be encouraged to write discursively about their development, are tricky to implement. Learning design is also affected by physical infrastructure (e.g., classroom layout) and decisions about technology (e.g., obligation to use the Virtual Learning Environment Blackboard; initiatives to support and share good practice in technology-enhanced learning).

The authors are able to develop an understanding of the learners' perspective—for example, their expectations, characteristics, and needs—from the way in which the programs themselves are framed. These are explicitly vocational, thus arousing expectations that they will be of practical use and not just theoretical. Past experience, student record systems, interactions with students during learning, student feedback, and evaluation all inform practice. The authors augment this in the IL classes by adopting an action research approach.

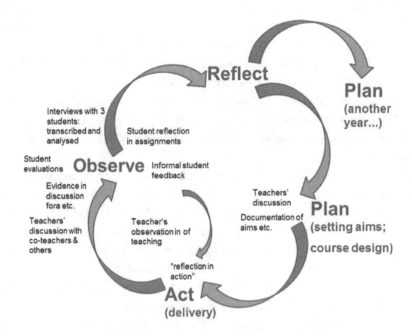

Figure 10.2. Action Research Cycle for the Information Literacy classes

Figure 10.2 shows the reflective action research cycle as it applies to the scholarship undertaken in this particular teaching context. It frames the iterative nature of class development, where experiences inform development year on year. The data for this action research is varied and includes

- interviews with three students who studied the distance learning IL module in 2015–17;
- student evaluations collected as part of the standard departmental process—these constitute important data for reflection but do not provide a complete picture (e.g., they may focus on minutiae of delivery or a teacher's personality);
- reflections on IL and on teaching, submitted by students as part of their assignments (as described in the next section of this case study);
- the authors' reflections *on action* (i.e., after the event) and *in action* (i.e., reflection while engaged in teaching, which may result in small adjustments to the learning design whilst learning is taking place);[15]
- the reflective discussions between module tutors at planning and post-delivery stages; and
- observations of discussion fora.

The interviews were framed by two phenomenographic studies supervised by the authors. The first developed a model of teachers' conceptions of themselves as teachers[16] and the second identified conceptions of continuing professional development.[17] These studies were used to stimulate discussion about how participants felt they had developed their approach to teaching over the course of the class and what effect the class had on their professional development as librarians. This aspect is described further when looking at the TLE as an object of learning.

It is easy to make too many assumptions about learners and learning and to yield to the influence of external factors automatically without questioning them. By working through the TLE model, the authors are able to recognize the context within which learning and teaching are constructed. The model is helpful in making one step back from one's own teaching to work through the factors that result in a class taught in a specific time and place (physical or virtual) to a specific group of students. It helps one to question: What is fixed? What can be changed? Why am I doing this? What would happen if things were done differently? Has something changed (e.g., the nature of the learners or the external environment) without me thinking about it? One can also go beyond the more tangible elements outlined in this case study to consider broader issues of, for example, marketization and globalization in education.

The TLE Model and Learning Design

In this section, the authors address a final element of the TLE model, "what students are expected to learn and understand," and then focus on the heart of the model, quality of learning achieved through constructive alignment.

When considering the focus of the classes' content, the intention was not to create a "teaching tips and tricks" class. The authors view both IL and teaching and learning as contextual, or relational,[18] and this ontological perspective underpins the learning goals of the class. Ultimately, it is not useful for students, who may go into a huge variety of sectors, institutions, and job roles to just learn a few generic "tips." Rather, this class aims to stimulate interest in theories that can act as a platform for future teaching and future continuing professional development for graduates. Additionally, the classes include students from outside the UK, and so it is important not to adopt a parochial view of IL.

Looking at accreditation statements, neither CILIP's PKSB nor the QAA subject benchmark gives detail about what IL is, although QAA's (2015) contextualization of IL within society provides support for the authors' presentation of IL as being important lifelong and life-wide—throughout life and for all aspects of life.[19]

In developing the curriculum, the authors have sought to find a balance between providing alternative perspectives on IL (so that learners can construct their own understanding of it) and of presenting their own perspective. Their own conceptions of teaching and IL are inevitably embedded in both the *what* (is taught) and the *how* (it is taught) of the classes.

The classes also aim to develop students' IL across the "six frames of informed learning."[20] Students build awareness of the world of information (content frame); they are introduced to the view that IL is a set of competencies and skills and develop their own through engaging in guided and reflective search activities (the competency frame); and they understand the relationship between IL and learning through collaboration, reflection, and learning design tasks (the learning to learn frame). They engage with the idea that IL is contextual and personal through research in the field and their own reflections (the personal relevance frame) and that IL is important to society (the social impact frame). Finally, the module activities promote the relational frame and the understanding that IL is complex and involves different ways of interacting with information.

A central feature of the TLE model is that constructive alignment should be included in the learning design. Constructive alignment is the systematic alignment of teaching and learning activities and assessment tasks with the learning outcomes for students, and this is done through active learning. It takes "outcome-based" learning one stage further in that the activities as well as the assessment are focused on the outcomes, so students are better supported to achieve them.[21]

There are two assessed pieces of work for the IL modules:

- **Assignment 1:** (a) Create an annotated bibliography on a topic negotiated with a tutor and (b) reflect on how personal IL has been developed through this activity.
- **Assignment 2:** (a) Work in a group to design and deliver an IL learning intervention (not assessed) and (b) critically reflect individually on the experience of designing and delivering this IL teaching and your development as a teacher.

An example of how constructive alignment has been effected in the modules is through the extensive use of small reflective tasks throughout the classes to support the final assessed tasks, both of which feature reflective writing. For example:

1. In the "Information Universe" week, where theoretical material around access to information and preferred sources is covered, students are asked to write reflectively on a specific incident where they searched for information, and these reflections are then reviewed in the light of the research material.
2. Students give their own definitions of IL in week one of the class and return to these statements later in the semester to debate whether their conceptions have changed.
3. Students take the Approaches to Teaching Inventory,[22] both to reflect on their own approach and to discuss their experiences of being taught as undergraduate learners.

The reflective exercises also help the authors understand more about the characteristics of the specific cohort of learners (their expectations, approaches, etc.) as they are invited to discuss their reflections with us either in class or on one of the class online platforms.

The TLE Model as an Object of Learning: Facilitating Reflective Practice

The IL classes aim to support students in being reflective about themselves as learners in order to develop reflective practice of teaching. As identified above, there is a significant focus on reflective activities and writing. Students are encouraged to engage with recognized instruments, such as the Revised Approaches to Studying Inventory (RASI) and VARK (Visual Aural, Read-Write & Kinesthetic),[23] as a way to reflect on their own styles of learning as a springboard for considering teaching.

The TLE model is introduced to students at the start of the class, to indicate the range of factors that a teacher needs to think about when designing learning, and reintroduced when focusing on learning, on approaches to teaching, and on learning design. The results of the interviews undertaken for the authors' action research and the reflective activities undertaken in class indicate that most students have had some experience of teaching but very few have engaged with any theories of teaching.

Interviewees were positive about the contribution the theoretical material made to their development: "This was one of the big things about your module, that it kind of gave me more of this theoretical background, and I can use it" (Participant 1), and both interview and informal student feedback have indicated that students are able to use this theoretical grounding as a basis for future development—e.g., undertaking a postgraduate certificate in learning and teaching.

The interviewees all reported a step-change in their teaching, conceptualized as a move from transmissive to more constructivist pedagogical style:

> For me it was opening my ideas to probably some of the more modern theories about how we can engage people, and I can see how for me those would be good models to use with people

when you're trying to work with people with different skill sets and different ideas and different backgrounds, that allowing them to explore it is much more an empowering experience for them. (Participant 2)

Interviewees had all changed their self-categorization of themselves as teachers[24] over the course of the class, and there has been deep reflection from many students in assignment two on this model as a prompt for the re-conceptualization of their approach to teaching.

However, class evaluations and observations would indicate that for some other students this threshold was deeply problematic. Although a reflective approach to learning was encouraged, some students found it difficult to recognize the teaching style that they had been involved in during the class. Not all students had the desire to become teachers of IL, and some found it difficult to accept that IL was a subject that could be studied. This feedback is valuable in challenging the authors to reflect on what they are doing and why they are doing in it, and to determine what needs to change. For example, the video,[25] which includes use of the TLE model, was introduced to make their intentions and practice more explicit and as a means to engage students in discussion.

Conclusion

In this case study, the TLE model has been used as a framework for reflections on the design and implementation of two IL classes. The model encourages educators to reflect on the whole situation of teaching, which includes the institutional and professional background, the educational philosophy of the educators, as well as the characteristics of the learners. In making these assumptions explicit, it promotes a questioning attitude toward teaching and supports educators in challenging themselves and the educational orthodoxy. This is particularly important in this case where students are themselves involved in activities to develop as teachers of IL. In writing this case study, the authors have reflected on the constructive alignment of assessment and learning activities in these modules. They have learned from this experience and hope that the case study will also be helpful to others in their own reflective practice.

ENDNOTES

1.   Noel Entwistle, Jennifer Nisbet, and Adrian Bromage, "Teaching-Learning Environments and Student Learning in Electronic Engineering," paper presented at Third Workshop of the European Network on Powerful Learning Environments, Brugge, September 30–October 2, 2004, https://www.academia.edu/3426418/Teaching-learning_environments_and_student_learning_in_electronic_engineering.

2.   Jan H. F. Meyer and Ray Land, "Threshold Concepts and Troublesome Knowledge: Linkages to Ways of Thinking and Practising within the Disciplines," in *Improving Student Learning—Ten Years On*, ed. C. Rust (Oxford: OCSLD, 2003), 412–24.

3.   Association of College and Research Libraries, *Framework for Information Literacy for Higher*

     Education (Chicago: Association of College and Research Libraries, 2016), http://www.ala.org/acrl/sites/ala.org.acrl/files/content/issues/infolit/Framework_ILHE.pdf.

4.   Dai Hounsell and Jenny Hounsell, "Teaching-Learning Environments in Contemporary Mass Higher Education," *British Journal of Educational Psychology Monograph Series II* 4 (2007): 91–111, https://www.researchgate.net/publication/233690366_Teaching-Learning_Environments_in_Contemporary_Mass_Higher_Education.

5.   Malcolm Tight, "Discipline and Theory in Higher Education Research," *Research Papers in Education* 29, no. 1 (2014): 93–110, https://doi.org/10.1080/02671522.2012.729080.

6.   Malcolm Tight, "Bridging the Divide: A Comparative Analysis of Articles in Higher Education Journals Published inside and Outside North America," *Higher Education* 53, no. 2 (2007): 235–53, https://doi.org/10.1007/s10734-005-2429-9.

7.   Malcolm Tight, "Higher Education Research as Tribe, Territory and/or Community: A Co-Citation Analysis," *Higher Education* 55, no. 5 (2008): 593–605, https://doi.org/10.1007/s10734-007-9077-1.

8.   Malcolm Tight, "Discipline and Theory."

9.   Paul Ramsden, "Improving Teaching and Learning in Higher Education: The Case for a Relational Perspective," *Studies in Higher Education* 12, no. 3 (1987): 275–86, https://doi.org/10.1080/03075078712331378062.

10.   CILIP, "My Professional Knowledge and Skills Base: Identify Gaps and Maximise Opportunities along Your Career Path," 2017, http://www.cilip.org.uk/page/pksb.

11.   Quality Assurance Agency for Higher Education, "Subject Benchmark Statement: Librarianship, Information, Knowledge, Records and Archives Management," *UK Quality Code for Higher Education Part A: Setting and Maintaining Academic Standards*, 2015, https://docplayer.net/12230814-Subject-benchmark-statement.html.

12.   Pamela Ann McKinney, "Information Literacy and Inquiry-Based Learning: Evaluation of a Five-Year Programme of Curriculum Development," *Journal of Librarianship and Information Science* 46, no. 2 (2014): 148–66, https://doi.org/10.1177/0961000613477677.

13.   Philippa Levy Sabine Little, Pam Mckinney, Anna Nibbs, and Jamie Wood, *The Sheffield Companion To Inquiry-Based Learning* (Sheffield: CILASS, Centre for Inquiry-based Learning in the Arts and Social Sciences, The University of Sheffield, 2010), https://www.sheffield.ac.uk/ibl/resources/sheffieldcompanion.

14.   The University of Sheffield, "Learning and Teaching at the University of Sheffield 2016–2021," 2016, https://www.sheffield.ac.uk/polopoly_fs/1.661828!/file/FinalStrategy.pdf.

15.   Donald Schon, *The Reflective Practitioner: How Professionals Think in Action* (New York: Basic Books, 1983).

16.   Emily Wheeler and Pamela Ann McKinney, "Are Librarians Teachers? Investigating Academic Librarians' Perceptions of Their Own Teaching Roles," *Journal of Information Literacy* 9, no. 2 (2015): 111–28, https://doi.org/10.11645/9.2.1985.

17.   Eva Hornung, "On Your Own but Not Alone: One-Person Librarians in Ireland and Their Perceptions of Continuing Professional Development," *Library Trends* 61, no. 3 (2013): 675–702, https://doi.org/10.1353/lib.2013.0007.

18.   Christine Susan Bruce, *Informed Learning* (Chicago: Association of College and Research Libraries, 2008).

19.   Sheila Webber and Bill Johnston, "Information Literacy: Conceptions, Context and the Formation of a Discipline," *Journal of Information Literacy* 11, no. 1 (2017): 156–83, https://doi.org/10.11645/11.1.2205.

20.   Christine Susan Bruce, *Informed Learning.*

21.   John Biggs and Catherine Tang, *Teaching for Quality Learning at University*, 4th ed. (Maidenhead: Open University Press, 2011).

22.   Keith Trigwell and Michael Prosser, "Development and Use of the Approaches to Teaching

Inventory," *Educational Psychology Review* 16, no. 4 (2004): 409–24, https://doi.org/10.1007/s10648-004-0007-9.

23. Thomas F. Hawk and Amit J. Shah, "To Enhance Student Learning," *Decision Sciences Journal of Innovative Education* 5, no. 1 (2007): 1–19.

24. Emily Wheeler and Pamela Ann McKinney, "Are Librarians Teachers?"

25. Pamela McKinney and Sheila Webber, "Teaching the Next Generation of Information Literacy Educators: Pedagogy and Learning," YouTube video, 23:25, April 6, 2017, https://youtu.be/JDr1DbJJKRA.

BIBLIOGRAPHY

Association of College and Research Libraries. *Framework for Information Literacy for Higher Education*. Chicago: Association of College and Research Libraries, 2016. http://www.ala.org/acrl/sites/ala.org.acrl/files/content/issues/infolit/Framework_ILHE.pdf.

Biggs, John, and Catherine Tang. *Teaching for Quality Learning at University*. 4th ed. Maidenhead: Open University Press, 2011.

Bruce, Christine Susan. *Informed Learning*. Chicago: Association of College and Research Libraries, 2008.

CILIP. "My Professional Knowledge and Skills Base: Identify Gaps and Maximise Opportunities along Your Career Path." 2017. http://www.cilip.org.uk/page/pksb.

Entwistle, Noel, Jennifer Nisbet, and Adrian Bromage. "Teaching-Learning Environments and Student Learning in Electronic Engineering." Paper presented at *Third Workshop of the European Network on Powerful Learning Environments, in Brugge, September 30–October 2, 2004*. https://www.academia.edu/3426418/Teaching-learning_environments_and_student_learning_in_electronic_engineering.

Hawk, Thomas F., and Amit J. Shah. "To Enhance Student Learning." *Decision Sciences Journal of Innovative Education* 5, no. 1 (2007): 1–19.

Hornung, Eva. "On Your Own but Not Alone: One-Person Librarians in Ireland and Their Perceptions of Continuing Professional Development." *Library Trends* 61, no. 3 (2013): 675–702. https://doi.org/10.1353/lib.2013.0007.

Hounsell, Dai, and Jenny Hounsell. "Teaching-Learning Environments in Contemporary Mass Higher Education." *British Journal of Educational Psychology Monograph Series II* 4 (2007): 91–111. https://www.researchgate.net/publication/233690366_Teaching-Learning_Environments_in_Contemporary_Mass_Higher_Education.

Levy, Philippa, Sabine Little, Pam Mckinney, Anna Nibbs, and Jamie Wood. *The Sheffield Companion To Inquiry-Based Learning*. Sheffield: CILASS, Centre for Inquiry-based Learning in the Arts and Social Sciences, The University of Sheffield, 2010. https://www.sheffield.ac.uk/ibl/resources/sheffieldcompanion.

McKinney, Pamela Ann. "Information Literacy and Inquiry-Based Learning: Evaluation of a Five-Year Programme of Curriculum Development." *Journal of Librarianship and Information Science* 46, no. 2 (2014): 148–66. https://doi.org/10.1177/0961000613477677.

McKinney, Pamela, and Sheila Webber. "Teaching the Next Generation of Information Literacy Educators: Pedagogy and Learning." YouTube video, 23:25. April 6, 2017. https://youtu.be/JDr1DbJJKRA.

Meyer, Jan H. F., and Ray Land. "Threshold Concepts and Troublesome Knowledge: Linkages to Ways of Thinking and Practising within the Disciplines." In *Improving Student Learning—*

Ten Years On, edited by C. Rust, 412–24. Oxford: OCSLD, 2003.

Quality Assurance Agency for Higher Education. "Subject Benchmark Statement: Librarianship, Information, Knowledge, Records and Archives Management." *UK Quality Code for Higher Education Part A: Setting and Maintaining Academic Standards*, 2015. https://docplayer.net/12230814-Subject-benchmark-statement.html.

Ramsden, Paul. "Improving Teaching and Learning in Higher Education: The Case for a Relational Perspective." *Studies in Higher Education* 12, no. 3 (1987): 275–86. https://doi.org/10.1080/03075078712331378062.

Schon, Donald. *The Reflective Practitioner: How Professionals Think in Action*. New York: Basic Books, 1983.

Tight, Malcolm. "Bridging the Divide: A Comparative Analysis of Articles in Higher Education Journals Published inside and Outside North America." *Higher Education* 53, no. 2 (2007): 235–53. https://doi.org/10.1007/s10734-005-2429-9.

———. "Discipline and Theory in Higher Education Research." *Research Papers in Education* 29, no. 1 (2014): 93–110. https://doi.org/10.1080/02671522.2012.729080.

———. "Higher Education Research as Tribe, Territory and/or Community: A Co-Citation Analysis." *Higher Education* 55, no. 5 (2008): 593–605. https://doi.org/10.1007/s10734-007-9077-1.

Trigwell, Keith, and Michael Prosser. "Development and Use of the Approaches to Teaching Inventory." *Educational Psychology Review* 16, no. 4 (2004): 409–24. https://doi.org/10.1007/s10648-004-0007-9.

University of Sheffield, The. "Learning and Teaching at the University of Sheffield 2016–2021," 2016. https://www.sheffield.ac.uk/polopoly_fs/1.661828!/file/FinalStrategy.pdf.

Webber, Sheila, and Bill Johnston. "Information Literacy: Conceptions, Context and the Formation of a Discipline." *Journal of Information Literacy* 11, no. 1 (2017): 156–83. https://doi.org/10.11645/11.1.2205.

Wheeler, Emily, and Pamela Ann McKinney. "Are Librarians Teachers? Investigating Academic Librarians' Perceptions of Their Own Teaching Roles." *Journal of Information Literacy* 9, no. 2 (2015): 111–28. https://doi.org/10.11645/9.2.1985.

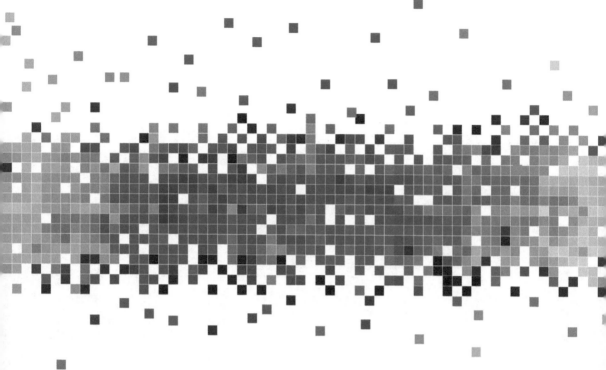

Section III
SoTL Research

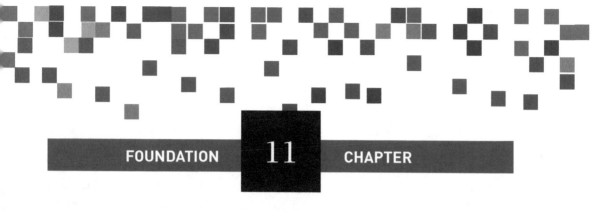

Inside/Outside/In-Between:

Librarians and SoTL Research

Emma Coonan

Introduction

"Are you a librarian engaged in the scholarship of teaching and learning?" inquires the call for case studies for this volume. Now there is a question to bring a librarian up short in their tracks: a source of some anxiety, certainly of self-questioning. It is a question that goes straight to the roots of librarian identity and the role we play in higher education.

Librarians rarely benefit from formal pedagogic training, yet on entering practice they often discover that teaching forms a major part of their professional identity. And, indeed, the nature of what they find themselves teaching may be equally unforeseen as, over time, librarians realize that the arena in which their vocation plays out is not, in fact, that of materials provision and resource access, the areas with which the profession is most closely identified. Teaching librarians do not work primarily with books or with the knowledge made tangible and contained in books but with the as-yet-unfixed, intangible, elusive knowledge under construction in people's heads. They find themselves delving not into database navigation but issues such as knowledge construction, active and reflective learning, and the part that information criticality can play in an individual's transformation and empowerment.

Lacking a frame of reference in which to evaluate, question, and affirm this work, however, librarians are often beset with an anxiety that relates deeply to their identity within the academy. Does this practice qualify as teaching? Even if it does, to what extent do librarians feel entitled to call themselves teachers? And are they ready to go a step further and call themselves not only teachers but *scholars of teaching*?

Both to support this developing pedagogic and scholarly identity and to develop a deeper understanding of these issues, a framework of practice is needed in which the teaching librarian can work and explore the meaning of this work—a conceptual scaffold to

understand their own practices, how and why they perform them, and how those practices are informed by other thinking and teaching they encounter. Librarians need a means "through which ... teaching can be something other than a seat-of-the-pants operation, with each of us out there making it up as we go."[1]

Such a mechanism would provide a stimulus through which librarians could not only teach but reflect on their teaching in a constructive and developmental way. It would provide the scaffolding to inquire into one's practice in a systematic, research-informed way and to collect and analyze evidence about it. And it would offer librarians an arena in which to share and receive feedback on their inquiries, which would spur further reflection, research, and dissemination.

The Scholarship of Teaching and Learning (SoTL) is precisely such a framework. It offers teaching librarians not only the tools and insights required to conduct formal inquiry into their practice, but also the means to confront deeper questions about themselves and their identities and about the roles they play and the responsibilities these roles bring. It imparts both the challenge and the tools to look at themselves as instructional librarians— that is, as educators—and to recognize and address all the responsibility that this role brings to reflect, to research, and to share these findings.

This chapter aims to show how and why engaging in SoTL research is beneficial for librarians and library staff, and to be candid about the challenges and rewards that the practice involves. It therefore looks at the practice of SoTL first from the outside, through published descriptions of SoTL research and the case studies included in this book. But it also explores what SoTL might feel like "from the inside"—the practical, intellectual, and affective implications that it holds for the teaching librarian community and how its members perceive their professional selves.

Finally, this chapter argues that librarians—because of the nature of their expertise, their position within the academy, and above all their involvement with information literacy—can make a unique contribution to SoTL research. Not only is SoTL good for librarians, therefore, librarians are good for SoTL!

But what is SoTL? And how is a librarian to know when they are doing it?

From the Outside In: SoTL as Practice

A quarter of a century after its first tangible appearance, the Scholarship of Teaching and learning still "appears endowed with multiple meanings."[2] Indeed, the literature is upfront about the variety and range of definitions of this practice and often seems to take a positive pleasure in describing SoTL in terms of what it is not. Kern et al.[3] point out, for instance, that an established core characteristic of SoTL is its non-identity with *excellent teaching*, which might be described as the effective teaching (or effective fostering of learning) of a field's subject matter. Another characteristic is its distinction from *scholarly teaching*, which Shulman defines as "teaching that is well grounded in the sources and resources appropriate to the field."[4] Both types of informed practice feed into SoTL, yet neither one, nor even the two in combination, constitute it.

The crucial difference appears to lie in which way the practice is orientated. The depictions of both "excellent" and "scholarly" teaching above look to the discipline as the locus where the quality and effectiveness of both the teaching and the learning are evaluated. Mastery of the subject knowledge is the lens through which these are measured. Both, therefore, face inward toward the knowledge and practices unique to the discipline. In contrast, common to all definitions of SoTL is an idea of going outward, beyond the borders of the individual discipline or subject field.

This "going outward" beyond the boundary of the discipline manifests in two ways: first and most important, is the commitment to look not only at *what* students are learning (the subject content) but the ways in which they learn—the processes through which knowledge is constructed, thresholds crossed, and complex understandings developed. As the mathematicians Bennett and Dewar write of their own work in SoTL, "Faculty use their disciplinary knowledge … to investigate a question about their students' learning, submit findings to peer review, and make them public for others in the academy to build upon."[5]

This "mak[ing] public for others … to build on" is the second way in which SoTL overspills the boundaries of the disciplines. A crucial element in all SoTL definitions is the requirement to make the findings of the work public so that others can both evaluate it and learn from it. In this, it conforms to one of the classic requirements of the scientific method, which holds that research is not research until it has been published. Indeed, Hutchings and Shulman's famous description of SoTL as a "going meta" corresponds with all the steps of formal scholarly research: "Faculty frame and systematically investigate questions related to student learning—the conditions under which it occurs, what it looks like, how to deepen it, and so forth—and do so with an eye not only to improving their own classroom but to advancing practice beyond."[6]

In focusing on the processes through which learning and teaching are carried out, and exploring questions such as whether that teaching and learning are taking place successfully, SoTL is a form of applied pedagogic research. However, it is not necessary to become an educational researcher to practice SoTL; in fact, it is crucial not to! By requiring teachers to stand back and tease apart the subject content from the processes through which their students learn it, SoTL overflows the boundaries of all disciplines, including education, to create a kind of extra-disciplinary "trading zone"[7] in which research dealing with learning in all subject fields can be explored and exchanged.

As Fanghanel notes, therefore, SoTL research is a form of inquiry "deeply anchored in the discipline and at the same time vibrantly interdisciplinary."[8] Its point of focus is *neither only* the subject knowledge that students master, which can be described exclusively in disciplinary terms, *nor* the processes of learning and teaching alone, which can be explored through educational research as a discipline in its own right, but the movement between the two. It is a dynamic process, a constant movement back and forth between the formal boundedness of discipline knowledge and the messier, freeform divagations involved in learning and constructing knowledge: those moments of transformation and reconceptualization when learners cross a threshold of understanding and "a qualitatively different conception of reality [becomes] established."[9]

Part of the difficulty in pinning SoTL down to a fixed definition is its own inherent lack of fixity. As a "systematic critical examination of an ever-changing object of inquiry,"[10] it could be argued that SoTL stands outside of disciplinarity itself, enacting a precarious dance across and between discipline knowledge, always carving out a contingent space for itself in the gaps between the established bodies of knowledge. And no one is better equipped for working beyond boundaries, in-between disciplines, than librarians.

THE LIMINAL LIBRARIAN

Instruction librarians frequently occupy a liminal position within the academy, falling organizationally between "academic" and "academic support." While in some countries it may be the norm for librarians to achieve academic tenure, in others their universities align them with administrative staff. Operationally, too, librarians' identity is often somewhat confused, being in continual movement on a spectrum of expertise at whose opposite poles are "information manager" and "educator." Teaching librarians frequently find themselves being expected to talk to students about the library when the learning content they have designed aims to engage learners in a negotiation around critical and contextual uses of information. Even when they are allowed to enact an educational role, they are often positioned toward the periphery of the discipline, not as an expert in the subject but an expert in the complex finding aids that contain (or, according to many users' perceptions, conceal) the subject literature.[11]

Although the teaching librarian's specialist field can be designated as information literacy (IL), this is not always a term that brings greater definition or visibility. Like SoTL, IL is an elusive entity to locate within academia and lends itself to a plurality of definitions. Unlike a discipline, it does not consist of a clearly bounded and externalized body of subject knowledge; rather, the teaching librarian's role is to enable learners to better understand, enact, and negotiate practices and values within a given discipline. IL is better thought of as a dynamic practice of contextual meaning-making[12] than a solid body of tangible or transmissible knowledge.

Teaching information literacy shows us that knowledge practices, information contexts, and even truth-values differ from discipline to discipline. This means that how information is constructed, communicated, consolidated, or contested operates differently in different fields. For librarians to call themselves "specialists in information" is really to do themselves and their profession a disservice: in reality, they are experts not in information but in how information is created and consumed in various highly situated and divergent contexts. Just like SoTL, IL takes place "in-between," in the gaps between the subject fields.

So, while the teaching librarian's position may seem from a traditional discipline-based point of view an uneasy or conflicted status, through the lens of SoTL practice, it emerges as a position of deep insight. Librarians have an advantage to being on the periphery of the discipline structure in that our teaching already takes place "in-between" subject knowledge, in the shadowier and less defined areas of developing academic understanding and practice. This can be seen clearly in the case study in this section, contributed by

Marshall and Wagner, who argue that

> librarians' insider-outsider perspectives as well as their frequent
> practice at traversing unfamiliar bodies of knowledge may make
> librarians especially well-situated to build bridges across the worlds
> of expert and novice.

The conceptual slipperiness of SoTL thus offers positive opportunities for librarians, who are experienced at negotiating the boundaries between discipline knowledge and Miller-Yeo and Young's extra-disciplinary "trading zone"[13] of learning processes and practices. Indeed, as a result of this agility in boundary-crossing, they may find themselves, as Marshall and Wagner imply, taking a leading role in making visible these processes.

ILLUMINATING EXPERTISE

In an article on the evolution of a SoTL community within their university, Boose and Hutchings note that "faculty have generally acquired their skills and approaches … over long periods of acculturation within their discipline's community of practice" and are therefore "so familiar with the steps they use to gather and process information, those steps are largely invisible to them."[14]

The "Decoding the Disciplines" work of Middendorf and Pace, which closely parallels SoTL thinking and research, is predicated on the metacognitive difficulty of exposing one's own expertise to analysis: "Faculty generally chose to go into fields where they were successful at that kind of thinking and have been working within that particular disciplinary framework for years. Therefore, they may have leaped almost automatically over obstacles that can prove daunting for novices."[15] It is notable that in its earliest versions, SoTL was conceived of as simply the "Scholarship of Teaching."[16] Only after a decade or so did its proponents recognize the need to explore the processes through which *learning* takes place as distinct from how a subject is taught. This recognition of learning as a separate entity from teaching illuminates the key role that SoTL research can play in helping faculty perceive and analyze the nature of their own expertise.

As noted above, much of the work that instructional librarians do lies in enabling students to understand and begin to embody for themselves the complex and situated practices peculiar to how their discipline deals with knowledge. Harp Ziegenfuss's change in instructional emphasis from the *how* of navigating databases to the *whys* of research as a process illustrates this approach, as do her endeavors to enable students to relate their prior experiences to learning about the research process. Librarians' expertise, therefore, lies in precisely the areas that a high level of disciplinary expertise may conceal from view. Librarians can thus play a catalytic role in helping faculty to bring to light the tacit thinking and understandings that on which their identity as experts is built.

The use of SoTL as a tool for exposing the hidden nature of disciplinary expertise can be seen in the case studies in this section by Wheeler et al., who use SoTL to explore ways of supporting their students' understanding of key business information literacy concepts, and Lacroix and Johnston, who use O'Brien's questions to probe into postgraduates' grasp and constructions of troublesome knowledge in the humanities. Similarly, Becker and Olcott note that a SoTL approach to their research was driven by the fact that "the outcome measured ... does not focus on content, but rather the application of skills such as critical thinking, information literacy, and the students' own reflections on their learning."

Again in this section, Marshall and Wagner directly address the issue of students' relationship with expert knowledge (and with those who model it), acknowledging their awareness of, yet also their separateness from expertise:

> One important theme ... was students' depictions of expertise and their accounts of negotiating expertise and how they negotiated expertise within the context of doing research. To begin with, one of the most enduring challenges facing instructor-librarians may be how to bridge the gap between students' lived experience and the often-daunting world of academic scholarship.

Indeed, Marshall and Wagner argue that librarians, too, need to understand and expose their own expertise, listening to learners when they describe the challenges and frustrations of working with information in new ways and to new ends. Marshall and Wagner encourage teaching librarians to seize the opportunities that students give them to "step outside of one's role as expert in order to remember what it was like to do research assignments for the first (and second and third) time. The opportunity for librarians to reflect and realign themselves with students is a crucial aspect of being an effective teacher."

Like all educators, teaching librarians have an obligation to bring the lenses of what they teach and how they teach into alignment, to explore the nature of their expertise, and find ways of bringing it to light—in the words of Wheeler et al., to "make ... learning visible."

SOTL: METHOD, METHODOLOGY OR MINDSET?

The practice of SoTL comes with an inescapable commitment to conducting research, as the classic definition by Hutching and Shulman, quoted above, underlines: "It requires a kind of 'going meta,' in which faculty *frame and systematically investigate* questions related to student learning."[17]

In line with this "going meta"—which, as described above, entails a moving beyond the thinking and methods that structure our own discipline—SoTL research methods offer an interesting counterpoint to the more traditional library research methods. Historically, library research has often tended toward quantitative approaches, with the survey method employed very frequently.[18] SoTL methods lean instead (or as well) toward more open, fluid, qualitative approaches such as ethnography, phenomenology, and phenomenography, with data collection methods such as in-depth interviews, observations, and assessment analysis.

The case studies by the authors in the SoTL Research section show how these methods operate and why they are effective for achieving "work that invites critical thinking about basic assumptions and purposes, and about the way we do our work as educators."[19] The methods employed range from Marshall and Wagner's ethnographic interviews with students to elicit their experiences of conducting research to the "lesson study" collaborative reflection carried out by Wheeler et al. with the aim of understanding and responding to how first-year students learn foundational business information literacy skills. Whitver's case study also focuses on the transformative potential of group reflection as a method to explore, in a structured manner, an aspect of teaching and learning—in this instance, the assessment rubric norming process.

Students' own assessment data (separated from the marking process) is the focus of the study by Bankston, Moberly, and Waltz, who analyzed the data for evidence of learners' ability to comprehend and judge the scientific papers they read. The collaboration resulted in a profound redesign of the course assignment format, how the course is taught, and how the librarian supports the developing understanding of the learners.

The study by Becker and Olcott also uses student assessment data. From their content analysis, they elicit rich data that cast new light on the assumptions teachers make about who their students are, how they learn, and how the teachers know their teaching has been effective.[20] Harp Ziegenfuss employed pre- and post-intervention surveys to gather data about students' learning experiences, including their anxieties about conducting research in the library, and shows how the information garnered has influenced her own perceptions and changed her ongoing instructional design.

SoTL methods can usefully complement the traditional range of methods used in library science; for instance, Lacroix and Johnston use both a survey and interviews within a phenomenological framework to evaluate their postgraduate course on scholarly communications. Similarly, in their study, Bowers and Yankovskyy employ surveys alongside observations and grounded theory to bring to light hidden disciplinary practices and threshold concepts across four separate courses.

Given the characteristic elusiveness of the field, it is no surprise to find that a semantic question mark hangs over the practice of SoTL research: can it be said that there are methods that are characteristic of SoTL or even a recognizable range of "SoTL methods"? Or should one, as Fanghanel avers, talk about SoTL itself as "a methodology for professional development"?[21]

The very richness of the literature suggests that it matters little whether each of us sees SoTL research as a method, a methodology, or simply a mindset. As Fanghanel notes, its importance lies in the fact that it not only equips educators with the framework and tools they need to carry out a structured inquiry into their own teaching practices, together with a fresh range of methods to inform their approach; it also provides them with a developmental praxis that enables them to continually deepen their learning about the nature of their own role.[22]

Boose and Hutchings argue that as they engage in reflection on their teaching, educators realize that students' learning is a matter of *seeing themselves as*—that learning is "as much about identity formation and self-assessment as about skill development."[23] This *seeing as* is a matter for teaching librarians, too, as they begin to negotiate the range of new identities SoTL offers them. In our research and reflection, we too continue to learn; what we are learning is to *see ourselves as* not only librarians but as teachers; not only teachers but as researchers and scholars. In doing so, the teaching librarian enters into an enriched identity combining teaching, researching, and learning, continually deepening their practice through an understanding of all three of these strands and the ways in which they are interwoven.

From the Inside Out: SoTL in Practice

The case studies in this section, and indeed in the entire volume, demonstrate that the nature of teaching librarians' expertise, their work with situated learning processes and information practices, and even their liminality in the academy, makes them ideally positioned to contribute to SoTL research. It is clear that doing so will open up new opportunities for librarians to deepen their own understanding as well as make a contribution to a new and dynamic field. SoTL offers an arena in which librarians' unique contribution to teaching and student learning can be both captured and built upon and their identity as scholars made known both in the literature and to their often-doubting selves, yet there is still some hesitation in the profession to embark upon it.

The methods may feel alien, but there are many exemplars available, in this volume and elsewhere. Likewise, the approach and focus may be outside the traditional library comfort zone, but there exist a well-tried map and compass[24] along with practical framing questions and principles[25] to guide our inquiries. Furthermore, teaching librarians have immediate field access to learners—although as Bowers and Yankovskyy acknowledge in this section, "Without consistent or long-term access to data about what students know, learn, fear, forget and need reinforcement on, many of the principles of SoTL can be abstractions."

It is true that longitudinal teaching opportunities remain relatively rare for librarians: the profession is still at the mercy of the "one-shot" session. In answer to this issue, however, the case study by Wheeler et al. demonstrates the value of a research approach that deliberately chooses to focus on a single lesson. They show that collaborative reflection on one teaching intervention can yield sufficient data for evidence-based reflection, investigation, and dissemination.

The opportunity to focus on a single learning event means that librarians forced to work in a one-shot scenario can still engage in SoTL research. However, Wheeler et al.'s solution does throw up a second potential barrier: the need for collaboration within SoTL research. All but one case study in this section are co-authored, most by a librarian-faculty partnership, and the one single-authored study provides a rich and stimulating picture of how not only teaching practice but also librarians' self-efficacy and confidence can be developed through group reflection in the service of SoTL.

While the cases in this section highlight the benefits of collaboration with faculty colleagues, a reflective practice with other librarians can be equally fruitful. As Whitver shows, it is the time spent in collegial reflection, experience sharing, and mutual support and development that matters for SoTL: "The act of teaching can be isolating and lonely.... . It is essential that librarians have dedicated time, not only to engage in personal reflection, but also to be able to talk through the experience in the classroom, share ideas, and problem solve." It is thus particularly unfortunate that the operational demands on our time often form a barrier to any kind of reflective practice. Teaching librarians may know very well that reflection "emancipates us from merely impulsive and routine action" and "enables us to know what we are about when we act,"[26] but it can be difficult to demonstrate the value of this activity to managers coping with day-to-day staffing demands and constraints, particularly those who are prone to measuring impact with a simple logic model.[27]

Ironically, it can be argued that reflection is itself an information literate practice, as it forces us to confront and encompass potentially unwelcome information (e.g., "that activity isn't working for my students"), but it is also—and for precisely the same reasons—a challenging and unsettling practice that may bring about emotional reaction, cognitive dissonance, and identity confusion. As Boose and Hutchings note dryly, "Careful examination of one's teaching can be risky."[28] It may be that teaching librarians find convincing their managers to let them take this first step into SoTL easier than convincing themselves.

> Whitver argues (in this section) that as teaching becomes more and more important within the field of librarianship, it is imperative that librarians find ways to develop confidence in their classroom practices.

The turning of one's critical gaze and analytic capabilities toward the self's own practice requires courage. It is an undertaking to not merely evaluate that practice but to develop and change it, and it is therefore a commitment to a lack of closure, a state of permanent beta. Paradoxically, SoTL's "long, loving look at reality"[29] is both what pushes us to take this step and what emboldens us to commit to it as a form of lifelong learning—not merely continuing but *continuous* professional development. Yet engagement with SoTL asks still more than this. Shulman's often-quoted definition of SoTL asks its practitioners to engage in a series of steps of which reflective practice is only the first: "To view teaching as serious, intellectual work, ask good questions about their students' learning, seek evidence in their classrooms that can be used to improve practice, and make this work public so that others can critique it, build on it, and contribute to the wider teaching commons."[30]

As noted above, SoTL research echoes the procedures of the scientific method, which carries with it a formidable commitment to rigorous research design, experimentation and analysis, validation, and dissemination. These are large, scary, formal words, and when taken in the abstract they imply large, scary, formal processes that can themselves appear insuperable barriers, perhaps prompting the response: "I'm a librarian, not a researcher!" Yet each of these steps forms the practical groundwork for the next. If once a librarian commits to seeing teaching as work that deserves a critical and reflective regard, their feet are already set on the SoTL pathway. The process of looking, the act reflecting on something, prompts the desire to pose questions about it. And because those questions bear on everyday practices and assumptions, it is almost impossible to avoid them once they have been asked: the questioner is inescapably driven to investigate, to explore, to affirm, or refute their beliefs. What SoTL asks of its proponents is to share the results of that inquiry, so that others can benefit from the researcher's insights and the researcher can benefit from their feedback.

In many ways, teaching librarians may find this last step the most difficult of all. Harder even than the "going meta"[31] of designing SoTL research is the "going public" of sharing findings in these new roles of scholar and researcher. Yet this exposure is essential in order to complete the cycle and deepen understanding further. This last step—the "contribut[ion] to the wider teaching commons"—is enfolded within the very first step Shulman[32] asks us to take: to make the commitment to see our own teaching as worthy of inquiry; and it returns us there to begin the cycle of research, reflection, and sharing anew.

In-Between: Dancing across the Boundaries

The evolution of the teaching librarian's identity, through these roles of reflective practitioner, scholar, and SoTL researcher, is an ongoing one: "I am never done becoming a teacher."[33] In embarking on SoTL research, a teaching librarian may find their way not only to a new understanding of their field and practices but to a new identity.

Yet, paradoxically, it can be postulated that no one consciously *decides* to embark on SoTL research. It is more likely that having turned that critical and reflective gaze on their teaching and learning practices, having made that courageous commitment to see their teaching as "serious, intellectual work," the librarian later discovers that what they are doing has a name: SoTL. In the act of asking, "Am I a librarian engaged in the Scholarship of Teaching and Learning?"—in the very moment of self-doubt that the question provokes— they discover that they have already begun, perhaps began long ago.

The case studies in this section show the range and the richness of SoTL research and the many rewards it offers for librarians who, in seeking to better understand their students' learning, also find that they have found a way to answer that question positively from their own position of precarity "in-between" discipline and non-discipline: in their "teaching in the gaps." Just as SoTL—and for that matter, IL—eludes a fixed definition, so ultimately does the teaching librarian. Engagement in SoTL opens the way into a rich, composite identity, one that embraces researcher and scholar as well as librarian; and, indeed, learner as well as teacher, in the continued exploration of what it means to be an educator.

ENDNOTES

1. Pat Hutchings and Lee S. Shulman, "The Scholarship of Teaching: New Elaborations, New Directions," *Change: The Magazine of Higher Learning* 31, no. 5 (1999): 14, https://doi.org/10.1080/00091389909604218.
2. Joelle Fanghanel, "Going Public with Pedagogical Inquiries: SoTL as a Methodology for Faculty

Professional Development," *Teaching and Learning Inquiry*, 2013: 59.

3. Beth Kern et al., "The Role of SoTL in the Academy: Upon the 25th Anniversary of Boyer's *Scholarship Reconsidered*," *Journal of the Scholarship for Teaching and Learning* 15, no. 10 (2015): 1–14, https://doi.org/10.14434/josotl.v15i3.13623.

4. Lee S. Shulman, "From Minsk to Pinsk: Why a Scholarship of Teaching and Learning?," *Journal of the Scholarship of Teaching and Learning* 1, no. 1 (2000): 50, quoted in Kern et al., "The Role of SoTL in the Academy: Upon the 25th Anniversary of Boyer's *Scholarship Reconsidered*."

5. Curtis D. Bennett and Jacqueline M. Dewar, "An Overview of the Scholarship of Teaching and Learning in Mathematics," *PRIMUS* 22, no. 6 (2012): 459, https://doi.org/10.1080/10511970.2011.585389.

6. Hutchings and Shulman, "The Scholarship of Teaching," 13.

7. Janice Miller-Young and Michelle Yeo, "Conceptualizing and Communicating SoTL: A Framework for the Field," *Teaching & Learning Inquiry* 3, no. 2 (2015): 38.

8. Fanghanel, "Going Public," 59.

9. Paul Ramsden, *Learning to Teach in Higher Education*, 2nd ed. (London: RoutledgeFalmer, 2003), 37, https://doi.org/10.1016/0307-4412(92)90210-D.

10. Fanghanel, "Going Public," 62.

11. See e.g., Karl V. Fast and D. Grant Campbell, "'I Still like Google': University Student Perceptions of Searching OPACs and the Web," *Proceedings of the American Society for Information Science and Technology* 41, no. 1 (September 22, 2005): 138–46, https://doi.org/10.1002/meet.1450410116.

12. Annemaree Lloyd, "Information Literacy Landscapes: An Emerging Picture," *Journal of Documentation* 62, no. 5 (2006): 570–83, https://doi.org/10.1108/00220410610688723.

13. Miller-Young and Yeo, "Conceptualizing and Communicating SoTL," 38.

14. David L. Boose and Pat Hutchings, "The Scholarship of Teaching and Learning as a Subversive Enterprise," *Teaching & Learning Inquiry* 4, no. 1 (2016): 8.

15. faculty who are deeply ingrained in their disciplinary research answer a series of questions to understand how students think and learn in their field. The cross-disciplinary nature of the process clarifies the thinking for each discipline. In the last twenty years, the call for faculty members to focus on critical thinking has led to a laudable effort on the part of faculty members and teaching support professionals to move the focus of courses to the higher levels of Bloom's (1956Joan Middendorf and David Pace, "Decoding the Disciplines: A Model for Helping Students Learn Disciplinary Ways of Thinking," in *New Directions for Teaching and Learning*, 2004, 5.

16. Ernest L. Boyer, *Scholarship Reconsidered: Priorities of the Professoriate* (Carnegie Foundation for the Advancement of Teaching, 1990); Hutchings and Shulman, "The Scholarship of Teaching."

17. Hutchings and Shulman, "The Scholarship of Teaching," 13, my emphasis.

18. Rebecca Halpern et al., "#ditchthesurvey: Expanding Methodological Diversity in LIS Research," *In the Library with the Lead Pipe*, March 11 (2015).

19. Boose and Hutchings, "The Scholarship of Teaching," 2.

20. Mia O'Brien, "Navigating the SoTL Landscape: A Compass, Map and Some Tools for Getting Started," *International Journal for the Scholarship of Teaching and Learning* 2, no. 2 (2008), https://doi.org/10.20429/ijsotl.2008.020215.

21. Fanghanel, "Going Public," 59.

22. Ibid.

23. Boose and Hutchings, "The Scholarship of Teaching," 8.

24. O'Brien, "Navigating the SoTL Landscape."

25. Peter Felten, "Principles of Good Practice in SoTL," *Teaching & Learning Inquiry: The ISSOTL*

Journal 1, no. 1 (March 1, 2013): 121–25, https://doi.org/10.20343/teachlearninqu.1.1.121.

26. John Dewey, *How We Think: A Restatement of the Relation of Reflective Thinking to the Educative Process*, rev. ed. (Boston: Heath, 1933).

27. Sharon Markless and David Streatfield, "How Can You Tell If It's Working? Recent Developments in Impact Evaluation and Their Implications for Information Literacy Practice," *Journal of Information Literacy* 11, no. 1 (June 5, 2017): 106, https://doi.org/10.11645/11.1.2201.

28. Boose and Hutchings, "The Scholarship of Teaching," 5.

29. Ibid., 8.

30. Lee S. Shulman, foreword to *Into the Classroom: Developing the Scholarship of Teaching and Learning*, 2006, ix.

31. Hutchings and Shulman, "The Scholarship of Teaching," 13.

32. Shulman, foreword, ix.

33. Lauren Hays, "Finding a Research Agenda When Teaching and Learning Is Your Passion," The Librarian Parlor, 2017, https://libparlor.com/2017/10/25/finding-a-research-agenda-when-teaching-and-learning-is-your-passion/.

BIBLIOGRAPHY

Bennett, Curtis D., and Jacqueline M. Dewar. "An Overview of the Scholarship of Teaching and Learning in Mathematics." *PRIMUS* 22, no. 6 (2012): 458–73. https://doi.org/10.1080/105 11970.2011.585389.

Boose, David L., and Pat Hutchings. "The Scholarship of Teaching and Learning as a Subversive Enterprise." *Teaching & Learning Inquiry* 4, no. 1 (2016): 1–12.

Boyer, Ernest L. *Scholarship Reconsidered: Priorities of the Professoriate*. Carnegie Foundation for the Advancement of Teaching, 1990.

Dewey, John. *How We Think: A Restatement of the Relation of Reflective Thinking to the Educative Process*. Rev. ed. Boston: Heath, 1933.

Fanghanel, Joelle. "Going Public with Pedagogical Inquiries: SoTL as a Methodology for Faculty Professional Development." *Teaching and Learning Inquiry*, 2013.

Felten, Peter. "Principles of Good Practice in SoTL." *Teaching & Learning Inquiry: The ISSOTL Journal* 1, no. 1 (March 1, 2013): 121–25. https://doi.org/10.20343/teachlearninqu.1.1.121.

Halpern, Rebecca, Christopher Eaker, John Jackson, and Daina Bouquin. "#ditchthesurvey: Expanding Methodological Diversity in LIS Research." *In the Library with the Lead Pipe* March 11 (2015).

Hutchings, Pat, and Lee S. Shulman. "The Scholarship of Teaching: New Elaborations, New Directions." *Change: The Magazine of Higher Learning* 31, no. 5 (1999): 10–15. https://doi. org/10.1080/00091389909604218.

Kern, Beth, Gwendolyn Mettetal, Marcia D Dixson, and Robin K Morgan. "The Role of SoTL in the Academy: Upon the 25th Anniversary of Boyer's Scholarship Reconsidered." *Journal of the Scholarship for Teaching and Learning* 15, no. 10 (2015): 1–14. https://doi.org/10.14434/ josotl.v15i3.13623.

Lloyd, Annemaree. "Information Literacy Landscapes: An Emerging Picture." *Journal of Documentation* 62, no. 5 (2006): 570–83. https://doi.org/10.1108/00220410610688723.

Markless, Sharon, and David Streatfield. "How Can You Tell If It's Working? Recent Developments in Impact Evaluation and Their Implications for Information Literacy Practice." *Journal of Information Literacy* 11, no. 1 (June 5, 2017): 106. https://doi.org/10.11645/11.1.2201.

Middendorf, Joan, and David Pace. "Decoding the Disciplines: A Model for Helping Students Learn

Disciplinary Ways of Thinking." In *New Directions for Teaching and Learning*, 1–12, 2004.

Miller-Young, Janice, and Michelle Yeo. "Conceptualizing and Communicating SoTL: A Framework for the Field." *Teaching & Learning Inquiry* 3, no. 2 (2015): 37–53.

O'Brien, Mia. "Navigating the SoTL Landscape: A Compass, Map and Some Tools for Getting Started." *International Journal for the Scholarship of Teaching and Learning* 2, no. 2 (2008). https://doi.org/10.20429/ijsotl.2008.020215.

Ramsden, Paul. *Learning to Teach in Higher Education*. 2nd ed. London: RoutledgeFalmer, 2003. https://doi.org/10.1016/0307-4412(92)90210-D.

12

At the Intersection of Theory and Experience:

How Qualitative Interviews Enrich the Scholarship of Teaching and Learning

Ann Marshall and Sarah Wagner

> "It is overwhelming thinking about a research paper. There's so much things that go into it. It is just overwhelming."
>
> —a sophomore liberal arts major

> "That paper I actually got it. [My professor] said it was really well done. I got to present it … this little no name kid presenting at this … convention."
>
> —a junior professional studies major

Introduction

The research process can be both overwhelming and exciting, as the quotations from the two students above illustrate. Taking the time to listen to students can tell volumes about who students are and how they learn, questions important to the Scholarship of Teaching and Learning (SoTL). This case study examines how qualitative methods can be used within SoTL, and, in particular, how student interview studies can meaningfully inform librarians' pedagogical practices. Often, librarians may get to know students on only an introductory basis; they may encounter the same students only once or twice a semester and have little exposure to students' written work. Given this context, open-ended, qualitative interviews can provide a much-needed depth of perspective and can lead to important

reflections on how students experience library instruction. In addition, librarians bring an important perspective to the field of SoTL, including a commitment to developing students' self-directed academic work within a complex research environment. This case study first considers the intersections between qualitative methods and SoTL, then it outlines the methods used, and finally, it discusses the student interviews from a SoTL perspective. The authors suggest that an ethnographic approach to understanding students' experience is rich with potential for the SoTL community and that instructional librarians have both much to gain and much to offer by engaging in these methods.

Literature Review

This case study is relevant to three overlapping areas of scholarship: qualitative methods in education, studies focused on the Scholarship of Teaching and Learning, and ethnographic research in library and information studies. Qualitative methods have deep roots within the field of education while also drawing heavily upon sociology and anthropology. For example, sociologists Stevens, Armstrong, and Arum identify a number of influential studies within higher education that, over decades, have explored the "experiential core of college life."[1] Examples include book-length studies which invoke a variety of qualitative methods, including interviews and participant observation on one or multiple campuses that are authored by a single person or team of researchers.[2] However, the majority of qualitative studies in education focus on elementary and high school-aged students, leaving higher education relatively neglected.[3] In addition, a number of education and sociology texts focus directly on qualitative research methods.[4]

By comparison, SoTL is a relatively new area of research but with wide breadth across academia. SoTL is loosely defined, but Felten suggests five principles of good practice: inquiry into student learning, grounded in context, methodologically sound, conducted in partnership with students, and appropriately public.[5] Similarly, O'Brien identifies four qualities of SoTL: concern for students and their learning; deliberate design for teaching and learning; systematic implementation, analysis and evaluation of the design; and contribution to SoTL knowledge and practice.[6] Since SoTL is not specific to any one discipline, SoTL may present important opportunities for librarians to collaborate with disciplinary faculty.[7] In addition, the involvement of multiple disciplines on SoTL projects can bring new approaches and expertise to the table.[8] Librarians have also engaged in SoTL research, and a sample of their work includes team-designed curriculum for writing courses,[9] in-depth assessment for instruction redesign,[10] and student-centered learning goals.[11] Placing students at the center of one's inquiry into learning is a key feature of SoTL and interviewing students seems particularly apropos for this goal.

Finally, both Dubicki[12] and Khoo, Rozaklis, and Hall[13] provide a review of the use of ethnographic methods in library settings, including studies that focus on students' research processes. Khoo, Rozaklis, and Hall describe ethnographic methods as longitudinal, which allow insights and theory to "emerge" over time.[14] They also discuss the intellectual foundations of ethnography, such as an emphasis on becoming "immersed" in others' perspectives and the "complex, in-situ" nature of ethnographic inquiry.[15]

Lanclos and Asher warn, however, that such methods may become "ethnographish," where researchers draw upon the methods of ethnography (with often useful results) but conducted in the short term, without the depth of perspective sought by ethnographers.[16] SoTL studies may be more vulnerable to this critique, with studies focused on a single course or semester and where the investigators, such as the authors of this study, juggle multiple responsibilities. However, Lanclos and Asher suggest that it is critical to not leave the "unfinished ethnographic moment" behind.[17] They call upon those interested in these methods to take risks, pursue long-term studies, seek institutional support, and collaborate with others.

Methods

The previous section discusses the traditions that inform this study's methodological approach, especially literature that applies qualitative methods to the student experience. The case study presented here is based on ten in-depth interviews conducted with undergraduates at Purdue University Fort Wayne, a mid-sized public university with undergraduate enrollment of just under 8,000 students, from June 2016 to May 2017. The study was approved by the university's institutional review board, and the authors recruited student volunteers through a combination of fliers, outreach to faculty and staff, and snowball sampling. In the open-ended interviews, undergraduates were asked about their research process, an approach based on a retrospective interview method.[18] The interviews began by inviting students to talk about a recent experience of doing research, especially a research-based assignment. The students were then asked to describe their process and the steps they took. The rest of the interview was based on this opening narrative, allowing students to elaborate on their examples and explanations. The interviews were transcribed and coded, prompting additional reflection on what students said and a consideration of both similarities and differences among the transcripts. The student interviewees included three first-year students, four sophomores, and three upper-class students, with a wide range of majors and minors, including the social sciences and applied fields such as business and education, among others.

Framing Expertise in Students' Language

This case study considers excerpts from the student interviews, especially as related to SoTL themes. In particular, the analysis focuses on the interviews from a single aspect of O'Brien's SoTL Compass: "Who are my students and how do they learn effectively?"[19] In addition, the authors were interested in O'Brien's idea of "going-meta—a kind of standing back from daily teaching and learning" to think more deeply about students' experiences and how those experiences might matter.[20] The authors also reflected on students' use of language and how issues of listening to students might enhance librarians' role as teachers.[21]

EXPERTISE AND STUDENTS' LIVED EXPERIENCE

One important theme in the interview transcripts was students' depictions of expertise and how they negotiated expertise within the context of doing research. To begin with, one of the most enduring challenges facing instructor-librarians may be how to bridge the gap between students' lived experience and the often-daunting world of academic scholarship. One student remarked:

> The one [article] that I found, I chose because one, it wasn't super long and two, it was understandable, whereas like some of them it's just like, "I can't read this." But I could actually understand it [this article].... It was something I could relate to.

This is likely a familiar sentiment and yet it draws attention to how students think about their own relationship to expertise. In this example, the language of scholarship is talked about as a barrier, limiting the students' choice of possible articles. Similarly, another student talked about choosing to bypass a potential research topic because, "I'm way too young, I haven't seen enough.... There was so much being talked about and like I couldn't figure out what was true or what was not true." Another student also talked about needing to transcend commonplace knowledge, stating, "You have to establish credibility" and, if you don't, "you could just be the average guy pulled off the street ... talking about something random that you have no clue about." Consider how this student talked out their assignments for one of their professors:

> I got that [good grade] on my last paper, and I was really stoked about that, because my teacher, he's a tough cookie. I swear, he's hard, he's a very smart guy too and he's very respectable, even though he's brought up some weird topics.

The language in this final example seems particularly evocative. The student provides a down-to-earth depiction of their professor as an expert and yet the student is also highly engaged and offers an outsider's perspective. The student is *both* a part of and not a part of the academic world that is described. The student is "stoked" to have done well on an assignment while still calling out aspects of academia as "weird." In each of these examples, students express a kind of separateness from, or not quite having access to, expertise, a sentiment heard unsurprisingly from first- and second-year students.

NEGOTIATING EXPERTISE AND THE ACRL *FRAMEWORK*

In other instances, the distance between students and scholarly knowledge seemed less stark, as students spoke of their own work as a kind of probing or negotiating of expertise.

In fact, there were times when concepts from the Association of College and Research Libraries (ACRL) *Framework for Information Literacy for Higher Education*[22] seemed to come alive in students' own depictions of their process:

> There is actually one set of articles I found, they were a play off of each other…. So this guy wrote this whole thing up on how successful the aspect of involving [the topic] was, but this other guy wrote a reflection on it. And it's kind of a cool little battle between the two of them. I got to incorporate that in the paper.

> When I have a question and I do reading … That is [like] asking the person who wrote the book a question. So I think that's probably how I do most of my research, is I try to find articles or papers and books of people who have done this research, and see what they say and….

Given early critiques of the ACRL *Framework* as jargon-heavy,[23] it seems important to consider the extent to which the ACRL *Framework* resonates with students' descriptions of their processes. The first example in the preceding paragraph vividly illustrates the frame Scholarship as Conversation in a student's own words and the second, while perhaps more ambiguous, brings the frame Research as Inquiry to mind. Note that these themes came up within students' larger stories about their research without any questions directed at the ACRL *Framework*. This affirms at least a degree of convergence between the threshold concepts identified in the ACRL *Framework* and what some undergraduates actually experience. The idea behind threshold concepts is that once students have rigorously grappled with the foundational theories or concepts inherent in a discipline or body of knowledge, then students' perspective undergoes an important transformation that makes possible a new depth of learning and pursuit of inquiry.[24] The two student statements discussed above are suggestive of students speaking the language of these core foundational ideas of information literacy, as outlined in the ACRL *Framework*, without being prompted to do so. Note, too, that with further analysis of these quotes, it is also difficult to categorize these student statements neatly into one specific ACRL frame. In other words, scholarly conversation and research as inquiry appear to be at work in both of these examples. In the first instance, an inquisitive mindset is what enabled the student to bring scholarly dialog into their own paper, and in the second example, the student's practice of asking questions of a text is certainly also an example of the student engaging in their own scholarly dialog.

However, the connections between the ACRL *Framework* and students' explanation of their processes were, at times, more diffuse and difficult tease out. For example, in which frame would one put the work of thesis statement development or argument, especially as related to the research process? One might say that it is either missing from the ACRL *Framework* or that it is, even if not stated, a part of all of the frames. The interviewees spoke of argument or thesis in varied but overlapping ways. For example, one upper-level student said that for all the papers this student writes, a thesis statement is expected. Another student said that developing an argument was a challenge because "I had, just all these ideas." A first-year student talked about argument as making "sure everything ties in with purpose." Even if not explicitly addressed in the ACRL *Framework*, these examples are a reminder that students' assignments often require them to view their research through the lens of a thesis or argument.

EXPERTISE AND STRIVING TO BE RIGHT

Students' descriptions of how they developed their arguments led to additional insights about how students negotiated expertise. For example, consider these two statements from a first-year student and sophomore respectively:

> I try to make sure I give enough examples as to why I'm right. And then give examples as to why I know I'm right. That's the fun part of it. If I was doing a persuasive paper, I wouldn't bash anything….

> Then before I did any research, I was like, "How am I going to get this flow from the top? … Then once you get them to flow together, you do a little bit of research. Sometimes you have to change a little bit in there. Then get the flow right.

In both of these examples, the students identified the role of evidence or research as a crucial part of their process. In addition, both students talked about striving toward getting it "right." For the first student, this meant being perceived as correct in their argument while the second student talked of trying to get the flow "right." Compared to the earlier examples of students' process as inquisitive, both of these accounts may appear somewhat formulaic, with a more rigid understanding of expertise. Yet both of the above examples also depict students grappling with important challenges. These two students were doing work that required a negotiation of both sources and argument as they endeavored to conceive what expertise looks like.

It may therefore be important for librarians to remember the challenge of negotiating expertise in these complex ways, especially as students also try to be true to themselves. For example, consider one student who said:

> I find it very challenging trying to relate the findings into like, an actual observation or into what we would say real world settings or like … an actual topic instead of just reporting on them.

Another student also spoke of how hard it can be to keep it all meaningful, stating, "After you keep working with it for so long, it just gets kind of mundane, and you're going through all these motions to get this crap done. And, it is hard to convince myself that I'm still interested." Yet another student similarly talked about how much work goes into a paper, saying, "I looked at the ten pages and I had a deep breath and it was like, 'I got some work to do.'"

While there were many potential themes to pursue in the interview transcripts, the idea of how students interacted with expertise seemed particularly thought-provoking. Although students talked about the mediation of expertise as both a challenge and at times as a barrier, these student accounts also provided insights into what it is like for students to incorporate expertise into their own work.

Library Instruction and the Negotiation of Expertise

This final section provides reflections on the student interviews from the vantage point of instruction. First, there is no doubt that librarians have expert knowledge to offer to students. Librarians come to their positions accomplished both academically and professionally and offer instruction about the research process and complex research tools. Hearing from students is important because it provides the opportunity to step outside of one's role as an expert in order to remember what it was like to do research assignments for the first (and second and third) time. This opportunity for librarians to reflect and to realign themselves with students is a crucial aspect of being an effective teacher and it can help librarians treat students with patience and dignity. In practical terms, just to imagine these students in one's classroom can remind librarians of students' potential and affirms that the work librarians do is important.

In addition, librarians may also have a unique relationship with expertise, and reflecting on this negotiation of expertise could also enhance librarians' pedagogical work. Librarians' insider-outsider perspectives as well as their frequent practice at traversing unfamiliar bodies of knowledge may make librarians especially well-situated to build bridges across the worlds of the expert and novice. For example, librarians might deliberately bring the language of both novice and expert into their classroom instruction. Also, by making the challenges of negotiating expertise explicit, librarians can more effectively create learning activities that better motivate students and create a safe space for students to face the complexities of research. Librarians can also effectively model, for both students and faculty, what it is like to work within an academic field where one is a beginner. Perhaps most important, this study also affirms how important it is to listen to students and how meaningful it can be for students to take the time to reflect. Such strategies can help librarians validate students' experiences of not knowing or feeling overwhelmed while also offering expert-based strategies for encountering new fields of knowledge.

This case study has also focused on how librarians' use of qualitative methods, and ethnography-inspired student interviews, in particular, can contribute to SoTL projects. O'Brien's SoTL Compass emphasizes the value of getting to know students and how they learn as well as reflecting on one's own teaching practice.[25] Taking the time to reflect on students' research methods and using those insights to inform teaching is a key aspect of SoTL, a practice the authors have found helpful for their own instruction. The approach taken here is just one of many ways that librarians might choose to apply qualitative methods within SoTL. For example, qualitative methods have been used to study questions of how students work with peers and ask for help, as well as students' specific encounters with research databases.[26] For this study, the student interviews led to deeper reflection about students' encounters with expertise and helped the authors become better oriented to students both within and beyond the classroom. Finally, this study has inspired the authors to be more thoughtful with their teaching, to be more aware of when students are struggling or stuck, and to develop a classroom environment which validates and supports students' experience of the research process.

ENDNOTES

1.　Mitchell L. Stevens, Elizabeth A. Armstrong, and Richard Arum, "Sieve, Incubator, Temple, Hub: Empirical and Theoretical Advances in the Sociology of Higher Education," *Annual Review of Sociology* 34 (2008): 131, https://doi.org/10.1146/annurev.soc.34.040507.134737.

2.　Howard S. Becker, Blanche Geer, and Everett C. Hughes, *Making the Grade: The Academic Side of College Life* (New Brunswick: Transaction, 1995); Ernest L. Boyer, *College: The Undergraduate Experience in America* (Princeton, NJ: Carnegie Foundation for the Advancement of Teaching, 2009); Richard J. Light, *Making the Most of College: Students Speak Their Minds* (Cambridge, MA: Harvard University Press, 2001); Rebekah Nathan, *My Freshman Year: What a Professor Learned by Becoming a Student* (Ithaca: Cornell University Press, 2005).

3.　Stevens, Armstrong, and Arum, "Sieve, Incubator, Temple, Hub," 132.

4.　Elliot W. Eisner, *The Enlightened Eye: Qualitative Inquiry and the Enhancement of Educational Practice* (Upper Saddle River, NJ: Merrill, 1998); Herbert J. Rubin and Irene S. Rubin, *Qualitative Interviewing: The Art of Hearing Data* (Los Angeles: Sage, 2016); Steven J. Taylor, Robert Bogdan, and Marjorie L. DeVault, *Introduction to Qualitative Research Methods: A Guidebook and Resource* (Hoboken, NJ: Wiley, 2016).

5.　Peter Felten, "Principles of Good Practice in SoTL," *Teaching & Learning Inquiry: The ISSOTL Journal* 1, no. 1 (2013): 121–25, https://doi.org/10.20343/teachlearninqu.1.1.121.

6.　Mia O'Brien, "Navigating the SoTL Landscape: A Compass, Map and Some Tools for Getting Started," *International Journal for the Scholarship of Teaching and Learning* 2, no. 2 (July 1, 2008), https://doi.org/10.20429/ijsotl.2008.020215.

7.　Michael Perini, "Enhancing Collaboration Through the Scholarship of Teaching and Learning," *Collaborative Librarianship* 6, no. 1 (January 2014): 52–55.

8.　Pat Hutchings, ed., *Opening Lines: Approaches to the Scholarship of Teaching and Learning* (Menlo Park, CA: Carnegie Publications, the Carnegie Foundation for the Advancement of Teaching, 2000).

9.　Daniel Bernstein and Andrea Follmer Greenhoot, "Team-Designed Improvement of Writing and Critical Thinking in Large Undergraduate Courses," *Teaching & Learning Inquiry: The ISSOTL Journal* 2, no. 1 (2014): 39–61, https://doi.org/10.20343/teachlearninqu.2.1.39.

10.　Asako Yoshida, "Information Literacy and Research Development Skills: Advancing Librarian's Participation in Pedagogical Research," *Qualitative & Quantitative Methods in Libraries*, no. 4 (December 2014): 865–77.

11.　Wendy Holliday, "Frame Works: Using Metaphor in Theory and Practice in Information Literacy," *Communications in Information Literacy* 11, no. 1 (January 2017): 4–20.

12. Eleonora Dubicki, "Writing a Research Paper: Students Explain Their Process," *Reference Services Review* 43, no. 4 (2015): 673–88, https://doi.org/10.1108/RSR-07-2015-0036.

13. Michael Khoo, Lily Rozaklis, and Catherine Hall, "A Survey of the Use of Ethnographic Methods in the Study of Libraries and Library Users," *Library & Information Science Research* 34, no. 2 (April 2012): 82–91, https://doi.org/10.1016/j.lisr.2011.07.010.

14. Khoo, Rozaklis, and Hall, "A Survey of the Use of Ethnographic Methods," 84.

15. Ibid., 83.

16. Donna Lanclos and Andrew Asher, "'Ethnographish': The State of the Ethnography in Libraries," *Weave: Journal of Library User Experience* 1, no. 5 (2016), http://dx.doi.org/10.3998/weave.12535642.0001.503.

17. Lanclos and Asher, "'Ethnographish,'" 2.

18. Nancy Fried Foster and Susan Gibbons, *Studying Students: The Undergraduate Research Project at the University of Rochester* (Chicago: Association of College and Research Libraries, 2007); Sarada George and Nancy Fried Foster, "Understanding How Undergraduates Work," in *Studying Students: A Second Look*, ed. Nancy Fried Foster (Chicago: Association of College and Research Libraries, 2013), 83–102.

19. O'Brien, "Navigating the SoTL Landscape."

20. Ibid., 3.

21. Susan Behrens and Ann Jablon, "Speaker Perceptions of Communicative Effectiveness: Conversational Analysis of Student-Teacher Talk," *Journal of College Science Teaching*, no. 3 (2008): 40–44.

22. "Framework for Information Literacy for Higher Education," Association of College & Research Libraries (ACRL), February 9, 2015, http://www.ala.org/acrl/standards/ilframework.

23. Ian Beilin, "Beyond the Threshold: Conformity, Resistance, and the ACRL Information Literacy Framework for Higher Education," *In the Library with the Lead Pipe*, February 25, 2015, http://www.inthelibrarywiththeleadpipe.org/2015/beyond-the-threshold-conformity-resistance-and-the-aclr-information-literacy-framework-for-higher-education/.

24. Gayle Schaub, Hazel Anne McClure, and Patricia Bravender, *Teaching Information Literacy Threshold Concepts: Lesson Plans for Librarians* (Chicago: Association of College and Research Libraries, 2015), 1–2.

25. O'Brien, "Navigating the SoTL Landscape."

26. Susan Thomas, Eamon Tewell, and Gloria Willson, "Where Students Start and What They Do When They Get Stuck: A Qualitative Inquiry into Academic Information-Seeking and Help-Seeking Practices," *The Journal of Academic Librarianship* 43, no. 3 (May 1, 2017): 224–31, https://doi.org/10.1016/j.acalib.2017.02.016.

BIBLIOGRAPHY

Association of College & Research Libraries. *Framework for Information Literacy for Higher Education.*" Association of College & Research Libraries (ACRL), February 9, 2015. http://www.ala.org/acrl/standards/ilframework.

Becker, Howard S., Blanche Geer, and Everett C. Hughes. *Making the Grade: The Academic Side of College Life.* New Brunswick: Transaction, 1995.

Behrens, Susan, and Ann Jablon. "Speaker Perceptions of Communicative Effectiveness: Conversational Analysis of Student-Teacher Talk." *Journal of College Science Teaching*, no. 3 (2008): 40–44.

Beilin, Ian. "Beyond the Threshold: Conformity, Resistance, and the ACRL Information Literacy Framework for Higher Education." *In the Library with the Lead Pipe*, February 25, 2015.

http://www.inthelibrarywiththeleadpipe.org/2015/beyond-the-threshold-conformity-resistance-and-the-aclr-information-literacy-framework-for-higher-education/.

Bernstein, Daniel, and Andrea Follmer Greenhoot. "Team-Designed Improvement of Writing and Critical Thinking in Large Undergraduate Courses." *Teaching & Learning Inquiry: The ISSOTL Journal* 2, no. 1 (2014): 39–61. https://doi.org/10.20343/teachlearninqu.2.1.39.

Boyer, Ernest L. *College: The Undergraduate Experience in America*. Princeton, NJ: Carnegie Foundation for the Advancement of Teaching, 2009.

Dubicki, Eleonora. "Writing a Research Paper: Students Explain Their Process." *Reference Services Review* 43, no. 4 (2015): 673–88. https://doi.org/10.1108/RSR-07-2015-0036.

Eisner, Elliot W. *The Enlightened Eye: Qualitative Inquiry and the Enhancement of Educational Practice*. Upper Saddle River, NJ: Merrill, 1998.

Felten, Peter. "Principles of Good Practice in SoTL." *Teaching & Learning Inquiry: The ISSOTL Journal* 1, no. 1 (2013): 121–25. https://doi.org/10.20343/teachlearninqu.1.1.121.

Foster, Nancy Fried, and Susan Gibbons. *Studying Students: The Undergraduate Research Project at the University of Rochester*. Chicago: Association of College and Research Libraries, 2007.

George, Sarada, and Nancy Fried Foster. "Understanding How Undergraduates Work." In *Studying Students: A Second Look*, edited by Nancy Fried Foster, 83–102. Chicago: Association of College and Research Libraries, 2013.

Holliday, Wendy. "Frame Works: Using Metaphor in Theory and Practice in Information Literacy." *Communications in Information Literacy* 11, no. 1 (January 2017): 4–20.

Hutchings, Pat, ed. *Opening Lines: Approaches to the Scholarship of Teaching and Learning*. Menlo Park, CA: Carnegie Publications, the Carnegie Foundation for the Advancement of Teaching, 2000.

Khoo, Michael, Lily Rozaklis, and Catherine Hall. "A Survey of the Use of Ethnographic Methods in the Study of Libraries and Library Users." *Library & Information Science Research* 34, no. 2 (April 2012): 82–91. https://doi.org/10.1016/j.lisr.2011.07.010.

Lanclos, Donna, and Andrew Asher. "'Ethnographish': The State of the Ethnography in Libraries." *Weave: Journal of Library User Experience* 1, no. 5 (2016). http://dx.doi.org/10.3998/weave.12535642.0001.503.

Light, Richard J. *Making the Most of College: Students Speak Their Minds*. Cambridge, MA: Harvard University Press, 2001.

Nathan, Rebekah. *My Freshman Year: What a Professor Learned by Becoming a Student*. Ithaca: Cornell University Press, 2005.

O'Brien, Mia. "Navigating the SoTL Landscape: A Compass, Map and Some Tools for Getting Started." *International Journal for the Scholarship of Teaching and Learning* 2, no. 2 (July 1, 2008). https://doi.org/10.20429/ijsotl.2008.020215.

Perini, Michael. "Enhancing Collaboration Through the Scholarship of Teaching and Learning." *Collaborative Librarianship* 6, no. 1 (January 2014): 52–55.

Rubin, Herbert J., and Irene S. Rubin. *Qualitative Interviewing: The Art of Hearing Data*. Los Angeles: Sage, 2016.

Schaub, Gayle, Hazel Anne McClure, and Patricia Bravender. *Teaching Information Literacy Threshold Concepts: Lesson Plans for Librarians*. Chicago: Association of College and Research Libraries, 2015.

Stevens, Mitchell L., Elizabeth A. Armstrong, and Richard Arum. "Sieve, Incubator, Temple, Hub: Empirical and Theoretical Advances in the Sociology of Higher Education." *Annual Review of Sociology* 34 (2008): 127–51. https://doi.org/10.1146/annurev.soc.34.040507.134737.

Taylor, Steven J., Robert Bogdan, and Marjorie L DeVault. *Introduction to Qualitative Research Methods: A Guidebook and Resource.* Hoboken, NJ: Wiley, 2016.

Thomas, Susan, Eamon Tewell, and Gloria Willson. "Where Students Start and What They Do When They Get Stuck: A Qualitative Inquiry into Academic Information-Seeking and Help-Seeking Practices." *The Journal of Academic Librarianship* 43, no. 3 (May 1, 2017): 224–31. https://doi.org/10.1016/j.acalib.2017.02.016.

Yoshida, Asako. "Information Literacy and Research Development Skills: Advancing Librarian's Participation in Pedagogical Research." *Qualitative & Quantitative Methods in Libraries*, no. 4 (December 2014): 865–77.

13

Instructor-Librarian Collaboration to Improve Students' Searching, Evaluation, and Use of Scientific Literature

Sarah Bankston, Micah J. Waltz, and Heather K. Moberly

Introduction

This case study is written by a writing instructor and two librarians. Across five semesters, they developed a learning environment to foster students' information and scientific literacy in a writing-intensive course.

In the literature of the Scholarship of Teaching and Learning (SoTL), Hutchings' "four questions" are frequently mentioned, these questions being broad categories of the SoTL work that occurs.[1] This project did not begin as a SoTL project, but rather as a project to identify approaches to foster scientific literacy in the scientific writing classroom, and, therefore, this project falls in the "what works" category of questions. This collaboration required reflection and iteration as questions about student learning evolved.

Finding and evaluating information is vital to comprehending and using scientific information to inform conclusions and perspectives. These skills are fundamental and involve at least three categories of a composite definition of scientific literacy: content knowledge, understanding scientific practices, and identifying and judging appropriate scientific expertise.[2] These same skills are crucial for the development of information literacy, the interrelated skills employed to discover, evaluate, and use information.[3] A core component of scientific literacy is drawing evidence-based conclusions. The development of information-seeking skills within the science classroom represents an intersection between the scientific processes involved in scientific literacy and the information-seeking aspect of information literacy.

Semester 0: Identifying the Need for Collaboration

Texas A&M University, a Tier One land-grant institution, is the sixth-largest university in the United States. The university requires undergraduate students to take two field-specific writing-intensive courses. In the undergraduate Biomedical Sciences program, one choice is VIBS 310: Biomedical Writing, a one-credit course that meets once a week for fifty minutes and focuses on writing for various audiences in biomedical fields. The major assignment includes outlining a biomedical review article, writing the introduction, and writing one of the body sections. Students are required to find and incorporate at least twelve scientific articles for this assignment—nine primary and three secondary. They often select review article topics that are relevant to their personal lives, such as pets, health issues, or job shadowing.

When the Instructor began teaching VIBS 310, he contacted his subject librarian, Librarian1, to guest lecture because of the intensive literature-searching component. In a previous course, the Instructor felt he could adequately break apart the searching process to teach it because of a background in pedagogy of teaching, relatives who were librarians, and past searching experience. However, students were unable to demonstrate competent searching skills in their final drafts. Upon reflection, the Instructor realized he was unable to explain the *why* and *how* of the searching process well enough for students to learn.

Semester 1: The Beginning

The Instructor invited Librarian1 to guest lecture. At the request of the Instructor, the library session was a one-shot guest lecture without hands-on activity time, covering "everything about the library and how to search." Following the lecture, the Instructor and Librarian1 discussed the possibility that adequate support for the assignment required a workshop-style class with hands-on experience. After evaluating student final drafts, the Instructor realized that the students would benefit from hands-on practice because they chose weak or tangentially related articles. Similar to the previous course he taught without Librarian1, it appeared the lecture had not significantly impacted students' learning. At the end of the semester, the Instructor and Librarian1 agreed on two things: the one-shot guest lecture would be replaced with a workshop-style searching session and Librarian1 would attend each class the next semester. This embedded-librarian model would test whether student learning was improved through increased librarian presence.[4] The "what works" question evolved from trying different approaches to find a way to enhance scientific literacy. The initial exploration addressed whether having a librarian involved in the class would improve student learning. This question changed after this semester to whether more intensive exposure to the librarian and library resources would have an impact on student learning.

The Instructor and Librarian1 brainstormed about why students struggled with their major project. Students could not demonstrate proficiency in searching the literature, understanding scientific articles, and evaluating study designs and evidence. The Instructor and Librarian1 identified two overarching themes based on common student errors: identifying primary and secondary scientific literature and finding appropriate scientific literature as evidence to support a point. These themes lay at the intersection of science literacy and information literacy.

The pair hypothesized that the fundamental problem was students' inability to comprehend and evaluate scientific papers. Students could not evaluate a paper's content and identify whether it was appropriate for their purposes,[5] which is a necessary skill for making a data-driven decision. To develop this skill,[6] the Instructor decreased didactic lecture time to incorporate class discussions about assigned scientific literature.[7]

Using backward design, the Instructor identified what students should know by the end of the semester[8] regarding reading and evaluating scientific literature and then developed an informal formative assessment using small-group discussions.[9] For the next semester, the Instructor structured these discussions around specific elements in assigned readings, such as good or bad examples of methodologies. During these discussions, the Instructor listened to the group conversations. After the discussion, the Instructor had the groups report back to address questions and confirm student understanding.

Semester 2: Reflection and Evolution

Librarian2 was hired during the summer between semester 1 and semester 2 and was assigned the embedded librarian role, with Librarian1 assisting as needed. Librarian2 attended each class session and provided informal formative feedback during group discussions of selected readings. Librarian2 also led the library instruction session about literature searching and distinguishing primary versus secondary literature. The library session was moved to a computer lab so that students could actively engage with the content of the lecture, and Librarian2 provided formative feedback on the students' literature searches.[10]

Librarian2 provided formative feedback via written comments on an annotated draft of each students' reference list. Specifically, she provided feedback to the students on the correct identification of each article as primary or secondary, their ability to articulate the intended use of each article through annotations, and the accuracy of their citations in the selected style. Feedback about students' annotated drafts was provided within one week, to be used while revising their drafts.[11]

Providing this feedback was difficult because students failed to provide context for their literature searches. Students were supposed to provide annotations that summarized the content and explained how they planned to use each article in their assignment. Librarian2 found that many students only provided a summary of the article content without explaining its relevance to their draft. Therefore, it was unclear whether they had focused their literature search appropriately, making it difficult to assess *why* each article was chosen and if it was appropriate for the student's topic.

Although the formative feedback assessed whether students understood the concept of primary and secondary literature and whether they could correctly identify and select them, it was not effective for evaluating students' understanding of applying the information found to support their scientific conclusions. Upon reflection, this feedback process was both time- and labor-intensive, requiring approximately forty hours during a single week of Librarian2's time to evaluate more than 500 references and annotations.

After turning in their assignment draft, students received feedback about the writing from a course teaching assistant (TA) in addition to Librarian2's feedback about the references. The drafts received comments and suggestions as formative feedback to help the students prepare the final version. Drafts either passed or failed. A passing or failing mark was a guideline for the students for how much additional time it would take to prepare the final version for grading. Although drafts were part of the assignment scaffolding, they were not designed to be included in grade calculations.

Due to limitations of the course management system software, the Instructor was unable to assess if changes made to the type, number, and use of references could be attributed to comments by the TA or Librarian2. Therefore, it was unclear whether students had used Librarian2's feedback. Additionally, when changes were made, it was unclear to the Instructor what the students' motivation was in choosing other sources: did they choose new sources in response to feedback or to avoid addressing feedback they didn't understand? Therefore, the Instructor was unable to assess whether they had learned to distinguish between primary and secondary sources. Since the final drafts were assigned numerical grades, they could not be quantitatively compared to the pass/fail drafts. Despite the feedback that was given, the Instructor did not notice improvement in how the references were used between the draft and final versions. In the last class of the semester, the students said the library lecture was useful and they found the formative feedback helpful because they felt they were able to identify more appropriate literature for their projects.

Semester 3: Reflection and Evolution

In preparation for semester 3, Librarian2 reflected on the embedding experience and decided that attending every class was not a wise use of time. Although student feedback indicated the librarian presence was helpful, often students looked to Librarian2 for additional writing support rather than library expertise. The Instructor and Librarian2 met and revised her role, deciding on strategic visits to the class for one library instruction session and three class-wide editing workshops that explicitly targeted incorporation of literature. Again, the "what works" question shifted because of student performance: would multiple structured and intentionally designed sessions involving the librarian improve student learning?

In semester 2, weekly discussions about assigned readings highlighted that students were struggling with identifying primary and secondary literature. To address this problem in semester 3, the Instructor added basic instruction about study design to help the students appropriately identify different types of primary and secondary literature.[12] The weekly discussions were modified to reinforce[13] students' ability to identify different types of primary and secondary literature before selecting articles for their assignment.

To provide contextualized feedback to students about their literature search and hold them accountable for this feedback, the Instructor and Librarian2 met individually with each student.[14] Each meeting was ten minutes, with fifty meetings scheduled in one week. The Instructor and Librarian2 each fulfilled specific roles to accomplish everything the meetings were intended to cover. The Instructor provided feedback about the scope of the students' topic as it related to the project. Librarian2 provided feedback about reference formatting. Both the Instructor and Librarian2 gave feedback about the students' identification of each of the twelve articles as primary or secondary and about whether they had selected the appropriate number of each type for the draft.

In the meetings, the Instructor and Librarian2 addressed misconceptions about primary and secondary article identification, talked students through scoping their assignments so they were not tackling topics that were overly large for the assignment, and corrected formatting errors.[15] Often, while the students were explaining why they had identified an article as primary or secondary, they would self-identify flawed logic and change their identification.[16]

These meetings were intense and exhausting, but there was marked improvement in the students' final drafts. Student misconceptions highlighted misunderstandings about the assignment. This was the first semester that most students correctly identified and used the required number of primary and secondary literature. With this change, there was a shift in how students supported their points. They started to use secondary articles to support broader statements and primary articles to incorporate specific data into the assignment.

The instruction about how to differentiate between primary and secondary literature also created unanticipated questions which the Instructor and Librarian2 addressed at the individual meetings. Instead of using only experimental studies and narrative reviews as seen in the final drafts in previous semesters, students were bringing different types of articles to the meetings such as case reports, systematic reviews, theses, patents, and conference proceedings.

Semester 4: Reflection and Evolution

Given the variety of literature types, the Instructor and Librarian2 realized that they needed to address identifying literature beyond obvious experimental studies. For example, students were bringing in systematic reviews and struggling with how to identify them. This was a surprise because, after the initial one-shot lecture in semester 1, the Instructor and Librarian1 had intentionally decided not to discuss systematic reviews because students were not using them. The evolution of the instruction created a cycle where students were becoming more adept with finding scientific literature and, in turn, were finding more article types, which raised more questions to be addressed in instruction. In his call to develop principles for good SoTL practice, Peter Felten notes that student learning should encompass "not only disciplinary knowledge or skill development, but also the cultivation of attitudes or habits that connect to learning."[17] As the semester progressed, the students internalized the discussions on study types and thus became more critical of the articles they found. Student learning moved past foundational skill acquisition (searching for literature and identifying article types) to an internalized discipline-specific attitude or disposition (questioning methodology and understanding the role of study design).

Three major changes were made to the course. First, Librarian2 addressed common source-identification misconceptions during the library instruction session. Second, the Instructor changed the assigned readings for the class, selecting articles that illustrated a specific point, such as a particular error within the paper. Third, the Instructor developed an entire lecture to teach students how to identify types of study design. This emphasized how study design relates whether the article is primary or secondary and the level of evidence associated with that type of article.

The Instructor and Librarian2 split the single meeting with each student into two meetings to create more timely and manageable meetings. The first meeting resembled the previous semester's meeting, with the pair meeting jointly with the student to focus on identification of primary and secondary literature and reference formatting. The Instructor and student focused on style and syntax during the second meeting.

The in-class discussions and the individual meetings built upon each other and reinforced the concept of primary and secondary literature identification, and students demonstrated competency with this skill. In the in-class group discussions, students correctly identified readings as primary or secondary most of the time. In the individual meetings, students came prepared with their chosen articles already identified, and most either accurately identified their articles or self-corrected based on discussion with the Instructor and Librarian2. Additionally, students began asking more sophisticated questions about their articles. These student meetings became timely interventions for individual misconceptions.[18]

In addition to consistently identifying primary and secondary literature accurately, students were more thoughtful about letting the content of the articles they selected drive their writing rather than cherry-picking articles to support the points they wanted to make. They displayed attitudes and habits indicative of discipline-specific practice. Indeed, these behaviors align with the Research as Exploration frame from the Association of College & Research Libraries (ACRL) *Framework for Information Literacy for Higher Education*, with students "synthesiz[ing] ideas gathered from multiple sources" and exhibiting an "open-ended exploration and engagement with information."[19] Students wrote their assignments from a perspective better informed by the scientific literature because they were approaching scientific literature to become informed about a topic rather than choosing literature based on what they wanted to say, which demonstrated an increased competency in scientific literacy.[20]

Semester 5: Reflection and Evolution

The Instructor, Librarian1, and Librarian2 decided to focus on student search strategies because students were no longer struggling with identifying primary and secondary literature. This resulted in major changes in the fifth semester.

The study-design lecture introduced in semester 4 was retained, and it was reinforced during class discussions by having students identify the study design of assigned primary articles.[21] How the students were taught to search was changed by flipping the searching lecture with extensive hands-on searching and preparing the students beforehand with a tutorial. The Instructor kept his syntax-and-style meeting and continued to individually meet with students about primary and secondary article identification. An additional individual meeting with the Instructor and one librarian or the other was added that focused on students' search strategies for their topic.

To flip the class, students were assigned the online *PubMed for Veterinarians* tutorial[22] prior to the class session. During the class, Librarian1 led a short session with mini-lectures and hands-on exercises about PubMed.[23] In the remaining class time, students searched for articles on their specific project, with feedback available from the Instructor, both librarians, and the course grader. This method combined just-in-time teaching with just-in-need learning in a hybrid approach: students used what they learned in their searching and received formative feedback.[24] The Instructor, librarians, and course grader addressed student questions and misconceptions while students were actively engaging in finding information for their project.[25] One advantage of having both the Instructor and librarians in the room is that when one could not answer a question, they could refer it to or consult with their colleagues. This modeled collaboration and use of different viewpoints while searching for articles, a critical component of information literacy.[26]

Meetings with individual students began the day after the searching lecture and spanned a two-week period. These meetings provided a new formative assessment to reinforce the skills taught in class. During these thirty-minute meetings, students sat at the computer with the Instructor and one of the librarians to demonstrate their search strategies. As students discussed their topics while searching, the Instructor and librarian helped brainstorm keywords and phrases to focus and re-scope their project as needed. Students used the new terms to search and discover whether there was sufficient literature for their re-scoped topic. Discussion of the searching was organic, with the student thinking aloud while they searched.

These time-intensive meetings actively engaged students with contextualized formative feedback about their project while they were working on it, facilitating just-in-need learning. Depending on the student's topic, the librarian introduced additional library databases. Most students were unaware of result filters or used them ineffectively. The Instructor and librarians showed students how to use PubMed Filters to refine results and Search Details to evaluate their search.

The final drafts students submitted were more focused than in previous semesters; students were no longer selecting a topic without reviewing the literature. The students used at least two articles per paragraph, supporting their main points. The logical flow between the ideas within their final drafts was also more cohesive because the literature they incorporated was appropriately focused. Students also used types of literature with appropriate levels of evidence to support their points.

Conclusion

This case study models how the instruction in a biomedical writing course has changed to better serve students' needs. When the Instructor started, the course did not emphasize searching the literature and evaluating information. However, through the evolving collaboration with librarians, the Instructor recognized students' lack understanding about how to search and evaluate information. Teaching students searching is teaching a skill. Reading and analyzing papers moves them toward information evaluation. Meeting with each student to teach how to search for their specific topic is contextualized learning that is both activity- and reality-centered, stimulating deeper learning and conceptual change that engages students.

The next iteration of the "what works" question will address the sustainability of these meetings. The searching meetings helped students with the assignment and three recurring themes emerged: understanding the assignment's parameters, choosing a topic of feasible scope, and learning how to search for the appropriate topic. In the next semester, individual meetings will be shifted to small group sessions to address these three themes in a sustainable and replicable model.

Through iterative design and focusing on "what works," the instructional collaboration moved from a static lecture to a dynamic hands-on experience. The resulting instructional experience not only exemplifies an opportunity for students to "be engaged in the cultural and social practices of particular communities or professions"[27] but also shows what librarians bring to the classroom.

ENDNOTES

1. Pat Hutchings, introduction to *Opening Lines: Approaches to the Scholarship of Teaching and Learning* (San Francisco: Jossey-Bass, 2000).
2. National Academies of Science, Engineering, and Medicine, *Science Literacy: Concepts, Contexts, and Consequences* (Washington, DC: The National Academies Press, 2016).
3. Association of College and Research Libraries, *Framework for Information Literacy for Higher Education*, accessed August 23, 2017, http://www.ala.org/acrl/standards/ilframework.
4. Rowland and Knapp, "Engaged Scholarship and Embedded Librarianship," *Journal of Higher Education Outreach & Engagement* 19, no.2 (2015): 15–34. http://openjournals.libs.uga.edu/index.php/jheoe/article/view/1432/856.
5. Association of College and Research Libraries, *Framework*; National Academies of Science, Engineering, and Medicine, *Science Literacy*, 33.
6. Reinders Duit and David F. Treagus, "Conceptual Change: A Powerful Framework for Improving Science Teaching and Learning," *International Journal of Science Education* 25, no. 6 (2003): 671–88, https://doi.org/10.1080/09500690305016.
7. Jennifer K. Knight and William B. Wood, "Teaching More by Lecturing Less," *Cell Biology Education* 4, no. 4 (2005): 298–310, https://doi.org/10.1187/05-06-0082.
8. Grant Wiggins and Jay McTighe, *Understanding by Design* (Alexandria, VA: Association for Supervision and Curriculum Development, 2005), 13–21.
9. Vanessa Barker and Robin Millar, "Students' Reasoning About Basic Chemical Thermodynamics and Chemical Bonding: What Changes Occur During a Context-Based Post-16 Chemistry Course?," *International Journal of Science Education* 22 no. 11 (2000): 1171–200, https://doi.org/10.1080/09500690050166742; Jo Handelsman, Sarah Miller, and Christine Pfund, *Scientific Teaching* (New York: W.H. Freeman and Company, 2007), 27.
10. Knight and Wood, "Teaching More by Lecturing Less," 298–310; Wiggins and McTighe, *Understanding by Design*, 142, 152–56, 168–70; Handelsman, Miller, and Pfund, *Scientific Teaching*, 52.

11. Steinar Killi and Andrew Morrison, "Just-in-Time Teaching, Just-in-Need Learning: Designing Towards Optimized Pedagogical Outcomes," *University Journal of Educational Research* 3, no. 10 (2015): 742–50, https://doi.org/10.13189/ujer.2015.031013.

12. National Academies of Science, Engineering, and Medicine, *Science Literacy*, 32–33.

13. Barker and Millar, "Students' Reasoning," 1171–200.

14. Killi and Morrison, "Just-in-Time Teaching," 742–50; Donna King and Stephen M. Ritchie, "Learning Science Through Real-World Contexts," in *Second International Handbook of Science Education*, ed. Barry J. Fraser, Kenneth Tobin, and Campbell J. McRobbie (New York: Springer, 2012), 69–79.

15. Killi and Morrison, "Just-in-Time Teaching," 742–50.

16. Phyllis C. Blumenfeld, Elliot Soloway, Ronald W. Marx, Joseph S. Krajcik, Mark Guzdial, and Annemarie Palincsar, "Motivating Project-Based Learning: Sustaining the Doing, Supporting the Learning," *Educational Psychologist* 26, no. 3–4 (1991): 369–98, https://doi.org/10.1080/00461520.1991.9653139; Handelsman, Miller, and Pfund, *Scientific Teaching*, 29–30.

17. Felten, "Principles of Good Practice in SoTL," 122.

18. Killi and Morrison, "Just-in-Time Teaching," 742–50.

19. Association of College & Research Libraries, *Framework*, 7.

20. National Academies of Science, Engineering, and Medicine, *Science Literacy*, 32-33.

21. Barker and Millar, "Students' Reasoning," 1171–200.

22. Lisa Keefe, Heather K. Moberly, and Micah J. Waltz, "PubMed for Veterinarians," last modified October 2016, http://oaktrust.library.tamu.edu/handle/1969.1/158203.

23. Paul Baepler, J. D. Walker, and Michelle Driessen, "It's Not About Seat Time: Blending, Flipping, and Efficiency in Active Learning Classrooms," *Computers and Education* 78 (2014): 227–36, https://doi.org/10.1016/j.compedu.2014.06.006; Keefe, Moberly, and Waltz, "PubMed for Veterinarians."

24. Kathleen A. Marrs and Gregor Novak, "Just-in-Time Teaching in Biology: Creating an Active Learner Classroom Using the Internet," *Cell Biology Education* 3 (2004): 49–61, https://doi.org/10.1187/cbe.03-11-0022; Gregor M. Novak, Evelyn T. Patterson, A. Gavrin, and R. C. Enger, "Just-in-Time Teaching: Active Learner Pedagogy with WWW," paper presented at IASTED International Conference on Computers and Advanced Technology in Education, Cancun, Mexico, May 1998, http://webphysics.iupui.edu/JITT/ccjitt.html.

25. Wiggins and McTighe, *Understanding by Design*, 152–56; Handelsman, Miller, and Pfund, *Scientific Teaching*, 52.

26. Association of College and Research Libraries, *Framework*; Blumenfeld, Soloway, Marx, Krajcik, Guzdial, and Palincsar, "Motivating Project-Based Learning," 369–98.

27. O'Brien, "Navigating the SoTL Landscape," 13.

BIBLIOGRAPHY

Association of College and Research Libraries. *Framework for Information Literacy for Higher Education."* Accessed August 23, 2017. 2015. http://www.ala.org/acrl/standards/ilframework.

Baepler, Paul, J. D. Walker, and Michelle Driessen. "It's Not About Seat Time: Blending, Flipping, and Efficiency in Active Learning Classrooms." *Computers and Education* 78 (2014): 227–36. https://doi.org/10.1016/j.compedu.2014.06.006.

Barker, Vanessa, and Robin Millar. "Students' Reasoning About Basic Chemical Thermodynamics and Chemical Bonding: What Changes Occur During a Context-Based Post-16 Chemistry Course?" *International Journal of Science Education* 22, no. 11 (2000): 1171–200. https://doi.org/10.1080/09500690050166742.

Blumenfeld, Phyllis C., Elliot Soloway, Ronald W. Marx, Joseph S. Krajcik, Mark Guzdial, and Annemarie Palincsar. "Motivating Project-Based Learning: Sustaining the Doing, Supporting the Learning." *Educational Psychologist* 26, no. 3-4 (1991): 369–98. https://doi.org/10.1080/00461520.1991.9653139.

Duit, Reinders, and David F. Treagust. "Conceptual Change: A Powerful Framework for Improving Science Teaching and Learning." *International Journal of Science Education* 25, no. 6 (2003): 671–88. https://doi.org/10.1080/09500690305016.

Felten, Peter. "Principles of Good Practice in SoTL." *Teaching & Learning Inquiry* 1, no. 1 (2013): 121–25. https://doi.org/10.20343/teachlearninqu.1.1.121.

Handelsman, Jo, Sarah Miller, and Christine Pfund. *Scientific Teaching.* New York: W.H. Freeman and Company, 2007.

Hutchings, Pat. Introduction to *Opening Lines: Approaches to the Scholarship of Teaching and Learning.* San Francisco: Jossey-Bass, 2000.

Keefe, Lisa, Heather K. Moberly, and Micah J. Waltz. "PubMed for Veterinarians." Pubmed for Veterinarian tutorial documents collection. Last modified October 2016. http://oaktrust.library.tamu.edu/handle/1969.1/158203.

Killi, Steinar, and Andrew Morrison. "Just-in-Time Teaching, Just-in-Need Learning: Designing Towards Optimized Pedagogical Outcomes." *University Journal of Educational Research* 3, no. 10 (2015): 742–50. https://doi.org/10.13189/ujer.2015.031013.

King, Donna, and Stephen M. Ritchie. "Learning Science Through Real-World Contexts." In *Second International Handbook of Science Education,* edited by Barry J. Fraser, Kenneth Tobin, and Campbell J. McRobbie, 69–79. New York: Springer, 2012. ProQuest Ebook Central.

Knight, Jennifer K., and William B. Wood. "Teaching More by Lecturing Less." *Cell Biology Education* 4, no. 4 (2005): 298–310. https://doi.org/10.1187/05-06-0082.

Marrs, Kathleen A., and Gregor Novak. "Just-in-Time Teaching in Biology: Creating an Active Learner Classroom Using the Internet." *Cell Biology Education* 3 (2004): 49–61. https://doi.org/10.1187/cbe.03-11-0022.

National Academies of Science, Engineering, and Medicine. *Science Literacy: Concepts, Contexts, and Consequences.* Washington, DC: The National Academies Press, 2016. https://doi.org/10.17226/23595.

Novak, Gregor M., Evelyn T. Patterson, A. Gavrin, and R. C. Enger. "Just-in-Time Teaching: Active Learner Pedagogy with WWW." Paper presented at IASTED International Conference on Computers and Advanced Technology in Education, Cancun, Mexico, May 1998. http://webphysics.iupui.edu/JITT/ccjitt.html.

O'Brien, Mia. "Navigating the SoTL Landscape: A Compass, Map and Some Tools for Getting Started." *International Journal for the Scholarship of Teaching and Learning* 2, no. 2 (2008): 1–20. https://doi.org/10.20429/ijsotl.2008.020215.

Rowland, Nicholas J., and Jeffrey A. Knapp. "Engaged Scholarship and Embedded Librarianship." *Journal of Higher Education Outreach & Engagement* 19, no.2 (2015): 15–33. http://openjournals.libs.uga.edu/index.php/jheoe/article/view/1432/856.

Wiggins, Grant, and Jay McTighe. *Understanding by Design.* Expanded 2nd ed. Alexandria, VA: Association for Supervision and Curriculum Development, 2005. eBook Collection (EBSCOhost).

14

Assessment of a One-Credit Course for Humanities Graduate Students:

A Phenomenological Approach to Identify Thresholds and Impacts

Denis Lacroix and Lindsay Johnston

In the fall of 2016, three librarians from the Humanities and Social Sciences Library at the University of Alberta (UofA) took on the challenge of teaching a one-credit scholarly communication course to new graduate students in the department of Modern Languages and Cultural Studies (MLCS). Three librarians delivered the five two-hour MLCS795 weekly classes from late October through November. The University of Alberta is a large Canadian University with five campuses and an enrollment of more than 38,000 students. The Faculty of Arts has more than 5,000 undergraduates and 800 graduate students. The University of Alberta Libraries is mandated to be a teaching library.

The Scholarship of Teaching and Learning (SoTL) movement provides the context and impetus for analyzing the effectiveness of the course through the lens of student learning and evaluation. Student feedback obtained in early spring 2017 through a survey and interviews has provided an understanding of student opinion of scholarly communication and how the course met their expectations. Findings have provided the authors with plans for improving the course for fall 2017.

Literature Review

Few articles in the literature focus on graduate student information literacy credit courses. Many articles focus on understanding how students find information but very few investigate

student perceptions or pedagogical approaches. Bruce's study,[1] with methodology and results closely resembling those for MLCS795, shows that students' perceptions of their information literacy course were favorable. Students who participated in interviews identified ways in which the coursework assisted the research process, including improved searching skills, better understanding of research intentions, and improved awareness of resources.

A more recent article by Madden[2] found that a humanities PhD information literacy course had clear benefits. The students ranked research resource discovery and evaluating information as the two most important topics covered during the module. All of the students in Madden's study indicated that the first year of the PhD is an appropriate time to take the module, as did the students in the MLCS795 study.

The literature did not provide a lot of guidance for the research team on how to structure the MLCS795 course. Cohen's 2016 survey[3] of librarians who taught credit courses at all levels of study revealed no consensus on the content or format of courses. Fisher's article[4] focuses on using the Association of College and Research Libraries (ACRL) *Framework for Information Literacy for Higher Education* to guide a credit-bearing course. She outlines eight weeks' worth of course content, which fosters the kinds of scholarly communication discussions that MLCS795 elicits.

Background

For many years at the start of fall term, the MLCS department partnered with UofA Libraries to offer a ninety-minute one-shot seminar for new MLCS graduate students. It took years of advocacy and prototyping with MLCS faculty to convince them that graduate students deserved more than a one-shot session. The main catalyst for change stemmed from the re-envisioning process that the MLCS department began in 2012. This resulted in a completely different approach: a portfolio model where students are encouraged to innovate and go beyond "the traditional thesis/dissertation as the only format for major capping project in graduate schools."[5] This model involves students taking three portfolio modules, two of which are mandatory: grant writing and information literacy.[6]

In March 2015, a Future of the PhD Conference, held at the University of Alberta, recommended some new directions for the humanities PhD, including digital humanities; the recommendations stated that "archival digitization, data compression for storage, and the importance of search indices"[7] in every discipline, should become part of a humanities PhD because "this digital revolution is as important as libraries."[8] Digital tools are "the library and printing press of our age."[9] In a similar vein, a recent Social Sciences and Humanities Research Council funded *White Paper on the Future of the PhD in the Humanities* says students should be given the opportunity to develop their "dialogical capacities"[10] and "discursive practices"[11] in the world of academia with a special emphasis on scholarly communication.

When MLCS795 was first conceived, its main focus was to be information literacy; however, the instructors felt that graduate students would benefit from learning information literacy concepts and skills within the wider context of scholarly communication. The Scholarship of Teaching and Learning asks, "What will my students need to grapple with?"[12] The MLCS795 course description responds that the course will "provide students with a practical understanding of the nature of professional conversations in their field and how to participate."[13] Information literacy is only one tool that contributes to the main objective of preparing students to engage ethically and effectively in the scholarly discourse of their chosen discipline. The majority of MLCS795 classes were devoted to scholarly communication objectives (see Appendix 14A). Only one class section focused on traditional library tools and search strategies. Information-seeking and finding were reinforced throughout the class sessions, but insofar as they helped achieve the greater goal of acculturating students to scholarly communication.

Scholarship of Teaching and Learning (SoTL) Methodology

Following the completion of the MLCS795 Information Literacy & Scholarly Communication Module, the course instructors implemented a SoTL study of the course's effectiveness with a phenomenological approach in order to answer O'Brien's Scholarship of Teaching and Learning question, "How do I know if my teaching and my students' learning have been effective?"[14] In other words, what impact does this scholarly communication course have on the research of incoming humanities graduate students? The study consisted of four participants, one MA and three PhDs (there were only four new MLCS graduate students in 2016). The students had a combination of Canadian and international degrees. They came with a range of previous information literacy training—from a mandatory course as an MA requirement to none at all. All were registered in comparative literature; however, the departmental focus is very interdisciplinary. All four students responded to an initial short survey, which was approved by the institution's research ethics board (see Appendix 14C). The three students who participated in interviews, chose the pseudonyms Fern, Robin, and Pat (see Appendix 14B).

Findings

The research project involved obtaining student perceptions regarding course expectations, content and outcomes, and readings and assignments. The key student perception findings are summarized below.

STUDENT COURSE EXPECTATIONS

The interviews began by asking students what they expected from the course (see Appendix 14B). While they had low expectations, they all ended up finding the course much more helpful than anticipated. Robin said she thought, "Ok, here we go with another MLA writing style course…. I really didn't expect anything from you guys." However, by the end, she could see how it fit into her development as a researcher: "So, I think this is a major course … how to find sources, how to become a researcher—very important. And I think this is a principle in the mentality of MLCS—they are trying to raise independent researchers, intellectual minds."

STUDENT PERCEPTIONS OF COURSE CONTENT AND OUTCOMES

The first survey question asked students to what extent the course met the U of A Faculty of Arts Vision and Mission statements.[15] All students agreed or strongly agreed that the course met three of the statements:

1.   Opens unexpected doors of opportunity
2.   Instills students with adaptable, critical skills sought after by top employers
3.   Prepares students to undertake ground-breaking research

Three survey participants also agreed that the course prepared them "to undertake creative activity," which was the fifth vision statement.

During the interviews, Fern linked these concepts to the ability to search more broadly and dig up a comprehensive set of resources on interdisciplinary topics. Similarly, Pat explained that the course helped her to hone her research skills and focus on asking the right questions, so she is better prepared to undertake her research. Robin referred to a digital humanities project presented in class and talked about how she found it inspiring as it led her to consider novel forms of creation and dissemination of research results from multiple disciplines.

The survey asked: "In terms of your studies and research, please rate each of the concepts included in the course from least important to most important" (see Appendix 14C, question 2). The four concepts that were rated with the highest importance by the participants were:

- discovering information using information seeking tools;
- citation;
- scholarly communication in the humanities; and
- evaluate information.

All ten course concepts were ranked as "most important" by at least one participant. None were ranked "not very" or "least important." The final six concepts that were ranked as most important or important by two or three respondents were:

- research data management;
- source types: scholarly/popular, primary/secondary;
- research methodologies/critical approaches;
- copyright;
- open access; and
- research metrics.

Open-ended responses to the following question shed a bit more light on the students' choices. The survey asked: "Please explain why the course concept(s) ranked as most important had the greatest impact in your scholarly activities." As one student explained, [the instruction] "gave me research skills after a long absence from Academia and a complete restructuring of research." The complete restructuring of research might refer not only to the comprehensive information databases now available to students but also to the contextualizing of this information in terms of scholarly communication, which becomes intricately intertwined for the student. Another student expressed how difficult it was to pinpoint a single course concept and referred to a number of concepts as being most impactful: "The materials on information seeking tools, citation and research metrics helped me to expand my bibliography and re-formulate some of my research questions; they were also helpful for evaluation of the sources. The training session on copyright helped me plan the preparatory stages of my project."

STUDENT PERCEPTIONS ON READINGS AND ASSIGNMENTS

During the interviews, student participants were asked about the readings from the UNESCO series "Open Access Curricula for Researchers and Library Schools."[16] As humanities researchers, students found the documents too technical. They consulted the readings for relevant sections as reference resources when working on assignments, but they found them too long to read in full. One student explained that a quick reference sheet on metrics to provide definitions and summarize uses would have been more useful.

The overall perception of the students on class assignments was favorable, but there was some disagreement. The students liked the creativity involved in the initial active learning exercise that required them to create a visual representation of their research, then explain their research focus to the class. Pat valued the first citation assignment; it introduced her to MLA style and to bibliographic citation after years away from academia. The other two students said they already knew how to cite, so it wasn't useful. However, they all made mistakes in their citations! In the next iteration of this course, the instructors plan to collect students' SSHRC application bibliographies and approach citation on an individual level with each student.

For the second class, the students had to identify an article and then analyze it using the usual criteria—purpose, audience, bias, etc.—plus the type of research method used. Fern didn't see the point to this assignment because the students' research questions and critical-thinking skills were already well-formed, though she did appreciate the focus on methods. Robin valued the assignment; she said it was the first time she had been introduced to these concepts and that learning to "ask the right questions" helped a lot in learning to evaluate what she reads.

Students struggled with the metrics assignment because metrics were new to them. Most of them saw the value in metrics but did not like the repetitive nature of finding different types of metrics for ten articles for their assignment. Publication metrics require more thought than what was required in class. In the next iteration, the instructors will try to design an assignment that asks students to choose a journal to publish in and explain how and why they have made that choice.

For the final assignment, students had to create a citation map and a 100-word data management summary. Pat said that the final assignment "brought out all the connections between the authors and the sources. And it was very illustrative in the way that it demonstrated how complex those connections were." She said that the final assignment highlighted that "the most important sources used for that picture were the least important for her actual project. Because they connected all the dots, but still they lacked that perspective that I need for doing my research." Robin initially felt that the mapping concept did not suit her way of thinking, but in the end, she said that it helped her to put parameters around her research, focus on her research question, and not be diverted by all of the peripherally related great ideas she comes across.

Threshold Concepts

Student comments in class and during the interviews revealed that there are concepts that proved troublesome, yet transformative, which researchers indicate as characteristics of threshold concepts.[17] Many of the troublesome concepts, if not all, became transformative once the students grasped them and understood their significance in their research. In general, scholarly communication (SC) was enlightening for students but difficult to grasp because of the innovative, creative, flexible, and sometimes nebulous concepts that make up SC. The concept map assignment, publication metrics, and research data management were SC concepts that were particularly noteworthy. These SC concepts were new to the students. They found them troublesome initially, but the more they engaged with them, the more they saw their importance in their scholarly work.

Citation styles had a love/hate effect on students. Some were glad and thankful they were covered in class and others found them too basic for a graduate-level course. However, students did say that MLCS795 enabled them to use citation style knowledge in working as research assistants and consulting with faculty.

The concept map assignment was also troublesome because it forced students to consider scholarly communication in a creative and perhaps unconventional way. It also appealed to some learning styles more than others. However, even those who are not visually inclined learners recognized the value of the astounding maps created by their classmates (see Appendix 14D). The map allowed one student to realize that the authors she considered most authoritative in her field had a very general approach, while the authors she actually needed to communicate with were lesser known and had more focused approaches.

Publication metrics are troublesome in their own right because of their multiplicity and the various tools used to produce them. Students are looking for easy solutions and quick evaluation methods and one-page cheat sheets. Unfortunately, evaluating a publication or a researcher is not usually straightforward. Students told us that they have used metrics since the course ended to select a journal to publish in and to track their own influence as authors. One student, who was looking through Researchgate or Academia.edu, noticed that a co-author had uploaded a paper without her knowledge and without permission. Another student explained that she had always dismissed numbers in the past, but the ability to apply metrics now gives her a bigger picture view of the discipline and individual researchers' place in it. Learning about metrics also made her realize that researchers can become too introverted, but metrics help researchers "look at their work from other people's eyes."

Research data management (RDM) is particularly troublesome for humanities scholars. As emerging academics, MLCS795 graduate students struggled to understand how "data" applied to them. Most understood at least theoretically how RDM may have some implications on their research, but practically it will take time for the theory to sink in. In class, students were given examples from real life U of A RDM humanities projects (e.g., Dr. Natalie Kononenko's Sanctuary Project[18]), which seemed overwhelming to students at first. When they took time to consider their work and research outputs from a RDM perspective, they recognized that even managing citations—so fundamental to the work of humanities researchers—requires time and planning.

The copyright guest lecture led one student to change her thesis proposal in light of copyright issues. Another student was a published fiction writer, who had quite a different take from the instructors' on access to information, copyright, and publishing. As academic librarians, the course instructors assumed that open access was a public good, which may be true for scholarly works but is not necessarily a shared value when considering works of fiction or art.

Conclusion

Based on the evidence from the student surveys, the students were very satisfied with the course. They appreciated the broader scholarly communication focus of MLCS795 and receiving a librarian's perspective on what academia is all about. By the time students were interviewed, they had accepted that librarians would force them out of their comfort zones. Creating the citation map, for example, scared them, but in the end, they mostly found it to be very useful for their research.

Humanities graduate students, however, had limits. A flipped classroom approach is a pedagogical approach that is at odds with the culture of the humanities discipline. Active learning is challenging with humanities graduate students; they are used to working independently, reflecting, investigating, and carrying out assignments and research on their own. They resisted the instructors' attempts to carry out in-class assignments and preferred to take them home and finish them. When asked in the interviews, none of the students responded favorably to the idea of a flipped classroom. They already felt overwhelmed by readings for their other courses and by the pressure of meeting grant application deadlines. They said things like they prefer to watch short videos in context in class and that they don't have time for more readings.

Students valued the course and its broader focus on scholarly communication. The instructors will revise it to improve concept retention and to include a stronger focus on digital humanities as well as the importance of communicating research to the wider community.[19] MLCS graduate students, because of their academic background and learning styles, challenged our understanding of effective pedagogies in regards to active learning and flipped classroom approaches. The effectiveness of the course became apparent in the benefits students identified, which include a better understanding of research intentions, new knowledge of metrics and their applications, and an improved awareness of resources that enhance students' ability to face the challenge of interdisciplinarity.

Appendix 14A: MLCS795 Course Guide and Description

MLCS 795 Information Literacy & Scholarly Communication

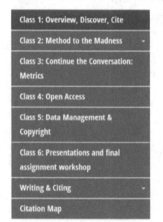

Class 1: Overview, Discover, Cite

Class 2: Method to the Madness

Class 3: Continue the Conversation: Metrics

Class 4: Open Access

Class 5: Data Management & Copyright

Class 6: Presentations and final assignment workshop

Writing & Citing

Citation Map

Syllabus

- Course Syllabus 2017

Readings, Handouts and Presentations

- Presentation Slides
- Class 1 - Summary

Preparing for MLCS 795

To prepare for the first class, please complete the following:

1. Information Literacy Tutorials:

- Where Do You Find Information (Tutorial)
- Putting a Search Together (Tutorial)
- Where to Start Searching (Tutorial)

2. Reading: UNESCO Scholarly Communications 1 - essential background for class content

3. Please provide Denis and Lindsay with a copy of the bibliography from your grant application. Email: Denis.Lacroix@ualberta.ca, Lindsay.Johnston@ualberta.ca (we have homework too!)

Assignments

- "What is your research?" Activity...

- Keywording Excercise (Due on October 31st 2017)
  1. complete Keywording exercise for your own research topic
  2. go to your worksheet where you identified 5 databases relevant to your topic & select 2 relevant databases that you have not used before to search
  3. use your completed Keywording sheet to search to search the new databases and export citations into RefWorks (minimum 5 citations from each database)
  4. in RefWorks, create a folder for your research topic, then add your citations there. Bring your completed Keywording sheet with the titles of the two databases and the list of references entered into RefWorks to class on October 31st 2017.

Appendix 14B: MLCS795 Study Interview Script

1. What were you expecting when you started the class?
   - Were there specific things that you thought you would learn?
2. What are your biggest challenges as a researcher? Can you comment on whether the course has helped in any way with those challenges?
   - Follow-up questions regarding specific topics covered during the course
3. Considering your most recent 3 months of course and research work, are there any parts of the course that stand out to you as particularly important? Please give some examples.

Please tell us what happened in a recent situation when you needed to
   - find information
   - evaluate information
   - create a citation
   - identify a source type
   - identify or select a research method
   - use metrics
   - publish or disseminate your research (scholarly communication)
   - manage your data
   - deal with a copyright issue
   - other

4. Please tell us what happened in a recent situation in your work as a researcher which was troublesome to you. Please explain how you tried to solve it.
5. Do you think you would have benefitted from a flipped classroom approach that would involve more readings and videos at home and more time for assignments and hands-on practice during class? We structured the course with 5 2-hour class sessions. We cut out a possible 6th class in recognition of the amount of work we required for the final assignment. Did this work for you or would you have benefitted from more class hours? [Possible follow-ups: Should there have been more guidance, hands-on time during class for assignments?]
6. Reflecting on the final assignment involving mapping out at least 10 bibliographic citations according to your research's concepts and outlining the scholarly conversations taking place among the cited scholars, how has this changed your outlook on your research? What impact has the assignment had on your literature review or your understanding of the area? If you could change the assignment, what would you modify to make it more relevant or useful?
7. What does digital humanities mean to you?
   - Follow-up questions: Did the course help you with your understanding? Should it have greater focus on digital humanities?

Appendix 14C: MLCS795 Survey Questions

Please find the survey questions here: https://goo.gl/Lqaiva

MLCS 795 Course Survey

Consent

Thank you for your interest in this study. By responding to this survey you are giving your consent to participate in this portion of the research study, *Engaging with Grad Students, Expanding our Role, Exploring Outcomes*, and affirming that you agree to the following:
• I have received and read the information letter on the study that was provided in the email invitation.
• I understand that I may withdraw from the study at any time prior to submitting my answers to the current survey, after which it will no longer be possible to identify my answers nor withdraw them.
• My participation in the study is voluntary and anonymous.
• My answers to the survey will be securely stored on password-protected servers at the University of Alberta for a minimum of 5 years.
• Only the two researchers mentioned in the information letter will have access to my answers.
• I understand that study results may be presented at conferences, published in professional journals, and/or presented in class lectures.
• I understand that there are no foreseeable risks to participating in this study nor are there any direct benefits.

1. To what extent do you agree or disagree that the course met the following elements of the Faculty of Arts Vision and Mission:

	Strongly Disagree	Disagree	Neutral	Agree	Strongly Agree
opens unexpected doors of opportunity	☐	☐	☐	☐	☐
instills students with adaptable, critical skills are sought after by top employers	☐	☐	☐	☐	☐
develops a passion for lifelong learning which forms a foundation for a lifetime of career success	☐	☐	☐	☐	☐
prepares students to undertake groundbreaking research	☐	☐	☐	☐	☐
prepares students to undertake creative activity	☐	☐	☐	☐	☐
instills the foundational skills that lead to change in a complex world	☐	☐	☐	☐	☐

2. In terms of your studies and research, please rank each of the concepts included in the course from lowest importance (1) to greatest importance (10)

☐	Discovering information using information seeking tools
☐	Source types: scholarly/popular, primary/secondary sources, BEAM
☐	Citation
☐	Research methodoligies/critical approaches
☐	Research Metrics
☐	Open Access
☐	Scholarly Communication in the Humanities
☐	Copyright
☐	Research data management
☐	Evaluate information

3. Please explain why the unit you ranked highest (10) in question 2 above has had the greatest impact on your scholarly activities.

4. Please explain why the unit you ranked lowest (1) in question 2 above has had the lowest impact on your scholarly activities.

5. Is there any content that was missing that you would have liked the course to cover? Please explain.

Appendix 14D: Sample Student Citation Concept Map

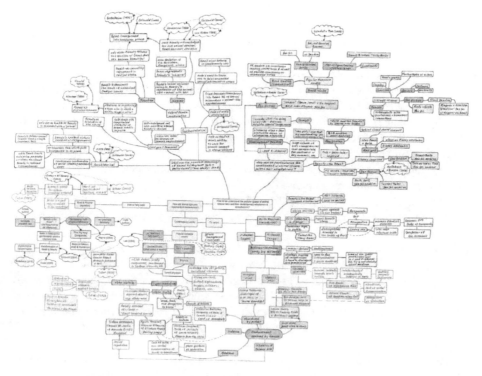

Gulcev, Liljana. Citation Concept Map for MLCS795, 2016. Reproduced with permission.

ENDNOTES

1. Christine S. Bruce, "Postgraduate Response to an Information Retrieval Credit Course," *Australian Academic and Research Libraries* 22, no. 2 (June 1991): 103–10, http://dx.doi.org/10. 1080/00048623.1991.10754723.

2. Ronan Madden, "Information Behaviour of Humanities PhDs on an Information Literacy Course," *Reference Services Review* 42, no. 1 (2014): 90–107, https://doi.org/10.1108/RSR-07- 2013-0034.

3. Nadine Cohen et al., "A Survey of Information Literacy Credit Courses in US Academic Libraries," *RSR: Reference Services Review* 44, no. 4 (2016): 564–82, https://doi.org/10.1108/ RSR-03-2016-0021.

4. Zoe Fisher, "Facing the Frames: Using the Framework as a Guide for a Credit-Bearing Information Literacy Course," *College & Research Libraries News* 8, no. 7 (July/August 2017): 354–58, https://doi.org/10.5860/crln.78.7.354.

5. Andriy Nahachewsky, *Backgrounder to the Graduate Transformation Proposal* (April 12, 2013).

6. For a full description, see: https://www.ualberta.ca/modern-languages-and-cultural-studies/ graduate-program-information/the-portfolio.

7. Anne Krook, "Trial is by What is Contrary: New Directions for the Humanities PhD," paper presented at *Future of the PhD Conference*, University of Alberta, Edmonton, Alberta, Canada

(March 20, 2015): 1, https://www.ualberta.ca/arts/-/media/arts/programs/graduate/documents/krook-documents/trial-is-by-what-is-contrary-delivery.pdf, 1.

8. Krook, "Trial is by What is Contrary," 13–14.

9. Ibid., 15.

10. Institute for the Public Life of Arts and Ideas, "White Paper on the Future of the PhD in the Humanities" (McGill University, December 2013): 4, http://iplai.ca/wp-content/uploads/2015/04/white_paper_on_the_future_of_the_phd_in_the_humanities_dec_2013_1.pdf.

11. Institute for the Public Life of Arts and Ideas, "White Paper," 4.

12. Mia O'Brien, "Navigating the SoTL Landscape: A Compass, Map and Some Tools for Getting Started," *International Journal for the Scholarship of Teaching and Learning* 2, no. 2 (2008): 2, https://doi.org/10.20429/ijsotl.2008.020215.

13. "Information Literacy and Scholarly Communication," *Modern Languages and Cultural Studies*, University of Alberta, Edmonton, Canada, https://www.ualberta.ca/modern-languages-and-cultural-studies/graduate-program-information/the-portfolio/modules/information-literacy-and-scholarly-communication.

14. O'Brien, "Navigating the SoTL Landscape," 4.

15. "About," Faculty of Arts, University of Alberta, accessed June 18, 2019, https://www.ualberta.ca/arts/about/.

16. "Open Access for Researchers," *Open Access Curricula for Researchers and Library Schools*, UNESCO, accessed February 26, 2018, http://www.unesco.org/new/en/communication-and-information/resources/publications-and-communication-materials/publications/publications-by-series/oa-curricula-for-researchers-and-library-schools/.

17. Lori Townsend et al., "Identifying Threshold Concepts for Information Literacy: A Delphi Study," *Communications in Information Literacy* 10, no. 1 (2016): 24, http://files.eric.ed.gov/fulltext/EJ1103398.pdf.

18. Angelique Rodrigues, "Sanctuary Project Preserving Ukrainian Religion in the Prairies, One Church at a Time," *WOA: Work of Arts* (April 17, 2015), http://www.woablog.com/2015/04/sanctuary-project-preserving-ukrainian-religion-in-the-prairies-one-church-at-a-time/.

19. See MLCS795 2018 course guide, https://guides.library.ualberta.ca/mlcs795_2018.

Bibliography

Banski, Erika, and Denis Lacroix. "'… in from the cold': Multicultural Researchers, Global Scholarship and the Library." Poster presented at the 74th IFLA World Library and Information Congress, Québec, Canada, August 2008. https://doi.org/10.7939/R3DJ58M49.

Bruce, Christine S. "Postgraduate Response to an Information Retrieval Credit Course." *Australian Academic and Research Libraries* 22, no. 2 (June 1991): 103–10. http://dx.doi.org/10.1080/00048623.1991.10754723.

Cohen, Nadine, Liz Holdsworth, John M. Prechtel, Jill Newby, Yvonne Mery, Jeanne Pfander, and Laurie Eagleson. "A Survey of Information Literacy Credit Courses in US Academic Libraries." *RSR: Reference Services Review* 44, no. 4 (2016): 564–82. https://doi.org/10.1108/RSR-03-2016-0021.

Fisher, Zoe. "Facing the Frames: Using the Framework as a Guide for a Credit-Bearing Information Literacy Course." *College & Research Libraries News* 8, no. 7 (July/August 2017): 354–58. https://doi.org/10.5860/crln.78.7.354.

Institute for the Public Life of Arts and Ideas. "White Paper on the Future of the PhD in the Humanities." McGill University. December 2013. http://iplai.ca/wp-content/uploads/2015/04/white_paper_on_the_future_of_the_phd_in_the_humanities_dec_2013_1.pdf.

Krook, Anne. "Trial is by What is Contrary: New Directions for the Humanities PhD." Paper presented at *Future of the PhD Conference*, University of Alberta, Edmonton, Alberta, Canada, March 20, 2015. https://www.ualberta.ca/arts/-/media/arts/programs/graduate/documents/krook-documents/trial-is-by-what-is-contrary-delivery.pdf.

Madden, Ronan. "Information Behaviour of Humanities PhDs on an Information Literacy Course." *Reference Services Review* 42, no. 1 (2014): 90–107. https://doi.org/10.1108/RSR-07-2013-0034.

Modern Languages and Cultural Studies. *Information Literacy and Scholarly Communication*. University of Alberta. Edmonton, Canada. https://guides.library.ualberta.ca/mlcs795_2018.

Nahachewsky, Andriy. *Backgrounder to the Graduate Transformation Proposal*. April 12, 2013.

O'Brien, Mia. "Navigating the SoTL Landscape: A Compass, Map and Some Tools for Getting Started." *International Journal for the Scholarship of Teaching and Learning* 2, no. 2 (2008). https://doi.org/10.20429/ijsotl.2008.020215.

Rodrigues, Angelique. "Sanctuary Project Preserving Ukrainian Religion in the Prairies, One Church at a Time." *WOA: Work of Arts*. April 17, 2015. http://www.woablog.com/2015/04/sanctuary-project-preserving-ukrainian-religion-in-the-prairies-one-church-at-a-time/.

Townsend, Lori, Amy R. Hofer, Silvia Lin Hanick, and Korey Brunetti. "Identifying Threshold Concepts for Information Literacy: A Delphi Study." *Communications in Information Literacy* 10, no. 1 (2016): 23–49. http://files.eric.ed.gov/fulltext/EJ1103398.pdf.

UNESCO. "Open Access for Researchers." *Open Access Curricula for Researchers and Library Schools*. Accessed February 26, 2018. http://www.unesco.org/new/en/communication-and-information/resources/publications-and-communication-materials/publications/publications-by-series/oa-curricula-for-researchers-and-library-schools/.

University of Alberta. "About." Faculty of Arts. Accessed June 18, 2019. https://www.ualberta.ca/arts/about/.

———. "Information Literacy and Scholarly Communication." *Modern Languages and Cultural Studies*. Accessed May 26, 2017. https://www.ualberta.ca/modern-languages-and-cultural-studies/graduate-program-information/the-portfolio/modules/information-literacy-and-scholarly-communication.

Uncovering the Comfort Levels of Students Who Are Conducting Library Research

Donna Harp Ziegenfuss

Introduction

Much research has been conducted on how students, especially first-year students, do library research.[1] The literature contends that college students regularly rely on Google and other common web-based resources that they are familiar with, rather than use proprietary library scholarly databases. In addition, students can feel overwhelmed or think because they can use web browsers, they will excel at library research.[2] When teaching information literacy in a variety of different instructional contexts such as one-shots or embedded in courses, librarians experience many examples of these teaching and learning challenges. However, by gathering data from these students about library research, librarians will get a better sense about student perceptions and anxiety about library research. But what is really underlying this level of discomfort? What are student expectations about library research? This case study presents findings gleaned and lessons learned from asking students about their perceptions and comfort levels related to conducting library research. Data were collected in thirty-one lower-level classes at a large public institution in the US Mountain West with an undergraduate enrollment of just less than 25,000 undergraduate students. Evidence collected was then used to re-evaluate and improve library information literacy instruction for the author in future semesters. In addition, data collected about what students think about doing research can also be used by librarians to redesign instructional sessions. In librarianship, there is a growing emphasis on taking an evidence-based practice (EBP) approach and reflect on research findings to generate new questions and inform changes in teaching practice.[3]

Literature Review

Project information literacy has been studying freshman students and how they use library resources since 2008 and have reported that 80 percent of students claim they do not often ask librarians for help.[4] Instead, students prefer to use open search engines such as Google and Wikipedia because they are familiar to them and they use them for personal research tasks.[5] The literature also contends that students think they have a high confidence level when it comes to doing academic research because they think if they know how to use Google and the Internet then they will know how to do academic research. Therefore, it becomes important for librarians to gather data about student learning experiences and library research perceptions of the students in front of them. Collecting data in a systematic way, as compared to an anecdotal approach, provides concrete evidence that can be integrated into decision-making processes. This rigorous practice of evidence-based decision-making can then be used to improve practice and rationalize change. Planning, teaching, and assessing one-shots, which has been the traditional approach to teaching research skills, does not often yield opportunities for librarians to engage and establish relationships with students.[6] Embedded librarianship, a growing instructional trend, where librarians partner with faculty and become embedded in a class on a more frequent basis, provides more opportunity for student-librarian interaction.[7] However, the reality is that there are many different library instruction formats occurring each semester at any given university or college that can depend on staffing, teaching and learning cultures, and relationships with faculty partners. Emerging strategies from the literature focus more on experiential sessions, more authentic assessment strategies, and more thoughtful design of library sessions using instructional design methods. Gathering student data about student perspectives on the research experience and library instruction can identify places where students get stuck and can also improve learning outcomes.[8] Collecting student feedback can also help to improve future library instruction planning, identify needs students still have after instruction, as well as make recommendations for improving instruction.

Methods

This SoTL project involved a classroom case study approach[9] driven by questions about student library research comfort levels. Anonymous survey data was collected in thirty-one lower-level class sections and provided student perspectives and insights about the academic research process. The population of students participating in this study was primarily freshmen and sophomores taking writing-intensive courses with a research component. The same librarian taught all classes, which included one-shots, embedded librarian sessions, accelerated sessions, as well as developmental courses. Library session pre- and post-surveys, which contained eight quantitative Likert-scale questions and several open-ended questions, were first pilot-tested in three sections of the same course, then administered in twenty-eight different sections. Pre-surveys were administered before the library sessions, and all post-surveys were collected during the last week of the semester.

Results

A total of 1,217 surveys were collected across three semesters. Mean Likert-scores for each pre-and post-Likert-question were calculated with SPSS. The lowest student comfort levels across all the different course section types were lack of comfort in (1) using the library catalog and (2) finding books in the library stacks. The two highest means showed students very comfortable using (1) Google and other web search engines, and (2) knowing what a citation is and using citations in writing. Although additional statistical analysis was done on the pre- and post-survey data, findings from the qualitative data yielded much more interesting results for uncovering student concerns and potential for improving library instruction. Seven hundred and ninety-six unique comments were coded, categorized, and analyzed. In the pre-survey, students were asked: (1) What are your expectations for the library session and doing research? and (2) What do you want to learn about library research? In the post-survey, students were asked: (1) What questions do you still have about doing library research? and (2) What was the most valuable thing you learned in this library research session? The comments were then coded using constant comparative qualitative methods[10] of coding and categorizing the comments line by line. Coding of the comments resulted in five categories: (1) learning about library research resources, (2) valuing library resources, (3) becoming a more effective/efficient researcher, (4) other library resources, tools, and support, and (5) expressing anxiety and needs.

Discussion and Conclusions

Although much research has been published on how students go about *doing* research and *using* library resources, this project focused on uncovering the perspectives and needs of student researchers learning to do academic research. The findings provided valuable evidence that led this librarian researcher to explore alternative teaching practices and redesign curriculum. Although the case study research findings are not new or earth-shattering related to habits of novice information literacy students, findings were invaluable for rethinking library research instruction to meet the students where they are in the library research process, for uncovering perceptions of novice researchers, and providing a framework for redesigning library instruction sessions and materials.

Uncovering Student Perceptions, Needs, and Concerns about Library Research

The biggest takeaway from this project for this author was the need to communicate explicitly more often with students about their library research needs and anxieties by taking time during instruction to be open to student comments and their concerns, and then acting on their comments to improve instruction. The coding and categories that emerged from the open-ended comments shed light on student library research anxiety and concerns. From experience, this librarian researcher knows that students rely heavily on open-web search engines to do research; in this study, the web-based tool comfort level score was the highest score in all sessions. It was also the score that changed the least from the pre- to post-survey. Student anxiety about doing library research became clear when they were asked to use tools they were not comfortable with. A comment that expresses this student library anxiety is: "How to use the college library … it's big and it scares me." Students also expressed concerns about not knowing where to start using library research tools and concerns about how using library-related tools required a different process and developing new skills. The pre-survey comments contained 63 percent of the anxiety codes. Therefore, formative classroom assessment techniques, or CATs,[11] are now incorporated into this researcher's library instruction sessions—even one-shot sessions. Students provide concepts they still do not understand (muddiest points) at the end of instruction so the instructor can provide additional resources or tutorials for those topics identified by students. In addition, presenting students with an opportunity during library instruction to reflect on their expectations and concerns about library research resulted in them asking new questions based on what they were learning about, which resulted in more engagement in the research process.

There were also pre-post differences in the language or vocabulary that students used to refer to research. In the pre-survey, students spoke in general terms about using the library, but in the post-survey, student comments reflect more honed responses citing specific library resources, like scholarly databases, books, and articles. In the post-survey, students had more questions about access and usage of specific library tools and resources and services that they did not know about before the session. Reflecting on the pre- to post-survey vocabulary differences resulted in changes to this author's teaching practice, such as being more explicit about using academic research vocabulary. As new vocabulary is defined and described, examples are provided to help them build new knowledge based on their prior web-based searching knowledge. Knowing how valuable the web-based tools are to this groups of students, Google hacks and tips were also included in the instruction sessions to help them see how the tools they commonly use could be used even more efficiently. Instead of discrediting web-tools, instruction now includes recommendations for why and when to use types of tools. In addition to better articulation and communication with students, future plans for research related to this finding also includes better integration of the ACRL frames into this student-centered approach to presenting library instructional materials.

Rethinking of the Presentation of Library Instructional Materials

In addition to including more explicit vocabulary and reflection so students can relate prior experiences to the academic research process, findings from this study also resulted in changes to how this instructor presents library instructional to the novice library researchers. Seventy-three percent of the student pre-survey expectation comments were related to students saying they wanted to become more efficient/effective researchers. In these pre-comments students also talked about how they wanted to be better at research but did not know how to do that. Reflection on this finding resulted in the author rethinking how instruction materials could be organized and presented to show them how to be more effective researchers. This resulted in less of a focus on clicking through a series of library tools, databases, and journals. This author redesigned the presentation of library instruction, "The Five Top Strategies for Being an Effective Researcher," and shifted the focus from *how* to use the library resources to *why* to use library resources. Instead of presenting a list of tools and databases, the library sessions are now designed around a framework for doing research in a more effective way. The five strategies being used are: (1) go abroad to start (use Google and Google Scholar), (2) dig down deeper (disciplinary databases), (3) mine good sources (for keywords and references), (4) develop a research toolbox (to stay organized with tools like citation management software and cloud storage tools), and (5) ask for help and use available support. For example, this instructor now uses Google Scholar to show students how to begin research by going broad and demonstrate the international scholarly conversation around their topic. Using this framework for one-shot presentations has appeared to help students follow a process for research. After working with this "Strategies for Effective Researcher" framework for planning library instruction for novice lower-level researchers, it became evident that this framework could be adapted for multiple library sessions and enhanced for graduate student library sessions.

Using this strategies framework also makes it is easier for this librarian to talk in non-library lingo to faculty partners and customize instructional sessions. Some faculty want a deeper dive into one or more of the strategies and it has become easier to design new instruction grounded in a process rather than a list of research tools to demonstrate. For example, using strategy #1, to begin by going broad, students do a broad scan around their topic using Google Scholar or more general databases and then use concept mapping to map out subtopics so they can create keywords to dive in deeper to their topic (strategy #2).

The survey results also included significant student comments about the students' perceptions for a need to practice to become good researchers. So, the process for instructional sessions for this instructor has evolved into briefly presenting one of the strategies and then turning it over to students to practice that strategy, even if for just brief a time in a one-shot session. In a fifty-minute one-shot, there is time for ten minutes on each effective research strategy.

Redesign of Library Instructional Materials: Beyond the Classroom Experience

Another valuable finding that came out of this research that has impacted this author's teaching practice was the realization that students needed continued support beyond the classroom experience. The open-ended comments from the end of semester post-survey demonstrated that now that students had learned about how to find and use databases, journals, books, and other library services, they had new and/or more complex questions about other library services and support. The largest category of coded comments in the post-survey questions was related to the category Other Library Resources, Tools, and Support. Students' questions reflected more advanced questions about resources and services the author had discussed in the session and questions about library services and resources I had not even talked about, which indicated that they had explored the library and what the library had to offer them post-instruction. Examples of comments coded in this category are: "What do I do when ILL is unable to get me a book?" and "How do I rent out one of the study rooms in the library for future use?" They did not know what questions to ask in the one-shot session, but they did have questions by the end of the semester post-survey.

To meet the needs of continued support for student post-instruction, an online support website was designed and implemented. Due to retirements and decreasing first-year student librarian teaching support, it was not feasible for a single librarian to provide continued support to all these classes. Therefore, the option of designing an online library resource in the university's learning management system, Canvas, to meet the needs of the many different types of library sessions appeared to be the only viable option. The website contains a library FAQ section to help students who said they did not know where to get started; it contains all the getting-started resources organized by questions like, How do I get started? Where can I find…? and How do I…? The design and organization of the FAQ section of the online resource resulted from the student comments about their anxiety with using the library and feeling that they did not know where to start in the research process. The top five strategies for effective research framework used in the face-to-face instruction are also posted here with additional links and resources so students can pick up where they left off in class. The online research materials in this section, are organized into the similar five strategies framework to help students feel comfortable about the content and see familiar strategies and resources so they can continue to learn about conducting library research on their own. To address the research findings of library anxiety and finding physical books in the library that emerged from the research as one of the most common student concerns, this open web resource also contains a step-by-step process about how to find a book in the library. In addition, a single flipped instruction class lesson with tutorials is included for other library instructors that can be used to help students find a book in the catalog and then bring the call number to class where they go out into the stacks as a group (to alleviate anxiety) to find books instead of meeting in a computer lab. This online resource also provides support in a variety of formats (text and video) to meet different student needs, such as self-directed modules and downloadable handouts. Each section of the online resource was developed to address the research themes, concerns expressed by students, or to answer questions students still expressed at the end of the semester.

In conclusion, data and evidence from this study were shared with faculty partners to help garner support for continued and expanded academic research instruction. Several faculty concerned about the low mean scores for students related to not being able to find physical books in the library have resulted in faculty scheduling additional flipped library sessions to go out into the book stacks. The resulting collaborative problem-solving and decision-making process between the librarian and faculty members has also set a new expectation for partnership processes going forward. For this librarian researcher, conducting this classroom research and sharing data and findings with faculty partners have resulted in strengthening faculty-librarian relationships and identified new areas for collaboration. New doors have also been opened for this librarian in the areas of online library instruction development and faculty-librarian conference presentations. This enhanced collaboration model around identifying problems and conducting research has resulted in a deeper and more meaningful focus on learner-centered teaching and student academic success that will hopefully result in the continued scholarship of teaching and learning classroom projects.

ENDNOTES

1. Lynn Sillipigni Connaway, Timothy J. Dickey, and Marie L. Radford, "'If It Is Too Inconvenient, I'm Not Going After It:' Convenience as a Critical Factor in Information-Seeking Behaviors," *Library & Information Science Research* 33, no. 3 (2011): 179–90.
2. Amy Gustavson and H. Clark Nall, "Freshman Overconfidence and Library Research Skills: A Troubling Relationship?," *College & Undergraduate Libraries* 18, no. 4 (2011): 291–306.
3. Denise Koufogiannakis, "Academic Librarians' Conception and Use of Evidence Sources in Practice," *Evidence-Based Library and Information Practice* 7, no. 4 (2012): 5–24.
4. Alison J. Head and Michael B. Eisenberg, "Lessons Learned: How College Students Seek Information in the Digital Age," *Project Information Literacy Progress Report 2* (December 1, 2009) (Seattle: University of Washington's Information School, 2009), accessed August 25, 2017, https://www.projectinfolit.org/uploads/2/7/5/4/27541717/pil_fall2009_finalv_yr1_12_2009v2.pdf.
5. Alison J. Head and Michael B. Eisenberg, "How College Students Use the Web to Conduct Everyday Life Research," *First Monday* 16, no. 4 (2011), accessed August 25, 2017.
6. Jen Salvo-Eaton, Susan Sanders, Gloria Tibbs, and Fu Zhuo, "Research Rescue: Beyond the One-Shot Instruction Session," *Brick & Click Libraries Symposium Proceedings* (November 1, 2013): 14–19.
7. Amy Van Epps and Megan Sapp Nelson, "One-Shot or Embedded? Assessing Different Delivery Timing for Information Resources Relevant to Assignments," *Evidence-Based Library and Information Practice* 8, no. 1 (2013): 4–18.
8. Kacy Lundstrom, Britt Anna Fagerheim, and Elizabeth Benson, "Librarians and Instructors Developing Student Learning Outcomes: Using Frameworks to Lead the Process," *Reference Services Review* 42, no. 3 (2014): 484–98; Joan Middendorf and David Pace, "Decoding the Disciplines: A Model for Helping Students Learn Disciplinary Ways of Thinking," *New Directions for Teaching and Learning* 2004, no. 98 (2004): 1–12.
9. James McKernan, *Curriculum Action Research: A Handbook of Methods and Resources for the Reflective Practitioner* (Oxfordshire, UK: Routledge, 2013).
10. A. Strauss and J. Corbin, *Basics of Qualitative Research Techniques* (Thousand Oaks, CA: Sage Publications, 1998).
11. Thomas A. Angelo and K. Patricia Cross, "Classroom Assessment Techniques," *A Handbook for Faculty* (Washington, DC: Office of Educational Research and Improvement, 1988).

BIBLIOGRAPHY

Angelo, Thomas A., and K. Patricia Cross. "Classroom Assessment Techniques." *A Handbook for Faculty*. Washington, DC: Office of Educational Research and Improvement, 1988.

Connaway, Lynn Sillipigni, Timothy J. Dickey, and Marie L. Radford. "'If It Is Too Inconvenient, I'm Not Going After It:' Convenience as a Critical Factor in Information-Seeking Behaviors." *Library & Information Science Research* 33, no. 3 (2011): 179–90.

Gustavson, Amy, and H. Clark Nall. "Freshman Overconfidence and Library Research Skills: A Troubling Relationship?" *College & Undergraduate Libraries* 18, no. 4 (2011): 291–306.

Head, Alison J., and Michael B. Eisenberg. "How College Students Use the Web to Conduct Everyday Life Research." *First Monday* 16, no. 4 (2011). Accessed August 25, 2017.

———. "Lessons Learned: How College Students Seek Information in the Digital Age." *Project Information Literacy Progress Report 2* (December 1, 2009). Seattle: University of Washington's Information School, 2009. Accessed August 25, 2017. https://www.projectinfolit.org/uploads/2/7/5/4/27541717/pil_fall2009_finalv_yr1_12_2009v2.pdf.

Jiao, Qun G., Anthony J. Onwuegbuzie, and Art A. Lichtenstein. "Library Anxiety: Characteristics of 'At-Risk' College Students." *Library & Information Science Research* 18, no. 2 (1996): 151–63.

Koufogiannakis, Denise. "Academic Librarians' Conception and Use of Evidence Sources in Practice." *Evidence-Based Library and Information Practice* 7, no. 4 (2012): 5–24.

Lundstrom, Kacy, Britt Anna Fagerheim, and Elizabeth Benson. "Librarians and Instructors Developing Student Learning Outcomes: Using Frameworks to Lead the Process." *Reference Services Review* 42, no. 3 (2014): 484–98.

McKernan, James. *Curriculum Action Research: A Handbook of Methods and Resources for the Reflective Practitioner*. Oxfordshire, UK: Routledge, 2013.

Middendorf, Joan, and David Pace. "Decoding the Disciplines: A Model for Helping Students Learn Disciplinary Ways of Thinking." *New Directions for Teaching and Learning* 2004, no. 98 (2004): 1–12.

Salvo-Eaton, Jen, Susan Sanders, Gloria Tibbs, and Fu Zhuo. "Research Rescue: Beyond the One-Shot Instruction Session." *Brick & Click Libraries Symposium Proceedings*. November 1, 2013: 14–19.

Soria, Krista M., Jan Fransen, and Shane Nackerud. "Library Use and Undergraduate Student Outcomes: New Evidence for Students' Retention and Academic Success." *portal: Libraries and the Academy* 13, no. 2 (2013): 147–64.

Strauss, Anslem, and Julia Corbin. *Basics of Qualitative Research Techniques*. Thousand Oaks, CA: Sage Publications, 1998.

Van Epps, Amy, and Megan Sapp Nelson. "One-Shot or Embedded? Assessing Different Delivery Timing for Information Resources Relevant to Assignments." *Evidence-Based Library and Information Practice* 8, no. 1 (2013): 4–18.

16

Using O'Brien's "Compass":

A Case Study in Faculty-Librarian Partnerships and Student Perceptions of Research and Writing in Anthropology and Sociology

Catherine Bowers and Shelly Yankovskyy

Introduction

For some librarians, the Scholarship of Teaching and Learning (SoTL) may seem beyond reach—without consistent or long-term access to data about what students know, learn, fear, forget, and need reinforcement on, many of the principles of SoTL can be abstractions. This case study describes one approach to the Scholarship of Teaching and Learning in the context of library instruction for upper-level anthropology and sociology classes at a regional comprehensive university in the southern United States with nearly 10,000 full-time students and an undergraduate full-time enrollment of about 8,000. The primary intention of this project is to build a sustainable and meaningful vein of library instruction across several courses within an anthropology and sociology program, specifically in an environment where library instruction has bypassed many students. O'Brien's Compass was utilized as a frame for understanding our ongoing work as well as the results of surveys and observations.[1] This case study reflects on the importance of balancing interdisciplinary thinking with discipline-specific resources.

Background and Theory

Research on faculty-librarian collaboration tends to focus on one course, such as introduction to composition or as a general call to action. Cassidy and Hendrickson describe a more

focused and customized contribution at the course level,[2] while others like Arrington and Cohen[3] and Kobzina[4] describe other aspects of collaboration and instruction. Lindstrom and Shonrock[5] suggest librarian-faculty collaboration is nowhere near the standard practice, as it ought to be. This case study highlights the value of diversifying library instruction and research support for students across four different courses in anthropology and sociology. The students enrolled in these classes were largely majors, except for one sociology course, which was required for healthcare administration majors. In the course of this partnership, a strong SoTL relationship was built on an ongoing commitment to macro- and micro-level collaboration.

This collaborative work has led to opportunities to both deepen majors' knowledge of their own discipline and communicate the transformative importance of discipline-specific practices, which aligns with some explanations of micro-level collaborations often found in the literature. Rader encourages librarians to build partnerships with faculty that might challenge typical academic models "in new and creative ways."[6] Rader's definition of information fluency presents the idea of information-seeking as holistic or even as a worldview, which parallels the idea of research as a process of enculturation.[7] This idea of enculturation is found in the broader research practice of learning to think within a discipline but is also an essential concept in anthropology. The partnership discussed in this case study focuses on strengthening disciplinary mindsets for new students and building on existing research practices for more experienced majors.

O'Brien offers an introductory overview and provides guidelines for SoTL projects.[8] Especially helpful is the analogy of a compass, four essential points of reference to guide pedagogical design, and apply the same "rigorous process of research," such as "design, inquiry, collection of evidence, analysis, documentation, contribution to knowledge, and critical review,"[9] to reflect on teaching and students' learning.

Data Collection and Method

During the course of this research, medical sociology (MedSoc) was taught twice and medical anthropology (MedAnth) once. In each of these classes, library instruction was scheduled around the fourth week of the semester. The librarian came to the classroom and gave a course-specific demonstration. These sessions started with library basics and quickly focused on disciplinary sources. Students were encouraged to schedule a research consultation for further help with the librarian if needed. Throughout the semester, the professor reminded the students of the library instruction; students often followed up with research consultations, which was already a popular service in the library. The professor further reinforced the importance of library research throughout the semester. In order to gauge student learning and teaching effectiveness, electronic surveys were conducted at the end of each semester in MedAnth and MedSoc. In these surveys, students were asked about their research and writing practices and were polled on information fluency; these surveys worked both as landmarks of students' perceptions and experiences and served as catalysts for future faculty-librarian partnerships. Core questions noted students' majors and intentions to attend graduate school and asked them to self-report on previous research experience. The MedAnth survey included discipline-specific questions to study students' experiences with methods such as ethnographic research.

The survey questions were edited between semesters, and awkwardly-worded or miscommunicated questions were revised for clarity and to minimize repetition. Grounded theory framed the coding of open-ended questions by themes, such as resource use, disciplinary mindset, writing or research insights, and future goals. The surveys were designed with the intention of documenting students in their actual experiences and own words, but it was the use of O'Brien's Compass that helped clarify the often-scattered piles of data collected in Qualtrics.

O'Brien's Compass as a Frame

For this collaboration, O'Brien's Compass[10] was essential for sense-making and continued exploration of SoTL. The Compass's "points of reference … [are] a set of interrelated questions that offer direction for the conceptualization, implementation, and evaluation of SoTL projects and activities."[11] O'Brien suggests using the Compass as a "touchstone and template for your own SoTL projects,"[12] which is exactly the approach adopted in this case study, point by point. This case study is situated within the context of the questions posed as the four points of the Compass due to their accessibility for both librarians and classroom faculty; the questions and answers are equally meaningful in guiding research as well as understanding evidence and evaluation.

WHAT WILL MY STUDENTS LEARN AND WHY IS IT SIGNIFICANT?

O'Brien states that the answer to the first of the four questions is culturally constructed within the discipline, specifically "within the ways of thinking and practice of the discipline, profession, or community of research and practice the students are being inducted into."[13] Additionally, to answer "what my students will learn," one has to consider threshold concepts as well as troublesome knowledge. Threshold concepts are "grounded within concepts that are *central* [sic] to that discipline's way of constructing knowledge and viewing the world,"[14] while troublesome knowledge conceptualizes the often difficult, turbulent, or uncertain paths through learning that present conflict with a known world of existing beliefs.[15] In order to address this first point of the Compass, it is necessary to explicitly lay out the culturally constructed practices of the disciplines involved.

WHAT WILL STUDENTS LEARN IN LIBRARY INSTRUCTION?

Students need to learn how to search effectively for topics, how to incorporate sources into writing, and how to engage with complex ideas. These are standard library instruction objectives, and when applied to MedSoc and MedAnth, they also activate concepts of disciplinary research. O'Brien exhorts educators to think broadly and suggests that students should learn more than content, invoking "ways of thinking and practice, threshold concepts, and troublesome knowledge."[16] Significant threshold concepts in sociology and anthropology are cross-cultural analysis, cultural relativism, cultural and social constructionism, inequalities, and establishing the authority of lived experience as information. In some cases, this includes brokering between relativism and activism.

For the librarian, active awareness of the assignments shaped the library instruction for each class. For the students in MedSoc, the idea that authority is constructed and contextualized and its related dispositions in the Association of College & Research Libraries (ACRL) *Framework for Information Literacy for Higher Education*, was intensely troublesome, as the students were outside their home discipline and mindsets. Students needed to know how to think about bridging disciplinary practices between majors, the idea of continual and progressive growth of expectations as they advance through their majors, and how to research complex ideas while building effective searches. Additionally, they should be able to find their way through the structures and streams of information. As some students remarked, it was difficult to navigate "between hardcore facts" and the headspaces of worldview and culture. Specifics for each class will be discussed in the next section. Some students, especially those enrolled in MedSoc who took a class for an outside major, needed to build a bridge between research mindsets, but others wanted to know how to build on what they might have learned in other anthropology or sociology classes.

WHAT ARE STUDENTS LEARNING IN MEDANTH AND MEDSOC?

For both courses, the major course learning outcomes and information literacy goals are similar. MedAnth stresses the idea that cultural belief systems play a role in perceptions of health, disease etiology and treatment, patient/healer interactions, and explanatory models. MedSoc reaches outside the biological paradigm of health and demonstrates that there is more to health than the cellular level. Both classes were assigned a research project, which meant library outcomes were drawn to meet a range of basic and advanced concepts. In the MedSoc course project, students were asked to use their sociological imaginations to understand how prejudice, discrimination, structural violence, and other inequalities play a role in outcomes.

Illness narratives are valuable social and cultural reflections on medical care, even though some medical researchers might debate their worth; this conflict works as an example of a threshold concept. By including it in the MedSoc class, the professor emphasized the disciplinary importance of an individual's worldview and lived experience; this presented a troublesome concept to students accustomed to dealing with numbers where disease is often conceptualized as a clearly defined event with a known etiology and treatment. Illness narratives were utilized in both classes to accomplish these tasks, and in

MedAnth, students wrote their own. Students in MedSoc read an assigned monograph of an illness narrative and then chose episodes from podcasts such as The *New York Times'* Patient Voices,[17] WNYC's *Only Human*,[18] and the official Médecins Sans Frontières/Doctors Without Borders/(MSF) podcast.[19] Using podcasts was an adaptation the professor made after learning that students did not have the skills to conduct interviews. Although they are distinct disciplines, anthropology and sociology share a disciplinary history, which means the "ways of thinking and practice of the discipline"[20] can constructively overlap in the classroom and library instruction, an idea underlined by the Anthropology and Sociology Section (ANSS) of ACRL in their information literacy standards.[21]

WHO ARE MY STUDENTS, AND HOW DO STUDENTS LEARN EFFECTIVELY?

The most important identifier in MedSoc and MedAnth students is their differences in major. For example, out of twenty-nine respondents in the fall 2016 MedSoc class, more than half (55 percent) of the respondents to the end of semester surveys were in their fourth year of college and the majority (86 percent) were in healthcare administration. Most students had previously written a research paper—34 percent just once and 45 percent more than once—though 20 percent had never written a research paper. A significant number of students (41 percent) self-identified as having very limited experience with library research. As a result, library instruction needed to respond to the range of student experience and create a quick, clear path between basics and disciplinary sources. Survey research allowed the authors to recognize the range of experience and not take core knowledge for granted.

In MedAnth, all but one student was in their third or fourth year, and that sole student claimed an "it's complicated" status. Less than a third of the students were anthropology majors, although unlike MedSoc, many students were majors in more closely related fields, which created less of a "tourist" mindset because transference of knowledge was more direct. In MedAnth, 57 percent of the class had written more than one research paper and no students reported never having written a research paper. Only 14 percent of MedAnth students self-described themselves as having limited research experience or skills.

O'Brien lists three foundational theories of learning: constructivism, social constructivism, and sociocultural theory.[22] To help students learn more effectively, teaching in this case study focused on constructivist principles, described as "primarily concerned with the individual learner and his/her processes of learning. Constructivist theory asserts that students learn by constructing and reconstructing their understandings about the world and phenomena, via a process of actively attempting to make sense of one's experiences."[23] In other words, "students are not simply constructing knowledge, or sharing meaning, they are learning to become competent members of a particular community."[24] Library instruction helps bridge the gap and communicates practices and expectations between majors and non-majors. Both MedSoc and MedAnth courses reinforce practices and standards in the classroom on a regular basis.

The MedSoc students had a choice between a research paper and writing an illness narrative. The research paper asked the students to apply approaches and ideas learned in the class to studies of current health problems. The majority of the healthcare administration students in the class chose to write a research paper, and this required students to research and engage with sociological sources. All of the MedAnth students wrote a research paper for their final project, which relied on library use and occasionally consultations with reference librarians. These consultations helped students reinforce searching skills and allowed them more time to talk through their topic ideas. Although the authors did not specifically track the efficacy of consultations, students reported increased success in locating relevant sources and more focused research topics. In contrast, the MedSoc students, who were less accustomed to social science research, did not reach out for consultations. This was reflected in the quality of their work, which showed less robust analysis and discussion. While the majority had written a research paper in the past, 41 percent of the students claimed very limited research experience and 20 percent had never written a paper at all. This finding might imply that continued reluctance to engage with the library created a closed loop where students continued to be unfamiliar with or unaware of research practices.

What Can I Do to Support Students to Learn Effectively?

O'Brien's third point of the Compass lays out three areas of pedagogical thinking: "teaching as design," "signature pedagogies," and "authentic assessment of learning."[25] This case study focuses on the pedagogical tactic of "signature pedagogies." Both MedAnth and MedSoc courses used a medical narrative assignment as part of the practice of learning insider and outsider, also known as emic/etic, perspectives on illness, health, and healing. For MedAnth specifically, the concept of "explanatory models"[26] as well as the illness narrative model were utilized to explore the subjective nature of illness; readers may be familiar with this model through Anne Fadiman's *The Spirit Catches You and You Fall Down* (1997).[27] End-of-semester surveys allowed students to elaborate on their experiences with these pedagogical tactics. One student wrote, "In the future it will allow me to reach people not only through numbers, but how those numbers are still humans. Those humans have ideas, and the only way to treat that situation is to understand those ideas." Another student commented, "Writing for business is putting down hardcore facts. However, with sociology, because of great diversity, there's [sic] more aspects to think about." These kinds of comments highlight the value of narrative as a signature pedagogy. Likewise, they can bridge the research experience from one discipline to another, an important skill to remember, especially in the context of a major that requires understanding the social dimensions of health and healing.

THE ROLE OF LIBRARY INSTRUCTION

In this collaboration, the librarian conducted all the library instruction sessions for MedAnth, MedSoc, and the professor's other upper-level classes. These sessions were conducted in the classroom with a projector and were introduced as special guest-lecturer sessions. Each session was planned together between the librarian and the professor to introduce library basics to anyone who might have missed them, as well as disciplinary resources, and specific sources for assignments. The library instruction followed the information literacy standards from the ANSS and emphasized the idea of ethics, key professional organizations, government documents and websites, and discipline-specific sources.[28] These were presented as resources for research and tools to learn to think within the discipline. Below is a table that describes the focus areas for the library instruction sessions for MedAnth and MedSoc:

Table 16.1. Comparison of library instruction content for MedSoc and MedAnth

Medical Sociology LI	Medical Anthropology LI
Library website, chat, research consult	Library website, chat, research consult
Research guides	Research guides, professional associations
Website evaluation	Website evaluation
CDC, Census data	eHRAF
Citing with ASA	Citing with Chicago
Searching databases, considerations about ethics and marginalized voices, and power imbalance	Searching research and multimedia databases, research ethics in anthropology, the role of voice and shifting ideas in the field.
Bridging the gap between disciplines (sociology and healthcare administration)	Using anthropology's "four fields" premise to search

Approximately one-third of each session was devoted to questioning what students already knew. This was conducted in a conversational manner, and students were able to connect library skills with specific assignments that some or all had completed in other classes. In these groups, they were able to share their library experiences with each other, rather than only hearing from the librarian or professor. The skills discussed among the students were woven into active discussions about how to search, develop a topic, find statistics strategically, and engage with the scholarly conversation.

How Do I Know If My Teaching and My Students' Learning Have Been Effective?

O'Brien lists three potential sources of evidence to answer questions of learning effectiveness: "ourselves, our peers, our students."[29] The majority of the data gathered here, such as students' descriptions of past experiences with research and writing, topic development, and discipline-specific values like confidentiality and ethical interviewing, focuses on assessing students' work and growth, although anecdotal observations were included. These informal observations were collected mostly from the professor, who was able to measure how much students learned by the questions asked after the library session; these questions reflected engagement with research and enthusiastic interest in bridging the researching and writing process. Much of the data used to determine learning and teaching effectiveness came directly from open-ended surveys administered at the end of each semester. The survey questions were worded in a way so as to benefit both classroom teaching and library instruction, and many questions included a text space for students to add a description (see Appendix 16A).

Using the concept of enculturation, research can be understood as a holistic practice that incorporates discipline-specific ways of thinking. Kain extends the idea of the sociological imagination to incorporate discipline-specific research into sociology classes, although the library's role is less visible in this scenario.[30] Attached to this is the idea that library skills used in research, such as database searching and source evaluation, are learned like culture: through both direct and passive channels. Library instruction is a direct channel, but students also learn to research through peer learning, practice, and failure. The survey for this case study asked students if they had to unlearn or adjust previously existing skills; this process of learning by trial and error is analogous to the practice of learning to think in the ways asked of them in medical sociology and medical anthropology.

Selected comments from student responses to open-ended survey questions highlight the range of experiences that gave the authors insight into the effectiveness of their teaching and if students recognized their own learning:

- MedAnth
  - Had to incorporate more of a worldly view
  - More learning about people rather than just disease
  - Shift in focus from the demographic view of health to culture-focused understanding
- MedSoc
  - Got to write about something I was passionate about and could use later in life
  - Writing from the sociological perspective was very hard
  - I think it pertained more toward sociology than healthcare administration major
  - Used to using non-peer reviewed sources
  - To not write in a business aspect
  - More help with the process [from professor and librarian]
  - Deeper look into the practices and morals of different cultures
  - Writing for business is putting down hardcore facts. With sociology, because of great diversity, there are more aspects to think about
  - Business people are horrible at writing, and that proves to be true
  - It was rather interesting seeing that there is a whole different side to some illnesses

After using content analysis to code for emergent themes, an inductive, grounded-theory approach to the open-ended questions revealed that students had to learn to use different formats, in this case, ASA and Chicago styles, as well as writing from new perspectives. They also noted an increased use of library resources and peer-reviewed articles. In turn, students felt this greatly expanded their understanding of their chosen topics.

Recommendations and Future Directions

Through working together over the course of several semesters, a few recommendations emerged for others undertaking similar work. When one plans for a partnership, they should plan for the big picture and not limit the scope of collaboration to one assignment or even just one class. Investments in programs are opportunities to continue to build upon prior classes and can strengthen the outcome for the student and the faculty. Using O'Brien's Compass helped the authors organize and streamline their teaching goals. The collaboration produced opportunities to diversify library instruction. It helped the authors reflect on students' learning, which in turn shaped teaching practice. The four points of the Compass provided both the librarian and the professor structure to review the ongoing questions of whether students are learning by providing a macro frame and structure for assessing the micro levels of learning and teaching. It could be imagined as zooming in and back out and then in again, to evolve and adapt to the needs of the specific students in a classroom at any moment.

Over the course of the five semesters that framed the larger scope of this research, the librarian and professor worked repeatedly with several of the same students in MedSoc and MedAnth as well as other classes not mentioned here. This provided a rare opportunity to gather anecdotal data and glean insights about the long-term roles of library instruction and research, leading to the primary purpose of this case study. Librarians can change the way they design library instruction if they know they will be able to build upon those same students' experiences. Additionally, repeated exposure will help to ensure continued practice in information fluency and a more solid outcome for disciplinary research skills.

Conclusion

Focusing on O'Brien's Compass model and navigation principles created clarity that has been invaluable to this research for all parties. First, many of O'Brien's top values, such as authenticity and inductive approaches, were already in general practice, so it was an easy fit to apply the framework of the Compass to this research. Second, valuing authenticity has been very liberating because it encouraged using disciplinary standards on terms that made sense in the classroom and in the library without feeling forced. When applied to research and data, this value made scaffolding across courses for library instruction more organic, and grounded theory became a more dynamic practice. Authentic assessment became more holistic when it extended from the confines of student achievement to a reflective practice for librarians and faculty. Finally, the librarian-faculty partnership framed the overarching SoTL value of discussing teaching and learning with interdepartmental peers. The original aim for sustainability and meaning became real as the students' learning moved to the foreground as an essential point of reference and research and classroom experiences could be shaped with more direction.

Appendix 16A: Research Questions

Core survey questions distributed in Medical Sociology and Medical Anthropology courses.

*Denotes a question with an open-ended response option.

**Denotes a strictly open-ended question.

1. What is your student classification?
   a. First year
   b. Second year
   c. Third year
   d. Fourth year
   e. It's complicated

2. What is your major?
   a. Anthropology
   b. Sociology
   c. Business/health care administration
   d. Other

3. Before taking [Medical Sociology/Medical Anthropology], had you written a research paper for any other college classes?*
   a. Yes, once. (If yes, which class?)
   b. Yes, more than once. Please list the classes.
   c. No, never.
   d. Other, please describe.

4. Please comment further on your research and writing experiences. For example, did you struggle with any part of the process, or multiple parts? Were there any funny (or scary!) stories from your research process? Please elaborate as desired.**

5. If you have previous research and writing experience, what, if anything, was different about researching or writing for [Medical Sociology/Medical Anthropology]?**

6. The authors of this survey are interested in assessing writing skills of students enrolled in sociology and anthropology classes. What writing skills have you learned or used in this class? Please select all that apply. [multi-answer option]
   a. How to write a research proposal
   b. How to write a bibliography or works cited list
   c. How to write an annotated bibliography
   d. How to choose an appropriate topic
   e. How to modify a topic
   f. How to incorporate data and information into a paper
   g. How to incorporate interviews into the final write-up
   h. How to incorporate field notes into the final write-up
   i. How to incorporate observations into the final write-up.
   j. Is there anything else you would like to add?

7. During the course of your research, did you struggle with confidentiality issues or ethical dilemmas?*
    a. Yes. Please elaborate in general terms.
    b. No.
    c. Other.
8. In this research process, do you feel confident that you were able to answer your initial research questions?
    a. Definitely yes.
    b. Probably yes.
    c. Might or might not.
    d. Probably not.
    e. Definitely not.
9. Did you have to unlearn, re-learn, or alter any existing research or writing skills during work for your [Medical Sociology/Medical Anthropology] project?**
10. In what ways do you think this research and writing [assignment] is important for your major? **
11. Are you planning to go to graduate school?*
    a. Yes! Please identify a program (e.g., anthropology, sociology, MBA).
    b. Not sure, I need to finish my current degree first.
    c. Not sure. I want to take time off and think about it.
    d. Definitely not.
12. Were you able to make connections between [Medical Sociology/Medical Anthropology] and your other classes for your major? Please elaborate.**
13. What research and writing advice do you have for future students of [Medical Sociology/Medical Anthropology]?**

ENDNOTES

1. Mia O'Brien, "Navigating the SoTL Landscape: A Compass, Map and Some Tools for Getting Started," *International Journal for the Scholarship of Teaching and Learning* 2, no. 2 (July 2008): 1.
2. Erin Dorris Cassidy and Kenneth E. Hendrickson, "Faculty–Librarian Micro-Level Collaboration in an Online Graduate History Course," *The Journal of Academic Librarianship* 39 (November 1, 2013): 458–63.
3. Nancy McBride Arrington and Adrienne Cohen, "Enhancing the Scholarship of Teaching and Learning through Micro-Level Collaboration across Two Disciplines," *International Journal of Teaching and Learning in Higher Education* 27, no.2 (2015): 194–203, http://www.isetl.org/ijtlhe/.
4. Norma G. Kobzina, "A Faculty—Librarian Partnership: A Unique Opportunity for Course Integration," *Journal of Library Administration* 50, no. 4 (May 2010): 293–314, https://doi.org/10.1080/01930821003666965.
5. Joyce and Diana D. Lindstrom, "Faculty-Librarian Collaboration to Achieve Integration of Information Literacy," *Reference & User Services Quarterly*, no. 1 (2006): 18, http://www.jstor.org/stable/20864595.

6. Hannelore B. Rader, "Building Faculty-Librarian Partnerships to Prepare Students for Information Fluency: The Time for Sharing Information Expertise Is Now," *College & Research Libraries News* 65, no. 2 (February 2004): 74–90.
7. Rader, "Building Faculty-Librarian Partnerships."
8. O'Brien, "Navigating the SoTL Landscape."
9. Ibid., 1
10. Ibid., 1
11. Ibid., 3
12. Ibid., 3
13. Ibid., 7
14. Ibid., 8
15. Ibid.
16. Ibid., 6-7.
17. Karen Barrow, *Patient Voices*, https://www.nytimes.com/column/patient-voices.
18. Mary Harris, *Only Human*, https://www.wnyc.org/shows/onlyhuman.
19. Médecins Sans Frontières/Doctors Without Borders, *Everyday Emergencies*, https://www.msf.org.uk/everyday-emergency-msf-podcast.
20. O'Brien, "Navigating the SoTL Landscape," 7.
21. ALA/ACRL/ANSS Instruction and Information Literacy Committee Task Force on Information Literacy Standards, "Information Literacy Standards for Anthropology and Sociology: Approved by the ACRL Board, January 2008," accessed November 9, 2017. http://www.ala.org/acrl/standards/anthro_soc_standards.
22. O'Brien, "Navigating the SoTL Landscape," 9–11.
23. Ibid., 10
24. Ibid., 11
25. Ibid., 12–13
26. Arthur Kleinman, *The Illness Narratives: Suffering, Healing, and the Human Condition* (New York: Basic Books, 1988).
27. Anne Fadiman, *The Spirit Catches You and You Fall Down* (New York: Farrar, Strauss and Giroux, 1997).
28. ALA/ACRL/ANSS Instruction and Information Literacy Committee Task Force on Information Literacy Standards, "Information Literacy Standards."
29. O'Brien, "Navigating the SoTL Landscape," 14.
30. Edward L. Kain, "Building the Sociological Imagination through a Cumulative Curriculum: Professional Socialization in Sociology," *Teaching Sociology* 27, no. 1 (1999): 1–16, http://www.jstor.org/stable/1319241.

Bibliography

Arrington, Nancy McBride, and Adrienne Cohen. "Enhancing the Scholarship of Teaching and Learning through Micro-Level Collaboration across Two Disciplines." *International Journal of Teaching and Learning in Higher Education* 27, no.2 (2015): 194–203. http://www.isetl.org/ijtlhe/.

Barrow, Karen. *Patient Voices*. https://www.nytimes.com/column/patient-voices.

Cassidy, Erin Dorris, and Kenneth E. Hendrickson. "Faculty–Librarian Micro-Level Collaboration in an Online Graduate History Course." *The Journal of Academic Librarianship* 39 (November 1, 2013): 458–63. 10.1016/j.acalib.2013.08.018.

Fadiman, Anne. *The Spirit Catches You and You Fall Down*. New York: Farrar, Strauss and Giroux, 1997.

Harris, Mary. *Only Human*. https://www.wnyc.org/shows/onlyhuman.

Kain, Edward L. "Building the Sociological Imagination through a Cumulative Curriculum: Professional Socialization in Sociology." *Teaching Sociology* 27, no. 1 (1999): 1–16. http://www.jstor.org/stable/1319241

Kleinman, Arthur. *The Illness Narratives: Suffering, Healing, and the Human Condition*. New York: Basic Books, 1988.

Kobzina, Norma G. "A Faculty—Librarian Partnership: A Unique Opportunity for Course Integration." *Journal of Library Administration* 50, no. 4 (May 2010): 293–314. https://doi.org/10.1080/01930821003666965.

Lindstrom, Joyce, and Diana D. Shonrock. "Faculty-Librarian Collaboration to Achieve Integration of Information Literacy." *Reference & User Services Quarterly* no. 1 (2006): 18. http://www.jstor.org/stable/20864595.

Médecins Sans Frontières/Doctors Without Borders. *Everyday Emergencies*. https://www.msf.org.uk/everyday-emergency-msf-podcast.

O'Brien, Mia. "Navigating the SoTL Landscape: A Compass, Map and Some Tools for Getting Started." *International Journal for the Scholarship of Teaching and Learning* 2, no. 2 (July 2008): 1.

Rader, Hannelore B. "Building Faculty-Librarian Partnerships to Prepare Students for Information Fluency: The Time for Sharing Information Expertise Is Now." *College & Research Libraries News* 65, no. 2 (February 2004): 74–90.

Mapping the Information Literacy Skills of First-Year Business Students:

A Journey Through Lesson Study

Norm Althouse, Peggy Hedges, Zahra Premji, and Justine Wheeler

Introduction

Academic campuses have become increasingly aware of the importance of the Scholarship of Teaching and Learning (SoTL). Similarly, there has been an increase in the awareness of opportunities for librarians to engage in SoTL. In particular, instruction librarians are committed to assessing and improving the learning opportunities of students. The knowledge gained through foundational skills in library research is critical to student success during their time at university and beyond.[1]

This case study chronicles the implementation of a lesson study (LS) project by two librarians and two teaching faculty at the Haskayne School of Business (HSB), University of Calgary. The University of Calgary is a multi-campus publicly funded university with more than 30,000 students. In this case study, the steps involved in creating and implementing the lesson study will be highlighted, including designing a lesson, ethical considerations, data collection, and data analysis. Additionally, the researchers' study findings will be discussed.

Context and Inquiry

At HSB, information literacy skills are initially introduced to undergraduate students in their mandatory first-year course, Strategy & Global Management (SGMA) 217. Students in the course are not only introduced to business as a professional and academic discipline,

but they are also becoming acculturated to the university environment. It is a foundational course that emphasizes skill development in the areas of communication, critical thinking, decision-making, and research skills. Furthermore, students are expected to complete a significant research project for the course. This comprehensive survey project challenges students to critically analyze a company and its corresponding industry within the context of multiple business perspectives. Specifically, students are required to examine their chosen company through such lenses as financial viability, global capacity, human resources, corporate governance, community relations, technology, and corporate culture.

Adding to the complexity, business research differs from research in other academic disciplines. Information sources are not highly structured or always evident. While students need to use academic articles and books in their research, they also rely heavily on corporate and commercial information, including financial statements, stock prices, market research reports, industry reports, corporate social governance data, brokerage firm analyst reports, and current news items. This information is not usually indexed or cataloged. As such, students need to be able to understand the nature of business information and how to apply this knowledge when conducting research.

For approximately fifteen years, a librarian has been involved in the creation and delivery of a one-shot face-to-face library instruction session for SGMA 217. This library session was delivered as a lecture, supplemented by an online library guide for the assignment. The content for the library session centered on discussing search techniques and highlighting common business information types and business databases. Despite positive feedback from students, anecdotal evidence suggests a high number of students from SGMA 217 continued to visit the library information desk with questions on how to start the research process. This led to an exploration of SoTL as a means of increasing student understanding and retention of key business information literacy concepts. Specifically, the research team of business librarians and teaching faculty wanted to investigate how first-year students most effectively learn foundational business information literacy skills.

Lesson Study

Lesson study was developed as a means for teachers to conduct systematic inquiry into their pedagogical practices within one contained lesson[2] or, as Cerbin and Kopp state, a small team works together to "design, teach, study, and refine a single class lesson."[3] Collaboration is one of the key aspects of LS; another key aspect is designing a study that makes learning visible. This is crucial because observation is a cornerstone of lesson study. Additionally, lesson study is an iterative process; in fact, it has been called a very specific type of action research.[4]

With this in mind, the LS in this case study incorporated a flipped classroom approach to encourage active learning. The flipped classroom approach is a teaching method that delivers lecture content prior to class time. Class time is then used to integrate learning into practical application activities.[5] Furthermore, during class time, the librarians are available to act as guides and help students overcome any roadblocks they encounter. Further benefits of a flipped classroom include more active learning, better use of class time, increased interaction between student and teacher, and student responsibility for learning.[6]

In relation to this lesson study, the research team was particularly attracted to the flipped classroom approach because it provided them with an opportunity to use in-class time to observe students work through activities based on what they learned from the online modules presented in the flipped instruction.

Lesson Design

For the flipped classroom, online modules introduced students to key information literacy concepts. The modules were designed using Bloom's Taxonomy to ensure that they were appropriate for new learners.[7] As such, the online modules focused on the cognitive domains of remembering and comprehending. The in-class activities also covered these two domains but also moved into the higher-level domain of application of knowledge.

In all, five online modules were created, each ranging from three to ten minutes in length. The content of the modules included an overview of the business information environment, including criteria for evaluating information; formulating a research plan; locating databases and research guides; synthesizing information and using critical thinking; and the basics of citing, plagiarism, and how to access the Business Library online citation guide. The online modules were linked to the learning objectives in the SGMA 217 course, particularly as they pertain to the group assignment. The course-level outcome aligned with this session stated that students would demonstrate effective secondary research methods and, more specifically, that they would learn business research skills. Each module concluded with multiple-choice quiz questions to reinforce important concepts and to provide interactivity.

These modules were accessible to students two weeks prior to the library workshop (for this LS). During the lesson, emphasis was placed on making learning visible through "talk-out-loud" activities in student groups and student presentations on learning. Data collection points were set up throughout the LS. Specifically, the research team collected and analyzed data from

1. descriptive statistics on student engagement in the online modules;
2. in-class observations;
3. in-class assignment worksheets;
4. a feedback form distributed immediately after the in-class session; and
5. an online feedback form distributed after students submitted their term project but before they received their grade.

Implementation: The Lesson

The in-class session consisted of three distinct activities, each with an introduction, a demonstration by the librarian, and time to work on the activity. Students worked on the activities in groups to encourage peer discussion and shared learning. Each group completed a worksheet (see Appendix 17A); the worksheets provided an overview of the three activities and space for students to provide answers and indicate their thought processes. The librarian collected the worksheets at the end of the lesson. Each activity ended with a review of learning in the form of student presentations or a debrief by the librarian.

The first activity asked students to summarize the online modules. The librarian assigned each group one of the five online modules to recap; they were given five minutes to discuss and summarize the two to three main takeaways for that module. Groups were randomly asked to present their summary to the class and the librarian filled in any gaps in their summaries. This activity sought to reinforce concepts introduced in the modules. This activity also allowed students who did not complete the online modules prior to class to catch up so that they could participate in the in-class activities.[8]

The second activity focused on formulating a research plan using a concept map. Students were assigned a question related to their course assignment, such as "How does the government impact your company?," and were asked to create a concept map. During this process, students identified keywords that could be used to search for information. Students were also asked to suggest possible creators or publishers of such information and the format this information would take. The end of this activity included debriefing the challenges students encountered during the process of creating their concept map.

In the third and last activity, students were asked to search business databases and evaluate one article or report of their choice. Each group was assigned two databases to search for information about their company that would help answer the assigned question. Students were then required to fill in a table on the in-class worksheet, including search terms, identifying information about the article or report they located, and an assessment of the credibility and bias of the information, using the criteria mentioned in the online modules.

Ethical Considerations

To ensure that the study complied with ethical research standards, the research team sought and received approval to conduct the study from their institutional Ethics Board. Student participation in the LS was voluntary and anonymous. Conceivably, during the lesson, a student could be identified by a professor or librarian; however, individual names were not recorded on the observation sheets, and this possibility was discussed in the informed consent form.

The consent form was sent to all students three weeks prior to the lesson. The students were asked to contact the investigators if they had any concerns; otherwise, it was requested that the students bring a signed consent form to the lesson. At the beginning of the lesson, the librarian reiterated the content of the informed consent form and provided extra copies for those students who had not brought a signed form. Additionally, because of the amount of data generated by this lesson study, the investigators only observed and collected data from two of the eight sections of the course. This meant that because all eight sections received the same lesson, if a student wanted to opt-out of the study, they could attend the lesson in a section that was not part of the study. Ultimately, no concerns were raised by any students.

Data Collection

The investigators collaborated on all of the data collection points. Most notably, the research team adhered to an observational protocol form provided by their university's Teaching & Learning Institute.[9] This form provided a template for the type of observations the observers should be recording. In LS, it is important to observe not how the teacher teaches but how the students engage with the lesson.[10] Consequently, the observers were recording affective elements such as whether the students appeared frustrated, engaged, or bored, and cognitive elements such as whether the students understood the assignment and were able to implement what they had just been taught. Elements were observed through facial expressions, language, and behaviors. Both the observed behaviors and possible cognitive or affective meaning was recorded. For instance, if a student was repeatedly checking their phone, this instance would be recorded along with the point in the lesson plan where this occurred. Furthermore, other affective or cognitive elements would be recorded, such as a bored facial expression or voicing confusion over the assignment. Observers were always a mix of librarians and teaching faculty. Additionally, for the observations, the team brought in one external instructor and one external librarian. It was hoped that this would result in richer observational data.

Data Analysis

In reviewing the data, the team found that the online statistics and data from the feedback forms were useful but limited in content. Very little additional analysis was required. In comparison, the activity sheets were analyzed by the librarians for concept recognition and understanding. Finally, the observational data was by far the most fulsome and richest data the team collected. In order to analyze this data, investigators were given copies of all of the written observations. Investigators then used an inductive content analysis approach to individually analyze the data. The research team then met with the director of the Teaching & Learning Institute to discuss each individual analysis.

Through discussion, reflection, and further interaction with the data, the team reached agreement on the concepts and themes emerging from the data. This led to a course of action for the next iteration of the LS.

Findings

The research team's analysis revealed that students had two main types of challenges: structural and conceptual. Structural challenges included motivating students to watch the online modules, distractions due to technology, and the need for more explicit instructions for each activity. Conceptual challenges included acculturating to the language of business and academia, understanding who creates and distributes business information, and connecting academic integrity to citations.

Table 17.1. Key Learning Challenges

Structural	Conceptual
1. Ensuring students are prepared for the library workshop	1. Acculturating to business/academic terminology
2. Minimizing non-class related use of technology and personal devices	2. Understanding the business information environment
3. Providing sufficient instruction for students to be able to be successful in class	3. Connecting academic integrity to citing

Revisions to the Lesson

The learning challenges identified and mentioned above led to changes in four major areas of the original lesson plan (see figure 17.1).

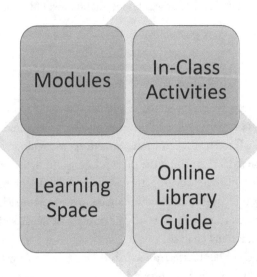

Figure 17.1. Aspects of the lesson changed after analysis

Observations from activity three highlighted that the students' level of knowledge about the business information environment was weak. Based on this, two of the online modules were restructured and revised. Module one became entirely focused on the business information environment. It was expanded to include common creators and common formats of business information, including brief descriptions of each producer and each format. This was intended to improve student understanding of the business information environment, including the content of each format type, the differences between how they are structured, and, consequently, how search practices vary depending on the format of the information. Since this module was now content-heavy, the criteria for evaluating information, which was formerly part of module one, was moved to the end of module two. Additionally, email communication to students more explicitly stressed the need to complete the modules prior to the lesson in order to fully benefit from the lesson.

The most extensive revision was to activity two. Observational data showed that students struggled to create a concept map. This was either due to a lack of understanding of the question itself or because students struggled with the terminology used in the questions, such as regulations or demographics. Analysis of the worksheets added to the evidence from observational data and crystallized for the research team that the concept map activity was not well-aligned or meeting the learning objectives for the lesson. Concept maps aid in research planning and may help generate keywords for use in searching. However, business information literacy requires students to navigate many different business formats, most of which do not require or support keyword searching. Instead, these formats require students to understand how to search by company name or identify the industry in which a company is situated.

As a result of these observations, activity two was changed to focus on the creators and formats of business information. In this new activity, students are provided with an infographic that describes six common creators of business information and six common formats of business information. Students are then asked to identify three possible creators of the information they need and the corresponding formats in which this information can be located. For example, if students are assigned the question "How competitive is company X in its industry," a possible source of relevant information is a financial statement, and the format of this information is an annual report. In addition, the question posed in the activity used accessible language, and the online library guide for the course was updated to include links to common business and academic words and phrases.

Activity three was also adjusted to ensure that students would be exposed to at least two different formats of information. In the first iteration of this session, half of a student group searched an article database and the other half searched an industry report database. Observational data showed that searching the article database was more intuitive for students than searching an industry report database. In order to overcome this, activity three was re-structured and broken down into two parts. In part one of this activity, all students will search an industry report database with explicit instructions on how to search using the industry name. In the second part of activity three, all students will search an article database with instructions on how to search for information on a company. This change was made with the intent of providing students with an understanding of the ways in which the different formats of information are structured within their respective databases and, therefore, how searching works across different formats of information and databases.

The above changes to the lesson plan were made in response to the conceptual issues identified by the data. In response to the structural issues identified, a couple of additional changes were also made. For example, previously, the lesson had taken place in an interactive learning studio. In this studio, students brought their own laptops to use during the lesson. In the second iteration, a computer lab with broadcasting technology was chosen as the classroom. Broadcasting software allows the teaching librarian to take control of the screens of the student desktop computers and broadcast the presentation or demonstration. This reduces the number of distractions available to students, particularly as personal devices no longer need to be present in the classroom. Finally, the instructions on the activity sheet were changed from paragraph to step-by-step bullet points.

The process of LS does not end after changes are implemented; rather, it can be continued in an iterative manner. The second iteration of LS is useful as it highlights which of the changes implemented are effective for overcoming their intended learning challenges. Observational data from the second iteration of this lesson showed that many of the changes were successful. For example, being more explicit about the need to complete the online modules before the class led to sessions with a greater number of prepared students, ultimately resulting in more meaningful peer learning, changing the classroom to one with broadcasting technology reduced distractions and led to improved student engagement, and the bullet point instructions were noticeably easier for students to follow.

Conclusion

Participating in SoTL projects is critical to better understanding how and what students learn. By using an LS approach to explore how to more effectively approach a business information literacy library workshop, the researchers were able to make evidence-informed adjustments to the workshop. Initial findings suggested that both structural and conceptual issues needed to be addressed in the research design. By using LS iteratively, the research team aims to continue to improve the lesson with a goal of strengthening information literacy skills within the HSB student population. And, ultimately, at its praxis, this means a more integrated introduction to business information literacy that emphasizes a foundational understanding of the concepts, issues, and technical skills students need in today's changing information ecosystem.

Appendix 17A: SGMA 217 Worksheet

SGMA 217 Worksheet - Fall 2017

Name: _____   Name: _____
Name: _____   Name: _____
Name: _____   Name: _____

Part 1: Online modules revisited

1a) Which module were you assigned? 1   2   3   4   5   (circle the module assigned)

1b) Briefly summarize the module you were assigned. (You may be asked to present your summary)

_____
_____
_____
_____
_____
_____

Part 2. Who would produce the information and what format would it be in

Your group has been asked to work on **bullet point 11** from your assignment (*Recent issues that have impacted the company and the industry*).

a) Read the information provided on the next page (*Who produces business information* and *An introduction to business information formats*).

b) Discuss within your groups:
 • Who would produce information about recent issues that have impacted your company and industry?
 • What format would this information be in?

c) Based on your discussion, please fill in the table (Table 1) below.

Who produces this information?	What format would this information be in?
Government	Industry report

Table 1: Who produces the information and what format would it be in

WHO PRODUCES BUSINESS INFORMATION

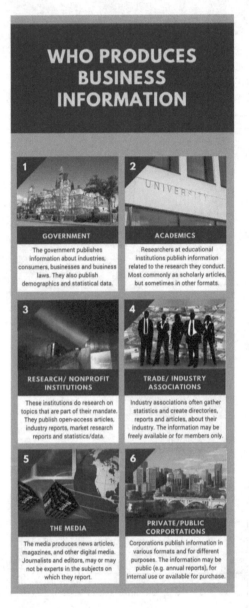

1 GOVERNMENT
The government publishes information about industries, consumers, businesses and business laws. They also publish demographics and statistical data.

2 ACADEMICS
Researchers at educational institutions publish information related to the research they conduct. Most commonly as scholarly articles, but sometimes in other formats.

3 RESEARCH/ NONPROFIT INSTITUTIONS
These institutions do research on topics that are part of their mandate. They publish open-access articles, industry reports, market research reports and statistics/data.

4 TRADE/ INDUSTRY ASSOCIATIONS
Industry associations often gather statistics and create directories, reports and articles, about their industry. The information may be freely available or for members only.

5 THE MEDIA
The media produces news articles, magazines, and other digital media. Journalists and editors, may or may not be experts in the subjects on which they report.

6 PRIVATE/PUBLIC CORPORATIONS
Corporations publish information in various formats and for different purposes. The information may be public (e.g. annual reports), for internal use or available for purchase.

AN INTRODUCTION TO BUSINESS INFORMATION FORMATS

BOOKS
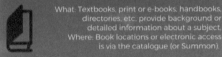
What: Textbooks, print or e-books, handbooks, directories, etc. provide background or detailed information about a subject.
Where: Book locations or electronic access is via the catalogue (or Summon).

ARTICLES
What: Scholarly, trade, magazine & news articles.
Where: Article databases (Business Source Complete, Canadian Business & Current Affairs, Proquest Business Collection, etc.), open access online (Globe & Mail, etc.).

INDUSTRY REPORTS
What: Focuses on an industry. May include details on industry size, operating environment, competition, barriers to entry, regulations, etc.
Where: Databases (e.g. IBISWorld, Passport, Mergent, NetAdvantage), government website (Industry Canada), trade association websites.

MARKET RESEARCH REPORTS
What: Information on consumer trends, profiles and behaviours.
Where: Databases (e.g. IBISWorld, Passport, etc.), Research institution/ nonprofit websites (e.g. PEW Research Center), government sites (e.g. Statistics Canada), or trade association websites.

COMPANY REPORTS

What: Report about any aspect of a company.
Example: company profiles, SWOT analysis, social responsibility report, investor report, Annual report.
Where: Databases (e.g. Thomson One, Business Source Complete, MSCI, etc.), company websites.

STATISTICS/FINANCIAL DATA

What: Demographics, statistics, financials & data.
Where: Government websites, databases (e.g. Mint global, Bloomberg, Capital IQ), Research institutions/ Nonprofits (e.g. PEW Research Center, etc.), Trade association websites.

Part 3. Let's get searching!

Within each group, split yourselves into two subgroups (2 to 3 people).

Instructions (sub-group 1)

a) Navigate to the SGMA 217 research guide (https://library.ucalgary.ca/guides/SGMA217) and read the section related to your bullet point.

Next, click on the "industry reports" link located within the text of bullet point 11 to go to a list of industry report databases.

b) Sub-group 1 will search the database called IBISWorld (listed in Table 2a below) for an industry report related to your company (using the industry name). **Hint: You need to know what industry your company operates in before you can search for industry reports.**

c) Once you have found a report related to your industry, please fill out table 2a below

Database 1	IBISWorld
Industry name	
Title of the report	
Date of the report	

Table 2a: Searching for information in an industry report database

d) Share your information with the other sub-group and demonstrate your search strategy. (You may be asked to present your information)

e) Now you will search another database called ABI/Business Premium Collection (as listed in table 3a below) for information about recent issues that have impacted your company (using the company name and other keywords, as necessary).

f) Once you have found one resource (article, report, etc), please fill out table 3a below.

Database 2	ABI/Business Premium Collection
Title of the resource	
Author of the resource	
Date of the resource	
Format of the resource (please tick one)	Book ☐ Article ☐ Industry report ☐ Market research report ☐ Company report ☐ Statistics/financial data ☐
Do you think the resource is … (optional)	Biased: Yes ☐ No ☐ Why?

Table 3a: Searching for information about your company

g) Share your information with the other sub-group and demonstrate your search strategy. (You may be asked to present your information)

Part 3. Let's get searching!

Within each group, split yourselves into two subgroups (2 to 3 people).

Instructions (sub-group 2)

a) Navigate to the SGMA 217 research guide (https://library.ucalgary.ca/guides/SGMA217) and read the section related to your bullet point.

Next, click on the "industry reports" link located within the text of bullet point 11 to go to a list of industry report databases.

b) Sub-group 2 will search the database called Netadvantage (listed in Table 2b below) for an industry report related to your company (using the industry name). Hint: **You need to know what industry your company operates in before you can search for industry reports.**

c) Once you have found a report related to your industry, please fill out table 2b below

Database 1	Netadvantage
Industry name	
Title of the report	
Date of the report	

Table 2b: Searching for information in an industry report database

d) Share your information with the other sub-group and demonstrate your search strategy. (You may be asked to present your information)

e) Now you will search another database called Business Source Complete (as listed in table 3b below) for information about recent issues that have impacted your company (using the company name and other keywords, as necessary).

f) Once you have found one resource (article, report, etc), please fill out table 3a below.

Database 2	Business Source Complete
Title of the resource	
Author of the resource	
Date of the resource	
Format of the resource (please tick one)	Book ☐ Article ☐ Industry report ☐ Market research report ☐ Company report ☐ Statistics/financial data ☐
Do you think the resource is … (optional)	Biased: Yes ☐ No ☐ Why?

Table 3b: Searching for information about your company

g) Share your information with the other sub-group and demonstrate your search strategy. (You may be asked to present your information)

ENDNOTES

1. Tiffini Travis, "From the Classroom to the Boardroom: The Impact of Information Literacy Instruction on Workplace Research Skills," *Education Libraries* 34, no. 2 (2011): 19.
2. Clea Fernandez, "Learning from Japanese Approaches to Professional Development: The Case of Lesson Study," *Journal of Teacher Education* 53 (2002): 394.
3. William Cerbin and Bryan Kopp, "Lesson Study as a Model for Building Pedagogical Knowledge and Improving Teaching," *International Journal of Teaching and Learning in Higher Education* 18, no. 3 (2006): 250.
4. Peter Dudley, *Lesson Study: A Handbook* (2012), 1, http://lessonstudy.co.uk/wp-content/uploads/2012/03/new-handbook-revisedMay14.pdf.
5. Sara Arnold-Garza, "The Flipped Classroom Teaching Model and Its Use for Information Literacy Instruction," *Communications in Information Literacy 8,* no. 1 (2014): 8, http://www.comminfolit.org/index.php?journal=cil.
6. Arnold-Garza, "The Flipped Classroom Teaching Model."
7. Benjamin S. Bloom, Max D. Engelhart, Edward J. Furst, Walker H. Hill, and David R. Krathwohl, *Taxonomy of Educational Objectives: The Classification of Education Goals. Handbook I: The Cognitive Domain* (New York: David McKay Co Inc., 1956).
8. Yunglung Chen, Yuping Wang, and Nian-Shing Chen, "Is FLIP Enough? Or Should We Use the FLIPPED Model Instead?," *Computers & Education* 79 (2014): 26.
9. Taylor Institute for Teaching and Learning, "Observation Guidelines for a Lesson Study Project," form, accessed November 2016, University of Calgary, Calgary, AB.
10. William Cerbin and Bryan Kopp, "Lesson Study as a Model for Building Pedagogical Knowledge and Improving Teaching," *International Journal of Teaching and Learning in Higher Education* 18, no. 3 (2006): 252.

Bibliography

Arnold-Garza, Sara. "The Flipped Classroom Teaching Model and Its Use for Information Literacy Instruction." *Communications in Information Literacy* 8, no. 1 (2014): 7–22. http://www.comminfolit.org/index.php?journal=cil.

Bloom, Benjamin S., Max D. Engelhart, Edward J. Furst, Walker H. Hill, and David R. Krathwohl. *Taxonomy of Educational Objectives: The Classification of Education Goals. Handbook I: The Cognitive Domain.* New York: David McKay Co Inc., 1956.

Cerbin, William, and Bryan Kopp. "Lesson Study as a Model for Building Pedagogical Knowledge and Improving Teaching." *International Journal of Teaching and Learning in Higher Education* 18, no. 3 (2006): 250–57.

Chen, Yunglung, Yuping Wang, and Nian-Shing Chen. "Is FLIP Enough? Or Should We Use the FLIPPED Model Instead?" *Computers & Education* 79 (2014): 16–27.

Dudley, Peter. *Lesson Study: A Handbook.* 2012. http://lessonstudy.co.uk/wp-content/uploads/2012/03/new-handbook-revisedMay14.pdf.

Fernandez, Clea. "Learning from Japanese Approaches to Professional Development: The Case of Lesson Study." *Journal of Teacher Education* 53 (2002): 393–405.

Taylor Institute for Teaching and Learning. "Observation Guidelines for a Lesson Study Project." Form, accessed November 2016. University of Calgary, Calgary, AB.

Travis, Tiffini. "From the Classroom to the Boardroom: The Impact of Information Literacy Instruction on Workplace Research Skills." *Education Libraries* 34, no. 2 (2011): 19–31.

If the Rubric Fits:

Library Instruction, Teaching Efficacy, and the Practice of Collective Reflection

Sara Maurice Whitver

> Beliefs of personal efficacy are the foundation of human agency. Unless people believe they can produce desired results by their actions, they have little incentive to act. It affects how they think, feel, act, and motivate themselves. Specifically, such beliefs regulate what people choose to do, how much effort they invest in what they undertake, how long they persevere in the face of obstacles and failure experience.... A high sense of personal efficacy pays off in performance accomplishments and emotional well-being. In group endeavors, people's shared beliefs in their collective efficacy affects the type of futures they seek to achieve and how much they accomplish as a group.
>
> —Albert Bandura, Social Cognitive Theory[1]

Critical Reflection and Efficacy for Librarian Teachers

As teaching becomes more and more important within the field of librarianship, it is imperative that librarians find ways to develop confidence in their classroom practices. Librarians frequently articulate a desire to improve their skills as teachers and to make their instructional efforts more effective. So how do librarians build personal and collective

217

efficacy in teaching? What methods are available to librarians within the classroom context that allow them to reflect on teaching and learning effectiveness? And how do librarians cultivate a local community of practice where they can receive peer feedback and develop norms? Albert Bandura's Social Cognitive Theory correlates belief in ability and effectiveness in praxis; when people believe in their ability, they will be more effective. This translates well to librarian teachers. When librarians believe in their ability to teach, they become more effective teachers. This efficacy can be developed by critically reflecting on one's teaching practice through the examination of student work.

Personal efficacy, or self-efficacy, can be defined as "an instructor's belief in their own ability to successfully gather and interpret student data for improving instruction."[2] Svinicki et al. suggest that teachers can develop self-efficacy by collecting and analyzing student data, and they found that teachers who scored high on self-efficacy were motivated to try new approaches to teaching. Likewise, librarian teachers can improve their efficacy in teaching by centering their inquiry on student learning. Booth suggests librarians can build self-efficacy through conscious self-reflection on student work that will, in turn, impact both the learning environment and student achievement.[3] Booth's assertion is that within this context self-reflection functions as a tool for iterative design, examining student work for the purpose of improving teaching. This practice is a hallmark quality in the Scholarship of Teaching and Learning (SoTL), as evidenced by O'Brien's SoTL Compass.[4] Librarians have to focus on improving their practice toward the goal of better student learning because without the student, "teaching" is pointless. O'Brien's Compass provides a heuristic for practitioners to examine the learning environment, using four foundational questions:

- What will my students learn and why is it worth learning?
- Who are my students and how do students learn effectively?
- What can I do to support students to learn effectively?
- How do I know if my teaching and my students' learning has been effective?

By using these questions as a frame for reflective inquiry when examining student data, librarians are able to identify problem areas in their lesson plans and recognize areas of difficulty for their students. When individual librarians reflect on work produced within their class sessions, they are able to consider the presentation of material and begin to imagine other ways of approaching concepts that, through a simple analysis of the evidence, appear to be bottlenecks for students. However, individual reflection and analysis is still a solitary and limited view into any one individual's teaching practice.

Brookfield asserts that in order to understand the complete picture, teachers must examine their practice in a multifaceted approach.[5] He offers four lenses for critical reflection: autobiography, students, colleagues, and theoretical literature. These lenses provide multiple perspectives with which to learn about one's teaching practice; the act of critically reflecting allows teachers to regard curricula "as constructed and tentative, as framed by human agency and therefore capable of being dismantled and reframed by teachers and students."[6] Brookfield describes this as "stance and dance," maintaining a stance of inquiry toward personal teaching practice while participating in a dance of experimentation and risk in the classroom.[7]

This case study is a snapshot of ongoing, routinized individual and group reflection at The University of Alabama Libraries. Librarians use worksheets as instruments for collecting student data and participate in rubric norming as a way to facilitate critical reflection on their teaching practices. End-of-semester workshops allow librarians to adapt Brookfield's theoretical framework of critical reflection for communal reflection. Applying O'Brien's SoTL Compass within each of Brookfield's lenses helps participants keep the focus of their practice on assessing and improving the learning environments they create for students, increasing both individual and collective efficacy within UA's library instruction program.

Establishing Community by Articulating Shared Outcomes

Oakleaf's "Staying on Track with Rubric Assessment" reports that institutions that implemented rubrics saw "substantial improvements in teaching information literacy concepts" and that the use of rubrics has impacted both librarian pedagogy and classroom curriculum.[8] Oakleaf's study participants reflected that rubrics were "empowering" and that they "facilitated valuable reflection on teaching practice."[9] While it is popular to use rubrics to assess student learning in information literacy,[10] it has also been noted that rubrics can be difficult to draft in order to produce valid assessment results,[11] and the quality of the results are only as good as the raters. Rubrics are a valued and useful tool for librarians who want to measure the impact that their instruction activities have on student learning, but perhaps they are even more useful as instruments for critical self-reflection and group reflection. When designed to facilitate teacher reflection in addition to measuring student learning,[12] rubrics offer librarians an opportunity to investigate their performance in the classroom, examine the design of their teaching activities, and when used in a group setting, to communicate about teaching practices, including successes and challenges in the classroom.

The University of Alabama is a flagship research university with an enrollment of 38,563 (freshman class of 7,404).[13] Following a model of integrating information literacy across the disciplines, all instruction librarians (a team of about sixteen) participate in the instruction program for first-year writing, partnering specifically with English (EN) 102. There are around 200 sections of EN 102 each academic year. The instruction program for EN 102 is highly structured in that instructors of record select from a menu of library instruction lesson options that have been specifically designed to support the learning goals of the course (see table 18.1). Each of the four "options" is described to the instructor of record as a set of learning outcomes and includes a short paragraph description of the conceptual ideas addressed within that lesson.

Table 18.1. Session Menu and Learning Outcomes for EN 102 Library Instruction

	Learning Outcome 1	**Learning Outcome 2**
Option 1	Students will use Scout to locate PDF, ebook, and physical book items in order to demonstrate an understanding of the different formats within the library's collections.	Students demonstrate an understanding of post-search limiters in order to strategically target format types and publication dates.
Option 2	Students will break a topic down into smaller components in order to engage in the iterative process of narrowing a research question.	Students will select terms related to their key concepts in order to develop a search strategy.
Option 3	Students will recognize different processes of source creation in order to choose sources that appropriately meet their research needs (editorial oversight, intended audience, review process).	Students will determine an author's expertise and the reputation of a publication in order to assess a source's credibility within their research assignment.
Option 4	Students will use controlled vocabulary and field-specific search options and limiters in order to retrieve topically relevant sources.	Students will combine search terms with Boolean operators in order to effectively interpret their research question into an effective search query.

EN 102 instructors can request up to three sessions from the menu in any order. Instruction is typically scheduled before the semester begins, and librarians partner with a class for the duration of the semester through both in-class instruction and out of class curriculum support and one-on-one student research consultations.

For the past five years, UA has used rubrics (see Appendix) to guide the lesson planning efforts of librarians who participate in instruction for first-year writing. To develop an assessment for this instruction program, the coordinator of library instruction (the author) drafted a list of skills based on an analysis of the campus' first-year writing curriculum. Through formal and informal channels, including round-robin draft revisions and informal conversations, a group of librarians then began collectively drafting rubrics that described two learning outcomes for each session option. Rubrics provided a way for librarians to communicate with each other and with instructors of record about learning outcomes. These rubrics help participating librarians to answer O'Brien's question, "Who are my students and how do students learn effectively?" and offer a way to provide consistency from librarian to librarian and class to class for such a large program.[14] As librarians work to compose performance indicators within rubrics, they actively engage in describing the skill levels based on their knowledge and experience of student performance as well as an understanding of the learning outcome; reflecting on student performance allows the librarian teachers to understand the learning outcomes through the lens of their experience with individual students.

Promoting Personal Efficacy Through Reflection

In her blog post, "The Ballad of the Sad Instruction Librarian," Farkas asserts, "I think about the people who want to improve, but don't have the time within their work day to develop professionally and improve or just don't know where to start."[15] Farkas mourns the lack of librarians' efficacy in teaching, suggesting that institutions should support librarians through the provision of time for reflection on teaching and opportunities to develop the practice of teaching. The anecdotes in Farkas' post serve to further highlight how alienated and unsupported librarians generally feel in the classroom.[16]

One of the goals of practicing individual and group reflection is to increase the individual efficacy of librarian teachers participating in instruction for first-year writing. Self-efficacy is developed through looking at student work and asking the questions, "Did these students understand what I was trying to teach them? And where am I encountering bottlenecks?" Brookfield recommends beginning critical reflections practices with the autobiographical lens asserting, "Insight and meaning for teaching that we draw from these deep experiences are likely to have a profound and long-lasting influence."[16] At UA, each librarian has the opportunity to use the rubric for lesson planning, in-class assessment, and, if they collect classroom artifacts of student work, as an evaluative measure for their teaching. When librarians use the established rubrics to score classroom artifacts such as worksheets, they are able to answer O'Brien's question, "How do I know if my teaching and my students' learning have been effective?"[17] Librarians at UA practice holistic scoring of student responses using Oakleaf's rubrics methodology in order to facilitate reflection on their classroom behavior. The results of this scoring practice enable librarians to make incremental changes to their personal teaching practice as well as informs programmatic adjustments. For example, one librarian teacher scored a set of worksheets and noticed that students had collectively scored lower when responding to questions about the publication process of a newspaper. This signaled an opportunity to refine questions about newspapers for class discussion. Another librarian recognized that worksheets were consistently left incomplete, leading to the realization that there was a pacing problem. This librarian was able to adjust the pacing within class and was also able to bring the issue up during rubric norming to see if anyone else was having difficulty covering the material within one class period. Each of these changes, while small in themselves, had a marked impact on the team.

Drafting rubrics in iterative collaboration has allowed participating librarians at UA to work as a team to achieve shared learning outcomes in which they have each invested. Worksheets are generated using these outcomes in order to facilitate the collection of student work for self-reflection and collective norming. Each librarian is responsible for submitting student work at designated points throughout the semester. While librarians are free to create original worksheets (see table 18.2), templates are also available. Worksheet templates suggest an order in which each learning outcome and associated skills and concepts might be addressed, but they do not dictate how.

Table 18.2. Examples of Topic Analysis (LO 1: Students will break a topic down into smaller components)

Narrowing Your Topic and Using Reference Tools

In this exercise, you will narrow your paper topic and prepare to start searching for sources. The steps in this exercise will not only aid you in narrowing your topic, they will prepare you to begin library research. This is not intended to be busy work, but rather a process of systematically preparing you for searching.

Step 1: Spend about 5 minutes freewriting to explore your paper topic. Think about what interests you about your topic, and also what you don't know. Freewriting is a type of brainstorming, and you are not expected to know everything. Just try to get some ideas onto the page-- this exercise is the foundation for the rest of our class today!

> State's rights depend on the issue at hand. There are many topics that states disagree on. For example, some states disagree with Obama's Affordable Care Act. Other states disagree with the idea of same-sex marriage. These two issues involve state's rights. Although the supreme court approved those two issues, some states disagree with one or both. So the question is, where do state rights lie?

Part 2: Narrowing Down Your Research Topic

WHEN?

Now	Future	

WHERE?

College Universities	United States	

WHO?

College Athletes		

WHAT?

Should college athletes recieve pay		

Part 3: Write your research question.

> Do college athletes in the United States deserve to be paid for their ability in the future?

For example, in Option 2: Methods for Approaching Research (see table 18.1), one librarian usually prompts students to analyze their research topic using W questions, while another typically chooses to ask students to participate in five minutes of free writing on their topic. While there is a lot of variation between these two classroom activities, both activities address the learning outcome: "Students will break a topic down into smaller components in order to engage in the iterative process of narrowing a topic" (see table 18.1). This diversity in teaching is captured through worksheets which are scanned and submitted for assessment. Worksheets allow librarians to arrange and present material according to their own teaching style, which is a priority in UA's program.

As librarians are assigned new liaison roles and take jobs at other libraries, the use of rubrics allows UA's program some consistency. Rotation is expected at a large university library, and while the number of librarians has remained constant, a few have participated only for about one year; some librarians have rotated out and then back into the program. The act of drafting and revising a rubric each semester also allows new librarians to gain an understanding of the existing program of instruction and connect with seasoned librarians who have participated for years. These activities have facilitated a deeper understanding of the goals and character of the program, achieving sustainability while promoting personal efficacy in teaching.

Iterative Design and Peer Feedback

The reflective practice of rubric norming within rubric drafting is an iterative process. Brookfield notes that "our colleagues serve as critical mirrors reflecting back to us images of our actions that often take us by surprise," suggesting that sometimes it is only through the joys and frustrations experienced by a peer that one can recognize successes and challenges within one's practice.[19] The act of teaching can be isolating and lonely; without support, librarian teachers can easily become disheartened and disconnected from the rest of their team. It is essential that librarians have dedicated time, not only to engage in personal reflection but also to be able to talk through their experience in the classroom, share ideas, and problem solve.

Half of a day is set aside as a norming session to facilitate formal group conversations about teaching throughout the semester. Worksheets, which have been completed by students throughout the semester, allow librarians to capture student data. Librarians scan and submit completed worksheets to the coordinator of library instruction by the end of the semester. Worksheets are important to UA's program because they allow librarians to demonstrate their diverse approaches within the classroom.

According to Holmes and Oakleaf's rules for norming rubrics,[20] the norming facilitator (usually the coordinator of library instruction) creates grading packets of selected worksheets from each of the four instruction options (table 18.1) and distributes them by email to librarians at least one week in advance of holding a rubric norming workshop. Holmes and Oakleaf assert that "the goal of norming is for the raters to come to consensus, not for the raters to agree with the facilitator," but sometimes even consensus among raters is difficult to achieve.[21] Norming activities are a cornerstone of the assessment plan, and librarians who participate in teaching first-year writing library instruction are required to participate. However, individual scores are not tabulated for students or librarian teachers. Rather, the exercise of norming is used as a platform for reflecting on teaching practices and examining student responses with the intention of improving instruction in the next semester.

During norming sessions, participating librarians discuss their individual approach to each of the sessions' learning outcomes. The norming facilitator takes detailed notes and asks specific questions (e.g., "Can you describe how you address this learning outcome or skill?" "Can you tell us more about the language you use to discuss this part of your lesson?"). It is essential during these workshops that the facilitator focuses the line of questioning to generate discussion about each librarian's approach to teaching specific areas of a given worksheet, prompt librarians to objectively discuss the connection between an area of the worksheet and its correlation to the rubric, and provide librarians with a platform for problem-solving and sharing successes in the classroom.

At the end of the session, participating librarians have the opportunity to make specific revision recommendations. Sometimes these recommendations have resulted in small adjustments in a performance indicator and sometimes in major revision or redrafting of a learning outcome. Before each semester begins, the coordinator of library instruction sends the revised rubrics to the entire team for final comments. Significantly, this formal documentation of the evolution of the program bears witness to the dedication and diversity of the librarians who have participated in this practice over the past five years. Influences on learning outcomes and performance indicators are visible from librarians who have been gone for several years; even if a librarian leaves, parts of their practice lives on with their colleagues through the revision of rubrics and worksheets. Over the years, participating librarians have been heavily influenced by the discourse surrounding approaches to concepts within a learning outcome. During one early norming session, it became apparent that each librarian at the table was struggling with teaching broad and narrow search terms. While only two librarians who participated in that conversation still participate in the program, the solutions that were brainstormed through that conversation have fortified the practice of brand-new librarians who enter the program years later. Experiences like these really illustrate the benefits of collective reflection.

Conclusion

Rubric norming is improved with practice, and although the rubrics have been in use for almost five years, this practice is not perfected. This case study has demonstrated that setting time aside for critically reflecting on teaching and learning through the use of rubric norming fosters community and shared practices that impact the program for years to come. Questions like O'Brien's "What can I do to support students to learn effectively?" are most effective when asked from a collective position supported through organizational values.[22] Much the same as Gola et al.[23] note, norming sessions at The University of Alabama Libraries often result in significant revisions to the performance indicators within the rubrics, and sometimes even the replacement of learning outcomes, as over the years librarians come to a clearer understanding of the needs of students. However, real benefits are seen when value is placed on the conversation that the rubric and worksheets generate among librarian teachers rather than seeking a perfect rubric with perfect performance indicators.

Appendix 18A: Rubrics for First Year Writing Instruction

Option 1: Searching Basics

In this session, students will learn to read Scout records to determine the material format, type, and location of the items within records, and how to sort and filter to search more strategically using post-search limiters. *This session will not cover controlled vocabulary or keywords (covered in Option 2), or advanced search strategies in Scout or in individual databases (covered in Option 4)*

Class activities for this session can include:
- Scout scavenger hunt for items of a specific format or material type
- Peer demonstration of multiple strategies for completing assigned basic search tasks
- Locating and retrieving a book from the shelf (encourages using the location limiter)

	No Attempt (0)	Beginner(1)	Intermediate(2)	Advanced(3)
Students will use Scout to locate PDF, ebook, and physical book items in order to demonstrate an understanding of the different formats within the library's collections		Student uses the names of formats ("PDF"; "ebook") as search terms in order to locate an item of that format in Scout..	Student recognizes the material type of content described in a Scout record, but might not understand when they encounter an index record or a record with a hyperlink in it.	Student understands how to access different item types within Scout; attempts to locate items described in Scout records that do not have items attached.
Students demonstrate an understanding of post-search limiters in order to strategically target format types and publication dates.		Student uses limiters but does not demonstrate an understanding of strategy for finding materials by format type or publication date.	Student uses limiters and indicates some strategy for finding materials by format type or publication date	Student demonstrates the ability to apply limiters strategically to find materials by format type or publication date

Option 2: Methods for Approaching Research

In this session, students will learn how to analyze a topic, use reference resources, and develop a search strategy for finding sources for their writing assignments.

Class activities for narrowing a topic or research question and identifying narrow and broad search terms can include:

- Diagramming a topic to identify subcategories
- Listing topically related narrow and broad search terms in a hierarchical list
- Answering 3-4 "w" questions (who, what, where, when)
- Negotiating these activities to develop a more narrowly-focused, answerable research question.

	No Attempt (0)	Beginner (0)	Intermediate (1)	Advanced (3)
Students will break a topic down into smaller components in order to engage in the iterative process of narrowing a research question.		Student identifies a broad research topic, but struggles to engage in narrowing activities.	Student engages in narrowing a topic through brainstorming but fails to appropriately narrow areas of focus.	Student successfully identifies components of a balanced research topic and is able to articulate it in an answerable question.
Students will select terms related to their key concepts in order to develop a search strategy.		Student extracts some obvious keywords or search terms from a topic. Student continues to use natural language and broad search terms to conduct research.	Student extracts obvious keywords/search terms from topic and identifies related search terms Student includes words that describe measurement such as greater, less, increase or words like complicated or challenges.	Student demonstrates keyword development skills by identifying relevant keywords as well as related broad and narrow terms that are topically relevant.

Option 3: Evaluating Sources

In this session, students will learn to assess a source for relevancy and authority to decide whether it meets the needs of their writing assignment. Students will engage in activities and conversations throughout this session to help them understand the nature of popular and academic publishing.

Issues of "Source Creation" can include:
- Primary and secondary sources (archival research will not be covered in this session)
- Publishing/review processes including editorial oversight (peer review; role of an editor of a magazine or newspaper; web publishing for a nonprofit or government site;
- Intended audience and original purpose of the source, and means of original dissemination

	No Attempt (0)	Beginner (1)	Intermediate (2)	Advanced (3)
Students will recognize different processes of source creation in order to choose sources that appropriately meet their research needs. • **Editorial oversight** • **Intended audience** • **Review process**		Student is unable to recognize the difference between various review processes or intended audience Student is unable to determine if a source meets the criteria outlined in the assignment.	Student is able to respond to questions about an editor's role and intended audience and make some general comments about the role of an editor and the review process. Student attempts to understand why these issues influence the source criteria outlined in their assignment	Student is able t articulate how publication proc editorial oversigh valued within ac research.` Student is able t comment on hov sources can be leveraged conte within their rese order to fulfil diff needs for their assignment.
Student will determine an author's expertise and the reputation of a publication in order to assess a source's credibility within their research assignment.		Student makes basic assumptions about a source's credibility but struggles to engage with metrics such as an author's background and the reputation of a publication.	Student is able to identify an author's expertise and background and moderately assess a publication's reputation but still struggles to contextualize a source's value.	Student engage issues of author expertise and publication repu and is able to successfully arti different values "credibility" withi different context

Option 4: Searching Strategically

In this session, students will be taught to execute advanced searches in selected databases and resources. Databases will be selected when the session is scheduled, and advanced options will be chosen according to the needs of the class topic and assignment.

	No Attempt (0)	Beginner (0)	Intermediate (0.5)	Advanced (1.0)
Students will use controlled vocabulary and field-specific search options and limiters in order to retrieve topically relevant sources		Student struggles to differentiate keywords from controlled vocabulary; student still incorporates elements of natural language; student is only aware of basic limiters.	Student identifies relevant subject terms and applies it appropriately using a search field OR student effectively locates limiters to strategically narrow their search.	Student identifies relevant subject terms and applies it appropriately using a search field AND student effectively locates limiters to strategically narrow their search.
Students will combine search terms with boolean operators in order to effectively interpret their research question into an effective search query		Student understands how to choose keywords but struggles to combine with operators.	Student uses AND effectively to combine their search terms.	Student is able to effectively use more than one operator; student is able to combine field searches with Boolean operators to execute a search that targets a focused set of results.

ENDNOTES

1. Albert Bandura, "Social-Cognitive Theory," in *Encyclopedia of Psychology*, Vol. 7 (Washington, DC; New York: American Psychological Association, 2000), 329.

2. Marilla D Svinicki, Kyle Williams, Kadie Rackley, Anke JZ Sanders, Lisa Pine, and Julie Stewart, "Factors Associated with Faculty use of Student Data for Instructional Improvement," *International Journal for the Scholarship of Teaching and Learning* 10, no. 2 (2016): 6.

3. Char Booth, *Reflective Teaching, Effective Learning: Instructional Literacy for Library Educators* (Chicago: American Library Association, 2011), 19.

4. Mia O'Brien, "Navigating the SoTL Landscape: A Compass, Map and some Tools for Getting Starting," *International Journal for the Scholarship of Teaching and Learning* 2, no. 2 (2008): 4.

5. Stephen Brookfield, *Becoming a Critically Reflective Teacher: The Jossey-Bass Higher and Adult Education Series* (San Francisco: Jossey-Bass, 1995), 29.
6. Brookfield, *Becoming a Critically Reflective Teacher,* 40.
7. Ibid.,42.
8. Megan Oakleaf, "Staying on Track with Rubric Assessment: Five Institutions Investigate Information Literacy Learning," *Peer Review* 13, no.4/1 (2011): 326.
9. Oakleaf, "Staying on Track."
10. Debra Hoffmann and Kristen LaBonte, "Meeting Information Literacy Outcomes: Partnering with Faculty to Create Effective Information Literacy Assessment," *Journal of Information Literacy* 6, no.2 (2012): 73.
11. Jos van Helvoort, Saskia Brand-Gruwel, Frank Huysmans, Ellen Sjoer, "Reliability and Validity Test of a Scoring Rubric for Information Literacy," *Journal of Documentation* 73, no. 2 (2017): 312.
12. John R. Ward and Suzanne S. McCotter, "Reflection as a Visible Outcome for Preservice Teachers," *Teaching and Teacher Education* 20 (2004): 244.
13. The University of Alabama, "Quick Facts," https://www.ua.edu/about/quickfacts.
14. O'Brien, "Navigating the SoTL Landscape," 10.
15. Meredith Farkas, "The Ballad of the Sad Instruction Librarian," October 11, 2017.
16. Ibid.
17. Brookfield, *Becoming a Critically Reflective Teacher,* 35.
18. Ibid.
19. Ibid.
20. Claire Holmes and Megan Oakleaf, "The Official (and Unofficial) Rules for Norming Rubrics Successfully," *Journal of Academic Librarianship* 39, no. 6 (2013): 600.
21. Holmes and Oakleaf, "The Official (and Unofficial) Rules."
22. O'Brien, "Navigating the SoTL Landscape," 12.
23. Christina H. Gola, Irene Ke, Kerry M. Creelman, and Shawn P. Vaillancourt, "Developing an Information Literacy Assessment Rubric: A Case Study of Collaboration, Process, and Outcomes," *Communications in Information Literacy* 8, no.1 (2014): 138.

Bibliography

Bandura, Albert. "Social-Cognitive Theory." In *Encyclopedia of Psychology*, vol. VII: 329–32. Washington, DC; New York: American Psychological Association, 2000. http://dx.doi.org/10.1037/10522-140.

Booth, Char. *Reflective Teaching, Effective Learning: Instructional Literacy for Library Educators.* Chicago: American Library Association, 2011.

Brookfield, Stephen. *Becoming a Critically Reflective Teacher.* The Jossey-Bass Higher and Adult Education Series. San Francisco: Jossey-Bass, 1995.

Farkas, Meredith. "The Ballad of the Sad Instruction Librarian." *Information Wants to Be Free,* October 11, 2017. https://meredith.wolfwater.com/wordpress/2017/10/11/the-ballad-of-the-sad-instruction-librarian/.

Gola, Christina H., Irene Ke, Kerry M. Creelman, and Shawn P. Vaillancourt. "Developing an Information Literacy Assessment Rubric: A Case Study of Collaboration, Process, and Outcomes." *Communications in Information Literacy* 8, no.1 (2014): 131–44. http://www.comminfolit.org/index.php?journal=cil&page=article&op=view&path%5B%5D=v8i1p131&path%5B%5D=192.

Hoffmann, Debra, and Kristen LaBonte. "Meeting Information Literacy Outcomes: Partnering with Faculty to Create Effective Information Literacy Assessment." *Journal of Information Literacy* 6, no.2 (2012): 70–85. https://ojs.lboro.ac.uk/JIL/article/view/LLC-V6-I2-2012-1.

Holmes, Claire, and Megan Oakleaf. "The Official (and Unofficial) Rules for Norming Rubrics Successfully." *Journal of Academic Librarianship* 39, no. 6 (2013): 599–602. https://doi.org/10.1016/j.acalib.2013.09.001.

Oakleaf, Megan. "Staying on Track with Rubric Assessment: Five Institutions Investigate Information Literacy Learning." *Peer Review* 13, no.4/1 (2011): 18. https://experts.syr.edu/en/publications/staying-on-track-with-rubric-assessment-five-institutions-investi.

O'Brien, Mia. "Navigating the SoTL Landscape: A Compass, Map and some Tools for Getting Starting." *International Journal for the Scholarship of Teaching and Learning* 2, no. 2 (2008): 1–20. https://doi.org/10.20429/ijsotl.2008.020215.

Svinicki, Marilla D., Kyle Williams, Kadie Rackley, Anke JZ Sanders, Lisa Pine, and Julie Stewart. "Factors Associated with Faculty use of Student Data for Instructional Improvement." *International Journal for the Scholarship of Teaching and Learning* 10, no. 2 (2016): 5. https://doi.org/10.20429/ijsotl.2016.100205.

Van Helvoort, Jos, Saskia Brand-Gruwel, Frank Huysmans, Ellen Sjoer. "Reliability and Validity Test of a Scoring Rubric for Information Literacy." *Journal of Documentation* 73, no. 2 (2017): 305–16. http://dx.doi.org/10.1108/JD-05-2016-0066.

Ward, John R., and Suzanne S. McCotter. "Reflection as a Visible Outcome for Preservice Teachers." *Teaching and Teacher Education* 20 (2004): 243–57. https://doi.org/10.1016/j.tate.2004.02.004.

19

How Do I Know If They Learned Anything?

Evidence-Based Learning and Reflective Teaching in a First-Year Learning Community

Jill Becker and Alison Olcott

Introduction

This case study illustrates the application of O'Brien's Scholarship of Teaching and Learning (SoTL) Compass[1] in the revision of curriculum to improve student learning in a first-year student learning community at the University of Kansas (KU). The University of Kansas is a four-year, public research university located in Lawrence, KS, offering 141 undergraduate majors in its ten degree-granting schools. In the fall of 2015, KU had an enrollment of 28,091 students of whom 19,224 were undergraduates and 4,187 were first-year students.

O'Brien's SoTL Compass represents an approach to SoTL research consisting of four interrelated questions that researchers can use to guide their teaching practice: "What will my students learn and why is it worth learning?," "Who are my students and how do students learn effectively?," "What can I do to support students to learn effectively?," and "How do I know if my teaching and my students' learning have been effective?" The authors of this case study used this Compass as a model to reflect on their teaching and their students' learning in an effort to modify and improve an integrated assignment for future iterations of the learning community. To align this project to the model, the authors modified O'Brien's Compass as illustrated in Figure 19.1.

This case study is organized around the four questions in the modified version (see figure 19.1) of O'Brien's SoTL Compass. First is a description of Learning Communities at KU and the students who are enrolled in the courses. Next, the authors explore their own

assumptions about their students and identify the key concepts and learning outcomes for the learning community. This is followed by an evidence-based analysis of student work on an integrated assignment from the first offering of the learning community in fall 2016. Finally, the authors discuss their revisions to the integrated assignment to improve learning in the second offering of the learning community in fall 2017.

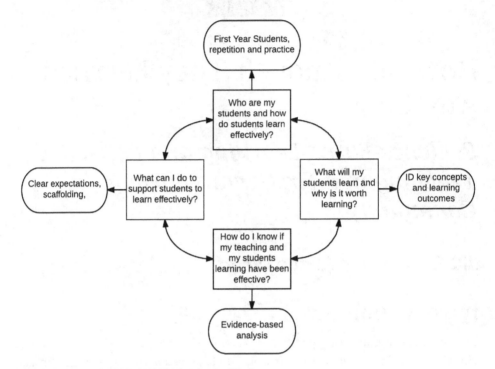

Figure 19.1. Modified O'Brien's SoTL Compass

Who Are My Students and How Do They Learn Effectively?

Learning Communities at KU are offered in one of two formats: residential or linked course. In residential Learning Communities, students enrolled in a small seminar course also live in the same residence hall. In a linked course learning community, a small seminar course is paired with a larger lecture course. This linked course learning community consists of a first-year orientation seminar (UNIV 101) taught by a librarian and a first-year geology course (GEOL 121) taught by a geology professor. Learning Communities at KU are designed to provide first-year students with high-impact educational experiences[2] in their first semester, including experiential learning, teamwork and problem-solving, as well as teaching students information literacy skills. These goals are met through an integrated assignment that assesses the transfer of skills, connection to experience and discipline, teamwork, reflection, self-assessment, and the application of information literacy skills.

While Learning Communities foster collaboration among students enrolled in the courses, they also require collaboration between the two course instructors. UNIV 101 supports GEOL 121 through the development of critical thinking, study skills, and information literacy. The connection between the two courses culminates in an integrated assignment that brings together key concepts from both courses and requires students to apply the concepts they have learned in both classes to new problems. Instructors who teach Learning Communities at KU participate in several course development workshops where they work together to design the integrated assignment. While these workshops did not explicitly use O'Brien's SoTL Compass, the questions "Who are my students and how do students learn effectively?" and "What will my students learn and why is it worth learning?" were central themes of these course development workshops.

Studies have revealed that teaching first-year students involves approaches that are different than teaching upper-level students; first-year students, particularly in their first semester, need to be offered classes that provide both academic rigor and scaffolded learning.[3] If first-year students are not offered challenging material, they will not engage with the material, and thus are not likely to persist;[4] however, the instructors also need to meet the students where they are and then structure the class so the students are guided to where they need to be. Effective first-year instruction, then, offers varied repetition, providing students multiple chances to practice and apply course material with prompt and detailed feedback as they are scaffolded toward deeper learning and understanding.[5]

Course development for Learning Communities at KU is cyclical in that both new and returning faculty and instructors participate in course design workshops in late spring and summer to prepare to deliver the courses in the fall semester. Since the authors of this chapter had already taught the learning community once, they utilized the course development workshops to examine the extent to which the integrated assignment both enabled and enhanced student learning.

What Will My Students Learn and Why Is It Worth Learning?

One of the core goals for the learning community is integrative learning. According to the Association of American Colleges & Universities (AAC&U) Integrative Learning VALUE Rubric,[6] "Integrative learning is an understanding and a disposition that a student builds across the curriculum and co-curriculum, from making simple connections among ideas and experiences to synthesizing and transferring learning to new, complex situations within and beyond the campus." The purpose of the integrated assignment is to bring together elements from both courses to make connections among ideas and experiences and to transfer learning to new situations. The integrated assignment for this learning community has four outcomes:

1. Connect experience and academic knowledge—students will synthesize connections between two museum visits (experiences) and their academic knowledge of geology.

2. Connect to discipline—students will demonstrate a deepened understanding of geology.

3. Transfer of skills—students will apply skills learned in one situation to a new situation.

4. Reflection and self-assessment—students will evaluate changes in their own learning over time.

When designing the integrated assignment for the fall 2016 semester, the course instructors both developed assignments that required students to visit a campus museum. In GEOL 121, students visited KU's Museum of Natural History where they examined fossils. In UNIV 101, students visited KU's Spencer Museum of Art where they selected a work of art that connected to GEOL 121 course content. The integrated assignment required students to write a short essay making connections between the two museum visits and geology. The researchers' hope was that this essay would meet outcomes one (connections to experience and academic knowledge) and two (connections to discipline). In addition to this essay, students completed an information literacy exam to meet outcome three (transfer of skills). There is an information literacy unit included in all UNIV 101 courses that introduces students to a variety of source types, teaches students to evaluate information sources for authority, and introduces students to the research cycle. For this exam, students were asked a series of questions that required them to transfer these skills to new questions related to geology. The final component was a short essay to meet outcome four (reflection and self-assessment). This essay asked students to reflect on both their individual strengths and how these strengths contributed to teamwork, group effectiveness, group challenges, and changes in learning over time.

The researchers identified the key concepts from both GEOL 121 and UNIV 101 that they wanted to see in their students' work. For GEOL 121, students should be able to recognize and evaluate how evolution and geological change are ongoing processes, and what implications these changes have on their daily lives. Students should also be able to discuss the frequency and effects of extinction on life and its evolution, including the possibility of a sixth mass extinction. Evidence of these key concepts would indicate a deepened understanding of geology. For UNIV 101, students should be able to apply information literacy skills to the context of geology, as reflected in their information literacy exam. In their final essay, they also should be able to reflect on their strengths, the strengths of their teammates, group effectiveness and challenges, and evaluate the changes in their own learning over the course of the semester.

How Do I Know If My Teaching and My Students' Learning Have Been Effective?

The evidence in this case study is the integrated assignments from the eight students who were enrolled in the learning community in the fall of 2016. It is important to note that the evidence-based analysis of student learning discussed in this case study was decoupled from the grading as it occurred months after the semester ended.

In order to determine whether or not teaching was effective, it was necessary to assess the students' written work. To do so, the researchers first worked together to identify the key concepts from both GEOL 121 and UNIV 101 that they wanted to see in the students' work (see table 19.1). These concepts were drawn from the learning outcomes for each class as well as the programmatic goals of the Learning Communities program at KU, and thus mastering these key concepts would indicate a deepened understanding of geology, information literacy, and the students' own strengths.

Table 19.1. Assessment of Students' Written Work

Concept	Class	Assignment Piece	Class Average of Instructor-assigned codes
Recognize and evaluate how evolution and geological change are ongoing processes and what implications these changes have on their daily lives.	GEOL 121	Art Minute	0.50
Discuss the frequency and effects of extinction on life and its evolution, including the possibility of a sixth mass extinction.	GEOL 121	Art Minute	0.375
Identifying source types	UNIV 101	Information literacy exam	0.375
Identifying primary research methods	UNIV 101	Information literacy exam	0.875
Understanding the research cycle	UNIV 101	Information literacy exam	0.45
Reading scholarly articles	UNIV 101	Information literacy exam	0.875
Explaining peer review	UNIV 101	Information literacy exam	0.50
Identifying an information need	UNIV 101	Information literacy exam	0.875
Connecting two objects	GEOL 121 UNIV 101	Connection to experience	0.625
Connect object to geology	GEOL 121 UNIV 101	Connection to experience	0.625
Deepen understanding of geology	GEOL 121 UNIV 101	Connection to experience	0.25
Deepen understanding of self	GEOL 121 UNIV 101	Connection to experience	0.50
Understanding the application of Strengths to their work	GEOL 121 UNIV 101	Self-assessment essay	0.625
Explaining group work successes and challenges	GEOL 121 UNIV 101	Self-assessment essay	0.50
Self-assessment of learning and change in learning	GEOL 121 UNIV 101	Self-assessment essay	0.75

Once the researchers agreed on the framework for what effective student learning would look like, student work was coded depending if students attained (1) or failed to attain (0) the goal. This coding was done individually by each faculty member and then any discrepancy between the two codes was discussed. This process ensured that the final assigned code reflected both disciplinary viewpoints (geology and information literacy) about what successful student learning looked like. These values were then averaged in each category across all of the students.

The integrated assignment began with a visit to the campus art museum. For this assignment (the Art Minute), students selected an artwork from the museum and wrote a short essay describing, in detail, how the selected piece connected with geology topics. The only guidance toward making connections to the discipline of geology was a bullet point in the assignment prompt that said, "Describe, in detail, how the selected piece connects with your Geology 121 topic." Only half of the students (0.50) recognized and evaluated how evolution and geological change are ongoing processes and what implications these changes have on the students' daily lives, and even fewer (0.375) discussed the frequency and effects of extinction on life and its evolution, including the possibility of a sixth mass extinction. On the whole, students exhibited a very superficial understanding of geology and loose connections, at best, between the two museum visits.

The next section of the integrated assignment was an exam that required students to apply information literacy skills to their geology course. For example, in UNIV 101, students were introduced to a variety of source types, including scholarly sources, learned about peer-review, discussed primary research methods, practiced reading scholarly research articles, and learned how to identify information needs. The exam included questions to test this knowledge. Based on the instructor-assigned codes, students generally demonstrated a good understanding of primary research methods (0.875), reading scholarly articles (0.875), and identifying an information need (0.875). One major shortcoming on this exam was students' understanding of source types (0.375). This was disappointing, considering several days were spent evaluating different source types in the context of UNIV 101. Another weak spot was students' understanding of the peer-review process with only half (0.50) of students attaining key concepts. Some students described peer-review as experts providing their thoughts and opinions rather than an expert review of evidence and facts. Additionally, when asked to outline the steps of the research process to a research question in the field of geology, some students (0.55) simply repeated the steps learned in UNIV 101 rather than frame the steps in the context of geology.

Finally, students were asked to write a reflection and self-assessment. Students fell short when discussing their own strengths (.625) and were even weaker (.50) when discussing the strengths of others and how this impacted group effectiveness and/or created challenges within the group. And while a majority of students (.75) did discuss how their learning changed over the course of the semester, their writing did not convey a realization that learning occurred nor any specific growth moments or deepened understanding of their learning.

What Can I Do to Support Students to Learn Effectively?

One of the main takeaways from the evidence-based analysis was the need to be more explicit in the integrated assignment prompt, to provide examples of the kinds of connections the instructors expect students to make, and to scaffold the steps toward the integrated assignment. Both instructors agreed to continue the museum visits because they are generally enjoyed by students and create an experiential learning opportunity. To make the experience more meaningful and targeted to the learning community, the instructors worked with the art museum staff to identify specific works from the collection that related to the themes from the geology course (climate change, evolution, extinction, etc.). The museum had a special exhibit containing works related to the environmental impact on soils that the class could visit as part of this assignment. In addition to limiting student choice of artwork to works connected to course content, students were also required to watch a video on climate change and focus on one reading from GEOL 121 in preparation for the art museum visit. Finally, to help the students make connections between both museum visits, the instructors asked the students to read an article on "Cabinets of Curiosities"[7] and write a concluding essay about museum collections and how they deepen understanding of course content. It is the researchers' expectation that scaffolding the assignment to include specific works of art and supporting materials to add context to the experience will provide the necessary structure for students to make deeper connections to geology.

The exam portion of the integrated assignment did not need much revision, but rather revisions were made to the delivery of this content throughout the information literacy unit in UNIV 101. The question on the exam about peer-review resulted in multiple student responses about the "opinions of experts." Next time, more time will be spent discussing source types in different disciplines and that peer-review is not about the thoughts and ideas of experts but rather about evidence and facts. Last, in the exam, students were asked to apply the steps of the research process to a hypothetical research question in geology. Most student responses just repeated the steps, rather than put the steps into a disciplinary context. The UNIV 101 instructor modified the portion of the information literacy unit that teaches the research cycle to include examples of research in different disciplines and asks students to think about these steps using real-life research examples. The research cycle is modeled by course instructors, and sample research questions are developed and discussed in class to provide an opportunity to practice articulating the steps with a discipline-specific example.

At the beginning of the semester, students were asked about their understandings of geology topics, including climate change, evolution, and extinction. For the new integrated assignment, students are presented with data collected from the class at the beginning of the semester and asked to discuss how their learning and understanding of these concepts have changed over the course of the semester. Additionally, the final portion of the new integrated assignment expands on learning in terms of information sources and communicating science. Students are asked to consider the types of information sources that expose the general public to science and compare these to the scholarly sources and readings from their GEOL 121 class. Through this new integrated assignment, the instructors hope to see the deepened understanding of geology that they did not see in the first offering of the learning community.

Conclusion

Using actual student work as data, the instructors assessed whether or not the goals of the learning community were met. What began with a simple "What worked, what didn't work?" question resulted in a redesign of learning experiences to better measure teaching effectiveness and student learning. Engaging in SoTL via assessment of student work in a learning community is ideal since the outcome measured through the integrated assignment does not focus on content but rather the application of skills such as critical thinking, information literacy, and the students' own reflections on their learning. In reviewing student work, the authors focused on the application of key concepts and how to improve both the integrated assignment prompt and the delivery of key concepts throughout both courses. This process was a good reminder of the need to be explicit and specific in assignment prompts, in particular for first-year students.

ENDNOTES

1. Mia O'Brien, "Navigating the SoTL Landscape: A Compass, Map, and Some Tools for Getting Started," *International Journal for the Scholarship of Teaching and Learning*, 2, no.2 (2008): 1.
2. George D. Kuh, *High-Impact Educational Practices: What They Are, Who Has Access to Them, and Why They Matter* (Washington, DC: Association of American Colleges & Universities, 2008).
3. Bette Lasere Erickson, Calvin B. Peters, and Diane Weltner Strommer, *Teaching First-Year College Students* (San Francisco: John Wiley & Sons, 2009).
4. Thomas F. Nelson Laird, Daniel Chen, and George D. Kuh, "Classroom Practices at Institutions with Higher-than-Expected Persistence Rates: What Student Engagement Data Tell Us," *New Directions for Teaching and Learning* 115 (2008): 85.
5. Erickson, Peters, and Strommer, *Teaching First-Year College Students*.
6. Association of American Colleges and Universities, "Inquiry and Analysis VALUE Rubric," 2009, https://www.aacu.org/value/rubrics/inquiry-analysis.
7. Melody Amsel-Arieli, "Cabinets of Curiosities (Wunderkammers)," *History Magazine* 13, no. 6 (August/September 2012): 40.

BIBLIOGRAPHY

Amsel-Arieli, Melody. "Cabinets of Curiosities (Wunderkammers)," *History Magazine* 13, no. 6 (August/September 2012): 40.

Association of American Colleges and Universities. "Inquiry and Analysis VALUE Rubric." 2009. https://www.aacu.org/value/rubrics/inquiry-analysis.

Erickson, Bette Lasere, Calvin B. Peters, and Diane Weltner Strommer. *Teaching First-Year College*

Students. San Francisco, CA: John Wiley & Sons, 2009.

Kuh, George D. *Excerpt from High-Impact Educational Practices: What They Are, Who Has Access to Them, and Why They Matter*. Washington, DC: Association of American Colleges & Universities, 2008.

Laird, Thomas F. Nelson, Daniel Chen, and George D. Kuh. "Classroom Practices at Institutions with Higher-than-Expected Persistence Rates: What Student Engagement Data Tell Us." *New Directions for Teaching and Learning* 115 (2008): 85–99.

O'Brien, Mia. "Navigating the SoTL Landscape: A Compass, Map, and Some Tools for Getting Started. *International Journal for the Scholarship of Teaching and Learning, 2*, no. 2 (2008): 1–20.

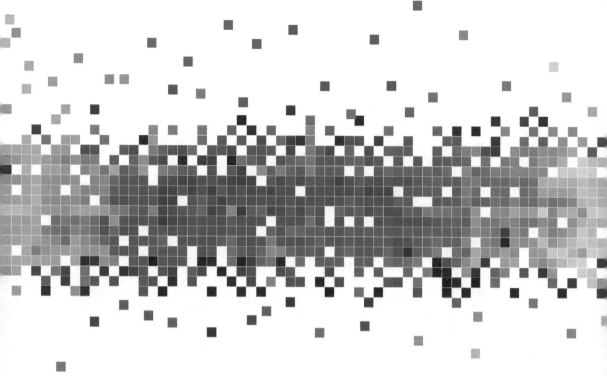

Section IV
SoTL as Professional Development

SoTL Difference:

The Value of Incorporating SoTL into Librarian Professional Development

Peter Felten, Margy MacMillan, and Joan Ruelle

This essay is the product of a collaboration between three authors who bring diverse understandings of SoTL, librarianship, and professional development. Writing this has been a form of professional development, encouraging the authors to think more deeply about discipline-based practices and how they connect to student learning, increasing understanding of each other's disciplines, and transforming that joint reflection into work that may impact teaching.

Introduction

The Scholarship of Teaching and Learning (SoTL) is by definition a form of professional development. In one of the first articles published on SoTL, Shulman[1] emphasized a "pragmatic" rationale for this form of inquiry: "By engaging in purposive reflection, documentation, assessment and analysis of teaching and learning, and doing so in a more public and accessible manner, we not only support the improvement of our own teaching" but we also contribute to a community of scholarly teachers. Put another way, SoTL always aims both to enhance individual practice and to contribute to the broader "teaching commons."[2]

The purposes of SoTL are clear, even though a canonical definition of SoTL does not exist.[3] That's not entirely surprising since SoTL is an applied form of scholarship that tends to take on the distinct "disciplinary styles" of its practitioners and has been adapted to a diverse set of "domains" around the world.[4] A historian doing SoTL at a US community college likely will—and probably should—ask different questions and use different research methodologies than a psychologist or a chemist—or a librarian—at a South African

research university. In an effort to make room in the "big tent" of SoTL for this variation, in 2011, three scholars at the Carnegie Foundation for the Advancement of Teaching crafted an expansive frame for this emerging field:

> The scholarship of teaching and learning encompasses a broad set of practices that engage teachers in looking closely and critically at student learning for the purpose of improving their own courses and programs. It is perhaps best understood as an approach that marries scholarly inquiry to any of the intellectual tasks that comprise the work of teaching.[5]

Echoing Shulman, this definition reinforces the connection between SoTL and professional development. This link now routinely appears in the literature. Educational developers around the world have critically analyzed the alignment between their field and SoTL.[6] And a recent major study by educational researchers took as a foundational premise that "faculty development, understood in the scholarship of teaching and learning (SoTL) sense, offers teaching faculty opportunities to learn new approaches, technologies, and more."[7] In short, SoTL is not a well-defined "thing" but its fundamental purpose is the improvement of teaching and learning; SoTL, thus, is at its core an approach to professional development for all those who teach in higher education, regardless of the setting.

Not all professional development, however, is SoTL; instead, SoTL enacts a distinctly scholarly approach to professional development. As such, SoTL-informed professional development reflects the essential criteria for any scholarly activity:[8]

1. clear goals—the activity has explicit and clear purposes;
2. adequate preparation—the activity draws on relevant scholarship and expertise;
3. appropriate methods—the activity is conducted in ways that align its goals and context, and that reflect good practice in the field;
4. significant results—the activity makes (or aims to make) a meaningful contribution to an area of study or practice;
5. effective presentation—the purposes, methods, and results of the activity are shared with appropriate audiences; and
6. reflective critique—those involved in the activity assess their experiences and outcomes to inform future action.

Scholarly professional development should embody these criteria, but they are not a simple recipe for individual action or strategic programming. Instead, these sketch the outlines of what scholarly professional development might be, leaving plenty of room for variation to reflect the local contexts and the particular needs of individuals and groups involved in this work.

Even within this diversity of practices and contexts, a growing body of evidence suggests that SoTL contributes to improved teaching and learning—that SoTL is an efficacious approach to professional development. Uncovering and documenting this connection has been vexing because it requires establishing a causal chain between SoTL, teaching practices, and student learning. Leading scholars have vigorously debated whether and how SoTL can be proven to yield enhanced student learning, as some see a compelling case[9] and others are more cautious.[10] Significantly, a recent longitudinal mixed-methods study at Carleton College and Washington State University provides rich and compelling evidence that engaging in SoTL-framed professional development contributes to significantly enhanced learning for undergraduates.[11] In short, research demonstrates that SoTL leads to positive changes in teaching behaviors and that these changes likely contribute to deepened student learning. This marks SoTL as an evidence-based approach to professional development for everyone who teaches in academic settings.

Finding a Way into SoTL

If SoTL sounds familiar to librarians, it should. As Cara Bradley noted in 2009, "The SoTL movement slightly reframes, but in large part reaffirms and validates, the type of research that many librarians already do."[12] A parallel statement could easily be made about SoTL reaffirming and validating but also reframing the kinds of professional development librarians already do. While methods of teaching and research are discussed in library conference sessions, countless articles, and an increasing number of webinars, MOOCs and other online learning opportunities that librarians count as professional development, SoTL adds layers of depth and breadth. SoTL provides opportunities to deepen understanding, practice, and contributions to higher education through prompting reflection, opening up new questions, and requiring librarians to explain themselves beyond the narrow confines of library literature. SoTL encourages librarians to broaden their horizons, their networks, and their concepts of teaching, learning, and research—and in so doing, to widen their sphere of influence.

Engaging in SoTL also leads inevitably to professional development for librarians. Whether reading or hearing about SoTL research, collecting materials to support it, or conducting it as a solo or collaborative activity, SoTL requires learning—exploring new methodologies, new literatures, and making new connections within and beyond the library, the institution, and existing personal networks. And while the most obvious connections between SoTL and librarianship may arise from information literacy work, the broader understanding of learners and learning that SoTL encourages can encompass all aspects of library operations from facilities design to policies, usability to staff training, and work in partnership with other campus units. Following Hutchings, Huber, and Ciccone,[13] SoTL encompasses the broad set of practices that engage librarians in any of the intellectual tasks that comprise the work of librarians in supporting learning.

Opportunities for librarians to engage SoTL as professional development can arise from multiple entry points such as existing interpersonal relationships, liaison roles with academic departments, formal and informal communities of practice, and reading the literature. Just as there is no single right way to do SoTL as a librarian, there also is no need to take extensive training before jumping in, nor is there only one way to begin engaging in SoTL. As a first step, however, it is useful to find out who is doing what with SoTL on campus. Librarians can look to their institution's teaching center or at faculty development opportunities around innovative pedagogy, higher education programs, and schools of education; in fact, most of the case studies in this section involved the campus center for teaching and learning as a resource or as a site for participation in SoTL. Librarians can leave the safe confines of the library, attend presentations about SoTL on campus, even (and especially) if they are the only librarian to do so. Not only will they learn more about SoTL but colleagues who did not expect their presence may gain a deeper understanding of the ways that librarians teach and the stake they have in student learning. Librarians can determine who is doing SoTL on campus, then engage these colleagues in conversation about their teaching just as liaisons do about research; at a minimum, they will appreciate the interest in their work, and these connections may develop into opportunities for future collaboration.

SoTL can be a solo pursuit, and often starts out that way as with any exploration of new domains. However, SoTL also benefits from collaboration, whether through communities of practice within the library where SoTL can provide a lens to study practices and innovations, such as the ACRL *Framework for Information Literacy for Higher Education*, or through conversations on Twitter with colleagues in faraway places who have similar interests. SoTL can provide a common language for these discussions and can also offer some epistemological distance from previous research or contentious positions, moving consideration beyond the library and into a broader arena of efforts to improve teaching and learning. Reading and discussing SoTL literature in order to apply it to library contexts exposes participants in such groups to different perspectives on issues that impact learning, potentially leading to less defensive discussions. There are several examples in this section and in the literature of library-based communities of practice that effectively applied a SoTL lens to the ACRL *Framework*, moving past debates within the profession to wider considerations of learning. For instance, DeFrain, Delserone, Lorang, Riehle, and Anaya provide a rich example of this in their case study. In their library-based community of practice, they developed a shared understanding of key learning bottlenecks, which led to collaborative SoTL research projects, the results of which fed back into the group's discussions and enriched understanding across the community. Other case studies in this section detail additional approaches to and benefits from using the Community of Practice theory and model. In some, like Fyn and Shinaberger's, Kirker's, and Laverty and Saleh's, the library participants become the learners studied in a SoTL project, a rewarding area for further research.

The most obvious benefit of engaging with SoTL as professional development is participation in wider communities of practice beyond the library. It quickly becomes apparent that librarians are not the only members of the academy who feel underprepared by their formal education for the teaching that is a regular part of their work (see the case studies by Durham, Hess, and Fyn and Shinaberger as examples). Nor are they the only ones who want to engage more deeply in scholarly teaching, in bringing theory to bear on practice. Participating in SoTL discussions, workshops, or research as a learner alongside others in the institution allows librarians to see and be seen as equally committed partners in advancing student learning. In their case study, Weeks and Johnson highlight this benefit both to the librarians, who learn more about disciplinary approaches to teaching by participating in these communities, and to the institutional colleagues who gain insights into library work and the strengths librarians can bring. This, in turn, can foster more integrated working relationships through which the library may gain a higher profile. Teaching faculty who learn about library teaching through collaborative partnerships and participation in communities of practice may be far better positioned to speak to the teaching impact of libraries than librarians themselves. In an environment where decision-makers may question the continuing relevance of libraries, developing meaningful connections across the institution and contributing more visibly to local and international understandings of student learning isn't just a benefit, it may be a requirement for survival.

The library also gains from knowledge brought back from these wider discussions or readings. Roxå, Mårtensson, and Alveteg[14] describe this as cluster-to-cluster communication, critical for enhancing teaching cultures on campus. While they acknowledge the usefulness of "brokers"—peripheral participants who serve as conduits between clusters of professionals—they highlight the need for "practitione rs with the interest and the capacity to do so from the centre of one cluster to the centre of another." Librarians involved in SoTL communities serve as bridges to the center of librarian communities in institutions, associations, or interest groups to strengthen mutual understanding. They contribute not just to the professional development of individual librarians but to the development of the profession itself. SoTL offers a rich network of connections across the academy and affirms teaching as a scholarly endeavor. The case study by Hess demonstrates how transformative this kind of role can be for both the library and broader campus supports for teaching. Seeing librarians active within SoTL reframes the profession's authentic scholarship as a contribution not just to libraries but to student learning—a fundamental purpose of higher education—in a way that librarians rarely recognize their own work.

Exploring the literature of SOTL through reading and collection development also provides opportunities to reframe professional development in promising ways. The case study by Cobolet, Grolimund, Hardebolle, Isaac, Panes, and Salamin alludes to the value of engaging with the wide array of literature about teaching that exists beyond library publications. Becoming familiar with SoTL, like any new liaison area, requires understanding how and where it is disseminated and accessed. Librarians' understanding of international publishing patterns and other aspects of scholarly communication can support SoTL work on campus by highlighting ways into the work for disciplinary specialists, illuminating gaps in the literature that suggest opportunities for future research and identifying potential venues for publication. Weeks and Johnson describe a SoTL project around rebuilding a course using open access resources in their case study, another area where librarians have much to contribute. SoTL research is widely dispersed through disciplinary and SoTL-based publications as well as on institutional websites and other online "gray literature" sites, making it a pleasantly challenging field to collect. Many new SoTL scholars (and, indeed, many experienced ones) are often less aware of the SoTL literature than that of their home disciplines, so librarians have a lot to offer in developing and promoting strong collections that support work on understanding learning within and across the disciplines. Through becoming members of SoTL communities, librarians can inform and strengthen SoTL work by deepening the relationship between research and the literature, developing greater familiarity with how other faculty conduct research inside and outside their home disciplines. In Durham's case study, she notes the range of ways into SoTL afforded by the literature, webinars, and a variety of formal and informal learning opportunities. Similarly, Cobolet et al. recount how a role supporting a journal group became a venue for much deeper library participation in campus SoTL initiatives.

The reliance on cross-disciplinary conversations is one of the critical differences between SoTL as professional development and most library scholarship. While some SoTL work, like information literacy (IL) research, is conceived of and disseminated for disciplinary insiders, much of it is developed to be communicated in the what Huber and Morreale[15] described as a "trading zone," with a focus on what will be useful for educators in multiple contexts. SoTL becomes a sort of common second language for many of its practitioners, a tool for exploring and understanding underlying similarities in teaching and learning concepts separate from the confusion of different disciplinary terms. This communication also demands a greater explanation, both what Huber and Hutchings[16] would call "thick description of context" and greater attention to explaining the rationale behind different ways of teaching and understandings of learning. All of this can make SoTL literature more accessible to readers new to the field. In writing up the results of SoTL, the requirement for thick descriptions has the added value of requiring librarians to articulate their own underlying assumptions and test them with a non-expert audience. Thinking through and decoding teaching motivations and processes, the rationale for the decisions made in teaching and how those decisions affect learning, is useful professional development in its own right.

Of course, reading the SoTL literature may also lead to further professional development as librarians integrate findings from research in non-library teaching into their own library practice. Doing so requires at the very least a deeper consideration of other teaching environments and may entail learning new teaching skills, developing alternative assessment methods, and integrating new technologies. The results of such changes may also spark SoTL investigations, but engaging in SoTL does not necessarily mean carrying out original research. Professional development rewards accrue from the time librarians start noticing the generative conversations SoTL provokes.

If a librarian does decide to take on a SoTL inquiry, professional development opportunities arise from asking new kinds of questions, exploring new ways of finding and analyzing evidence, and disseminating work to audiences beyond librarians. SoTL welcomes research that uses a wide variety of methodologies from close reading to statistical analysis and examines teaching and learning in a wide range of settings, including libraries. Librarians who present at SoTL conferences report feeling very much at home, and their sessions and posters attract attention from those who teach across the academy.[17] Librarians in many contexts are conducting SoTL investigations either on their own or in partnership with faculty outside of the library, and several of the case studies in this section provide evidence of the benefits of this work, both in terms of contributing to knowledge and improving learning and also in terms of developing collaborative relationships across institutions.

Reframing SoTL as Library Professional Development

Peter Felten, one of the authors of this essay, has developed "5 Principles of Good Practice in SoTL" that may help distinguish SoTL from other approaches to teaching, learning, and professional development. SoTL,[18] he suggests, has five essential characteristics:

- Inquiry focused on student learning
- Grounded in context
- Methodologically sound
- Conducted in partnership with students
- Appropriately public

Each of these characteristics carries with it opportunities for librarian professional development. Considering a focus on student learning brings requirements for understanding forms of evidence and deeper insights into what learning is, how it looks, and how all the attendant factors beyond what the teacher is doing may affect it. To be grounded in context requires the researcher to understand more deeply the environment in which they teach and the learners with whom they work, uncovering the factors that make learning in this situation unique and those transferable to or from the settings of other studies. To do work that is methodologically sound may require deeper engagement with familiar methods, or an exploration of new methods, and a clear understanding of how they align with research questions.[19] To truly work in partnership with students may provide some of the greatest opportunities for professional development and engage some aspects of critical practice as researchers negotiate power dynamics and ethics in developing questions, methods, and dissemination that considers the students as those to practice research *with* rather than *on*.[20] Finally, making work appropriately public, as Durham notes in her case study, may stretch skills in new directions and engage librarians with unfamiliar discourses in disciplinary conferences, student-facing blogs and reports to audiences beyond librarianship. In any mode, librarians must consider what they need to decode for non-librarian audiences, a highly productive form of reflection. Below are three examples of what library SoTL projects could look like and the kinds of professional development they might lead to.

- A liaison librarian who has a longstanding partnership with a faculty member senses that their comfortable groove has become a rut. After discussing their ideas at a SoTL community of practice meeting and gaining several ideas from peers, they investigate the transfer of learning from the workshop to the assignment by asking students to complete a research log, reflecting on specific prompts as they complete their major research assignment. The first prompt asks students to describe their approach to finding information for their everyday activities, to assist the researchers in understanding more about this particular group of students. The final reflection prompt asks students to describe a research project they would commission from the librarian or faculty member about how students use information. The reflections aim to illuminate several bottlenecks in learning that will inform teaching in subsequent iterations of the course and could be the subject of future studies. The researchers schedule follow-up focus groups led by a senior student, asking what students recalled and used from the workshop, and what, if anything, they transferred to work in other classes. The researchers also analyze the students' coursework using grounded theory and close reading to see what markers they could establish that linked the processes outlined in the research logs in the final products. The librarian, the faculty member, and the student research partner present their findings informally to the student participants over a voluntary coffee and doughnuts meeting, at a workshop during the library faculty professional development day, and at a SoTL conference. For this presentation, they meticulously write up the assignments and activities in the class as well and develop a demographic profile of the students to ground the study in context; in doing so, using data from the study, they discovered opportunities to improve the flow of the course through better scaffolding of the activities.

- The librarian develops greater familiarity with IRB protocols, qualitative methods, designing effective prompts for reflection, research partnerships, writing for publication in SoTL journals, and using social media for wider dissemination, including hosting a Twitter chat.
- A library dean is seeking greater collaboration with other campus academic units to support student success, particularly the writing center, a math tutoring lab, and career services, all of which are now located in a new building with the library. Her key questions focus on what differences students perceive between these supports, what they expect from them in terms of impact on learning, and what they see as the costs and benefits to learning associated with asking for help from these personnel; for instance, is there any stigma attached to asking for help with writing or math? She develops a collaborative study involving personnel from the library and the other areas. Groups of students in each year of study are surveyed electronically about their awareness and use of each campus service to get a large-scale view of issues and sentiment. The survey includes two free response questions for each support area: Who do you think benefits from the service? How does the service impact learning? Data from the survey is supplemented by having trained students interview a representative sample of students to identify patterns in perceptions, barriers, and motivations. Results are disseminated through infographics at each service

point, in meetings with every level of university administration, during workshops with faculty and staff, in new student orientation materials, and in presentations at national conferences. Results also are used to inform marketing efforts aimed to influence student perceptions of both academic help-seeking behaviors and the services of each academic support unit. All of the research partners enhance their skills in survey development, statistical analysis, ethical research, interviewing, and dissemination—and a stronger community is created among the various units and people who work in the new building.

- A librarian wonders why students have trouble with generating synonyms to use in a search. He reads SoTL work on vocabulary building, tries something new in class, documents how students employ the new approaches he has taught, and tells his colleagues about the results. In this simple case, the librarian gains familiarity with SoTL literature, experiments with a new teaching method, and better understands student search behaviors. He also serves as something of a role model for his peers who may now develop their own SoTL inquiries, and his new knowledge contributes to improved teaching across the library.

Conclusion

In the early publication on SoTL introduced at the beginning of this chapter, Shulman[21] asked a fundamental question: *Why* are we doing SoTL at all? He reminded his readers that they already were plenty busy and already should be engaged in professional development. Academic librarians are familiar with calls to do more with less, to better demonstrate the value librarians contribute to institutions, to respond to existential threats raised by claims that libraries are no longer necessary, to constantly stay current through engaging in multiple forms of library-focused professional development, and to continue to be engaged scholars and contributors to the profession. So why should librarians make the extra effort to be active in SoTL?

Shulman argued—and the authors of this chapter agree—that SoTL *deepens* individual efforts and *connects* professional development to a broader teaching commons. SoTL improves teaching on a day-to-day basis, whether it be for-credit classes, one-shot instruction sessions, ongoing collaborations with teaching faculty or the one-to-one teaching in research consultations. SoTL also deepens what professional development means for librarians. In librarianship, professional development is often understood as development of the individual professional (through participation in webinars, trainings, and professional societies). Through collaborations, communities of practice, and the literature, the common language of SoTL integrates library-based teaching more firmly into the wider discussions in higher education, building stronger communities among librarians while simultaneously raising librarians' profile as teachers and scholars even as it deepens their practice.

It can be difficult sometimes for librarians to justify the time, or, in some cases, funding, for professional development that does not carry an explicit library connection. If it is necessary to make the case to oneself or to administrators, SoTL provides a pathway to explicitly connect library teaching to student learning in a way that may be both understood and valued by faculty colleagues and administration across the institution. That pathway serves the development of both the individual professional and the profession as a whole. It embeds librarians' work within scholarly networks and communities that connect individual efforts to the long-term aspirations of libraries and higher education to transform students through better understanding of how they learn.

ENDNOTES

1. Lee Shulman, "From Minsk To Pinsk: Why A Scholarship of Teaching and Learning?," *Journal of the Scholarship of Teaching and Learning* 1, no. 1 (2000).
2. Mary Taylor Huber and Pat Hutchings, *The Advancement of Learning: Building the Teaching Commons*, A Carnegie Foundation Report on the Scholarship of Teaching and Learning in Higher Education; Carnegie Foundation Special Report (San Francisco: Jossey-Bass, 2005).
3. Mary Taylor Huber and Sherwyn P. Morreale, Carnegie Foundation for the Advancement of Teaching, and American Association for Higher Education, *Disciplinary Styles in the Scholarship of Teaching and Learning: Exploring Common Ground* (Washington, DC: American Association for Higher Education, 2002).
4. S. Booth and L. C. Woollacott, "On the Constitution of SoTL: Its Domains and Contexts," *Higher Education*, June 6, 2017, 1–15, https://doi.org/10.1007/s10734-017-0156-7.
5. Pat Hutchings, Mary Huber, and Anthony Ciccone, "Getting There: An Integrative Vision of the Scholarship of Teaching and Learning," *International Journal for the Scholarship of Teaching and Learning* 5, no. 1 (January 1, 2011), https://doi.org/10.20429/ijsotl.2011.050131.
6. Johan Geertsema, "Academic Development, SoTL and Educational Research," *International Journal for Academic Development* 21, no. 2 (April 2, 2016): 122–34, https://doi.org/10.1080/1360144X.2016.1175144; Natasha Kenny, Celia Popovic, Jill McSweeney, Kris Knorr, Carolyn Hoessler, Shirley Hall, Nobuko Fujita, and Eliana El Khoury, "Drawing on the Principles of SoTL to Illuminate a Path Forward for the Scholarship of Educational Development," *The Canadian Journal for the Scholarship of Teaching and Learning* 8, no. 2 (June 16, 2017), https://doi.org/10.5206/cjsotl-rcacea.2017.2.10; Peter Felten and Nancy Chick, "Is SoTL a Signature Pedagogy of Educational Development?," *To Improve the Academy* 37, no. 1 (2018), 4-16, https://doi.org/10.1002/tia2.20077.
7. William Condon, Ellen R. Iverson, Cathryn A. Manduca, Carol Rutz, Gudrun Willett, Mary Taylor Huber, and Richard H. Haswell, *Faculty Development and Student Learning: Assessing the Connections*, Scholarship of Teaching and Learning; Scholarship of Teaching and Learning (Bloomington: Indiana University Press, 2016).
8. Charles E. Glassick, Mary Taylor Huber, Gene I. Maeroff, Ernest L. Boyer, and Carnegie Foundation for the Advancement of Teaching, *Scholarship Assessed: Evaluation of the Professoriate*, 1st ed., A Special Report; Special Report (Carnegie Foundation for the Advancement of Teaching) (San Francisco: Jossey-Bass, 1997).
9. Hutchings, Huber, and Ciccone, "Getting There"; Daniel Bernstein, "How SoTL-Active Faculty Members Can Be Cosmopolitan Assets to an Institution," *Teaching & Learning Inquiry: The ISSOTL Journal* 1, no. 1 (2013): 35–40, https://doi.org/10.2979/teachlearninqu.1.1.35.
10. Keith Trigwell, "Evidence of the Impact of Scholarship of Teaching and Learning Purposes,"

Teaching & Learning Inquiry 1, no. 1 (March 1, 2013): 95–105, https://doi.org/10.20343/teachlearninqu.1.1.95.

11. Condon et al., *Faculty Development and Student Learning*.
12. Cara Bradley, "The Scholarship of Teaching and Learning: Opportunities for Librarians," *College & Research Libraries News* 70, no. 5 (2009): 276–278.
13. Hutchings, Huber, and Ciccone, "Getting There."
14. Torgny Roxå , Katarina Mårtensson, and Mattias Alveteg, "Understanding and Influencing Teaching and Learning Cultures at University: A Network Approach," *Higher Education: The International Journal of Higher Education and Educational Planning* 62, no. 1 (July 2011): 99–111, https://doi.org/10.1007/s10734-010-9368-9.
15. Huber et al., *Disciplinary Styles in the Scholarship of Teaching and Learning*.
16. Huber and Hutchings, *The Advancement of Learning*.
17. Charissa Jefferson, Margy Elizabeth MacMillan, Ann Manginelli, Caitlin McClurg, and Brian Winterman, "ISSOTL 2016: Exploring Opportunities for Librarians," *Journal of Information Literacy* 11, no. 1 (June 5, 2017): 227, https://doi.org/10.11645/11.1.2174.
18. Peter Felten, "Principles of Good Practice in SoTL," *Teaching & Learning Inquiry: The ISSOTL Journal* 1, no. 1 (2013): 121–25, https://doi.org/10.2979/teachlearninqu.1.1.121.
19. Janice Miller-Young and Michelle Yeo, "Conceptualizing and Communicating SoTL: A Framework for the Field," *Teaching & Learning Inquiry* 3, no. 2 (September 1, 2015): 37–53, https://doi.org/10.20343/teachlearninqu.3.2.37.
20. Alison Cook-Sather, Catherine Bovill, and Peter Felten, *Engaging Students as Partners in Learning and Teaching* (San Francisco: Jossey-Bass, 2014).
21. Shulman, "From Minsk To Pinsk."

BIBLIOGRAPHY

Bernstein, Daniel. "How SoTL-Active Faculty Members Can Be Cosmopolitan Assets to an Institution." *Teaching & Learning Inquiry: The ISSOTL Journal* 1, no. 1 (2013): 35–40. https://doi.org/10.2979/teachlearninqu.1.1.35.

Booth, S., and L. C. Woollacott. "On the Constitution of SoTL: Its Domains and Contexts." *Higher Education*, June 6, 2017, 1–15. https://doi.org/10.1007/s10734-017-0156-7.

Bradley, Cara. "The Scholarship of Teaching and Learning: Opportunities for Librarians." *College & Research Libraries News* 70, no. 5 (2009): 276–278.

Condon, William, Ellen R. Iverson, Cathryn A. Manduca, Carol Rutz, Gudrun Willett, Mary Taylor Huber, and Richard H. Haswell. *Faculty Development and Student Learning: Assessing the Connections*. Scholarship of Teaching and Learning; Scholarship of Teaching and Learning. Bloomington: Indiana University Press, 2016.

Cook-Sather, Alison, Catherine Bovill, and Peter Felten. *Engaging Students as Partners in Learning and Teaching*. San Francisco: Jossey-Bass, 2014.

Felten, Peter. "Principles of Good Practice in SoTL." *Teaching & Learning Inquiry: The ISSOTL Journal* 1, no. 1 (2013): 121–25. https://doi.org/10.2979/teachlearninqu.1.1.121.

Felten, Peter, and Nancy Chick. "Is SoTL a Signature Pedagogy of Educational Development?" *To Improve the Academy* 37, no. 1 (2018), 4–16. https://doi.org/10.1002/tia2.20077.

Geertsema, Johan. "Academic Development, SoTL and Educational Research." *International Journal for Academic Development* 21, no. 2 (April 2, 2016): 122–34. https://doi.org/10.1080/1360144X.2016.1175144.

Glassick, Charles E., Mary Taylor Huber, Gene I. Maeroff, Ernest L. Boyer, and Carnegie Foundation for the Advancement of Teaching. *Scholarship Assessed: Evaluation of the Professoriate*.

1st ed. A Special Report; Special Report (Carnegie Foundation for the Advancement of Teaching). San Francisco: Jossey-Bass, 1997.

Huber, Mary Taylor, and Pat Hutchings. *The Advancement of Learning: Building the Teaching Commons*. A Carnegie Foundation Report on the Scholarship of Teaching and Learning in Higher Education; Carnegie Foundation Special Report. San Francisco: Jossey-Bass, 2005.

Huber, Mary Taylor, Sherwyn P. Morreale, Carnegie Foundation for the Advancement of Teaching, and American Association for Higher Education. *Disciplinary Styles in the Scholarship of Teaching and Learning: Exploring Common Ground*. Washington, DC: American Association for Higher Education, 2002.

Hutchings, Pat, Mary Huber, and Anthony Ciccone. "Getting There: An Integrative Vision of the Scholarship of Teaching and Learning." *International Journal for the Scholarship of Teaching and Learning* 5, no. 1 (January 1, 2011). https://doi.org/10.20429/ijsotl.2011.050131.

Jefferson, Charissa, Margy Elizabeth MacMillan, Ann Manginelli, Caitlin McClurg, and Brian Winterman. "ISSOTL 2016: Exploring Opportunities for Librarians." *Journal of Information Literacy* 11, no. 1 (June 5, 2017): 227. https://doi.org/10.11645/11.1.2174.

Kenny, Natasha, Celia Popovic, Jill McSweeney, Kris Knorr, Carolyn Hoessler, Shirley Hall, Nobuko Fujita, and Eliana El Khoury. "Drawing on the Principles of SoTL to Illuminate a Path Forward for the Scholarship of Educational Development." *The Canadian Journal for the Scholarship of Teaching and Learning* 8, no. 2 (June 16, 2017). https://doi.org/10.5206/cjsotl-rcacea.2017.2.10.

Miller-Young, Janice, and Michelle Yeo. "Conceptualizing and Communicating SoTL: A Framework for the Field." *Teaching & Learning Inquiry* 3, no. 2 (September 1, 2015): 37–53. https://doi.org/10.20343/teachlearninqu.3.2.37.

Roxå, Torgny, Katarina Mårtensson, and Mattias Alveteg. "Understanding and Influencing Teaching and Learning Cultures at University: A Network Approach." *Higher Education: The International Journal of Higher Education and Educational Planning* 62, no. 1 (July 2011): 99–111. https://doi.org/10.1007/s10734-010-9368-9.

Shulman, Lee. "From Minsk To Pinsk: Why A Scholarship of Teaching and Learning?" *Journal of the Scholarship of Teaching and Learning* 1, no. 1 (2000): 48–53.

Trigwell, Keith. "Evidence of the Impact of Scholarship of Teaching and Learning Purposes." *Teaching & Learning Inquiry* 1, no. 1 (March 1, 2013): 95–105. https://doi.org/10.20343/teachlearninqu.1.1.95.

21

Finding Common Ground:

Developing Partnerships Between the Academic Library and Campus Teaching Center to Advance Teaching and Learning

Amanda Nichols Hess

Introduction

While academic librarians can seek professional development to be effective educators, they may discount their own valuable knowledge that could help other instructors develop how they think about SoTL. In this chapter, the author highlights how she worked as a part of her institution's Center for Excellence in Teaching and Learning (CETL) to provide campus-wide faculty development grounded in SoTL. This partnership involved collaborating with other faculty developers and disciplinary faculty to expand instructors' knowledge and use of Universal Design for Learning (UDL) in teaching. As part of this partnership, she provided a year-long learning community, a three-part campus-wide workshop series, and a number of standalone resources for ongoing use. The author explains how these tools were designed, developed, and deployed as she worked with CETL to further SoTL on her campus. As librarians consider putting SoTL into practice, this kind of formal relationship outside academic libraries offers a unique kind of opportunity for cross-institutional common ground around teaching and learning.

SoTL and Academic Libraries

While Michael Perini asserted that SoTL had "not made tremendous headway into conversations on librarian roles and activities,"[1] in fact the opposite is true. Based on Sharon

K. Naylor's definition, which classified SoTL as "a movement that conceptualizes teaching as a scholarly work ... and involves the formal study of teaching and/or learning and the scholarly communication of such work,"[2] many of librarianship's scholarly conversations are grounded in SoTL concepts. Several publications—including *Communications in Information Literacy* and the *Journal of Information Literacy*—focus solely on advancing the "research, theory, and practice ... of information literacy in higher education,"[3] and other prominent journals such as *College and Research Libraries, the Journal of Academic Librarianship,* and *portal: Libraries and the Academy* welcome submissions that consider the formal study of academic librarians' teaching practices. While many articles that conceptualize and communicate information literacy instruction as a scholarly work are published annually, librarians have also researched SoTL-specific ideas such as adult learning theories,[4] high-impact practices,[5] and engaging in professional development around teaching.[6] While SoTL in name may still be gaining traction, then, academic librarians have engaged with its core tenets in many ways for some time.

From this professional foundation around teaching and learning as a scholarly area, academic librarians have knowledge and experience to share with other post-secondary instructors. To this end, some libraries and librarians have partnered with institutional offices, centers, or faculty groups specifically focused on supporting these endeavors. Trudi E. Jacobson first examined these partnerships systematically across different institutions; she found that such cross-campus relationships most often were librarian-initiated and involved either library-centric workshops for others (e.g., faculty, staff, teaching assistants, graduate students) or offering training for library staff.[7] At the time of her inquiry, Jacobson also found that librarians saw growth potential in such partnerships, especially to offer more in-depth or SoTL-focused activities, such as collaborating on grants, co-sponsoring events, or developing courses in tandem.[8] From this initial examination of library-teaching center partnerships, other scholars have shared how they built relationships with their institution's teaching organization, whether for library-centric[9] or faculty-focused[10] professional development. While Candice Dahl considered whether liaison-type relationships would be fruitful for libraries and administrative units such as teaching and learning centers,[11] no scholarship has focused on how more formal working arrangements between a librarian and the campus teaching center might advance SoTL and benefit the library academic library more broadly.

A SoTL-Centered Partnership in Practice
LIBRARIAN-TEACHING CENTER RELATIONSHIP

The author, who works as an academic librarian at Oakland University (OU) in Rochester, Michigan, engaged in this kind of formal relationship with her institution's Center for Excellence in Teaching and Learning (CETL) during the 2016–2017 academic year. OU is a public, Carnegie-classification doctoral research institution with an enrollment of approximately 16,000 undergraduate and 3,500 graduate students.[12] Although both OU and the OU Libraries focus on teaching as central to their respective missions, the working partnership between the libraries and CETL did not develop overnight. Beginning in 2012, the author connected with CETL as both a participant and presenter. Her experiences led to a growing interest in faculty development and a professional relationship with CETL's director; during the 2015–2016 academic year, she served as the author's mentor in her PhD program in Educational Leadership, and in this capacity, the CETL director encouraged the author to learn more about SoTL and faculty development as a field.

From these experiences, the author felt equipped to apply for one of CETL's Faculty Fellowships in 2016–2017. At OU, this role offers faculty members interested in the SoTL opportunities to facilitate year-long learning communities (called faculty development institutes, or FDIs), plan and provide an international teaching-centric conference, and collect and analyze teaching-centric data integral to CETL's mission.[13] This position comes with a partial release of duties for the fall and winter semesters and reinforces CETL's mission to be "fully faculty-driven … [in promoting] teaching and learning excellence" on campus.[14]

SOTL-GROUNDED FACULTY DEVELOPMENT

As a faculty fellow, the author's work focused on Universal Design for Learning (UDL). Developed and advanced by the Center for Applied and Special Technologies and the National Center on Universal Design for Learning, UDL offers a framework around which instructors can structure learning to reduce barriers and increase access for all students.[15] Practically, instructors who consider the UDL philosophy in their teaching offer students multiple means of information representation, engagement in course experiences and material, and action or expression to demonstrate their learning.[16] While the author was not an expert on UDL, her work as an academic librarian brought valuable perspective to this topic. She had expertise in the information resources that the faculty could use to provide multiple means of representation in their courses; she had background knowledge in learning and motivation theories, and her interest in instructional technology and online instruction meant she could help faculty identify both low- and high-tech ways to use UDL in their teaching.

The author worked with the CETL director, other faculty developers, and OU faculty and staff to provide three types of professional learning activities. First, she led a year-long FDI in which a group of instructors and staff worked to use UDL to support OU's increasingly diverse student population's learning needs. Second, she provided a three-part workshop series on UDL open to all on OU's campus. And third, she partnered with CETL's director and virtual faculty developer to design and develop resources (e.g., job aids, videos) on UDL that could be used during and after her tenure as a faculty fellow. Each of these professional learning offerings advanced SoTL to impact faculty's teaching and students' learning experiences at OU.

YEAR-LONG FDI

The author's year-long FDI, comprised of between eight to twelve faculty and staff, used the faculty learning community model to structure their work. This scaffold is a well-established, SoTL-focused professional development practice across higher education.[17]

The group engaged in face-to-face, online synchronous and asynchronous sessions over the course of the 2016–2017 academic year. They began by focusing on the three UDL principles (providing multiple means of representation, engagement, and action/expression) in depth. The author and the participants shared ways they were already incorporating these principles into instruction; they then discussed how they could push these practices further to foster student success. Following each meeting, the author shared SoTL scholarship related to the questions or issues discussed so participants could develop best practices within their own disciplinary areas. She also provided scholarly and pedagogical resources useful for participants as they dealt with technological, administrative, workload, and support issues related to using UDL. Once the FDI members had built UDL knowledge, they shifted to applying these understandings in their practices. As they did this, the author led online synchronous or asynchronous monthly meetings that focused on discussing UDL case studies[18] and participants' progress, work, questions, or issues in implementing UDL. All FDI content was available in a shared virtual course (see figure 21.1), and all face-to-face and virtual sessions were recorded so participants could review discussions at any time.

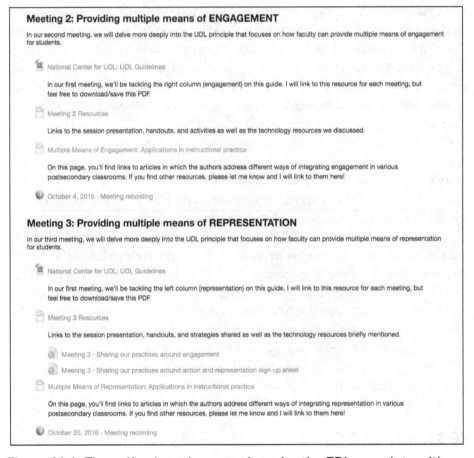

Figure 21.1. The online learning repository for the FDI, complete with UDL resources and meeting recordings.

THREE-PART WORKSHOP SERIES

In addition to the year-long FDI, the author also provided a three-part workshop series for the campus community. As with other librarian-teaching center partnerships, these workshops focused on building knowledge about UDL. In these sessions, the author offered an introduction to the UDL principles and scholarly foundation, examples of UDL in practice shared by FDI participants, and micro-, meso-, and macro-level UDL challenges, both at OU specifically and in higher education more broadly. These workshops were recorded and made available on the CETL website.[19] To promote these sessions, the author worked with CETL's virtual faculty developer to create and send several email-based teaching tips to all faculty and staff subscribed to CETL's email updates (see figure 21.2). These messages contained short, focused strategies designed for a wide audience with varied UDL knowledge and offered another way to reinforce SoTL across campus.

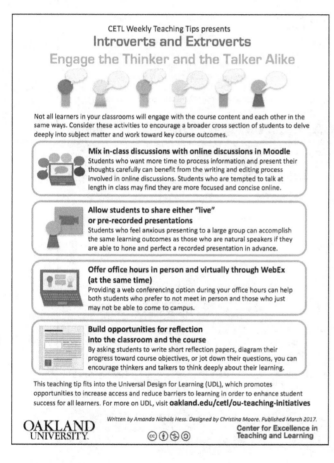

Figure 21.2. A sample email promoting the UDL workshop series, with text by the author and graphics by CETL's virtual faculty developer.

FREESTANDING INSTRUCTIONAL RESOURCES

While the bulk of her faculty fellow work involved designing and offering formal, structured professional learning opportunities for faculty, the author also worked with CETL's director and virtual faculty developer to create standalone resources on UDL. They developed a number of "quick notes" on UDL, which offered succinct and adaptable guidance on integrating these principles into teaching (see figure 21.3). Two of these resources provided the basics of UDL, including information on its place in curriculum/learning design and broad options for applying the three UDL principles in diverse classrooms. Three follow-up quick notes delved into these ideas, providing both general applications for a variety of learning environments and targeted strategies for specific groups of learners (e.g., international students, English language learners, nontraditional students, and students with anxiety).[20] From these quick notes, the author and the virtual faculty developer also created a series of videos to further promote and share UDL strategies for instruction.[21]

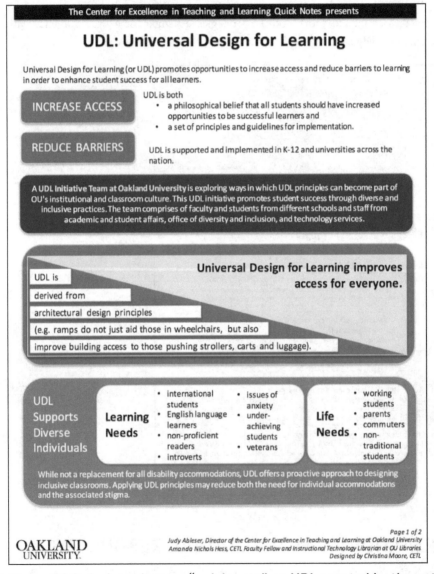

Figure 21.3. An introductory "quick note" on UDL created by the author, CETL's director, and the virtual faculty developer.

Key Takeaways and Conclusion

From this formal librarian-teaching center partnership grounded in SoTL, there were several important lessons learned. These takeaways may help other librarians as they consider SoTL in their work:

- Consider librarians' unique perspective only librarians can share. Because academic librarians' scholarship often focuses on pedagogical practicalities, they are uniquely positioned to give voice to SoTL at their institutions. They also see the cross-section faculty, staff, and students' needs. Academic librarians interested in SoTL partnerships with an institutional teaching center should consider their own existing expertise in this area and identify ways it can help others grow as educators.

- Formalize partnerships to maximize results (and equitable work responsibilities). The contributions the author made in faculty development, but also in professional service activities around SoTL, would not have been feasible without a formal working relationship with CETL. Although other librarians may engage in single faculty development sessions or workshop series, having a position—and release time—can foster more meaningful and long-lasting contributions. Other academic librarians may find it valuable to explore the possibilities of an in-house, residency, or fellowship program with their institution's SoTL-focused entity rather than simply adding new responsibilities to already-packed workloads.

- Determine how the academic library can benefit from such partnerships and use these pieces to gain internal buy-in. OU Libraries' administration supported the author's work as a faculty fellow in part because it offered the libraries several unique opportunities. It provided a new way to voice libraries' value in SoTL across campus; Ms. Hess could advocate for the libraries' presence in teaching initiatives while also sharing the resources available for supporting high-quality teaching at OU. Her work with CETL also could directly impact the libraries' information literacy instruction: the author shared her increased SoTL knowledge with her colleagues in an effort to promote their own personal instructional growth. For other academic librarians interested in finding common ground with a teaching or learning center, outlining the potential benefits to the library and its staff may help to get administrative and colleagues' support.

- Ensure personal and professional goals or benefits are met in any working partnerships. The author's work as a CETL faculty fellow helped her enhance her SoTL knowledge in faculty development, but being a part of the FDI and learning alongside faculty helped her reflect on her own teaching practices through a UDL lens. For example, she reframed how she presented instructional content, reconsidered the supplementary or additional online information she offered to students in addition to classroom instruction, and more intentionally approached engaging them in the content matter. For other academic librarians looking to build these professional partnerships, they should consider what they may get out of such work and then regularly reflect on their experiences to ensure personal, professional, scholarly, or other goals are addressed.

The author's formal, albeit temporary, role with OU's CETL had myriad mutual benefits for advancing SoTL within the library and across campus. Other academic librarians can use this partnership model to develop their instructional presence, build relationships with faculty, and be included in important campus conversations about learning. This work can also help faculty members in other disciplines to develop deeper understandings of the library's role in twenty-first-century student success and its diverse teaching-centric resources. Librarians' unique expertise and experiences leveraged in this way may help institutions provide richer, more dynamic learning environments. Other librarians should ponder how similar, mutually beneficial SoTL partnerships could be established at their own institutions.

ENDNOTES

1. Michael Perini, "Enhancing Collaboration through the Scholarship of Teaching and Learning," *Collaborative Librarianship*, 6, no. 1 (2014): 52-55, accessed July 24, 2017, https://digitalcommons.du.edu/collaborativelibrarianship/vol6/iss1/8/.

2. Sharon K. Naylor, "Scholarship of Teaching and Learning," in *Greenwood Dictionary of Education*, ed. John William Collins and Nancy P. O'Brien (Santa Barbara, CA: ABC-CLIO, 2011), 412.

3. "Aims and Scope," *Communications in Information Literacy* Editorial Board, accessed June 18, 2019, https://pdxscholar.library.pdx.edu/comminfolit/about.html#aimsandscope.php?journal=cil&page=about&op=editorialPolicies#focusAndScope.

4. See, for instance, Donald L. Gilstrap, "Why Do We Teach? Adult Learning Theory in Professional Standards as a Basis for Curriculum Development," *College & Research Libraries*, 74, no. 5 (2013): 501–18, accessed July 24, 2107, https://doi.org/10.5860/crl12-334; Lindsay Roberts, "Research in the Real World: Improving Adult Learners Web Search and Evaluation Skills through Motivational Design and Problem-Based Learning," *College & Research Libraries*, 78, no. 4 (2017): 527–51, accessed July 24, 2017, https://doi.org/10.5860/crl.78.4.527.

5. See, for instance, Merinda Kaye Hensley, "A Survey of Instructional Support for Undergraduate Research Programs," *portal: Libraries and the Academy*, 15, no. 4 (2015): 719–62, accessed July 24, 2017, https://doi.org/10.1353/pla.2015.0047; Catherine Fraser Riehle and Sharon A. Weiner, "High-Impact Educational Practices: An Exploration of the Role of Information Literacy," *College & Undergraduate Libraries*, 20, no. 2 (2013): 127–43, accessed July 24, 2017, https://doi.org/10.1080/10691316.2013.789658.

6. See, for instance, Sheril J. Hook, Marianne Stowell Bracke, Louise Greenfield, and Victoria A. Mills, "In-House Training for Instruction Librarians," *Research Strategies*, 19, no. 2 (2003): 99–127, accessed July 24, 2017, https://doi.org/10.1016/j.resstr.2003.12.001; Amanda Nichols Hess, "A Case Study of Job-Embedded Learning," *portal: Libraries and the Academy*, 16, no. 2 (2016): 327–47, accessed July 24, 2107, https://doi.org/10.1353/pla.2016.0021; Scott Walter, "Instructional Improvement: Building Capacity for the Professional Development of Librarians as Teachers," *Reference & User Services Quarterly*, 45, no. 3 (2006): 213–18, accessed July 24, 2017,

7. Trudi E. Jacobson, "Partnerships between Library Instruction Units and Campus Teaching Centers," *Journal of Academic Librarianship,* 27, no. 4 (2001): 311–16, accessed July 24, 2017, https://doi.org/10.1016/S0099-1333(01)00217-8.
8. Jacobson, "Partnerships."
9. See, for instance, Robert Behary, Leslie Lewis, and Bridget Euliano, "Implementing a Promotional Process for Academic Librarians," *Collaborative Librarianship*, 5, no. 3 (2013): 211–15, accessed July 24, 2107, http://digitalcommons.du.edu/collaborativelibrarianship/vol5/iss3/7/; Loanne Snavely and Nancy Dewald, "Developing and Implementing Peer Review of Academic Librarians' Teaching: An Overview and Case Report," *Journal of Academic Librarianship*, 37, no. 4 (2011): 343–51, accessed July 24, 2017, https://doi.org/10.1016/j.acalib.2011.04.009.
10. See, for instance, Danuta A. Nitecki and William Rando, "A Library and Teaching Center Collaboration to Assess the Impact of Using Digital Images on Teaching, Learning, and Library Support," *VINE*, 34, no. 3 (2004): 119–25, accessed July 24, 2017, https://doi.org/10.1108/03055720410563487.
11. Candice Dahl, "Library Liaison with Non-Academic Units: A New Application for a Traditional Model," *Partnership: The Canadian Journal of Library and Information Practice and Research*, 2, no. 1 (2007): 1–12, accessed July 24, 2017, https://journal.lib.uoguelph.ca/index.php/perj/article/view/242#.WXYi_9MrL48.
12. "Oakland University Fast Facts," Oakland University Communications and Marketing, accessed January 4, 2018, https://www.oakland.edu/Assets/Oakland/ucm/files-and-documents/pdfs/OU-Fast-Facts.pdf.
13. "About CETL Faculty Fellows," Oakland University Center for Excellence in Teaching and Learning, accessed July 24, 2017, http://wwwp.oakland.edu/cetl/top-links/contact-us/#tab-2.
14. "About CETL Faculty Fellows," Oakland University.
15. "What is UDL?," National Center on Universal Design for Learning, accessed July 24, 2017, http://www.udlcenter.org/aboutudl/whatisudl.
16. Ibid; "About Universal Design for Learning," Center for Applied and Special Technologies, accessed July 24, 2017, http://www.cast.org/our-work/about-udl.html#.WXYxpdMrL48.
17. See, for instance, Milton D. Cox, "Faculty Learning Communities: Change Agents for Transforming Institutions into Learning Organizations," *To Improve the Academy* 19 (2001): 69–93; Oscar T. Lenning and Larry H. Ebbers, *The Powerful Potential of Learning Communities: Improving Education for the Future, ASHE-ERIC Higher Education Report* (Washington, DC: George Washington University, 1999).
18. "Case Stories," MERLOT ELIXR, accessed July 24, 2017, http://elixr.merlot.org/case-stories?noCache=747:1500921293.
19. These recordings can be accessed at www.oakland.edu/cetl/virtual.
20. These documents can be accessed at https://oakland.edu/cetl/resources/#tab-5.
21. These videos can be accessed at https://oakland.edu/cetl/virtual/#tab-3.

BIBLIOGRAPHY

Behary, Robert, Leslie Lewis, and Bridget Euliano. "Implementing a Promotional Process for Academic Librarians." *Collaborative Librarianship*, 5, no. 3 (2013): 211–15. http://digitalcommons.du.edu/collaborativelibrarianship/vol5/iss3/7/.

Center for Applied and Special Technologies. "About Universal Design for Learning." Accessed July 24, 2017. http://www.cast.org/our-work/about-udl.html#.WXYxpdMrL48.

Communications in Information Literacy Editorial Board. "Focus and Scope." Accessed July 24, 2017. http://

comminfolit.org/index.php?journal=cil&page=about&op=editorialPolicies#focusAndScope.

Cox, Milton D. "Faculty Learning Communities: Change Agents for Transforming Institutions into Learning Organizations." *To Improve the Academy* 19 (2001): 69–93.

Dahl, Candice. "Library Liaison with Non-Academic Units: A New Application for a Traditional Model." *Partnership: The Canadian Journal of Library and Information Practice and Research*, 2, no. 1 (2007): 1–12. https://journal.lib.uoguelph.ca/index.php/perj/article/view/242#.WXYi_9MrL48.

Gilstrap, Donald L. "Why Do We Teach? Adult Learning Theory in Professional Standards as a Basis for Curriculum Development." *College & Research Libraries*, 74, no. 5 (2013): 501–18. https://doi.org/10.5860/crl12-334.

Hensley, Merinda Kaye. "A Survey of Instructional Support for Undergraduate Research Programs." *portal: Libraries and the Academy*, 15, no. 4 (2015): 719–62. https://doi.org/10.1353/pla.2015.0047.

Hook, Sheril J., Marianne Stowell Bracke, Louise Greenfield, and Victoria A. Mills. "In-House Training for Instruction Librarians." *Research Strategies*, 19, no. 2 (2003): 99–127, https://doi.org/10.1016/j.resstr.2003.12.001.

Jacobson, Trudi E. "Partnerships between Library Instruction Units and Campus Teaching Centers." *Journal of Academic Librarianship*, 27, no. 4 (2001): 311–16. https://doi.org/10.1016/S0099-1333(01)00217-8.

Lenning, Oscar T., and Larry H. Ebbers. *The Powerful Potential of Learning Communities: Improving Education for the Future, ASHE-ERIC Higher Education Report* (Washington, DC: George Washington University, 1999).

MERLOT ELIXR. "Case Stories." Accessed July 24, 2017. http://elixr.merlot.org/case-stories?noCache=747:1500921293.

National Center on Universal Design for Learning. "What is UDL?" Accessed July 24, 2017. http://www.udlcenter.org/aboutudl/whatisudl.

Naylor, Sharon K. *Greenwood Dictionary of Education*, 2nd ed., s.v. "Scholarship of Teaching and Learning." Santa Barbara: ABC-CLIO, 2011.

Nichols Hess, Amanda. "A Case Study of Job-Embedded Learning." *portal: Libraries and the Academy*, 16, no. 2 (2016): 327–47. https://doi.org/10.1353/pla.2016.0021.

Nitecki, Danuta A., and William Rando. "A Library and Teaching Center Collaboration to Assess the Impact of Using Digital Images on Teaching, Learning, and Library Support." *VINE*, 34, no. 3 (2004): 119–25. https://doi.org/10.1108/03055720410563487.

Oakland University Center for Excellence in Teaching and Learning. "About CETL Faculty Fellows." Accessed July 24, 2017. http://wwwp.oakland.edu/cetl/top-links/contact-us/#tab-2.

Oakland University Communications and Marketing. "Oakland University Fast Facts." Oakland University Communications and Marketing. Accessed January 4, 2018. https://www.oakland.edu/Assets/Oakland/ucm/files-and-documents/pdfs/OU-Fast-Facts.pdf.

Perini, Michael. "Enhancing Collaboration through the Scholarship of Teaching and Learning." *Collaborative Librarianship*, 6, no. 1 (2014): 52–55. https://digitalcommons.du.edu/collaborativelibrarianship/vol6/iss1/8/.

Riehle, Catherine Fraser, and Sharon A. Weiner. "High-Impact Educational Practices: An Exploration of the Role of Information Literacy." *College & Undergraduate Libraries*, 20, no. 2 (2013): 127–43. https://doi.org/10.1080/10691316.2013.789658.

Roberts, Lindsay. "Research in the Real World: Improving Adult Learners Web Search and Evaluation Skills through Motivational Design and Problem-Based Learning." *College & Research Libraries*, 78, no. 4 (2017): 527–51. https://doi.org/10.5860/crl.78.4.527.

Snavely, Loanne, and Nancy Dewald. "Developing and Implementing Peer Review of Academic Librarians' Teaching: An Overview and Case Report." *Journal of Academic Librarianship,* 37, no. 4 (2011): 343–51. https://doi.org/10.1016/j.acalib.2011.04.009.

Walter, Scott. "Instructional Improvement: Building Capacity for the Professional Development of Librarians as Teachers." *Reference & User Services Quarterly,* 45, no. 3 (2006): 213–18. https://www.jstor.org/stable/20864516.

22

Five Concrete Collaborations to Support SoTL Across Campus

Noémi Cobolet, Raphaël Grolimund, Cécile Hardebolle, Siara Isaac, Mathilde Panes, and Caroline Salamin

Introduction

As experts in information literacy, university librarians often conduct instruction sessions for students and faculty. As has been observed with university teachers,[1] it seems likely that most librarians will have become instructors via a learning-by-doing[2] or "apprenticeship of observation"[3] approach. An examination of one's own personal practice, informed by the Scholarship of Teaching and Learning (SoTL) literature, offers a strong basis for improving the teaching of information literacy and underlying beliefs about learning. This case study discusses how the development of a collaboration between the Library and the Teaching Support Centre at the Ecole Polytechnique Fédérale de Lausanne (EPFL) has led to the introduction of SoTL into the library's teaching practice.

This case study uses five concrete examples to illustrate how the collaboration shed new light on the library's instructional practices, how the use of SoTL enabled some intuitive knowledge to be formalized and other practices to be challenged and adapted to incorporate more evidence-based teaching strategies. It also shows how, beyond the positive impact for the library training team, the relationship was beneficial to the Teaching Support Centre through the support it received from the library around monitoring, using, and managing literature on teaching and learning. The case study explores the specific characteristics of these successful collaborations, and some persistent challenges, with the intention to provide readers with insight on how to foster similar dynamics in their own academic environments.

EVIDENCE-INFORMED TEACHING

EPFL is a renowned research-intensive technical university located in the French-speaking part of Switzerland. The institution comprises five schools, two colleges, twenty-one institutes, and 357 laboratories. There are more than 10,000 students, from undergraduates to doctoral students, and more than 300 faculty. Over the years, EPFL librarians have developed expertise in information literacy, copyright rules, publishing, and research data. Parallel to individual support for faculty and students on these topics, library staff also provide formal information literacy instruction. This situation has led to the creation of a team of teaching librarians. This team handles most of the instructional efforts of the library: it carries out the majority of the one-shot courses (which can be from two hours to half-day-long sessions) and supports other librarians in delivering instruction.

In 2012, the teaching librarians felt the need to have a clearer understanding of students' prior knowledge, especially in the field of plagiarism. They also wanted to improve interactivity in a forty-five-minute course about good citation practices. With the idea of using interactive questioning in class, they contacted the teaching advisors from the Teaching Support Centre to access clickers and to investigate the potential educational advantages offered by this technology. The challenge of formulating effective clicker questions stimulated a first foray into educational literature on this topic. Because teaching was not part of the Swiss Library and Information Science (LIS) curriculum until recently, librarians had to develop teaching skills while on the job. This first contact with the literature was an important step in developing a more evidence-based pedagogical practice, which in turn allowed the EPFL librarians to implement more interactive and collaborative sessions for students.

While the initial inclusion of the clickers reshaped the course, the data generated by the clickers about the students' prior knowledge and evolving understanding of information literacy also stimulated the librarians' reflections about teaching. For instance, the clicker data showed that students understood the rules on avoiding plagiarism but struggled to apply their understanding in practice.[4] It also revealed that while students knew they have to cite sources used for their work, they did not clearly see how to do it. In addition, students appeared to misunderstand the rules regarding the reuse of pictures and graphs.[5] Based on these observations, the librarians created new activities and games to help students deal with different contexts (homework, in-class presentation, self-publication on the web, scientific publication) and the rules to apply to each case. Progressively, the training offered by the librarians improved on an evidence-based and iterative trajectory.

SUPPORT FOR STUDENTS ON INFORMATION LITERACY AND OTHER TRANSVERSAL SKILLS

The Teaching Support Centre and the Library were involved in the design of a new interdisciplinary course for first-year bachelor's degree students, which included the development of information literacy, teamwork, and oral communication skills. A review of the literature reinforced the motivation to integrate such skills into students' disciplinary courses in order to maximize their perceived relevance to students and thus their application across the curriculum.[6] In response to the logistical challenges of reaching 1,700 students across twelve sections of the course, the Teaching Support Centre and the library developed a series of videos and application exercises available online to complement students' project work. Feedback from students on the first version of the resources was lukewarm, and many students appeared to have been unaware of their existence, indicating a lack of integration with the classroom sessions taught by the disciplinary instructors. In response to this feedback, a second version of the resources used testimonies from the first cohort of students on the difficulties they encountered in order to increase the contextualization of the skills in terms of the specific project tasks required of students. This approach draws on the "near peer role model" technique found to be beneficial in other contexts.[7]

Feedback from students and from the course teaching team has been positive, and the collaboration has enabled increased contact between first-year students and the library. As part of the feedback on the fourth iteration of the course, students were asked to list the two most important difficulties they had experienced in completing their project. The data indicated that the resources offered by the library are meeting most students' needs but that intragroup communication and coordination are continuing challenges.

This data-led approach has been a valuable angle for SoTL-informed discussions with the teaching team. Further, the disciplinary teachers have engaged in the SoTL approach, including publishing on the course[8] in addition to articles authored by the Teaching Support Centre.[9] The partnership with the Teaching Support Center has provided the librarians with increasing opportunities to understand best practices for collecting data and using feedback from students. Not only has this specific first-year course been improved by such an iterative, collaborative, and data-driven approach, but this process has also enabled librarians to develop a more research-based approach to their teaching practice.

LITERATURE MONITORING

At the end of 2014, two new colleagues joined the library teaching team. As part of their preparation for teaching workshops, the new librarians read extensively in LIS and educational literature. This encouraged the rest of the team, who then started to share literature by email. An initial meeting was organized for team members to share the most relevant sources and tools they were using. This resulted in the development of a shared systematized literature watch with Inoreader (https://www.inoreader.com/). The current teaching and learning literature monitoring combines multiple sources, including annual reports (e. g., Innovating Pedagogy annual reports of the UK's Open University, http://www.openuniversity.edu/), teaching community blogs (e.g., https://ciel.unige.ch/), Twitter accounts of practitioners (e.g., @clauersen, https://twitter.com/clauersen), and practical "how to" books that are particularly useful for building new teaching activities. Additional books on teaching have been acquired[10] and made directly available to all staff and teachers via the library collection. The library now plans to develop a feed on information literacy for engineers in higher education for colleagues outside the institution. Building on their experience, the librarians have also helped to teach advisors to develop their reference management and literature monitoring activities.

Employing teaching and learning literature has proved to be a great experience for the librarians: they have been inspired in the preparation of their courses and have begun to participate in wider education-focused meetings and events such as the Swiss Faculty Development Network conference (http://www.sfdn.ch/). This has also demonstrated, in particular to departmental faculty, that the library teaching team is proactive and employs a reflective methodology to its own instructional work. This provides the librarians with research experience that facilitates their understanding of faculty research and pedagogical practices.

SCIENTIFIC INFORMATION LITERACY CLUB

The shared literature monitoring process strongly improved the circulation of ideas through the library teaching team. However, a moment dedicated to face-to-face discussion was missing. Relevant literature was discussed informally but there was no structured follow-up. The library teaching team needed a devoted meeting to pool its findings, to critically assess them, and to reflect on the possibility of applying them to its teaching activities. As a first step, a new kind of informal meeting—the "scientific information literacy club"—was scheduled for the library teaching team. As the name suggests, the concept is inspired by journal clubs. Each month, a team member volunteers to facilitate a session. The aim is to present a book, a report, a game, or any pedagogical tool that might prompt the team to develop innovative teaching activities. Articles providing models and frameworks are also presented as bases to compare and evaluate practices.[11] After the presentation, the team discusses ways to integrate the game, activity, or theory presented in an upcoming course. The meeting provides a time dedicated to exploring ideas before trying them out in class, creating a bridge between literature and teaching activities. Trying and discussing instructional strategies in advance of class sessions also enabled the team to receive feedback, which is essential to fine-tune the design of a course. The quality of teaching increased as librarians continuously experimented with new pedagogical approaches.

After a few monthly sessions, the library teaching team—in a spirit of sharing and openness—started to invite other colleagues to present on topics connected to teaching. For example, a collection development librarian reported on conference presentations she attended related to gamified activities, and a member of the Center for Digital Education introduced learning analytics. In order to further these discussions, the librarians hope to eventually include faculty members. Teaching librarians collaborate with faculty on a regular basis to instruct students in information literacy, but deeper pedagogical questions are rarely addressed explicitly. Including faculty in these discussions would open up the possibility of increasing each other's comprehension of instructional best practices and have a positive impact on upcoming partnerships.

Building on the success of this model, teaching librarians also hope to begin to measure the effectiveness of the teaching activities emerging from the monthly meetings. Formal data collection will enable the team to adapt instruction to specific student and curricular needs, to develop models, and to share expertise with colleagues beyond the walls of the institution.

INTERDISCIPLINARY TEACHING DEVELOPMENT

In many research-intensive institutions, graduate teaching assistants are the first line of contact with students.[12] Like many others, the Teaching Support Centre at EPFL has developed specific training for graduate teaching assistants.[13] However, because their teaching duties typically involve supervising students in laboratories or responding to questions during exercise sessions, teaching assistants rarely have the opportunity to structure a complete teaching sequence. To provide them both with a space to practice and a first contact with a teaching community,[14] the Teaching Support Centre created the TeachDev group, a community of practice composed of doctoral candidates and post-docs.

The group functions like a journal club dedicated to teaching, with each session centered on an interactive mini-lesson facilitated by a member of the group. Topics have included student motivation, assessment, stereotype threat, multiple intelligences, and a talk about a SoTL project undertaken by a doctoral candidate.[15] These lessons provide an ongoing opportunity for microteaching practice, which has been shown to be among the most effective techniques for improving teaching skills,[16] particularly for developing interactive teaching strategies. They enable graduate students to design and facilitate lessons as part of their pedagogical development, and several alumni of the community now hold teaching or academic positions. The collaborative nature of the group also provides rich opportunities for feedback on the lesson and its implementation, and, given the value of feedback in learning,[17] this is worth underlining on its own. With participants from multiple departments, the TeachDev community is helping to spread the SoTL approach across the institution.

Librarians became progressively involved in the group, first as attendees then as full participants. They taught mini-lessons on the use of games in information literacy training and on a peer-based tool to support collaborative professional development. The group has benefited from the information literacy expertise of the librarians, and, in turn, has helped to assess the pedagogical material created by the librarians, which allowed librarians to get feedback on new teaching methods. These lessons were also an opportunity for the librarians to gain greater insight into doctoral students' training needs. More generally, the participation of the librarians in this group facilitated the integration of their work into the development of students' information literacy skills across the institution.

Limits and Perspective

As stated earlier, both the library and the Teaching Support Centre consider this partnership successful in the sense that it has led to concrete implementations of SoTL-driven initiatives. These initiatives have progressively led to a more systematic use of evidence from the literature on teaching and learning, data collection to inform decisions, and microteaching opportunities and feedback to transform practices. The initiatives have also resulted in an increased attention to internal and external dissemination of teaching best practices and findings.

However, there were challenges and limitations to this approach. A first challenge to overcome was that academic research was not part of the job description of the librarians or of the teaching advisors. Although most of them have academic research skills, a deficiency of such skills has been identified as an impediment in other contexts.[18] Allocating time and resources to the different initiatives described above was therefore difficult because the tasks were not part of everyday formal responsibilities. It required effort not to cancel the meetings because they were never a priority, especially during busy periods of the academic calendar. Many of the discussions around evidence-based teaching methods, plagiarism, reference management, collaborative writing, and studying support happened during lunch and coffee breaks. An initial limit of the approach is therefore the motivation of the individuals involved to dedicate part of their time to additional work beyond their duties. The good personal relationships that grew up slowly between the teaching advisors and the librarians played an important role. Another factor that kept both teams motivated was that both were convinced that investing in developing SoTL-related skills and making this visible by publishing was also a way to open the path toward an official incorporation of academic research in the job descriptions of members.

While SoTL was not part of the original mission of the library teaching team, there was a shared belief that having solid evidence to support information literacy instruction was important. And this belief fueled a desire to work together, building on the shared practice of reviewing each instructional session in order to identify areas for improvement. Initial contact with SoTL concepts occurred at different moments for members of the team, and the realization that many activities had been permeated by a SoTL approach came later. In turn, this awareness also stimulated an increased use of literature, data, and reflection to improve teaching and to develop new approaches in support of student learning. The development of similar initiatives would likely occur more rapidly with an explicit intention to use SoTL.

Another challenge actually came from the success of the group at establishing a friendly and motivating atmosphere. With a growing number of participants, it was no longer possible for everyone to work on all initiatives. It is also important to note that, more generally, not all members of the library and of the Teaching Support Centre have been involved in the developments described in this chapter, although they were informed of the ongoing partnership. As the two units recruit new staff and more explicitly draw on SoTL to improve their pedagogical practices, a question remains about how to involve new arrivals in the initiatives. In addition, making these initiatives stable over the long term is a question the teams still need to address.

Conclusion

This case study has presented five concrete examples of SoTL-informed activities resulting from collaborations between the library and the Teaching Support Centre at Ecole Polytechnique Fédérale de Lausanne in Switzerland. While this list is not exhaustive, it illustrates how the nature of the collaboration between the two services has evolved from guide to partner in the co-facilitation of workshops, conferences, and a community of practice for teaching assistants. In discussing both the successes and challenges of this work, the authors hope to provide librarians with insights on how to reproduce similar partnerships in their own institutions.

After five years, the cross-fertilization between the two teams has led to a more collaborative monitoring of literature on teaching and learning, an increased use of this evidence in the design of instruction offered by both services, and the development of a more systematic way to collect data to inform pedagogical decisions. More generally, the different initiatives have spurred the development of a more reflective, evidence-based, and data-driven approach to teaching, which is an increasingly important part of the overall culture of a research-intensive institution such as the EPFL.

ENDNOTES

1. Lee S. Shulman, "Signature Pedagogies in the Professions," *Daedalus*, 134, no. 3 (2005): 52–59, accessed May 11, 2018, https://doi.org/10.1162/0011526054622015.
2. Theresa Westbrock and Sarah Fabian, "Proficiencies for Instruction Librarians: Is There Still a Disconnect Between Professional Education and Professional Responsibilities?," *College & Research Libraries*, 71, no. 6 (2010): 569–90, accessed May 11, 2018, https://doi.org/10.5860/crl-75r1.
3. Michaela Borg, "The Apprenticeship of Observation," *ELT Journal*, 58, no. 3 (2004): 274–76, accessed May 11, 2018, https://doi.org/10.1093/elt/58.3.274.
4. Noémi Cobolet and Raphaël Grolimund, "Avoiding Plagiarism: The Road to Autonomy," Swiss Faculty Development Network Conference 2017, Lausanne, 2017, accessed May 11, 2018, http://infoscience.epfl.ch/record/225666.
5. Caroline Salamin et al., "What Students Answer When Discussing About Citation Practices," *Zenodo*, February 10, 2017, accessed May 11, 2018, https://doi.org/10.5281/zenodo.290155.
6. For a review, see Debra Bath et al., "Beyond Mapping and Embedding Graduate Attributes: Bringing Together Quality Assurance and Action Learning to Create a Validated and Living Curriculum," *Higher Education Research & Development*, 23, no. 3 (2004): 313–28, accessed May 11, 2018, https://doi.org/10.1080/0729436042000235427.
7. Mary C. Murphy, Claude M. Steele, and James J. Gross, "Signaling Threat: How Situational Cues Affect Women in Math, Science, and Engineering Settings," *Psychological Science*, 18, no. 10 (2007): 879–85, accessed May 11, 2018, https://doi.org/10.1111/j.1467-9280.2007.01995.x; Susan D. Nickerson et al., "Identification Matters: Effects of Female Peer Role Models Differ By Gender Between High and Low Mathematically Identified Students," Conference on Research in Undergraduate Mathematics Education, San Diego, 2017.
8. Adrian Holzer et al., "Early Awareness of Global Issues and Development of Soft Skills in Engineering Education: An Interdisciplinary Approach to Communication," in *2014 Information Technology Based Higher Education and Training (ITHET)*, 2014, 1–6, accessed May 11, 2018, https://doi.org/10.1109/ITHET.2014.7155697; Adrian Holzer et al., "Gamifying Knowledge Sharing in the Humanitarian Context," in *Proceedings of the 7th Annual Symposium on Computing for Development*, ACM DEV '16 (New York: ACM, 2016), 21:1–21:4, accessed May 11, 2018, https://doi.org/10.1145/3001913.3006630.
9. Siara Isaac and Roland Tormey, "Undergraduate Group Projects: Challenges and Learning Experiences," *QScience Proceedings*, 2015, no. 4 (2015): 19, accessed May 11, 2018, https://doi.org/10.5339/qproc.2015.elc2014.19; Roland Tormey et al., "The Formal and Hidden Curricula

of Ethics in Engineering Education," 43rd Annual SEFI Conference, Orléans, 2015, accessed May 11, 2018, https://infoscience.epfl.ch/record/210646.

10. e.g., John Hattie, *Visible Learning: A Synthesis of over 800 Meta-Analyses Relating to Achievement* (London: Routledge, 2009); Jake Carlson and Lisa Johnston, eds., *Data Information Literacy: Librarians, Data, and the Education of a New Generation of Researchers*, Purdue Information Literacy Handbooks (West Lafayette, IN: Purdue University Press, 2015).

11. Igor Mayer et al., "The Research and Evaluation of Serious Games: Toward a Comprehensive Methodology," *British Journal of Educational Technology*, 45, no. 3 (2014): 502–27, accessed May 11, 2018, https://doi.org/10.1111/bjet.12067.

12. Donald H. Wulff and Ann E. Austin, eds., *Paths to the Professoriate: Strategies for Enriching the Preparation of Future Faculty*, The Jossey-Bass Higher and Adult Education Series (San Francisco: Jossey-Bass, 2004).

13. Roland Tormey, Cécile Hardebolle, and Siara Isaac, "The Teaching Toolkit: Design and Evaluation of a One-Day Pedagogical Workshop for Engineering Graduate Teaching Assistants," *Submitted*, 2017.

14. Sharon Dotger, "Exploring and Developing Graduate Teaching Assistants' Pedagogies via Lesson Study," *Teaching in Higher Education*, 16, no. 2 (2011): 157–69, accessed May 11, 2018, https://doi.org/10.1080/13562517.2010.507304.

15. Manuel Aprile, "Using ConcepTests During Exercise Sessions" (The Scholarship of Teaching and Learning SoTL): developing teaching through research, Zurich, 2016).

16. Hattie, *Visible Learning*.

17. Ibid.

18. Fay Patel, "Promoting a Culture of Scholarship among Educational Developers: Exploring Institutional Opportunities," *International Journal for Academic Development*, 19, no. 3 (2014): 242–54, accessed May 11, 2018, https://doi.org/10.1080/1360144X.2013.805693; Tony Harland and David Staniforthb, "Academic Development as Academic Work," *International Journal for Academic Development*, 8, no. 1–2 (2003): 25–35, accessed May 11, 2018, https://doi.org/10.1080/1360144042000277919.

BIBLIOGRAPHY

Aprile, Manuel. "Using ConcepTests during Exercise Sessions." Zurich, 2016.

Bath, Debra, Calvin Smith, Sarah Stein, and Richard Swann. "Beyond Mapping and Embedding Graduate Attributes: Bringing Together Quality Assurance and Action Learning to Create a Validated and Living Curriculum." *Higher Education Research & Development*, 23, no. 3 (2004): 313–28. Accessed May 11, 2018. https://doi.org/10.1080/0729436042000235427.

Borg, Michaela. "The Apprenticeship of Observation." *ELT Journal*, 58, no. 3 (2004): 274–76. Accessed May 11, 2018. https://doi.org/10.1093/elt/58.3.274.

Carlson, Jake, and Lisa Johnston, eds. *Data Information Literacy: Librarians, Data, and the Education of a New Generation of Researchers*. Purdue Information Literacy Handbooks. West Lafayette, IN: Purdue University Press, 2015.

Cobolet, Noémi, and Raphaël Grolimund. "Avoiding Plagiarism: The Road to Autonomy." Lausanne, 2017. Accessed May 11, 2018. http://infoscience.epfl.ch/record/225666.

Dotger, Sharon. "Exploring and Developing Graduate Teaching Assistants' Pedagogies via Lesson Study." *Teaching in Higher Education*, 16, no. 2 (2011): 157–69. Accessed May 11, 2018. https://doi.org/10.1080/13562517.2010.507304.

Harland, Tony, and David Staniforthb. "Academic Development as Academic Work." *International Journal for Academic Development*, 8, no. 1–2 (2003): 25–35. Accessed May 11, 2018. https://doi.org/10.1080/1360144042000277919.

Hattie, John. *Visible Learning: A Synthesis of over 800 Meta-Analyses Relating to Achievement.* London: Routledge, 2009.

Holzer, Adrian, Samuel Bendahan, Isabelle V. Cardia, and Denis Gillet. "Early Awareness of Global Issues and Development of Soft Skills in Engineering Education: An Interdisciplinary Approach to Communication," In *2014 Information Technology Based Higher Education and Training (ITHET)*, 1–6, 2014. Accessed May 11, 2018. https://doi.org/10.1109/ITHET.2014.7155697.

Holzer, Adrian, Bruno Kocher, Isabelle Vonèche Cardia, Jorge Mazuze, Samuel Bendahan, and Denis Gillet. "Gamifying Knowledge Sharing in the Humanitarian Context." In *Proceedings of the 7th Annual Symposium on Computing for Development*, 21:1–21:4. ACM DEV '16. New York: ACM, 2016. Accessed May 11, 2018. https://doi.org/10.1145/3001913.3006630.

Isaac, Siara, and Roland Tormey. "Undergraduate Group Projects: Challenges and Learning Experiences." *QScience Proceedings*, 2015, no. 4 (2015): 19. Accessed May 11, 2018. https://doi.org/10.5339/qproc.2015.elc2014.19.

Mayer, Igor, Geertje Bekebrede, Casper Harteveld, Harald Warmelink, Qiqi Zhou, Theo van Ruijven, Julia Lo, Rens Kortmann, and Ivo Wenzler. "The Research and Evaluation of Serious Games: Toward a Comprehensive Methodology." *British Journal of Educational Technology*, 45, no. 3 (2014): 502–27. Accessed May 11, 2018. https://doi.org/10.1111/bjet.12067.

Murphy, Mary C., Claude M. Steele, and James J. Gross. "Signaling Threat: How Situational Cues Affect Women in Math, Science, and Engineering Settings." *Psychological Science*, 18, no. 10 (2007): 879–85. Accessed May 11, 2018. https://doi.org/10.1111/j.1467-9280.2007.01995.x.

Nickerson, Susan D., Katie Bjorkman, Sei Jin Ko, and David Marx. "Identification Matters: Effects of Female Peer Role Models Differ by Gender Between High and Low Mathematically Identified Students." San Diego, 2017.

Patel, Fay. "Promoting a Culture of Scholarship among Educational Developers: Exploring Institutional Opportunities." *International Journal for Academic Development*, 19, no. 3 (2014): 242–54. Accessed May 11, 2018. https://doi.org/10.1080/1360144X.2013.805693.

Salamin, Caroline, Noémi Cobolet, Raphaël Grolimund, and Pascale Bouton. "What Students Answer When Discussing About Citation Practices." *Zenodo*. February 10, 2017. Accessed May 11, 2018. https://doi.org/10.5281/zenodo.290155.

Shulman, Lee S. "Signature Pedagogies in the Professions." *Daedalus*, 134, no. 3 (2005): 52–59. Accessed May 11, 2018. https://doi.org/10.1162/0011526054622015.

Tormey, Roland, Cécile Hardebolle, and Siara Isaac. "The Teaching Toolkit: Design and Evaluation of a One-Day Pedagogical Workshop for Engineering Graduate Teaching Assistants." *Submitted*, 2017.

Tormey, Roland, Ingrid Le Duc, Siara Ruth Isaac, Cécile Hardebolle, and Isabelle Vonèche Cardia. "The Formal and Hidden Curricula of Ethics in Engineering Education." Orléans, 2015. Accessed May 11, 2018. https://infoscience.epfl.ch/record/210646.

Westbrock, Theresa, and Sarah Fabian. "Proficiencies for Instruction Librarians: Is There Still a Disconnect Between Professional Education and Professional Responsibilities?" *College & Research Libraries*, 71, no. 6 (2010): 569–90. Accessed May 11, 2018. https://doi.org/10.5860/crl-75r1.

Wulff, Donald H., and Ann E. Austin, eds. *Paths to the Professoriate: Strategies for Enriching the Preparation of Future Faculty.* The Jossey-Bass Higher and Adult Education Series. San Francisco: Jossey-Bass, 2004.

Breaking New Ground:

Librarians as Partners in a SoTL Fellowship

Thomas Weeks and Melissa E. Johnson

In spring 2015, the Office of Faculty Development and Teaching Excellence (OFDTE) at Augusta University, a mid-sized public research university with approximately 8,300 students located in Augusta, Georgia, called for applicants for a newly created, year-long Scholarship of Teaching and Learning (SoTL) Fellowship. This program was the first of its kind in the University System of Georgia. OFDTE envisioned the fellowship as a community of practice for those interested in learning more about the research methods used in SoTL and developing a research project based on their own teaching practice. An increased focus on research for all faculty at the university prompted the authors, librarians at Augusta University, to apply for the inaugural cohort which started in fall 2015. One of the librarians developed a project exploring student learning using methods influenced by the Association of College & Research Libraries (ACRL) *Framework for Information Literacy for Higher Education*. The other collaborated with a faculty member from the Department of English and Foreign Languages to explore the creation of an American literature survey course using open access materials and to investigate the students' engagement with the various text formats. Also included in this cohort were teaching faculty in the fields of physics, math, psychology, and epidemiology. In this case study, the librarians will share their experiences during their fellowship and the benefits and challenges of conducting SoTL research.

Librarian SoTL Fellowship Projects

During the first semester of the fellowship, the members met once a week to discuss what constitutes SoTL and various topics in research design. This was also when the fellows

developed their projects with constant feedback from the other members of the cohort. In the second semester of the fellowship, spring 2016, the participants conducted their projects, again with the help of the community of fellows. In order for the librarians at Augusta University to be able to conduct their SoTL research, it was beneficial to collaborate with other faculty on campus. Although there is a robust library instruction program at the university, the majority of the classes are one-shot instruction sessions. By working with several of the English professors, the librarians had an opportunity to utilize English classes, the subject area that tends to have the most library instruction sessions, to conduct their SoTL research.

For his project, the first author collaborated with two different freshman composition instructors to conduct his research involving the ACRL *Framework*. He explored how incorporating one of the frames into a one-shot library instruction session for a freshman composition course would affect student learning. The author taught four library instruction sessions for two different English composition instructors. One section for each instructor received a traditional, skills-based lesson (the control group), while the other section emphasized conceptual knowledge using a lesson developed from the frame Authority is Constructed and Contextual (the experimental group). The impetus for the project resides in the notion that both skills-based and conceptual knowledge are necessary for becoming information literate, but many times skills- or tool-based instruction is what is expected by course instructors. Because of the conceptual focus of the ACRL *Framework* and its set of knowledge practices and dispositions, the author questioned the effectiveness of instruction focusing on only one form of delivery for student learning.

The second author had previously discussed the use of Open Educational Resources (OERs) in a literature course with an English professor. The author is the Affordable Learning Georgia (ALG) Library Coordinator for Augusta University. ALG is an initiative begun by the University System of Georgia to "promote student success by providing affordable textbook alternatives."[1] The program provides access to and highlights many open resources for use in classes. By reducing or alleviating textbook costs and access issues for students, the initiative hopes to increase retention, progression, and graduation. One of the challenges in providing these freely available materials in literature classes is that many of the key texts that are being studied are still under copyright. The ability to create a survey class in literature using only freely available texts and how students engage with these texts became the genesis of the joint SoTL project between the author and the English professor with whom she collaborated. Literature is traditionally a print-heavy subject area, so the desire to study the students' interaction with the material was also an interest. As noted by Michael Levine-Clark, "Humanists prefer print to electronic."[2] This was reaffirmed eight years later by Mizrachi who stated that "studies show student preferences for reading academic material in print remain consistent."[3] This project sought to confirm these assertions in an American literature survey course.

While results were mixed, the projects still helped answer questions surrounding teaching practice for both librarians. Both were able to utilize some of the information gathered from their SoTL projects to influence their teaching. In addition, these projects led to further areas of inquiry and future research opportunities.

Benefits and Challenges of Conducting SoTL Research and Participating in a SoTL Community

In addition to working with English faculty who provided the classes to conduct the research, the fellowship presented opportunities for the librarians to collaborate closely with faculty fellows from other disciplines and to learn about and discuss instructional techniques specific to their fields. The director of OFDTE, a psychology professor, also provided guidance to the fellows and conducted workshops in various aspects of research methodology. All of the fellows, however, brought different skills and abilities to the fellowship from their respective fields. The physics, math, and epidemiology faculty helped the others with their statistical knowledge, advising which analyses to run and assisting with the identification of significant results. Additionally, the fellows provided insight into the pedagogies specific to their disciplines. For example, the librarians learned about Visual Python and its use in physics education and the effectiveness of Process Oriented Guided Inquiry Learning (POGIL) activities for mathematics. The librarians were also able to discuss the importance of information literacy for various disciplines and ways to incorporate it into their classes.

During the semester while the fellows developed the projects, they provided feedback to one another on their proposals, making suggestions for improvement, asking questions, and giving advice. The weekly meetings included workshops on research design, compiling statistics, and conducting library research. The authors led the session about library research, which not only informed the faculty of new ways to search for relevant resources and discover subscriptions they did not know were available but also provided the librarians with insight into how differently the faculty in various fields access resources for their literature reviews. Another session that proved especially helpful for the fellows was how to navigate the Institutional Review Board (IRB). A faculty member who was on the IRB but not a part of the fellowship provided assistance clarifying the information about the projects and reviewing the submissions prior to uploading them into the IRB online network.

One of the benefits of participating in the community of fellows has been increased visibility for librarians as partners and resources for the work of SoTL. Librarians were able to engage faculty with their knowledge of library resources and the literature review process, which helped create a formal relationship between librarians and OFDTE. The first author has continued offering a session on reviewing the literature to subsequent cohorts of fellows and was recently named the liaison to OFDTE. In fall 2017, he began offering research consultations to those working on literature reviews related to SoTL projects. Additionally, he was asked to serve on OFDTE's Advisory Board, a position that exposes a greater number of campus colleagues to librarian involvement in SoTL work. By being involved in the work of SoTL through opportunities like the fellowship program, not only can librarians gain greater access to the spaces in which faculty discuss issues of teaching and learning, they can become part of the conversation and contribute their knowledge and expertise. The authors' experiences with SoTL inspired other library faculty to apply for the SoTL Fellowship and engage with SoTL projects more broadly. The success and visibility of librarians in SoTL at Augusta University can be directly attributed to participation and involvement with OFDTE's professional development programs.

Throughout this fellowship, the participation and involvement between librarians and teaching faculty were successful. However, there are occasions when teaching faculty fail to view librarians as faculty researchers and potential partners for projects. Although the authors did not encounter this issue, it may arise when librarians collaborate with faculty researchers. William Walters notes that "although librarians are counted as faculty at more than half of all U.S. colleges and universities, the differences between librarians and regular faculty can be seen in their responsibilities, backgrounds, benefits, and working conditions."[4] Walters also indicates that there is a "gap between librarians and regular faculty, in terms of scholarly expectations and performance."[5] At Augusta University, however, research and publication are required for all librarians. They have faculty status but are not on the tenure track. By having librarians participate in the SoTL Fellowship with other campus faculty, it promotes and ensures an understanding that librarians have similar scholarly expectations placed upon them. Dr. Deborah Richardson, the director of OFTDE, agrees. When asked what she saw as the benefits of librarians participating in SoTL, she stated, "I think it makes other faculty aware that librarians are faculty in a way that they often [do not] grasp otherwise. I think the role of doing SoTL research is absolutely connected to what [librarians] do anyway ... [it is] just making what [they] do anyway more scholarly."[6] This sentiment is confirmed by Perini, who states, "By discussing or writing about instructional methodologies with academic colleagues, individuals (including librarians) are networking and making professional connections."[7] The authors were able to utilize their SoTL projects to enhance the professional connections they had on campus and to learn about teaching methodologies in other disciplines. Perini confirms, "SoTL offers librarians the prospect of increased knowledge of cross-disciplinary instructional methods, collaborative opportunities, and abundant research possibilities."[8] This is evidenced by the continued relationships that were afforded by the librarians' participation in the SoTL Fellowship.

One challenge for librarians participating in SoTL is conducting the research itself. Kennedy and Brancolini surveyed academic librarians about their engagement with research. They found that "several of the obstacles of conducting research are: reported lack of time to complete a research project, unfamiliarity with the research process, lack of support for research (both emotional and monetary), lack of access to research, lack of confidence, discouraging jargon, inadequate education in research methods, and lack of motivation."[9] Although the authors were familiar with the research process and had the support and confidence to complete their projects, they found the lack of time to be one of the biggest impediments. This aligns with the results reported by Kennedy and Brancolini.[10] Richardson confirms this assertion:

> Even though people theoretically have time that their chair has
> committed to them to work on the project, that sometimes works

and it sometimes [does not]. And I think one of the challenges in the Fellowship, though [the Fellows] would know better than I do, is just finding the time to do the things [they] need to do.... Finding the time to just put the effort in to get that writing project done, or to finally develop or to get the IRB proposal together.[11]

In fact, the fellowship application required the chair's authorization and signature; it stated, "I understand that his/her activity will require approximately 10% of the Fellow's time for fall 2015 and spring 2016. If accepted into the Fellowship program, this faculty member will be expected to develop research skills in the context of their teaching activities and will complete at least one SoTL project, suitable for peer review and publication or presentation."[12] Despite the head librarian giving permission for the two librarians to dedicate 10 percent of their time to their SoTL projects, in reality, that 10 percent was in addition to their daily work. Where teaching faculty can sometimes receive a course release for their participation, the librarians in this case still had to perform their regular duties while conducting this additional research. The authors recommend conducting research that can integrate current job duties with projects they are interested in pursuing. For example, the first author was already working on integrating the ACRL *Framework* into library instruction, while the second author promotes the implementation of open access materials into the curriculum. Because the research was closely aligned with job duties, some aspects of the SoTL projects could be easily incorporated into daily work.

Despite the added workload, the fellowship was and continues to be beneficial in regard to professional development. Conducting the research for both projects exposed the authors to more advanced research methods than either had previously experienced. By having the responsibility for designing and implementing these projects, they built upon their foundations in not only conducting but conveying their results to larger audiences. Both authors presented their SoTL projects at Augusta University's Faculty Development Day. Additionally, the first author presented his initial findings at the Georgia International Conference on Information Literacy and is also in the process of composing an article with the final results of his study for publication. The second author and her SoTL partner presented at the University System of Georgia's Teaching and Learning Conference and conferred their preliminary results at the Rocky Mountain Modern Language Association Conference. They are also working to author a publication conveying their final results.

Conclusion

Richardson indicated that professional development was one of the goals set forth in establishing the fellowship. She states that it is one of the benefits she sees for faculty who participate:

Clearly, it's their professional development ... and I mean in an informal way just a kind of way to learn things—learn things about teaching and learning, as well as learn more about research. I hope that it has a positive impact on the CV and *that* is pretty explicit in the call for applications, that the expectation is that anybody who does this will do presentations and publications and hopefully beyond this university and do it elsewhere. And so it is intended to help their professional development in that more formal way giving them entries for the *vita*. It also provides, because the group at the table is interdisciplinary, the opportunity for people to make connections with other people that they might not have otherwise made is, I think, excellent.[13]

The SoTL Fellowship provided faculty members from a variety of disciplines insight into the practice of other teachers. The librarians were able to see how some of the teaching faculty are applying unique teaching and research techniques that they otherwise may not have known about. Being involved in such an endeavor allowed the librarians to make connections and offer their expertise in ways they had not previously been afforded. In addition, learning from others involved in the program helped the librarians develop skills in research design and data analysis. By partnering with OFDTE and participating in the SoTL Fellowship, the librarians increased their visibility as researchers and partners on campus and greatly expanded their professional development beyond the library discipline. In conducting SoTL research, the authors gained the confidence and skills to develop additional projects and were inspired to find new avenues for exploring future teaching and learning opportunities. While the results garnered from this research were beneficial, the confidence and skills the authors obtained through working on these SoTL projects helped them expand how research can influence their work.

ENDNOTES

1. "About Us," Affordable Learning Georgia, accessed November 5, 2017, http://www.affordablelearninggeorgia.org/about/about_us.
2. Michael Levine-Clark, "Electronic Books and the Humanities: A Survey at the University of Denver," *Collection Building* 26, no. 1 (2007): 12, https://doi.org/10.1108/01604950710721548.
3. Diane Mizrachi, "Undergraduates' Academic Reading Format Preferences and Behaviors," *The Journal of Academic Librarianship,* 41 (2015): 310, https://doi.org/10.1016/j.acalib.2015.03.009.
4. William H. Walters, "Faculty Status of Librarians at U.S. Research Universities," *The Journal of Academic Librarianship* 42, no. 2 (2016): 161, https://doi.org/10.1016/j.acalib.2015.11.002.
5. Walters, "Faculty Status," 167.
6. Deborah Richardson (Director of Faculty Development & Teaching Excellence, Augusta University), in discussion with the authors, August 2017.
7. Michael Perini, "Enhancing Collaboration through the Scholarship of Teaching and Learning," *Collaborative Librarianship* 6, no. 1 (2014): 53, https://digitalcommons.du.edu/collaborativelibrarianship/vol6/iss1/8/.
8. Perini, "Enhancing Collaboration," 54.
9. Marie R. Kennedy and Kristine R. Brancolini, "Academic Librarian Research: A Survey of

Attitudes, Involvement, and Perceived Capabilities," *College & Research Libraries* 73, no. 5 (2012): 432, http://crl.acrl.org/index.php/crl/article/view/16252.

10. See Kennedy and Brancolini, "Academic Librarian Research," 440.
11. Richardson, discussion.
12. Application to participate in Scholarship of Teaching and Learning Fellowship, Augusta University, April 2015.
13. Richardson, discussion.

BIBLIOGRAPHY

Affordable Learning Georgia. "About Us." Accessed November 5, 2017. http://www.affordablelearninggeorgia.org/about/about_us.

Kennedy, Marie R., and Kristine R. Brancolini. "Academic Librarian Research: A Survey of Attitudes, Involvement, and Perceived Capabilities." *College & Research Libraries* 73, no. 5 (2012): 431–48. http://crl.acrl.org/index.php/crl/article/view/16252.

Levine-Clark, Michael. "Electronic Books and the Humanities: A Survey at the University of Denver." *Collection Building* 26, no. 1 (2007): 7–14. https://doi.org/10.1108/01604950710721548.

Mizrachi, Diane. "Undergraduates' Academic Reading Format Preferences and Behaviors." *The Journal of Academic Librarianship* 41 (2015): 301–11. https://doi.org/10.1016/j.acalib.2015.03.009.

Perini, Michael. "Enhancing Collaboration through the Scholarship of Teaching and Learning." *Collaborative Librarianship* 6, no. 1 (2014): 52–55. https://digitalcommons.du.edu/collaborativelibrarianship/vol6/iss1/8/.

Walters, William H. "Faculty Status of Librarians at U.S. Research Universities." *The Journal of Academic Librarianship* 42, no. 2 (2016): 161–71. https://doi.org/10.1016/j.acalib.2015.11.002.

24

DiYing Your Own Framework:

Partnering with a CTL to Construct Local Learning Outcomes

Amy Fyn and Jenn Marshall Shinaberger

Introduction

The adoption of the *Framework for Information Literacy for Higher Education*[1] by the Association of College & Research Libraries' (ACRL) executive board in January 2016 motivated library instruction programs to deeply explore the *Framework* and carefully evaluate its impact on a local level. A coordinator of library instruction and the director of a Center for Teaching and Learning (CTL) used Scholarship of Teaching and Learning (SoTL) as a method to investigate designing learning outcomes for a library instruction program that incorporates the ACRL *Framework*. The authors trace the design process followed by Kimbel Library and the Center for Teaching Excellence to Advance Learning (CeTEAL) at Coastal Carolina University (CCU). They argue that a SoTL framework can be used by academic librarians as a model for contextualizing the ACRL Frames and designing local learning outcomes.

SoTL as Professional Development

The ACRL *Framework*'s Appendix[2] noted that the frames provided opportunities for librarians to collaborate with other colleagues on their campus when developing instructional content for information literacy. One of the opportunities suggested by the ACRL *Framework* document is SoTL research. SoTL research is inquiry that is context-based, systematic, and evidence-based, follows ethical practice and shares findings publicly for colleagues to review, critique, and use.[3] The characteristics of SoTL research provided

a valuable model within which the authors began their research. As scholar-practitioners, the authors grounded an examination of the ACRL frames in SoTL research to contribute to professional dialogue around information literacy. The authors used the SoTL inquiry process, drawing upon two instructional design models, Understanding by Design (UbD) and Idea-Based Learning (IBL), in addition to evidence-based practice, in order to design professional development workshops for instruction librarians.

Faculty development that occurs around significant change within a profession and discipline, such as the adoption of the ACRL *Framework,* can benefit from examination through the SoTL lens. In this case study, the authors found several advantages to this approach: taking SOTL research to the program level, partnering with one another, and making our work public, in the SoTL tradition, so that others could benefit from our experiences.

Elton[4] discusses the important connection between continuing professional development and SoTL. Using SoTL as professional development allows practitioners to stand at "the intersection of content and pedagogy that brings together the wisdom of practice on a topic-by-topic, idea-by-idea practice."[5] Weimer sets out two broad categories of SoTL research in which practitioners engage: wisdom-of-practice scholarship and research scholarship. The wisdom-of-practice scholarship classification, called the "how-to literature of teaching" contains four entries: personal account of change, recommended practices reports, recommended-content reports, and personal narratives.[6] This case study is a recommended practices report within the wisdom-of-practice classification and relies on the experience of the authors, evidence-based research, and reflective practice and is within the recommended-practice approach to SoTL.

Project Background

This case study is written from the point of view of an academic librarian and a faculty developer who brought together their background and experiences to work on the issue of localizing the ACRL frames. The authors used a SoTL inquiry process as a guide to apply evidence-based practice to development workshops for librarians through which they examined the ACRL frames. This case study is positioned at the crossroads of several distinct fields: information literacy and library instruction, educational (faculty) development, and instructional design.

The authors of the ACRL *Framework* recommended that academic libraries collaborate with their campus Center for Teaching and Learning (CTL) to implement the *Framework* and to share their instruction materials with other librarians. The challenge faced by information literacy programs is that the ACRL *Framework* document, unlike the rescinded *Information Literacy Competency Standards for Higher Education* (2000),[7] lacks a standardized set of learning outcomes which libraries can draw on to determine competency in a set of skills. No longer given a one-size-fits-all model developed by a professional organization, librarians and information literacy programs were tasked with determining how the ACRL *Framework*'s concepts applied at their own institution.

ACRL provided little initial guidance for implementing the *Framework* beyond recommending discussions with partners who support or contribute to curricula initiatives on college campuses. To date, presentations and publications about implementing the *Framework* have focused on changes made to one-shot sessions[8] and individual courses or assignments,[9] with little published about the process used by information literacy programs that have successfully implemented the *Framework* at a program level. This case study addresses this gap in the existing library literature and practice. In the next section, the authors detail how one library partnered with a CTL to address the problem of constructing local learning outcomes for novice and expert learners using SoTL as inquiry and professional development.

DiYing the ACRL *Framework*: A Case Study

Coastal Carolina University (CCU) is a mid-sized, public liberal arts institution in the southeast Atlantic region with approximately 10,000 students, primarily undergraduates. CCU's Kimbel Library has a dedicated instruction program that works with faculty to provide course-integrated one-shot sessions to all levels of students and offers a set of credit-bearing research courses available to undergraduate students. CeTEAL is CCU's faculty development center and provides professional development for effective teaching, scholarship, and service.

Kimbel Library's instruction program is modeled in part on professional guidelines such as the *Characteristics of Programs of Information Literacy that Illustrate Best Practices: A Guideline*.[10] Following the recommendations from the ACRL *Framework's* supporting materials, instruction librarians at CCU's Kimbel Library prepared to explore the *Framework* and consider its relevance to the local community by engaging in discussions. The description, knowledge practices, and dispositions of one frame were reviewed each month during instruction meetings. Librarians shared how they addressed aspects of a frame within existing one-shot research sessions, and they individually and collectively considered how, when, and even if each frame had a place in their work with students. Librarians recognized that their instructional approaches should adapt in some ways in response to the ACRL *Framework*, moving away from teaching skills and moving toward guiding learners as they approach threshold concepts so they can produce, collaborate, and distribute information. In the next section, the authors describe the decisions made in the design of the in-house workshops.

Designing Professional Development Workshops for the ACRL *Framework*

Librarians at CCU have a strong relationship with the campus's faculty development center, CeTEAL. To expand the library's community of practice developing around the ACRL *Framework*, the coordinator of library instruction partnered with the director of CeTEAL to design workshops that would address some of the challenges presented by the *Framework*. The primary goals of this professional development workshop series were to develop learning outcomes for the library's information literacy program based on the *Framework* and to create a sense of ownership of the new focus within the department. The plan was to expand on the conversational approach of the previous year to more intentionally discuss and develop local outcomes for multiple levels of students.

Figure 24.1 shows the steps of the SoTL research cycle the authors used as a guide for developing a research question, gathering evidence-based models and approaches, implementing professional development workshops, adjusting the workshops, reflecting with lessons learned, and disseminating the results.

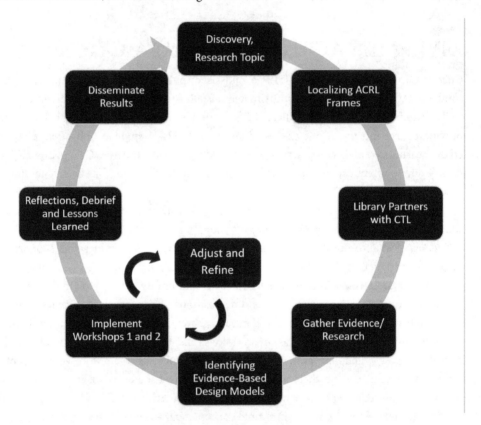

Figure 24.1. The SoTL research process showing how evidence-based practice and professional development were used by a coordinator of library instruction and a faculty developer.

The SoTL research cycle requires that research is rooted in evidence-based methods. The authors explored several design models and approaches in which to ground the development of local learning outcomes including Understanding by Design (UbD) and, for the second workshop, Idea-Based Learning (IBL).[11] The director of CeTEAL recommended the use of UbD, as the development of the ACRL *Framework* was informed by elements of backward design.

UbD is a curricular design model which uses the backward design approach, beginning with the end and asking what students should be able to do as a result of the instruction. The first stage of UbD—Key Design Elements—contains six steps:

1. Unpacking goals
2. Identifying big ideas
3. Developing essential questions
4. Developing understandings
5. Considering misunderstandings
6. Identifying key knowledge and skills

Using UbD as an evidence-based practice, the authors applied Stage 1 to develop learning outcomes for the information literacy program. UbD allows for entry into the design model at any point but seems to presume that unpacking goals or outcomes is the first step as most of the examples in the UbD text begin with state standards in K-12 education. The authors found UbD's focus on unpacking learning outcomes first conflicted with the ACRL *Framework*'s directive to develop local learning outcomes as the end result. They decided to enter the UbD model at the second step, "Identifying big ideas," since there were no outcomes to unpack, and ended at the "Unpacking goals" (student learning outcomes in this case) step of Stage 1 in the UbD model.

The authors worked through steps of Stage 1, using the frame Information has Value to conceptualize how this process would play out in the workshop setting. The CeTEAL director identified relevant templates from the Key Design Elements in Stage 1 of UbD[12] that would guide the participants in engaging with individual frames, and the coordinator gave feedback on which would work best to apply to the *Framework*. The next section discusses the first professional development workshop and adjustments made as a result of participant feedback.

Creating Program Outcomes: Understanding by Design

Six instruction librarians and the director of the faculty development center met to consider implications of the ACRL *Framework*'s approach to information literacy programs. The instruction coordinator set the expectation that the participants would complete activities leading to the creation of learning outcomes to complement or replace the ACRL Information Literacy Standards-based outcomes of the library's information literacy program. The CeTEAL director led the workshops so all librarians, including the instruction coordinator, could grapple with larger questions inherent in localizing the *Framework*.

The CeTEAL director began with a brief overview of the day's plan and introduced how to apply an instructional design process to the *Framework*. Next, she explained each of the Key Design Elements before guiding the librarians through Stage 1 of UbD. Using the Information Has Value frame as the example, the group considered their experiences working with students both in instruction settings and during reference desk interactions. They identified "big ideas" related to Information Has Value, developed "essential questions," framed "big ideas" and "understandings," and listed the "misunderstandings" often observed when working with students in regard to the value of information. The group completed the remaining parts of UbD by "identifying knowledge and key skills." At the end of these steps, they drafted several potential learning outcomes for Information Has Value, ranging in ability from novice to expert. Next, the librarians were split into two groups to repeat the backward design process for an additional frame, again starting with a description of "big ideas." At the end of the workshop, the group had drafted several outcomes related to three of the six frames.

During the professional development workshops, the authors encountered mixed feelings from the participants toward working with the frames, which is representative of the response the ACRL *Framework* received from the broader community of academic librarians. By the end of the session, some participants were confused or disengaged, while the process resonated with others who were enthusiastic. One librarian expressed disappointment that after all this work, the group drafted some knowledge and skills very similar to the ACRL *Information Literacy Competency Standards*. Feedback from participants noted that the UbD process was time-consuming and may not be worth the effort since most of the library instruction sessions are fifty minutes, while the process took much longer than fifty minutes. Librarians struggled with the abstract nature of the first steps of UbD. The authors noted that there were two new concepts—the frames **and** UbD—which posed significant challenges. Nevertheless, the group put forth an incredible amount of effort to participate in the workshop. Conversations and work shared in group reports indicated conscientious interaction with the *Framework* and with each other were ongoing.

The authors recognized the need to clarify the goals of the professional development series in order to encourage further engagement with the ACRL *Framework* and library instruction goals. Based on the results, a new theoretical approach was also needed to fully meet the needs of the instruction program. Since SoTL inquiry is an iterative process, the authors reflected on the first professional development workshop and made adjustments for the second workshop. Planning began immediately to improve the method used before the next workshop to gain more buy-in from participants.

Creating Program Outcomes: Idea-Based Learning

For the second workshop, the authors reevaluated their strategy in order to address some of the participant disconnect observed in the first workshop. The authors also changed their overall approach to the workshop, leading with a much more structured agenda. To provide additional context for the workshop, the coordinator of library instruction emphasized that the purpose of the series was not only to develop program-wide learning outcomes that incorporated the ACRL *Framework*, but also to reflect on current teaching practice as part of professional development and growth. After a brief review of the previous workshop's outcomes, the CeTEAL director introduced Idea-Based Learning (IBL) as an alternate method.

Like UbD, IBL is a backward design model. As shown in figure 24.2, IBL differs from UbD in that it is written by a faculty developer for a higher education audience. Idea-Based course design is inspired by UbD but takes into account how college and university faculty design courses.

Understanding by Design (UbD) : Stage 1 Steps—Key Design Elements	Idea-Based Learning (IBL) Stage 1 Steps—Identify Desired Results
Step 1. Unpack Goals	
Step 2. Identify the Big Ideas	Step 1. Big Ideas
Step 3. Develop Essential Questions	
Step 4. Develop Understandings	Step 2. Enduring Understandings
Step 5. Consider Misunderstandings	Step 4. Student Background—Identify where students struggle the most with the course
Step 6. Identify Key Knowledge and Skills	
	Step 3. Create Learning Outcomes

Figure 24.2. A comparison of the Stage 1 steps of Understanding by Design (UbD) and Idea-Based Learning (IBL).

IBL begins with developing "big ideas," creating "enduring understandings," creating "learning outcomes," and identifying "areas where students struggle the most in a course." Step 3 of IBL differs from UbD in that there are not always goals or contents standards as there are in the K-12 education. The final step of Stage 1 in IBL, considering "student background" is similar to "considering misunderstandings" in the UDL method.[13]

As there is overlap between UbD and IBL models—both are rooted in backward design—the CeTEAL director recommended using IBL for developing potential program outcomes based on the remaining three frames. To transition materials from the UbD approach of the first workshop to the new IBL approach, the CeTEAL director transferred the UbD steps from the first professional development workshop— "identifying big ideas," "enduring understandings," "essential questions," "misunderstandings and learning outcomes"—into an IBL template detailed in figure 24.3. Librarians filled gaps within the design matrix as the first activity of the second workshop. This bridging activity was designed to acknowledge the work completed in the first workshop before introducing IBL.

Big Ideas	Enduring Understandings	Learning Outcomes	Common Misconceptions	Essential Questions
Citation Practices	Citation is important because _____.	Locate and retrieve citations from databases.	Information practice doesn't carry into real life.	Why cite? Why bother? Why do library databases have value?
Commodification of Information	Information has value and commodification of information.	Recognize the need for value of information.	Information is easily accessible. No one cares about my personal info.	Why use or don't use Google?
	Value of info changes with the context.	Recognize the value of curated library resources.	All information is valued the same.	You can find an objective source. What kind of info do you value or trust?
	Author/ creator has value.	Recognize the value of one's own contribution and contributions of others.	Teacher/ creator won't know if I use it. Information is free and easily accessible. Info has no author.	What is an example of plagiarism? Why is plagiarism a bad thing?
	Responsibility of the consumer, creator, and owner.	Recognize the rights and responsibilities of the creator, consumer, and contributor.		How would you respond if you created _____?
		Identify a plurality of history in primary sources.	Everyone has a voice and is heard.	What groups or voices did you find (or not find)?
	Not all have access to info dissemination and creation resources/ discovery resource.	Articulate societal factors that may systematically marginalize or are underrepresented.		What are some barriers to info access?

Figure 24.3. Example of an Idea-Based Learning (IBL) design plan from a professional development workshop exploring the ACRL frame, Information Has Value.[14]

Next, the six librarians paired up and were assigned one frame to reflect on and draft suggested outcomes for novice and expert learners. Some pairs combined elements of a frame's knowledge practice with a disposition as a starting point to writing an outcome that either fit current students or represented a future goal for them. The authors observed that librarians were more engaged in drafting potential outcomes when beginning with the ACRL *Framework* language. This activity wrapped up the program-level portion of the workshop, and the outcomes were recorded for future incorporation into the program-level assessment plan.

Changing Directions: Using the SLO-Frame Grid

The workshop then shifted focus from abstract, big-picture thinking toward a specific strategic focus of the information literacy program. First-year programs are the foundation of Kimbel Library's instruction program, which historically provides research instruction to over 90 percent of first-year composition courses. The established standards-based learning outcomes for these courses, ENGL 101 and ENGL 102, were updated prior to the workshops as part of an earlier project to acknowledge the program needs. In this segment of the second workshop, librarians reconsidered each learning outcome for the first-year composition program through the lens of the *Framework* by using a student learning outcome grid modeled after Wohlmut's SLO-Frame Grid.[15] In this grid, learning outcomes are given on one axis, and the other axis lists each frame (see figure 24.4). Participants reflected how

INFORMATION LITERACY FRAMES	*Novice Level* ENGL 101 SLO 2: Students should be able to develop keywords and synonyms
Authority is Constructed and Contextual	In order to
Information Creation as a Process	In order to
Information has Value	In order to
Research as Inquiry	In order to
Scholarship as Conversation	In order to
Searching as Strategic Exploration	In order to
Framework Workshop Worksheet 1 August 2017	
From Wohlmut, P., *Meeting Your Class at the Crossroads: Using SLO/Frame Grids to Tailor Information Literacy Instruction.* Information Literacy Advisory Group of Oregon (ILAGO). Oregon IL Summit 2017. <https://ilago.wordpress.com/oregon-il-summit-2017/>	

Figure 24.4. Example of an SLO-Frame Grid used to explore the relationship between a library learning outcome for a first-year composition course and the ACRL frames.

each first-year composition learning outcome could be viewed through the lens of each frame. Participants applied each frame to the established learning outcomes by adding the phrase "in order to" and completing the sentence by writing a statement related to each frame. The end result was student learning outcomes which had each been individually considered in relation to each frame. The librarians much preferred this approach due to its direct, practical application to their daily work in comparison to developing program-wide outcomes. This activity concluded the second workshop.

Lessons Learned

SoTL requires reflection upon the research process. The authors offer several considerations based on the development and implementation of the professional development workshops. Librarians had varying levels of familiarity with the ACRL *Framework*, which was expected. The group also had different levels of buy-in, both for the *Framework* and for considering the program-level outcomes, based on personal interest and experience with library instruction at CCU. In a sense, the small group was representative of the conversations about the *Framework* taking place on professional listservs and blog posts. Based on the experiences of the two workshops, the authors recommend the following:

- Emphasize the professional and local goals in terms of how this work will benefit individuals and the program to bridge any gaps in creating the initial community.
- Discuss the professional obligation of participating in the discussion of how the frames apply locally.
- Model an activity first to set expectations for any independent or group work. Skipping this step leads to different understandings and work product for each group.
- Take the time to provide a firm grounding in backward design models. Not all librarians are familiar with instructional design, yet they need to learn enough about the theories in the field of instructional design in order to fully apply ACRL recommendations for tailoring the *Framework* to local interests.
- In retrospect, the director of CeTEAL determined that the UbD design model was too rooted in K12 standards-based education. She recommends IBL as the better model for higher education.
- Consider demographics when designating pairs or groups for activities. Mixing experienced and novice librarians and varying levels of instruction backgrounds creates solid group dynamics and allows for the participants to learn from each other.
- Scheduling professional development workshops facilitated by a CTL gives librarians the time and space away from the typical daily schedule to have appropriate time to consider the implications of the frames in a local context and permits librarians to serve as subject matter experts during the design process.

- The more concrete approach of examining existing outcomes for courses with one-shots commonly taught by librarians and considering them through the lens of the frames was the most successful portion of the workshops. Program-level outcomes presented a greater challenge.
- Be flexible in planning. If one approach or model does not work with a group, find another model that fits better.
- Use change as an opportunity to reflect on professional practice and teaching practice for scholarship and intellectual contributions. SoTL methods of investigation provide opportunity for research during times of change.

The SoTL research cycle used to contextualize the ACRL *Framework* facilitated a deeper conversation as librarians considered ideas, questions, understandings, and misunderstandings related to information literacy. On a program level, the SoTL-based workshops resulted in a retooling of instruction meetings to place more focus on pedagogy and teaching demonstrations, based on librarian feedback. On an individual level, librarians have used elements of the *Framework* to develop student learning outcomes and activities for one-shot sessions, spoken about the *Framework* with faculty in other disciplines, and used and considered distributing lesson plans in SoTL outlets such as Project CORA and the ACRL Sandbox. These are all promising steps toward further integration of a SoTL mindset to enhance library instruction research at the one-shot and program level.

Conclusion

This case study has discussed the experiences of a library partnering with a CTL to design professional development workshops to consider how the ACRL frames can be applied to a local context. Work undertaken in the partnership between librarians and the Center for Teaching Excellence to Advance Learning at Coastal Carolina University points to the need for further research into design models that can be used to assist library instruction programs in creating meaningful local learning outcomes based on the ACRL frames. The authors used SoTL to guide their process so their experiences could serve as an example for other academic libraries to develop professional development workshops to localize learning outcomes. SoTL provides an invaluable model for academic librarians to develop a reflective and evidence-based practice approach to improving teaching and learning and can inspire them to disseminate their research as a way to contribute to professional dialogue in their field.

ENDNOTES

1. Association of College and Research Libraries, *Framework for Information Literacy for Higher Education*, accessed October 21, 2017, http://www.ala.org/acrl/standards/ilframework.
2. Association of College and Research Libraries, *Framework*.
3. Cathy Bishop-Clark and Beth Deitz-Uhler, *Engaging in the Scholarship of Teaching and*

Learning: A Guide to the Process, and How to Develop a Project from Start to Finish (Sterling, VA: Stylus Publishing, 2012).
4. Lewis Elton, "Continuing Professional Development in Higher Education: The Role of the Scholarship of Teaching and Learning," *International Journal for the Scholarship of Teaching and Learning,* 3 no. 1 (2009), Article 28, https://doi.org/10.20429/ijsotl.2009.030128.
5. Ron Brandt, "On Research on Teaching: A Conversation with Lee Shulman," *Educational Leadership* 49, no. 7 (April 1992): 14, http://www.ascd.org/ASCD/pdf/journals/ed_lead/el_199204_brandt2.pdf.
6. Maryellen Weimer, *Enhancing Scholarly Work in Teaching & Learning: Professional Literature That Makes a Difference* (San Francisco, CA: Jossey-Bass, 2006).
7. Association of College and Research Libraries, *Information Literacy Competency Standards for Higher Education,* accessed October 21, 2017, https://alair.ala.org/handle/11213/7668.
8. Patrick Wohlmut, "Meeting Your Class at the Crossroads: Using SLO-Frame Grids to Tailor Information Literacy Instruction," PowerPoint, ILAGO conference, Washington State University, Vancouver, WA, May 13, 2017; Patricia Bravender, Hazel McClure, and Gayle Schaub, *Teaching Information Literacy Threshold Concepts: Lesson Plans for Librarians,* (Chicago: ACRL, 2015); Heidi Buchanan and Beth McDonough, "Right on Time: Best Practice in One-Shot Instruction," in *The New Information Literacy Instruction: Best Practices,* eds. Patrick Ragains and M. Sandra Wood (Lanham, MD: Rowman and Littlefield, 2016).
9. Mahrya Carncross, "Redeveloping a Course with the Framework for Information Literacy for Higher Education," *College & Research Libraries News* 76 no. 5 (2015): 248–73; Allison Hosier, "Creating Learning Outcomes from Threshold Concepts," *College and Undergraduate Libraries* 24 no. 1 (2017): 1–13.
10. Association of College and Research Libraries, *Characteristics of Programs of Information Literacy that Illustrate Best Practices: A Guideline,* accessed October 21, 2017, http://www.ala.org/acrl/standards/characteristics.
11. Grant Wiggins and Jay McTighe, *Understanding by Design* (Alexandria, VA: Association for Supervision and Curriculum Development, 2004); Lee Shulman, "Signature Pedagogies in the Professions," *Daedalus: Journal of the American Academy of Arts and Sciences,* 134 (2005), 52–59; Edmund Hansen, *Idea-Based Learning: A Course Design Process to Promote Conceptual Understanding* (Sterling, VA: Stylus, 2011).
12. Wiggins & McTighe, *Understanding by Design.*
13. Edmund J. Hansen, *Idea-Based Learning: A Course Design Process to Promote Conceptual Understanding* (Sterling, VA: Stylus Publishing, 2011).
14. Ibid.
15. Wohlmut, "Meeting Your Class."

BIBLIOGRAPHY

Association of College and Research Libraries. "ACRL Information Literacy Framework Sandbox." 2016. http://sandbox.acrl.org/.
———. "Characteristics of Programs of Information Literacy that Illustrate Best Practices: A Guideline." 2012. http://www.ala.org/acrl/standards/characteristics.
———. *Framework for Information Literacy for Higher Education.* 2015. http://www.ala.org/acrl/standards/ilframework.
———. "Information Literacy Competency Standards for Higher Education." 2000. https://alair.ala.org/handle/11213/7668.
Bishop-Clark, Cathy, and Beth Dietz-Uhler. *Engaging in the Scholarship of Teaching and Learning: A*

Guide to the Process, and how to Develop a Project from Start to Finish. Sterling, VA: Stylus Publishing, 2012.

Boyer, Ernest L. *Scholarship Reconsidered: Priorities of the Professoriate.* Princeton, NJ: Carnegie Foundation for the Advancement of Teaching, 1990.

Brandt, Ron. "On Research on Teaching: A Conversation with Lee Shulman." Educational Leadership 49, no. 7 (April 1992): 14–19.

Elton, Lewis. "Continuing Professional Development in Higher Education: The Role of the Scholarship of Teaching and Learning." *International Journal for the Scholarship of Teaching and Learning*, 3, no. 1 (2009), Article 28. https://doi.org/10.20429/ijsotl.2009.030128.

Hansen, Edmund J. *Idea-Based Learning: A Course Design Process to Promote Conceptual Understanding.* Sterling, VA: Stylus Publishing, 2011.

Shulman, Lee. "Signature Pedagogies in the Professions." *Daedalus: Journal of the American Academy of Arts and Sciences*, 134, no. 3 (2005): 52–59.

Weimer, Maryellen. *Enhancing Scholarly Work in Teaching & Learning: Professional Literature That Makes a Difference.* San Francisco, CA: Jossey-Bass, 2006.

Wiggins, Grant, and Jay McTighe. *Understanding by Design.* Alexandria, VA: Association for Supervision and Curriculum Development, 2004.

Wohlmut, Patrick. "Meeting Your Class at the Crossroads: Using SLO-Frame Grids to Tailor Information Literacy Instruction." PowerPoint, ILAGO conference, Washington State University, Vancouver, WA, May 13, 2017. https://ilago.files.wordpress.com/2017/04/wohlmut-ilago-2017-slideshow.pptx.

Re-centering Teaching and Learning:

Toward Communities of Practice at the University of Nebraska-Lincoln Libraries

Erica DeFrain, Leslie Delserone, Elizabeth Lorang, Catherine Fraser Riehle, and Toni Anaya

The scholarship of teaching and learning (SoTL) presents important opportunities that can transform learning, but many academic librarians at the University of Nebraska-Lincoln (UNL) struggle to find a scholarly center when their teaching roles are frequently that of external collaborator. Challenges such as access to student data, meaningful evaluations of instruction, limited opportunities for funding and professional development, and uncertainty over how to negotiate for these have contributed to librarians remaining on the periphery of SoTL work. Hoping to overcome some of these hurdles, UNL librarians are developing a community of practice (CoP) around teaching and learning.

In the summer of 2016, UNL librarians began developing new collaborative structures and practices to increase and encourage library-wide professional development, and this case study captures and reflects upon these attempts. This discussion has three goals: (1) to present the emerging efforts in the UNL Libraries to develop a more intentional CoP around teaching and learning, (2) to outline three recent, multidisciplinary SoTL projects in which librarians played critical roles, and (3) to reflect on how this CoP is inspiring librarians to be more systematic in approaches to teaching, in analyzing these efforts, and in sharing these outcomes and findings broadly.

Developing Collaborative Models of Instruction at UNL Libraries

Unlike many of its peer universities, UNL, a member of the Big Ten Academic Alliance and a Carnegie R1 institution, does not currently have a Center for Teaching and Learning; a previous center was closed due to budget cuts in 2000. Despite this setback, teaching and learning initiatives on this campus of 26,000 students are still institutionally valued and incentivized, and they occur across many units. Some of these initiatives have been out of reach to the majority of librarians, who have faculty status but generally do not teach credit-bearing courses. For example, the faculty-led Peer Review of Teaching Project has guided hundreds of UNL faculty through the process of developing reflective course portfolios, but only faculty teaching semester-length classes are eligible to apply.[1] For the other initiatives in which librarians were eligible and had participated, they typically did so in isolation from one another along traditional liaison lines.

Struggling to meet the demands of a growing student body with only twenty-two liaisons, librarians began seeking alternatives to the siloed structure of the liaison program and its approach to teaching that would foster greater collaboration and social interaction. Inspired by Belzowski, Ladwig, and Miller's application of Wenger's CoP theory in an academic library,[2] they formalized a mission statement for the liaison program, explicitly stating the program's movement toward a CoP and a SoTL culture.[3] Next, they launched a series of voluntary professional development initiatives centered on teaching and pedagogy. In 2016, two librarians introduced Practicing Pedagogies, a bi-monthly, internal workshop series, designed to provide teaching support and peer review for curriculum development and instruction.[4] The series has covered topics such as reflective practice, active learning, embodied pedagogy, and assessment theory. There will also be a two-day Practicing Pedagogies retreat for academic teaching librarians across Nebraska during summer 2018, which will provide opportunities for librarians to participate in sharing, discussion, and professional development programming related to teaching and learning, as well as for the development of personal teaching philosophies and teaching portfolios.

At the same time as the emergence of Practicing Pedagogies, librarians also began initiating campus-wide events that would help situate UNL Libraries directly within external conversations about teaching and learning. With support from the dean, UNL Libraries sponsored a campus-wide program that featured a keynote and panel discussion of three librarians connected with the Instruction Matters: Purdue Academic Course Transformation (IMPACT) program.[5] The event drew more than seventy attendees, including administrators, teaching faculty, and librarians from around the Midwest. Later that year, UNL Libraries appointed Alison Head of Project Information Literacy as Visiting Scholar for 2016–2017.[6] This was the first time UNL Libraries had ever bestowed such an appointment, which provided a unique opportunity for librarians and faculty from the entire University of Nebraska's four-campus system to engage with Head about research methods and students' information literacy needs. With additional financial support from the University Research Council, librarians again hosted a well-attended campus-wide program, which included a keynote by Head and a panel discussion titled "Critical Literacies for the Mass Information Age," which included four UNL faculty.[7]

Building Connections through the SoTL

While UNL librarians' teaching practices are shifting toward a more community-oriented approach, more collaborative research partnerships are also forming. The following librarian-led and librarian-engaged SoTL projects, based in three UNL colleges, highlight challenges and opportunities of these multidisciplinary collaborations, provide some preliminary findings, and demonstrate how the SoTL CoP is shifting the boundaries of UNL Libraries' liaison program.

INFORMATION LITERACY SKILLS FOR FIRST-YEAR INTERNATIONAL STUDENTS

When the Office of Academic Affairs at UNL launched an internal SoTL grant competition in 2016, DeFrain, a social sciences librarian, and Anaya, the multicultural studies librarian and instruction coordinator, immediately began discussing how they could use this opportunity to better understand the information literacy needs of UNL's international students. They shared their interest with other liaison librarians who had worked closely with this population and realized their interests and concerns were broadly held. Due to an established relationship, they reached out to the faculty coordinators of U.S. Education in the Age of Globalization (CYAF 121), a course required by all international students during their initial year of study, and let them known of their interest in using SoTL methods to evaluate the course. The coordinators enthusiastically agreed, and together they submitted a successful funding proposal.

Focusing on this course was a strategic choice for the librarians: it is offered year-round (making it ideal for iterative assessment), enrolls approximately 150 students each academic year, and implements a standardized syllabus. The course's main objective is to help international students adjust to life in the United States by emphasizing student success skills and campus resources, university expectations, and a comparative exploration of global cultures. As the course was not assigned to any individual liaison, numerous librarians had assisted with it over the years, providing instruction and tours of the library.

Despite this longstanding relationship, librarians sensed that their efforts were not supporting course objectives. They struggled to provide support for students working on a difficult writing assignment, which required a minimum of five scholarly sources for an essay comparing educational systems of their home country, the United States, and one other nation. They were also challenged by the time spent supporting the course. Librarian in-class instruction, initially scheduled for twice a semester, often resulted in additional visits and individual reference consultations as instructors responded to the students' ongoing struggles. Devoting multiple class periods to library-related instruction negatively impacted progress toward other learning objectives, and the unclear outcomes of the information literacy sessions in relation to student needs and assignment objectives was a concern. As a third challenge, librarians felt ill-prepared to effectively teach this diverse group of students, given their wide range of English fluency.

With the format of the Visiting Scholar and Practicing Pedagogies programs as a model, DeFrain and Anaya used part of the funds to bring in an outside expert to help facilitate conversations about teaching between the librarians and the course coordinators. This was the first in-depth conversation the librarians had ever had with the coordinators about the course and was a tremendous opportunity to discuss goals and obstacles.

Almost immediately, the value of the project and the strengthening of the community of practitioners involved was evident. Initial conversations between the librarians and the instructors revealed shared values around teaching and learning and a commitment to experimentation and continuous assessment of the course. The instructors welcomed the librarians as partners, granting them access to student data, inviting their feedback, and modifying the curriculum based on project findings. After DeFrain and Anaya presented about the project at UNL's Spring 2018 Teaching and Learning Symposium, a new department approached them about conducting a similar study in the future.

RESEARCH AND INFORMATION LITERACIES ACROSS UNDERGRADUATE CURRICULA IN THE COLLEGE OF ARCHITECTURE

While DeFrain and Anaya were working on their project, two other librarians were invited to collaborate on another SoTL study, also funded by the Office of Academic Affairs. Two College of Architecture faculty, who coordinated the required first-year Design Thinking (DSGN 110) and capstone Design Research (ARCH 489) courses, were frustrated that students' understanding and abilities in information literacy and research practices seemed no better in their final year than in their first. Upon receiving notification of funding to improve undergraduate information literacy across the college's curricula, they sought out the architecture librarian, Kay Logan-Peters, Riehle, the learning resources design librarian, and two instructional designers, to create the research team.

A challenge for the research team was to define the study. Course improvement was a goal, but the faculty also wanted to understand students' development of information literacy competencies throughout their programs. The research team considered a variety of methodologies and consulted with UNL Libraries' Visiting Scholar Alison Head on several occasions during the project design phase, an opportunity that was valuable not only for consultation specific to the project but also as professional development for the librarians in particular. Ultimately, the team decided on a two-fold focus: (1) the integration of information literacy in the first and final-year courses and (2) the college's approach to information literacy on a broader scale. The focus on each course's design supported specific changes related to course learning outcomes. The latter objective acknowledged that student engagement with information literacy would not be limited to these two required courses. The research team designed a two-part study involving curriculum analyses for both courses and a qualitative exploration of the college faculty's approach to information literacy and their perceptions of students' information literacy abilities.

The researchers invited all faculty within the college to participate in semi-structured interviews, using an interview protocol designed by the research team. The librarians conducted the interviews to facilitate open discussion since both architecture instructors are college administrators. Meanwhile, the instructors completed curriculum alignment exercises for each of their respective courses with guidance from the instructional designer and librarians. Using a backward design approach[8] and with learning outcomes identified for each course, each instructor mapped outcomes relevant to research and information literacy to course assessments and activities in order to identify gaps in the course designs and to make changes accordingly.

In DSGN 110, mapping information literacy outcomes to design thinking learning outcomes generated an "a-ha moment" for the instructor. A major course goal is that students value information in the design process; the Information Has Value frame from the Association of College & Research Libraries (ACRL) *Framework for Information Literacy for Higher Education* resonated with the instructor.[9] Furthermore, design thinking process stages and outcomes such as Empathize, Define, Ideate, and Test, mapped to information literacy outcomes related to determining information needs, accessing and evaluating information, and using information effectively for a specific purpose. In collaboration with the librarians, the instructor worked from these connections to more thoughtfully and explicitly integrate information literacy skills and competencies throughout the course.

The librarians co-designed and led two in-class sessions focused on framing and scoping design problems and conducting research to support design challenges as students embarked upon their first major projects. As pre-work for these sessions, students engaged with pieces providing professional perspectives about design research, including methods for collecting information and the value of research to their design processes. Librarians assigned introductory research-related tutorials on topics such as navigating the libraries website, determining the credibility of information, and searching effectively in a major multidisciplinary database. They also created a tailored online research guide for students to refer to throughout the course. These efforts were significant, as the architecture librarian had not previously been involved with the course. The context of the SoTL project and the new collaboration between the architecture and learning resources design librarian helped spark creativity so that librarians could envision a different way to contribute to this key course in the program's curriculum.

Collaborating on this research project and related teaching efforts and sharing the process with colleagues within and outside UNL Libraries have contributed to librarians' professional development and supported our developing CoP. The research team anticipates that sharing the study's findings will spark strategic conversations among college faculty about the role of and approach to information literacy in the curricula. In the meantime, one of the study's co-PIs participated in the panel following Head's Visiting Scholar keynote, offering insights related to information literacy in general and as relevant to her course and the SoTL project. Logan-Peters and Riehle also shared about the project at a recent internal event, during which librarians and staff members present on their research projects.

RESEARCH AND INFORMATION LITERACIES FOR HISTORY UNDERGRADUATES

Librarians working within history courses at UNL noticed challenges similar to those identified by College of Architecture faculty. In particular, Lorang, a humanities librarian, and Delserone, the government information librarian, recognized that approaches to research and information literacies within the history curriculum did not seem to lead to students' growth and expertise with regard to finding, using, and creating information. Two long-term goals emerged from their participation in the visit by Purdue's IMPACT team and the readings and discussions from the Practicing Pedagogies series: (1) developing scaffolded learning opportunities for students, appropriate to the level and composition of the course, and (2) gaining experience in reflective, critical practices for librarians to improve their teaching. Along with these goals, librarians' observations of students and discussions with history instructors strongly informed and influenced their approach.

Prior to the project, a significant challenge was the divergence between history faculty expectations, student preparation, and the instruction that librarians traditionally provided. For example, both librarians consistently received the same request from instructors—an introduction to the libraries' resources and services—regardless of course level, content, or student backgrounds and experience with research. In general, faculty assumed that students learned the research process elsewhere and that the completion of a research project created a competent, confident student-researcher. Given these assumptions, faculty requested instruction about specific resources and services rather than teaching toward the research process and essential dispositions such as the identification, synthesis, and evaluation of information environments.

In response, the librarians identified strategic courses within the history curriculum where they might partner with instructors to engage students in fundamental learning about the research process and associated information environments, as well as build students' confidence in their abilities to do research. The librarians considered courses that were foundational to departmental curriculum, motivated students to consult with librarians, and/or were part of a curricular sequence. They identified The Historian's Craft (HIST 250) and Rights and Wrongs in American Legal History (HIST 340) as candidates.

HIST 250 is a major requirement; students usually take it early in their program, and a minimum of four sections are taught each academic year. The humanities librarian contacted the primary instructor, who agreed to collaborate on a more deliberate integration of information literacy and the research process into the course. Lorang assembled a team that included Delserone, Riehle, and the university archivist. Delserone identified HIST

340, an upper-level legal history course, as a potential avenue for introducing government information literacy into the history curriculum; students in this course frequently requested assistance. A meeting between the librarians and the legal history instructor identified a sequence of five courses that could benefit from a similar integration. When the College of Arts and Sciences announced an internal funding opportunity for curriculum improvement in spring 2017, the librarians initiated writing a successful proposal in collaboration with the legal history instructor to implement the work over a two-year period.

Each team identified challenges students typically faced in the courses and then determined learning objectives and demonstrable activities students should be able to complete if the teaching and learning were successful. The challenges students faced in both courses were very similar, so the teams worked from similar objectives and goals. The objectives and practices fell broadly under the categories of asking questions, distinguishing among and using different types of sources, and attributing information. The legal history team added goals related to the nuances of legal and upper-level historical research (e.g., legislative chronologies).

The librarians took the lead in these particular areas but in collaboration with the instructors of record. The teams amended existing coursework and assignments to better achieve particular goals and outcomes. Both teams recognized the value of increased time with librarians as well as the pairing of in-person teaching with virtual learning opportunities. Students completed interactive tutorials, created by the humanities librarian, which asked them to embrace curiosity as central to historical research, learn strategies for asking historical research questions, and link those questions to information needs and sources. These tutorials required students to participate at each point in the process and to reflect on their responses. The government information librarian created an online course guide to provide students with key resources for historical research and several narrated videos which demonstrated the why and how of searching for relevant digital sources.

The projects are ongoing, with formal assessment of the first iteration underway. Anecdotally, both librarians noted increased requests by students for research assistance after the course integrations began; outside of formal consultations, several students volunteered that they found the legal history materials useful. Both history instructors reported stronger final projects in both courses than in previous semesters. However, many variables (e.g., students' prior experiences, the link between student completion of the virtual modules and performance on research assignments) are awaiting analysis. Students did well in performing and documenting the research process within the virtual modules—which asked them to consider their particular research for the course—but further assessment is necessary to see whether students successfully transferred and applied learning from the modules to their research projects more broadly. Ongoing assessment work will inform refinement of the pedagogies, teaching materials, and learning opportunities for both courses. Next steps include sharing results from this first stage of collaboration within the UNL Libraries and with colleagues in history. Preliminary assessment information, including feedback from the history instructors, supports further implementation, such as working with the history capstone course as well as other courses in which students require learning opportunities in legal historical research and government information.

Conclusions

Creating a CoP around teaching and learning at UNL Libraries has required a cultural shift but the benefits are many. The internally organized professional development opportunities and multidisciplinary, formal SoTL projects detailed in this case study provided opportunities for reflection, clarification, and sharing regarding teaching identities, practices, and findings. Librarians at UNL identify as scholar-practitioners, emphasizing "cooperation, collegiality, and collaboration"[10] and the integration of daily practice, research questions, and critical reflection. The reflective practices and intentional teaching and learning activities associated with SoTL map to the scholar-practitioner model; for some librarians with teaching apportionments, SoTL may be an essential part of their professional practice and/or scholarly output. Further, the cultivation of a CoP—which situates learning as social participation[11]—among the librarians taking part in these projects disassembles the silos of librarians' instruction efforts.

The collaborations of disciplinary faculty and librarians at UNL are encouraging. Across the three SoTL projects featured, librarians engaged at all levels of the undergraduate curriculum and within three of the university's seven colleges. This experience suggests that the CoP has fostered more thoughtful, deeper, and intentional integration of research and information literacy competencies in courses and curricula. The accomplishments to date also suggest that librarians are ideal initiators and leaders of SoTL projects. In each project, librarians established themselves as equal partners in SoTL, either by participating actively once brought into a team or by initiating the project with disciplinary faculty.

Finally, the CoP provides support for librarians to grow professionally as teachers, through opportunities to read, discuss, and present ideas, and develop curricula alongside colleagues. It also creates an environment that engages librarians to view the liaison program's and UNL's instructional efforts more holistically. This bringing together of people, expertise, and approaches has the potential to create new synergies and connections, with UNL Libraries and librarians playing a major role.

ENDNOTES

1.   Paul Savory, Amy Goodburn, and Amy Burnett, "Developing and Integrating a Campus Program for Scholarship of Teaching and Learning Initiatives," *Industrial and Management Systems Engineering Faculty Publications*, 2006, 40.

2.   Nora Belzowski, J. Parker Ladwig, and Thurston Miller, "Crafting Identity, Collaboration, and Relevance for Academic Librarians Using Communities of Practice," *Collaborative Librarianship* 5, no. 1 (2013): 2.

3.   John Seely Brown and Paul Duguid, *The Social Life of Information: Updated, with a New Preface* (Harvard Business Review Press, 2017), 109.

4.   Lorna Dawes and Elizabeth Lorang, "Practicing Pedagogies: Summer Teaching Summit," accessed February 27, 2018, http://unl.libguides.com/Practicing_Pedagogies/Summit.

5.   Troy Fedderson, "Visiting Scholar Program Hosts Purdue Speakers," University Communications, accessed February 28, 2018, https://news.unl.edu/newsrooms/unltoday/article/visiting-scholar-program-hosts-purdue-speakers/.

6.   Craig Chandler, "Alison Head is Visiting Scholar in University Libraries," University Communications, accessed February 27, 2018, https://news.unl.edu/newsrooms/today/article/alison-head-is-visiting-scholar-in-university-libraries/.

7.   Troy Fedderson, "Panel Discussion on Critical Literacies Is March 16," University Communications, accessed February 28, 2018, https://news.unl.edu/newsrooms/today/article/panel-discussion-on-critical-literacies-is-march-16/.

8.   Grant P. Wiggins and Jay McTighe, *Understanding by Design*, Expanded 2nd ed. (Alexandria, VA: Association for Supervision and Curriculum Development, 2005).

9.   Association of College & Research Libraries (ACRL), *Framework for Information Literacy for Higher Education* (Chicago, January 11, 2016), http://www.ala.org/acrl/standards/ilframework.

10.   Tom Sharpe, Monica Lounsbery, and Tom Templin, "Cooperation, Collegiality, and Collaboration: Reinforcing the Scholar-Practitioner Model," *Quest* 49, no. 2 (1997): 214–28.

11.   Etienne Wenger, *Communities of Practice: Learning, Meaning, and Identity*, Learning in Doing: Social, Cognitive, and Computational Perspectives (Cambridge: Cambridge University Press, 2008), 4.

BIBLIOGRAPHY

Association of College & Research Libraries (ACRL). *Framework for Information Literacy for Higher Education*. Chicago, January 11, 2016. http://www.ala.org/acrl/standards/ilframework.

Belzowski, Nora, J. Parker Ladwig, and Thurston Miller. "Crafting Identity, Collaboration, and Relevance for Academic Librarians Using Communities of Practice." *Collaborative Librarianship* 5, no. 1 (2013): 2.

Brown, John Seely, and Paul Duguid. *The Social Life of Information: Updated, with a New Preface*. Harvard Business Review Press, 2017.

Chandler, Craig. "Alison Head Is Visiting Scholar in University Libraries." University Communications. Accessed February 27, 2018. https://news.unl.edu/newsrooms/today/article/alison-head-is-visiting-scholar-in-university-libraries/.

Dawes, Lorna, and Elizabeth Lorang. "Practicing Pedagogies: Summer Teaching Summit." Accessed February 27, 2018. http://unl.libguides.com/Practicing_Pedagogies/Summit.

Fedderson, Troy. "Panel Discussion on Critical Literacies Is March 16." University Communications. Accessed February 28, 2018. https://news.unl.edu/newsrooms/today/article/panel-discussion-on-critical-literacies-is-march-16/.

Fedderson, Troy. "Visiting Scholar Program Hosts Purdue Speakers." Accessed February 27, 2018. https://news.unl.edu/newsrooms/unltoday/article/visiting-scholar-program-hosts-purdue-speakers/.

Savory, Paul, Amy Goodburn, and Amy Burnett. "Developing and Integrating a Campus Program for Scholarship of Teaching and Learning Initiatives." *Industrial and Management Systems Engineering Faculty Publications*, 2006, 40.

Sharpe, Tom, Monica Lounsbery, and Tom Templin. "Cooperation, Collegiality, and Collaboration: Reinforcing the Scholar-Practitioner Model." *Quest* 49, no. 2 (1997): 214–28.

Wenger, Etienne. *Communities of Practice: Learning, Meaning, and Identity*. Learning in Doing: Social, Cognitive, and Computational Perspectives. Cambridge: Cambridge University Press, 2008.

Wiggins, Grant P., and Jay McTighe. *Understanding by Design*. Expanded 2nd ed. Alexandria, VA: Association for Supervision and Curriculum Development, 2005.

26

Cultivating Teacher-Librarians through a Community of Practice

Maoria J. Kirker

As teaching continues growing as an integral component of librarianship, sustaining and developing pedagogical skills becomes a pressing need for librarians. In library departments where instructional staff with limited training in instruction must teach, providing opportunities to learn, discuss, and practice aspects of teaching is critical. In 2015, under the shadow of the emerging Association of College and Research Libraries' *Framework for Information Literacy for Higher Education*, librarians and staff of Gateway Teaching and Learning Services, a department focused on new and transfer students at George Mason University, created a series of internal professional development activities to unpack and implement the ACRL *Framework* into their instructional practice. These included a bi-weekly scholarship roundtable focused on each of the six frames and a workshop series intended to build instructional activities related to the frames and provide a space for constructive peer feedback.

Throughout this professional development series, participants answered a series of surveys about the effectiveness of the readings and workshops to determine the formats' efficacy for developing individuals' theoretical and practical knowledge about the *Framework*. The benefits of implementing a SoTL study were two-fold. First, participants wanted to capture if this format could provide adequate professional development on the *Framework*. Secondly, these activities took a considerable amount of time away from regular job duties. By using SoTL methods to assess participants' learning, participants felt that it might produce evidence to support the collective learning and benefits of the group, as well as provide a case for expanding it to the larger library community at George Mason University.

These regular roundtable discussions and workshops created an environment that fostered the development of a community of practice based on shared work and goals. Communities of practice offer a lens through which to view these professional development activities. Through this lens, this case study examines how a community of practice focused

on pedagogy, educational theory, and instructional praxis created a space for experts and novices to informally learn from one another.

Communities of Practice

Characterized by mutual engagement, joint enterprise, and a shared repertoire, communities of practice form around a group of people invested in the social knowledge construction of a particular skill or learning process.[1] In other words, communities of practice use a shared vocabulary as members learn from one another in a particular domain—e.g., information literacy instruction. Traditionally, communities of practice emerged from apprentice-based fields such as midwifery or tailoring. However, the term can be applied to informal learning communities within other professional and academic contexts. These social learning communities are driven by collaboration[2] and may include sharing work or ideas or observing each other's work. Central to communities of practice are learning skills and concepts, but the building and transfer of cultural knowledge within the community enable them to thrive. In this sense, cultural knowledge can be understood as local norms or practices within a group. For example, one library may approach teaching information literacy from a teacher-centered pedagogy while another may focus on active learning. A community of practice allows space for novice members of the library staff to learn those norms and practices from expert members. Novice members may be experienced teaching librarians but new to the community of practice. These communities allow the transfer of cultural knowledge through professional socialization, observation, and informal learning activities.[3] Members of the community of practice create the professional identity not only of the community but also of the individuals within the community through active, social participation.[4]

The relationship between novice and expert members of a community of practice is critical to understanding how they collectively function as an informal learning community. Lave and Wenger coined the term "legitimate peripheral participants" to describe this relationship. Legitimate peripheral participants learn the sociocultural practice of the community to gain full participation within it.[5] Through participation and learning from the expert members of the community of practice, legitimate peripheral participants gain mastery and expertise. Expert members must grant access to newcomers, who are judged on their ability to participate in discussions and the learning process by expert members of the group. Learning through a community of practice requires access to participation.[6] Critical to the success of a community of practice is also the acceptance that membership roles will fluctuate. Based on the goals or focus of a community of practice and participation levels, full participant and legitimate peripheral participant status may alternate.[7]

In addition to transferring cultural knowledge among expert and novice members of a community of practice, these informal learning communities dedicate themselves to the continuous learning of a skillset.[8] Academic libraries have incorporated community of practice models as informal professional development tools to varying degrees. Examples of communities of practice include the temporary creation of a learning community for a specific purpose, such as integrating information literacy into a university curriculum,[9] and building communities of practice for more general purposes, such as training teacher-librarians.[10] By the nature of how communities of practice operate, they can become insular. SoTL offers an opportunity to make the work and knowledge production of a community of practice public. This publicizing of work can be done locally[11] or nationally and internationally through SoTL networks.[12]

Gateway Instruction Roundtable

George Mason University is a multi-campus, public research university in Fairfax, Virginia serving approximately 21,000 undergraduate FTE and 5,400 graduate FTE. Gateway Teaching and Learning Services (Gateway) is a unit within Research and Educational Services at George Mason University Libraries that supports undergraduates in general education courses and assists graduates, faculty, and community members in familiarizing themselves with the libraries. While staffing levels fluctuate, there are usually three or four instruction librarians and four or five full-time instruction specialists teaching information literacy skills within Gateway. These specialists are full-time staff members with 15 to 40 percent of their job responsibilities dedicated to instruction. Instruction specialists are hired with either instruction or library experience and thus arrive at Gateway with varying knowledge of information literacy constructs, pedagogy, and educational theory. These specialists help teach 100- and 300-level general education courses, notably freshman and junior-level English composition. Gateway Roundtable was created to provide a space where staff and librarians could learn more about teaching and learning from each other's experiences and expertise.

The Roundtable began in 2014 when instruction was the sole function of Gateway. An instruction specialist wanted to create a regular time for those who teach information literacy to gather and discuss instructional theory rather than instructional practice, which most discussions about teaching had centered around. Although discussions on theory often seemed irrelevant to members of the community, these types of conversations are critical to engaging within a research or teaching community.[13] Members of the Roundtable read scholarship on teaching and learning and then discuss the readings in the style of a graduate seminar. The goal of this is to spur creativity for instructors to apply in their practice.

Since its creation, the Gateway Instruction Roundtable meets bi-weekly during low instruction times of the academic calendar. At the conclusion of a discussion, the community or an individual library instructor selects a theme for the next Roundtable, such as sociocultural learning theory, agnotology, teaching research questions, and problem-based learning. After a theme is chosen, an instructor volunteers to select two or three short readings related to the theme. Roundtable members read the articles or book chapters and bring a list of discussion topics or questions. The instruction and assessment librarian facilitates discussion as necessary. This overarching structure follows general best practices of community of practice: designating an internal facilitator, balancing between over- and under-structuring, and incorporating a social component to learning.[14] In cases where the Roundtable discussion lends itself to practical classroom applications, the facilitator schedules a workshop. Library instructors either individually or collaboratively prepare a lesson plan, activity, or assessment related to the week's theme to present. The workshop provides a space to brainstorm ideas, pilot learning activities, and receive constructive feedback from colleagues.

The decision to have separate components—theoretical discussions and workshops— of the community of practice was intentional and based on the professional development needs of the group. The Roundtable wanted discussions to focus on theory. Since librarianship is a field built on practice, members of the community felt space and time was needed to discuss the aspects of instruction often overlooked in formal library school and in day-to-day work. By separating time to discuss theory and time to discuss practice, the community of practice felt careful consideration for both critical aspects would follow and naturally build off one another. It provides an opportunity to connect theory and practice as instructors create new learning activities or re-evaluate existing materials.

The *Framework* Project

In preparation for the implementation of the Association of College & Research Libraries' *Framework for Information Literacy for Higher Education*, the Gateway Roundtable tackled threshold concepts and the draft frames in the spring and summer of 2015. During seven discussions, members of the Roundtable read and discussed two to three publications selected by the instruction and assessment librarian about threshold concepts, Scholarship as Conversation, Authority is Constructed and Contextual, Information Creation as a Process, Information Has Value, Research as Inquiry, and Searching as Strategic Exploration. One goal was for the library specialists, who expressed feelings reflective of legitimate peripheral participation, to learn from the knowledge and experience of the librarian experts. This targeted approach to learning about the *Framework* and its implications in the classroom had the following objectives:

- Build a working knowledge of the ACRL *Framework* and threshold concept theory.
- Articulate how instructors can apply the *Framework* in their information literacy instructional practice.
- Feel comfortable discussing the *Framework* and threshold concepts with library peers and instructional faculty.

Roundtable members felt a need to assess whether or not this approach to learning about the *Framework* was effective. This emerged partially from a fear that the amount of time these activities took would not be viewed favorably by upper library administration, as well as visions of expanding the roundtable format beyond Gateway and to the instruction librarian community-at-large at George Mason University. To this aim and to determine if participants met these outcomes, Roundtable members participated in a SoTL study. Before beginning the *Framework* program, members could voluntarily participate in a pre-survey assessing their knowledge of threshold concepts and frames, as well as their application to information literacy instruction. After each Roundtable discussion, members completed a follow-up survey related to the specific frame. Following the discussion of the final frame, members completed a post-survey about the cumulative experience.

Results

At the onset of the *Framework* Roundtable series, five librarians[15] and five library specialists actively participated in the bi-weekly discussions. Six of these members completed the pre-survey. While participation in the Roundtable remained stable each week, participation in the follow-up surveys dwindled during the project. Follow-up survey responses varied from one to five participants. For each survey, participants answered the following questions:

- How well do you understand the following concept/frame (e.g., threshold concepts, information has value, etc.)?
- Please describe what the frame "[insert name of frame]" means in relation to information literacy instruction.
- Please describe how you could apply the frame "[insert name of frame]" in the library classroom.

Low response rates make it difficult to discern how well the Roundtable discussions helped improve participants understanding of the *Framework*, but there appears to be a general trend toward a better understanding after the discussion. A library specialist with little instruction experience reported a growth in understanding of the *Framework* in each of the post-discussion surveys. Another library specialist with more instruction experience shifted from abstract and theoretical discussions about the *Framework* to practical descriptions and applications in the post-discussion surveys. A librarian shifted from thinking about teaching the *Framework* from a static, lecture-based perspective to a dynamic, student-centered pedagogy.

Where the Roundtable succeeded most was creating a comfortable, social environment to discuss pedagogy, learning theory, and classroom practices. In addition to identifying where particular instructors could use more professional development in their instruction, the post-discussion surveys also highlighted areas of success for inexperienced instructors. Responses indicated increased levels of confidence in teaching information literacy aligned with the *Framework*. They also showed where participants moved from surface-level understanding to nuanced interpretations of the *Framework*. With this information, the Roundtable can shape future readings and workshops to better meet the professional development needs of its members. While the SoTL study described here concluded, it calls to attention the importance of regular surveying of the community of practice. While group discussions and workshops may highlight aspects of learning, they often fail to capture nuanced understanding and growth. By regularly surveying participants, the Gateway Instruction Roundtable group can continue growing through this social enterprise.

The Future of the Gateway Instruction Round Table

Since the *Framework* project, the Gateway Instruction Roundtable continues to meet and discuss publications related to the theory and practice of information literacy instruction, as well as educational theory in general. Maintaining a community such as this requires time, sustained interest by all of its members, and trust among colleagues to respectfully listen to each other. If the community members actively participate and contribute to discussions, the benefits to regular discussions can create ripple effects in individual instruction.

The Gateway Instruction Roundtable it is not without its challenges. The greatest difficulty has been maintaining adequate participation. The number of possible Roundtable participants varies from ten to fifteen depending upon vacant positions. In order for the discussions to be active and engaging, a minimum of five participants who have read the week's publications is desired. Given how workloads fluctuate in academic libraries, this can be difficult to sustain each week. Participation often wavers during times of the semester where instructors may experience high levels of burnout. The end of the fall semester, the busiest time of the year for Gateway, and the end of the summer when the group has met consistently for a few months, tend to see the largest drop in participation. Keeping up with the readings while staying on top of increasing workloads remains a challenge for Roundtable members.

While participation remains the most consistent challenge, a couple of challenges within the discussion also regularly occur: civility and the dichotomy between theory and practice. In this instance, civility refers to the tendency for some group members to argue with their colleagues about their ideas. While this is often done respectfully, there are moments of passionate disagreement, which can cause discomfort among the other members. In the worst cases of this, the disagreements result in a member feeling alienated, unheard, or temporarily ceasing participation. While this behavior is not encouraged, and in some cases reprimanded, it is also unavoidable when working with dedicated instructors who are passionate about student learning and may vary in communication style preference. Discussions in the Roundtable primarily center on theoretical discussions, but these often bleed into practical implications for teaching information literacy. This dichotomy is often at odds with members of the group who see this space as strictly for theoretical discussions. In a field built on practice, discussions that move between theory and practice are unavoidable. To try to alleviate these issues, the community incorporated workshops to focus on the practical nature of information literacy instruction. Participation in this SoTL study began to open conversations about the intersection of theory and practice in unanticipated ways. The results of the third survey question, "Please describe how you could apply the frame [insert name of frame] in the library classroom," reveal that Roundtable members used the theoretical discussions to the application phase. Building on these discussions as the Roundtable continues will be critical to continued success and professional development.

These challenges aside, the roundtable format creates an opportunity for professional development for all of those who choose to participate. It allows for legitimate peripheral participants without a library science degree or extensive instructional experience to learn about instructional theory, pedagogy, and practice in a collaborative setting where everyone involved is interested in sharing and learning from each other. The goal of the roundtable discussions continues to be pulling these legitimate peripheral participants into the fold of the community of practice by sharing information and expert knowledge, fostering relationships between community members, and creating a shared context through a common language.[16] Within Gateway, these goals continue as new librarians and library specialists join the department. Those instructors new to teaching can learn from their colleagues through this informal professional development community.

In addition to creating internal professional development opportunities, one of the Gateway Instruction Roundtable's greatest successes has been fostering a space for collaboration. The Roundtable affords an opportunity not only to share ideas but also to create collaborative projects among colleagues. Through the group discussions, two instructors may realize their shared interest in developing a learning activity and begin working together. In this way, the Roundtable creates opportunities for shared work, which enhances departmental morale and teamwork.[17] In Gateway Teaching and Learning, the hallmark example of this is the collaborative creation of a departmental teaching philosophy and student learning outcomes. Small-scale examples include the creation of a problem-based learning activity and a fake news workshop for students.

Conclusion

Since the conclusion of the *Framework*-based Gateway Instruction Roundtable discussions, the community of practice continues. With occasional librarian and library specialist turnover the roundtable format allows for newcomers to acclimate to the existing culture through legitimate peripheral participation during discussions. The format allows for new ideas to emerge, new and varied opportunities for shared work, and membership status to shift based on the current topic of discussion. Gateway Teaching and Learning Services now consists of more library specialists who do not have teaching experience with teaching responsibilities. The Gateway Instruction Roundtable provides an opportunity for low-cost, internal professional development to these novice teachers. By participating in the community of practice, these newcomers not only learn from the experts but also contribute their diverse skill sets and experiences to the community.

ENDNOTES

1. Jean Lave and Etienne Wenger, *Situated Learning: Legitimate Peripheral Participation*, Learning in Doing (New York: Cambridge University Press, 1991), 98.
2. Nora F. Belzowski, J. Parker Ladwig, and Thurston Miller, "Crafting Identity, Collaboration, and Relevance for Academic Librarians Using Communities of Practice," *Collaborative Librarianship* 5, no. 1 (2013): 11.
3. Noriko Hara, *Communities of Practice: Fostering Peer-to-Peer Learning and Informal Knowledge Sharing in the Work Place*, vol. 13, Information Science and Knowledge Management (Berlin:

Springer, 2009), 117, http://link.springer.com/chapter/10.1007/978-3-540-85424-1_7.

4. Jeff Jawitz, "Academic Identities and Communities of Practice in a Professional Discipline," *Teaching in Higher Education* 14, no. 3 (June 2009): 241–51, https://doi.org/10.1080/13562510902898817.

5. Lave and Wenger, *Situated Learning*, 37.

6. Ibid.

7. Ibid., 53; Anne Lloyd, "No Man (or Woman) Is an Island: Information Literacy, Affordances and Communities of Practice," *The Australian Library Journal* 54, no. 3 (August 1, 2005): 233, https://doi.org/10.1080/00049670.2005.10721760.

8. Hara, *Communities of Practice*, 13:118.

9. Chris Moselen and Li Wang, "Integrating Information Literacy into Academic Curricula: A Professional Development Programme for Librarians at the University of Auckland," *Journal of Academic Librarianship* 40, no. 2 (March 2014): 116–23, https://doi.org/10.1016/j.acalib.2014.02.002.

10. Malia Willey, "Library Instructor Development and Cultivating a Community of Practice," in *Advances in Librarianship*, ed. Anne Woodsworth and W. David Penniman, vol. 38 (Bingly, England: Emerald Group Publishing Limited, 2014), 83–100; Lisa Shamchuk, "Professional Development on a Budget: Facilitating Learning Opportunities for Information Literacy Instructors," *Partnership: The Canadian Journal of Library & Information Practice & Research* 10, no. 1 (January 2015): 1–14.

11. Renee L. Michael, "Sustaining the Scholarship of Teaching and Learning: A Campus-Based Community of Practice," *Transformative Dialogues: Teaching & Learning Journal* 6, no. 2 (December 2012): 1–10; Stephanie E. August and Jacqueline Dewar, "SoTL and Community Enhance One Another to Create Impact At Loyola Marymount University," *Transformative Dialogues: Teaching & Learning Journal* 4, no. 1 (July 2010): 1–15.

12. Elizabeth Marquis, Mick Healey, and Michelle Vine, "Building Capacity for the Scholarship of Teaching and Learning (SoTL) Using International Collaborative Writing Groups," *International Journal for the Scholarship of Teaching & Learning* 8, no. 1 (January 2014): 1–34.

13. Jonathan Tummons, "Theoretical Trajectories within Communities of Practice in Higher Education Research," *Higher Education Research & Development* 31, no. 3 (June 1, 2012): 307, https://doi.org/10.1080/07294360.2011.631516.\\uc0\\u8221{} {\\i{}Higher Education Research & Development} 31, no. 3 (June 1, 2012

14. Kristin J. Henrich and Ramirose Attebury, "Communities of Practice at an Academic Library: A New Approach to Mentoring at the University of Idaho," *The Journal of Academic Librarianship* 36, no. 2 (March 2010): 161, https://doi.org/10.1016/j.acalib.2010.01.007.

15. The author of this chapter is one of the five librarians, but did not participate in the study.

16. E. L. Lesser and J. Storck, "Communities of Practice and Organizational Performance," *IBM Systems Journal* 40, no. 4 (2001): 831–41.

17. Hara, *Communities of Practice*, 13:119.

BIBLIOGRAPHY

August, Stephanie E., and Jacqueline Dewar. "SoTL and Community Enhance One Another to Create Impact at Loyola Marymount University." *Transformative Dialogues: Teaching & Learning Journal* 4, no. 1 (July 2010): 1–15.

Belzowski, Nora F., J. Parker Ladwig, and Thurston Miller. "Crafting Identity, Collaboration, and Relevance for Academic Librarians Using Communities of Practice." *Collaborative Librarianship* 5, no. 1 (2013): 3–15.

Hara, Noriko. *Communities of Practice: Fostering Peer-to-Peer Learning and Informal Knowledge Sharing in the Work Place*. Vol. 13. Information Science and Knowledge Management. Berlin: Springer, 2009. http://link.springer.com/chapter/10.1007/978-3-540-85424-1_7.

Henrich, Kristin J., and Ramirose Attebury. "Communities of Practice at an Academic Library: A New Approach to Mentoring at the University of Idaho." *The Journal of Academic Librarianship* 36, no. 2 (March 2010): 158–65. https://doi.org/10.1016/j.acalib.2010.01.007.

Jawitz, Jeff. "Academic Identities and Communities of Practice in a Professional Discipline." *Teaching in Higher Education* 14, no. 3 (June 2009): 241–51. https://doi.org/10.1080/13562510902898817.

Lave, Jean, and Etienne Wenger. *Situated Learning: Legitimate Peripheral Participation*. Learning in Doing. New York: Cambridge University Press, 1991.

Lesser, E. L., and J. Storck. "Communities of Practice and Organizational Performance." *IBM Systems Journal* 40, no. 4 (2001): 831–41.

Lloyd, Anne. "No Man (or Woman) Is an Island: Information Literacy, Affordances and Communities of Practice." *The Australian Library Journal* 54, no. 3 (August 1, 2005): 230–37. https://doi.org/10.1080/00049670.2005.10721760.

Marquis, Elizabeth, Mick Healey, and Michelle Vine. "Building Capacity for the Scholarship of Teaching and Learning (SoTL) Using International Collaborative Writing Groups." *International Journal for the Scholarship of Teaching & Learning* 8, no. 1 (January 2014): 1–34.

Michael, Renee L. "Sustaining the Scholarship of Teaching and Learning: A Campus-Based Community of Practice." *Transformative Dialogues: Teaching & Learning Journal* 6, no. 2 (December 2012): 1–10.

Moselen, Chris, and Li Wang. "Integrating Information Literacy into Academic Curricula: A Professional Development Programme for Librarians at the University of Auckland." *Journal of Academic Librarianship* 40, no. 2 (March 2014): 116–23. https://doi.org/10.1016/j.acalib.2014.02.002.

Shamchuk, Lisa. "Professional Development on a Budget: Facilitating Learning Opportunities for Information Literacy Instructors." *Partnership: The Canadian Journal of Library & Information Practice & Research* 10, no. 1 (January 2015): 1–14.

Tummons, Jonathan. "Theoretical Trajectories within Communities of Practice in Higher Education Research." *Higher Education Research & Development* 31, no. 3 (June 1, 2012): 299–310. https://doi.org/10.1080/07294360.2011.631516.

Willey, Malia. "Library Instructor Development and Cultivating a Community of Practice." In *Advances in Librarianship*, edited by Anne Woodsworth and W. David Penniman, 38:83–100. Bingly, England: Emerald Group Publishing Limited, 2014.

Cultivating a Librarians' Community of Practice:

A Reflective Case Study

Corinne Laverty and Nasser Saleh

As librarians engage in new and evolving roles, there is a growing need to unite information literacy educators to extend and share their learning about evidence-based teaching. Although liaison librarians are typically assigned to multiple departments and may be dispersed across a campus, they are encouraged to demonstrate their impact on learning. Mechanisms for quality control and accountability, such as the Quality Assurance Framework mandated for higher education in Ontario, Canada,[1] have resulted in a new emphasis on assessment for librarians. The Ontario Council of University Libraries established a formal Quality Assurance Community which developed a template for writing academic reviews and suggests measures for demonstrating the library contribution to student learning outcomes. In support of information literacy development, it is recommended that librarians collect data that measures learning and formally report these findings to academic units as part of the cyclical program review process. While some individuals have tested different approaches to gathering this data, librarians are not necessarily trained in assessment methods, and assessment of information literacy may not be coordinated systematically across a program or a campus.

In response to these challenges, a librarian Teaching & Learning Working Group was formed at an Ontario university of 25,000 students. The original goal for the group was to develop effective information literacy assessment practices to gather data for quality assurance reports. However, regular meetings and conversations gradually evolved into a community of practice. This case study unravels what a community of practice looks like in action and traces its evolution from a task-oriented working group into a knowledge-based community of practice. The most significant enablers of the community are examined and the value of the learning fostered by the community itself is described. This analysis is an

example of the Scholarship of Teaching and Learning (SoTL) in that its intention is to study an approach to professional development to help librarians improve their own teaching practice in order to enable students' information literacy development. The purpose of the Teaching & Learning Working Group addresses Ernest Boyer's original concern regarding teaching scholarship when he proposed that "pedagogical procedures must be carefully planned, continuously examined, and relate directly to the subject taught."[2] He suggests that educators must be scholars in the realm of their own teaching to ensure that it evolves and transforms in creative new directions. Although librarians at many institutions do not have the opportunity to study student learning in the context of their own courses, they do need to assess what students learn as a result of librarian-led workshops and library instructional materials.

What is a Community of Practice?

The idea that practical knowledge can be transferred through social interaction in settings that relate to the application of that knowledge or practice was first referred to as a "community of practice" (CoP) by Jean Lave and Etienne Wenger.[3] A CoP is a group of individuals who come together to learn about something and who, through their learning interactions, develop relationships and build a sense of connectedness to one another and to their purpose.[4] Motivation to learn and share is central to the group,[5] and learning may take many forms, such as problem-solving, exchanging and comparing information and stories, seeking the experiences of others, discussing initiatives, mapping knowledge and identifying gaps, and creating tools. This practice offers the library a mechanism for developing scholarly approaches to teaching and as a pathway to invigorating learning and professional development across the organization.

Communities of practice originate from situated learning theory and exemplify a social learning system.[6] Wenger describes how learning takes place on two levels in this system through individual engagement with others in conversation and shared activities and also by means of the co-creation of artifacts which are the expression of personal and collaborative learning.[7] Over time, this synergy between participation and demonstration of learning develops the essence of community as a result of shared competence, belonging, and awareness of purpose. The word "practice" captures this dynamic and living system where meaning is continually and synergistically negotiated. This practice can be further described through the language of situated learning theory. Individual learning in a community is "situated" in that it is shaped by the cultural norms of those who belong to the practice and a symbiotic relationship ensures as the individual is inducted into the community becoming a member who in turn shapes the practice.[8] CoPs are especially well-suited to the library environment where service provision in a changing information landscape calls for situated learning akin to cognitive apprenticeship.[9]

Although a CoP is inherently fluid and constantly evolving,[10] some features directly impact its cultivation and sustainability. Wenger, McDermot, and Snyder propose seven principles for establishing and fostering a CoP:[11]

1. Design for evolution. Communities are organic and function within a central domain but not with specific terms of reference as in a "working group."
2. Open a dialogue between inside and outside perspectives. Bring in ideas from supporting units.
3. Invite different levels of participation. Acknowledge that members will participate in different ways and for various reasons.
4. Develop both public and private community spaces. Connect through meetings, small groups, one-on-one conversations, and online communication and resource sharing.
5. Focus on value. Communities thrive on the value they bring to the members, the group, and the institution, and the nature and worth of that value emerge over time.
6. Combine familiarity and excitement. Create a place where members ask questions and share opinions but are also challenged with divergent thinking and new ideas.
7. Create a rhythm for the community. Establish regular meeting patterns to ensure momentum and vibrancy.

The Teaching and Learning Working Group

The Teaching and Learning Working Group was composed of five core volunteer members. They were given Terms of Reference outlining tasks, including professional development on teaching for librarians. The group adopted a "process approach" (table 27.1) to conceptualize what the librarians needed to know to meet the assessment requirements for quality assurance. Working from the end target of having librarians apply more informed and meaningful approaches to assessment and incorporate assessment evidence into library quality assurance reports, the group identified a set of five sequential learning stages forecasted to achieve the group's goals (shown in table 27.1 under Process Approach). This orientation toward knowledge-building rather than as task-delivery transpired during ongoing discussions about the requirement for professional development. By framing the task as a learning process and applying a scholarly lens to that process, we inadvertently shifted toward a community of practice framework to accomplish meaningful and sustained learning. We could have simply listed possible PD topics and planned their delivery. Instead, we explored what we knew about how people learn and how we could apply that to our context. Following an inquiry-based model, we asked questions such as:

- How does institutional context reflect the need for scholarly teaching?
- How do we go about applying scholarship to our teaching?
- How can this learning be scaffolded to build skills gradually?
- What type of learning environment best supports this learning?
- How can we sustain learning and support over time?

This exploration enabled us to separate core learning concepts and then sequence how they could be introduced to allow time for personal practice and group interaction. Once our learning plan was initiated, the collective community of learners began to shape the process through their own collegial interactions and feedback.

Table 27.1. The Process Approach of the Working Group

Contextual Analysis		
Quality Assurance Requirements • collect evidence • incorporate evidence in reports	**Theories of Teaching & Learning** • backward design • assessment as learning • student engagement	**Librarian Needs** • analyze departmental needs • write learning outcomes • develop assessment tools • align teaching methods
Process Approach		
1. Investigate information literacy needs within departments. 2. Develop information literacy outcomes and curriculum. 3. Map information literacy learning outcomes to program/course curriculum. 4. Assess information literacy outcomes. 5. Develop teaching strategies that support student achievement.		
Workshops		
2011	Preparing for program assessments Learning outcomes: understanding by design (2 sessions)	
2012	Introduction to Curriculum mapping (2 sessions) Learning outcomes for graduate students Introduction to assessment of student research competencies Assessment using multiple choice and open-ended questions Assessment roundtable	
2013	Developing learning outcomes for the learning commons Active learning and student engagement Designing rubrics for inquiry-based learning: addressing both process and product Information literacy assessment plan	
2014	Liaison librarians' and support for blended and online courses Designing online tutorials Gathering statistics with Google Analytics Collecting e-resource usage statistics Developing videos with Camtasia (2 sessions) Introduction to threshold concepts	
2015	Narrating a PowerPoint in Camtasia	
Intended Outcomes	Incorporate evidence of student learning in quality assurance reports. Adopt a backward design approach to planning instruction. Apply student engagement techniques during instruction. Gather assessment of learning data during instruction.	

As a means of rooting the process in evidence-based methods that support the achievement of student learning goals, we drew on three foundational learning principles. The backward design approach to curriculum[12] prescribes setting desired learning outcomes and alignment with assessment methods prior to choosing learning activities. Use of assessment as learning[13] emphasizes the use of formative feedback to help students develop their own self-assessment skills and gradually develop their learning abilities. Learner engagement through problem-based and interactive activities is also a hallmark of good instruction[14] and constructivist learning.[15] These three principles informed our outcomes for the training program as well as our own delivery of it and they exemplify a scholarly approach to teaching. The intention of *scholarly teaching* is to change teaching practice by studying and contextualizing the research literature in order to apply ideas in the classroom and ultimately improve student learning. The distinguishing feature of SoTL is the production of scholarship where changes in practice and student learning are systematically studied as educational research.[16] Our learning goal was to introduce scholarly teaching practices and embrace them in our own delivery of content. In retrospect, this goal prompted our first step toward initiating our own authentic SoTL research project.

This process approach was also informed by a Theory of Change model. "A theory of change articulates how a project or initiative is intended to achieve outcomes through actions, while taking into account its context" and can also be used as a project evaluation plan.[17] The elements of the project are illustrated following the components of a theory of change model:[18]

- Analyze the challenge in the present context (contextual analysis).
- Identify outcomes and impacts for the intervention describing how they will address the challenge (intended outcomes).
- Develop a theory outlining how to move from the current state to the desired state (learning theories and process approach enacted with workshops/meetings/supporting resources).

Participants' Feedback: Evidence of a Community of Practice in Action

Our learning program served twenty-two liaison librarians and extended over four years (September 2011 to February 2015) during which time the group hosted twenty-two events driven by an assessment of librarian needs and the direction provided by participants. Average attendance at each event was sixteen people. Guiding members of the Working Group scheduled meetings every two weeks and supported librarian events by developing resources such as ACRL information literacy standards with examples of learning outcomes, a map of IL in all courses across campus, an action plan template for guiding IL instruction, a LibGuide outlining the process approach, and internal how-to documents on teaching (examples of assessment, outcomes, learning materials). These materials were made available on a shared wiki and in the university repository.

During the process approach, feedback forms were collected following sessions that included knowledge sharing and interaction to capture reflections on learning and support needs going forward. Short-term feedback at meetings was gathered using open-ended questions and long-term feedback on impact was gathered in one-minute papers, summaries from disciplinary library units, and individual action plans.

Twenty-two sessions were offered over forty-one months. Three were practice sessions and three were led by individuals outside the liaison librarian pool, including specialists on accessibility, instructional design, teaching, collection management, and information technology. Feedback was gathered after sixteen face-to-face meetings, which included presentations, discussion, and interactive problem-solving, using three questions:

1. What was the most important thing you learned today?
2. What is one thing you still don't understand?
3. How can the Teaching and Learning Group support your teaching?

The anonymous feedback from question three was analyzed to better understand the enablers and success factors of the growing community of practice. The outcome was eleven categories grouped into four overarching themes that characterized our CoP. For each category, the number of coded comments within that category is indicated.

- Community building: 107 comments relating to establishing relationships and learning from one another (categories: create a learning environment (n=44), build knowledge (e.g., provide expertise and content) (n=38), share ideas and experience (e.g., "someone to chat with," "free-flowing questions") (n=25))
- Personal growth: forty-seven comments relating to individual development (categories: provide opportunities for self-reflection (e.g., comments on personal change) (n=33); provide personal help (n=14))
- Leadership and organization: forty-six comments relating to the role of the core group in organizing opportunities to meet and share (categories: organize meetings and workshops (n=28), provide a strategy to achieve learning goals (n=14), advocate for librarians (n=4))
- Supporting tools: forty comments relating to creating and sharing resources (categories: create learning materials (e.g., assessment examples, communication toolkit, lists of learning outcomes) (n=18), provide online participatory spaces (n=12), share resources (n=10))

This analysis describes a single community of practice in action. Its most significant enablers were community-building features, opportunities for personal growth, a leadership and organizational infrastructure underpinning the community as an evolving and continuing entity, and provision of a range of supporting tools. These enablers clearly map onto the core characteristics of a CoP[19] and the principles by which it is fostered.[20] These are illustrated in table 27.2. Aspects of community-building that were most remarked on included those relating to facilitating participatory sessions with interactivity, discussion, problem-solving, modeling of real examples in context, with underlying and supportive expertise from others.

Table 27.2. CoP case study enablers mapped against principles for establishing and fostering CoPs

Principles for Establishing and Fostering CoP (Wenger, McDermot, and Snyder, 2002)	Summary of Enablers in CoP Case Study
Design for evolution	Adopted process approach; organic and flexible; knowledge-driven
Dialogue between inside and outside perspectives	Liaised with supporting colleagues/units external to the group (e.g., accessibility hub, student writing, technology support, instructional design, online learning)
Invite different levels of participation	Core group took on a leadership role to organize and sustain; other members adopt roles such as leading workshops, creating tools
Develop public and private community spaces	Regular meetings and workshops, online communication via listserv and resource sharing via a repository (e.g., presentations, guides, teaching ideas, examples, scenarios) and public LibGuide
Focus on value	Community building; authentic learning in shared practice; developing an identity
Combine familiarity and excitement	Personal growth through reflection; inclusivity and belonging through interaction; enacting change in practice
Create a rhythm for the community	Regular gatherings to share and discuss over four years

The community of practice enabled professional development apart from conventional PD scenarios. The learning environment could be described as one of apprenticeship where learning focused on becoming a practitioner rather than learning about practice. Members weren't engaged in acquiring abstract knowledge as isolated individuals using resources that were separated from practice. Instead, learning was fostered by access to the community and its members and the enculturation that resulted from a situated, shared, contextual practice that related to an authentic workplace. The constructivist learning approach within the group triggered divergent views, spontaneous thinking, and proactive innovation and interpretation. Social constructivism further supported learning following Vygotsky's zone of proximal development[21] where collaboration with more experienced or knowledgeable peers further enables problem-solving and enriches learning.

SoTL Project Sparked by Community of Practice

An unintended outcome that was sparked by the community of practice was a SoTL project involving collaborative investigation of librarian assessment practices across twenty-one universities in Ontario. Scholarship on teaching and learning is frequently triggered by intrinsic motivation when practitioners decide to examine challenges in their own classrooms.[22] Most academic librarians do not have the luxury of developing their teaching during an entire course where student learning can be observed over time. Without sustained opportunities for instruction, there are significant challenges in progressing along the trajectory from good teaching to scholarly approaches originating in the research literature to becoming SoTL researchers in our own right. Social networks can also be transformative in developing a positive institutional culture toward SoTL. Williams describes how a community of practice offers a sustained mechanism for providing expertise and knowledge-sharing that has the potential to bridge micro (individual), meso (departmental), and macro (institutional) levels in postsecondary education.[23]

This last outcome supports the strong correlation outlined in a study measuring the relationship between good teaching and scholarly teaching and between scholarly teaching and SoTL.[24] It also highlights the power of a community learning together. As our community of practice continued to explore an evidence-informed approach to teaching, the group members were motivated to learn about approaches to engaging librarians in learning about assessment across other institutions. The learning environment was conducive to critically reflective practice because it was fluid and self-transforming. In studying how others have investigated their own teaching, it isn't much of a leap to pose questions about one's own practice. Had it been slated as a two-hour PD presentation, the transition toward SoTL thinking would have been unlikely. Instead, the escalation of learning prompted questions that became the impetus for a research study.

A provincial survey of fifty-three teaching librarians completed in 2014 helped to inform the group's approaches to their professional development needs. Analysis of survey results revealed that library staff engaged in teaching have a very wide baseline of pedagogical knowledge and abilities. Many people have not had sufficient training in this area. Every institution addresses information literacy development in different ways and there is no consistent approach to professional development for teaching librarians. With regard to quality assurance, the library is not automatically included in quality assurance processes unless there is a dedicated advocate representing the library voice. This study confirmed the need for professional development in assessment and teaching practices.

Moving Forward

This case study seeks to provide an understanding of how a community evolved from a task-oriented working group into a knowledge-based community of practice. The community was facilitated by group leaders through workshops and social interactions resulting in a learning environment that fostered trust and sharing. These features proved conducive to learner-driven professional development by providing continuing, collegial, and contextually relevant meetings with clear goals for teaching and learning. The emerging CoP included librarians with different levels of experience in different stages of their careers who do not often work directly with one another. The group-driven process also exemplifies the role of SoTL as a professional development area in creating a dynamic knowledge-based professional practice in academic libraries. Our group interactions led us to deeper questions about our own practice and provoked us to think about how we could actually study it. Without these enduring and rich conversations, we might not have been compelled to initiate a formal SoT project.

This case study confirmed findings in the reviewed literature in that it is entirely possible that a community of practice may form in an organization without its members being fully aware of its formal existence. However, the most significant aspect of the CoP framework is in helping us to understand the essential characteristics of social learning and how they can be applied to the larger concept of developing a learning organization.

ACKNOWLEDGMENTS

The authors extend their thanks to the other librarian members of the core Working Group: Sylvia Andrychuk, learning and research services librarian (humanities and social sciences) and Suzanne Maranda, head librarian, Health Sciences Library, Queen's University, Kingston, Ontario, Canada.

ENDNOTES

1. Ontario Universities Council on Quality Assurance, *Quality Assurance Framework*.
2. Ernest L. Boyer, "Scholarship Reconsidered: Priorities of the Professoriate" (Princeton, NJ: Carnegie Foundation for the Advancement of Teaching, 1990), 23–24.
3. Jean Lave and Etienne Wenger, *Situated Learning: Legitimate Peripheral Participation* (Cambridge: Cambridge University Press, 1991), 98.
4. Etienne Wenger, Richard Arnold McDermott, and William Snyder, *Cultivating Communities of Practice: A Guide to Managing Knowledge* (Boston, MA: Harvard Business School Press, 2002), 34.
5. Elayne Coakes and Steve Clarke, "The Concept of Communities of Practice," in *Encyclopedia of Communities of Practice in Information and Knowledge Management*, ed. Elayne Coakes and Steve Clarke (Hershey, PA: Idea Group Reference, 2011), 92.
6. Valerie Farnsworth, Irene Kleanthous, and Etienne Wenger-Trayner, "Communities of Practice as a Social Theory of Learning: A Conversation with Etienne Wenger," *British Journal of Educational Studies* 64, no. 2 (2016): 1–3. https://doi.org/10.1080/00071005.2015.1133799.
7. Etienne Wenger, *Communities of Practice: Learning, Meaning, and Identity* (Cambridge: Cambridge University Press, 1998), 179–80.
8. Jean Lave, "Situating Learning in Communities of Practice," *Perspectives on Socially Shared Cognition* 2 (1991): 63–82.
9. Jong-Ae Kim, "Integrating Communities of Practice into Library Services," *Collaborative Librarianship* 7, no. 2: 47.
10. Peta Dzidic, Emily Castell, Lynne D. Roberts, Peter J. Allen, and Michelle Quail, "Reflections on the Emergence and Evolution of a Scholarship of Teaching and Learning Community of Practice within a Research-Intensive Higher Education Context," in *Communities of Practice* (Singapore: Springer Nature, 2017), 23–24.
11. Wenger, McDermott, and Snyder, *Cultivating Communities of Practice*, 51–63.
12. Grant Wiggins and Jay McTighe, *Understanding by Design* (Alexandria, VA: Association for Supervision and Curriculum Development, 1998), 7–19.
13. Lorna Earl and Steven Katz, *Rethinking Classroom Assessment with Purpose in Mind* (Winnipeg, MB: Manitoba Education, Citizenship and Youth, 2006), 41–54.

14. Arthur Chickering and Zelda Gameson, "Seven Principles for Good Practice in Undergraduate Education," *American Association of Higher Education Bulletin* 39, no. 7 (1987): 1.

15. Susan Cooperstein and Elizabeth Kocevar-Weidinger, "Beyond Active Learning: A Constructivist Approach to Learning," *Reference Services Review* 32, no. 2 (2004): 141–42, https://doi.org/10.1108/00907320410537658.

16. Laurie Richlin and Milton D. Cox, "Developing Scholarly Teaching and the Scholarship of Teaching and Learning through Faculty Learning Communities," *New Directions for Teaching and Learning* 2004, no. 97 (2004): 127–128.

17. Karen Laing and Liz Todd, *Theory-Based Methodology: Using Theories of Change in Educational Development, Research and Evaluation* (Newcastle, England, 2015), 4.

18. Patricia Rogers, "Theory of Change," *Methodological Briefs: Impact Evaluation*, 3.

19. Wenger, McDermott, and Snyder, *Cultivating Communities of Practice*, 27–40.

20. Ibid., 51–63.

21. David W. L. Hung and Der-Thanq Chen, "Situated Cognition, Vygotskian Thought and Learning from the Communities of Practice Perspective: Implications for the Design of Web-based E-learning," *Educational Media International* 38, no. 1 (2001): 5.

22. George Gordon, "SoTL and the Quality Agenda," *International Journal for the Scholarship of Teaching & Learning* 4, no. 2 (Ju)ly 2010): 1.

23. Andrea L. Williams, Roselynn Verwoord, Theresa A. Beery, Helen Dalton, James McKinnon, Karen Strickland, Jessica Pace, and Gary Poole, "The Power of Social Networks: A Model for Weaving the Scholarship of Teaching and Learning into Institutional Culture," *Teaching and Learning Inquiry: The ISSOTL Journal* 1, no. 2 (2013): 54.

24. Susan Vajoczki, Philip Savage, Lynn Martin, Paola Borin, and Erika D H Kustra, "Good Teachers, Scholarly Teachers and Teachers Engaged in Scholarship of Teaching and Learning: A Case Study from McMaster University, Hamilton, Canada," *The Canadian Journal for the Scholarship of Teaching and Learning* 2, no. 1 (2011): Article 2, 13.

BIBLIOGRAPHY

Boyer, Ernest L. "Scholarship Reconsidered : Priorities of the Professoriate," 23–24. Princeton NJ: Carnegie Foundation for the Advancement of Teaching, 1990.

Chickering, Arthur, and Zelda Gameson. "Seven Principles for Good Practice in Undergraduate Education." *American Association of Higher Education Bulletin* 39, no. 7 (1987): 3–7. https://doi.org/10.1016/0307-4412(89)90094-0.

Coakes, Elayne, and Steve Clarke. "The Concept of Communities of Practice." In *Encyclopedia of Communities of Practice in Information and Knowledge Management*, edited by Elayne Coakes and Steve Clarke, 92. Hershey, PA: Idea Group Reference, 2011.

Cooperstein, Susan, and Elizabeth Kocevar-Weidinger. "Beyond Active Learning: A Constructivist Approach to Learning." *Reference Services Review* 32, no. 2 (2004): 141–48. https://doi.org/10.1108/00907320410537658.

Dzidic, Peta, Emily Castell, Lynne D. Roberts, Peter J. Allen, and Michelle Quail. "Reflections on the Emergence and Evolution of a Scholarship of Teaching and Learning Community of Practice within a Research-Intensive Higher Education Context." In *Communities of Practice*, 219–239. Singapore: Springer Nature, 2017.

Earl, Lorna, and Steven Katz. *Rethinking Classroom Assessment with Purpose in Mind*. Winnipeg, MB: Manitoba Education, Citizenship and Youth, 2006.

Farnsworth, Valerie, Irene Kleanthous, and Etienne Wenger-Trayner. "Communities of Practice as a Social Theory of Learning: A Conversation with Etienne Wenger." *British Journal of*

Educational Studies 64, no. 2 (2016): 139–60. https://doi.org/10.1080/00071005.2015.1133 799.

Gordon, George. "SoTL and the Quality Agenda." *International Journal for the Scholarship of Teaching & Learning* 4, no. 2 (July 2010): 1–6.

Hung, David W. L., and Der-Thanq Chen. "Situated Cognition, Vygotskian Thought and Learning from the Communities of Practice Perspective: Implications for the Design of Web-based E-learning." *Educational Media International* 38, no. 1 (2001): 3–12.

Kim, Jong-Ae. "Integrating Communities of Practice into Library Services." *Collaborative Librarianship* 7, no. 2: 47.

Laing, Karen, and Liz Todd. *Theory-Based Methodology: Using Theories of Change in Educational Development, Research and Evaluation*. Newcastle, England, 2015.

Lave, Jean. "Situating Learning in Communities of Practice." *Perspectives on Socially Shared Cognition* 2 (1991): 63–82.

Lave, Jean, and Etienne Wenger. *Situated Learning: Legitimate Peripheral Participation*. Cambridge: Cambridge University Press,1991.

Ontario Universities Council on Quality Assurance. "Quality Assurance Framework—Ontario Universities Council on Quality Assurance." Accessed October 29, 2017. http://oucqa.ca/ resources-publications/quality-assurance-framework/.

Richlin, Laurie, and Milton D. Cox. "Developing Scholarly Teaching and the Scholarship of Teaching and Learning through Faculty Learning Communities." *New Directions for Teaching and Learning* 2004, no. 97 (2004): 127–35.

Rogers, Patricia. "Theory of Change." *Methodological Briefs: Impact Evaluation* (2). 2014.

Smith, Brenda, and Leva Lee. "Librarians and OER: Cultivating a Community of Practice To Be More Effective Advocates." *Journal of Library and Information Services in Distance Learning* 11, no. 1–2 (2017): 106–22. https://doi.org/10.1080/1533290X.2016.1226592.

Vajoczki, Susan, Philip Savage, Lynn Martin, Paola Borin, and Erika D H Kustra. "Good Teachers, Scholarly Teachers and Teachers Engaged in Scholarship of Teaching and Learning: A Case Study from McMaster University, Hamilton, Canada." *The Canadian Journal for the Scholarship of Teaching and Learning* 2, no. 1 (2011): Article 2. http://dx.doi.org/10.5206/ cjsotl-rcacea.2011.1.2.

Wenger, Etienne. *Communities of Practice : Learning, Meaning, and Identity*. Cambridge: Cambridge University Press, 1998.

———. "Practice, Learning, Meaning, Identity." *Training* 34, no. 2 (1997): 38–39. https://doi. org/10.2277/0521663636.

———. "Communities of Practice and Social Learning Systems: The Career of a Concept." In *Social Learning Systems and Communities of Practice*, 179–98. London: Springer, 2010.

Wenger, Etienne, Richard Arnold McDermott, and William Snyder. *Cultivating Communities of Practice: A Guide to Managing Knowledge*. Boston, MA: Harvard Business School Press, 2002.

Wiggins, Grant, and Jay McTighe. *Understanding by Design*, Alexandria, VA: Association for Supervision and Curriculum Development, 1998.

Williams, Andrea L., Roselynn Verwoord, Theresa A. Beery, Helen Dalton, James McKinnon, Karen Strickland, Jessica Pace, and Gary Poole. "The Power of Social Networks: A Model for Weaving the Scholarship of Teaching and Learning into Institutional Culture." *Teaching and Learning Inquiry: The ISSOTL Journal* 1, no. 2 (2013): 49–62.

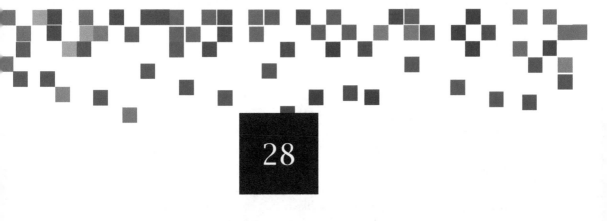

28

SoTL as Professional Development:

Participating in the Scholarship of Teaching and Learning as an LIS Graduate Student

Erin Durham

The Scholarship of Teaching and Learning (SoTL) provides valuable pedagogical training to graduate students embarking on careers in academic and research libraries. Although SoTL is fairly new to information professionals, it is a discipline that can fill a recognized gap in LIS programs nationwide. Many LIS programs do not offer courses in pedagogical training even though information literacy instruction is an essential component of the mission and services of academic libraries. As an evidence-based pedagogical discipline, SoTL can serve as a valuable complement to the professional development of LIS graduate students. Practitioners and researchers in SoTL encourage student-centered pedagogical methods, reflection, interdisciplinary collaborations, and shared teaching practice.[1] This case study explores benefits, strategies, and recommendations for engaging in SoTL as an emerging library professional.

The Scholarship of Teaching and Learning and the ACRL *Framework*

With the adoption of the Association of College & Research Libraries' (ACRL) *Framework for Information Literacy for Higher Education* in 2016, information literacy instruction has welcomed a shift from skills-based database demonstrations to an emphasis on critical thinking. In order to help students navigate complex information structures, librarians need

to be able to engage students in inquiry-based, participatory learning. Indeed, the adoption of the *Framework* spurred a revision of the ACRL proficiencies of instruction librarians in April 2017. The change in role titles from "instructional librarian" to "teaching librarian" reveals the centrality of teaching to information literacy positions. Teacher librarians are emboldened to embrace "a learner-centered approach, encouraging learners to be agents in their own learning."[2] It is clear that young professionals preparing for careers in academic teaching positions are expected to be able to actively engage students in their teaching, and yet the vast majority of LIS programs do not offer a course in pedagogy.

Evidence-based teaching practices from the SoTL literature can help fill the education gap. While many information professionals have discussed the importance of pedagogical training for teaching librarians, SoTL is a fairly new discipline to librarians. SoTL practitioners ask questions related to the teaching process, design and implement classroom interventions, reflect upon outcomes, and share the results with the greater community. The variety of ways to engage with SoTL ranges from reflection and implementation of classroom interventions to formal peer-review research studies.[3] In her work, "Navigating the SoTL Landscape: A Compass, Map and Some Tools for Getting Started," Mia O'Brien describes four principles of SoTL research practices. She emphasizes the importance of (1) centering research questions around student needs, (2) creating a "deliberate design" or research plan that engages with SoTL inquiry, (3) applying the design in the classroom and analyzing the findings, and (4) sharing the research findings in order to "contribute … to SoTL knowledge and practice."[4] While participants may be drawn at first to the reflective benefits of evidence-based teaching practice, they may later advance to more formal research projects.

Drawing from the author's experience of participating in SoTL as an LIS graduate student, this case study explores how young professionals can engage with SoTL communities to effectively provide learner-centered instruction. Evidence-based pedagogy skills can be cultivated both through informal reflective practice and more formally designed SoTL projects.[5] After discussing how the author progressed through stages of SoTL research, general strategies and recommendations for participating in SoTL as an emerging library professional are provided.

SoTL and the Graduate Student Experience

In the course of her work as a graduate assistant at the Teaching and Learning Services unit at the University of Maryland (UMD) Libraries, the author taught information literacy (IL) sessions for first-year students at the University of Maryland, College Park. This university serves more than 41,000 students, has an average annual budget of $1.9 million, and is the major public research institution in the state.[6] The Teaching and Learning Services unit oversees the large-scale information literacy program at UMD Libraries by serving close to four thousand undergraduate students each year in one-shot and occasional two-shot information literacy sessions of the required English 101 Academic Writing course. In preparation for teaching IL sessions, the author participated in pedagogy training developed by the Head of the Teaching and Learning Services unit and the First-Year Experience Librarian for the Research and Teaching Fellowship program at the University of Maryland, College Park. This program is designed to mentor LIS graduate assistants and fellows who teach information literacy sessions at UMD Libraries and prepare them for careers as academic instruction librarians. The mentorship program comprises of readings in evidence-based pedagogical theory and practice, discussion board postings, journal club discussions, a teaching-as-research project, and teaching observations and reflections.[7]

In addition to participating in the Research and Teaching Fellowship program as a graduate assistant, the author also joined the University Teaching and Learning Transformation Center (TLTC) training program. This program enables graduate students from all disciplines to participate in pedagogy workshops, take a credit-bearing pedagogy course, develop a teaching philosophy, and engage in a teaching-as-research project. Three levels of graduate student participation are offered—associate, practitioner, and scholar— in order to scaffold pedagogy skills through increasing levels of proficiency.[8] The author first learned of SoTL while participating in these professional development programs and was immediately drawn to the discipline's commitment to educational inquiry and student-centered teaching.

Encouraged by her readings and classroom reflections from both the library Teaching and Research Fellowship program and TLTC professional development program, the author thought about ways to better empower the undergraduate students she taught in one-shot information literacy sessions. The author noticed that many students seemed hesitant to voice questions about their research in class. In order to encourage student inquiry, the author placed a sticky note at each of the desks before the start of class and asked students to write down a question as they settled into their seats. During the middle of the session, the author collected the student responses and organized the search strategy portion of the class based on the questions they asked. By initiating this simple teaching intervention, the author worked to give voice to even the shyest of students and transform the classroom environment to one of student-directed learning. She was inspired by her pedagogy readings and trainings to make changes to her teaching in order to involve more active learning techniques.[9] As the author continued with her pedagogy studies, she discovered ways in which her classroom intervention aligned with critical feminist pedagogy. As scholars bell hooks and Maria Accardi discuss, feminist pedagogy centers student perspective in the classroom and empowers students to contribute to a co-constructed learning community.[10] Using sticky notes in the classroom was a means of welcoming all student perspectives in addition to those who already felt comfortable sharing their questions aloud in the classroom.

Knowing that shared pedagogy practices are an important part of the teaching community, the author included her intervention as part of a poster she presented on active learning in one-shot library sessions at the 2017 Library Orientation Exchange (LOEX) instruction conference.[11] This experience, which involved observing the classroom environment, developing a simple teaching intervention, and sharing knowledge with the greater teaching community, can highlight a path forward for LIS students to advance the quality of their teaching. While the author's project was based on teaching reflections and a simple classroom intervention, she found that her foray into active learning interventions invigorated her one-shot information literacy sessions, increased her confidence as a teacher, and inspired future plans to develop a more formal research and teaching scholarship project.

During her final year as an LIS student, the author developed and implemented a SoTL project as part of her professional development program. After noticing that many students struggled to apply information literacy concepts from classroom group activities to their individual research assignments, the author reflected on ways to encourage student self-directed learning. What materials or activities could be provided in the classroom to help students apply general concepts to their individual research assignments? Drawing upon literature regarding self-regulated learning, the author decided to include space in the lesson for students to reflect on their own research process. She developed a class handout based on the Teaching and Learning Services lesson outline to guide students through the process of setting a personal research goal, narrowing their research topic, and selecting keywords. It was important to the author that the class session remain a collaborative space, and she designed the handout as a resource to complement class discussions and group activities rather than replace them.[12]

The author outlined her teaching-as-research project in a two-page proposal that included her research questions, a brief discussion of related literature, description of the classroom intervention, and method for collecting student responses. She created a survey using Google forms to collect student reflections regarding the usefulness of the handout and their progress on their research topics. After meeting with an advisor in the University Teaching and Learning Program to review her project proposal, the author submitted a description of her project and assessment methods to the Institutional Review Board (IRB) at the University of Maryland. During the process of implementing the handout in her IL sessions, the author observed the classroom environment. How did the inclusion of the handout change the dynamics of the class session? How did it help or hinder students as they worked on their individual research assignments? After evaluating her reflections and the student responses, the author submitted a final report of the teaching-as-research project for the University Teaching and Learning Program practitioner certificate. A week later, she shared classroom strategies for empowering student-directed learning at a campus research and learning conference.[13]

The experience of designing, implementing, and evaluating a SoTL project allowed the author to better understand the needs of her students and adjust her teaching in efforts to advance their research progress. The author was able to reflect on her teaching experience and formulate a research question relating to student needs. She developed a classroom intervention that engaged with pedagogical literature. She implemented the design in the classroom, evaluated results, and shared her practice of encouraging student self-directed learning with the campus community.

The author's project can be understood in relation to the SoTL research steps recommended by O'Brien (see table 28.1). By pursuing her project, the author developed a greater ability to support student-directed learning and now looks forward to advancing future SoTL projects as a teaching librarian.[14]

Table 28.1. Research Process for SoTL Project

O'Brien's SoTL Research Steps[15]	1) Center a research question on student needs.	2) Create a research plan.	3) Apply the research design and analyze results.	4) Share research findings.
Author's SoTL Research Project	1) Author reflected on classroom instruction and developed research question. What materials could be provided in the classroom to help students apply general concepts to their individual research assignments?	2) Developed a handout to guide students through the research process, prepared the collection of student responses using Google forms, wrote a two-page research proposal, cleared research design with campus IRB.	3) Implemented the handout in sessions of ENGL 101, compared student responses in sessions with and without the handout, reported findings to the University Teaching and Learning Center.	4) Presented a lightning talk on strategies for empowering student-directed learning at campus Innovations in Teaching and Learning Conference.

Recommendations for Graduate Student Engagement in SoTL

There are many points of entry to the SoTL community. Whether or not one has accessibility to a formal professional development program, LIS graduate students everywhere can still engage in valuable SoTL experiences. At its heart, the discipline of SoTL seeks to improve the quality of the learning experience. LIS students can seek out part-time employment, an internship, or summer work that features teaching responsibilities or collaboration with an instruction librarian at an academic library. Hands-on teaching experience brings SoTL principles and projects to life. While completing LIS coursework, it is valuable for graduate students to find out if their institution supports a teaching and learning center.[16]

LIS students in any program can build a portfolio of teaching sessions they have observed, maintain a reflective teaching journal, and request mentorship from a teaching librarian, supervisor, or faculty member. Emerging professionals can develop a SoTL project organized according to O'Brien's categories of research, such as centering inquiry on student learning, creating a research design, applying the intervention in the classroom, analyzing results, and sharing findings with the SoTL community. Building pedagogical knowledge builds confidence to seek out teaching opportunities, whether in LIS class projects or through internship and employment experience. Developing a teaching project and sharing results at a graduate conference or during a poster presentation session can set a course for future student-centered teaching.[17]

When designing a SoTL project for the first time, it can be very helpful to consult a practical guide. McKinney provides a step-by-step approach in her work *Enhancing Learning through the Scholarship of Teaching and Learning: The Challenges and Joys of Juggling*. Felten discusses best principles and practices of the discipline, and O'Brien distills complicated aspects into a helpful framework. A robust journal literature supplies examples and case studies of SoTL research. When applying SoTL to library information literacy sessions, it can be helpful to read how librarians have participated in SoTL in a variety of reference and teaching roles.[18]

Finally, it is important to share teaching practices and classroom interventions with the greater SoTL community. While publishing a full-length article might seem daunting to new SoTL practitioners, there are a variety of other scholarship opportunities. LIS graduate students may first decide to present their findings in a poster session. Some of the major SoTL conferences include the International Society for Teaching and Learning, SoTL Commons, and the Lilly Conferences on Evidence-Based Teaching and Learning. In addition, the Library Orientation Exchange, LOEX, highlights best library information literacy praxis and reserves the poster session for graduate student and fellow presentations.[19]

Sharing SoTL research with a broader community builds professional networks and equips LIS graduate students to conduct future research as academic librarians. The author found that contributing to scholarly teaching and learning conversations provided opportunities to build connections with faculty across campus. While presenting her lightning talk on empowering student autonomy in the classroom, the author was placed on the same panel with an English instructor who taught in the first-year academic writing program that partnered with the library. The interdisciplinary nature of SoTL allows for a shared vocabulary of pedagogy practices that can help cultivate relationships across campus departments. In addition, the author's experience proved valuable during the job search, as she was able to discuss examples of her scholarly interests and research activities.

Regardless of whether LIS students participate in SoTL in a formalized program or through personalized professional development, the process of learning evidence-based practices, designing research projects, and sharing results with colleagues can advance sound information literacy practices. The author found that the experience of engaging in SoTL allowed her to formulate teaching and research interests while transitioning from LIS student to library professional. The SoTL literature and teaching interventions complement the shift from skills-based information literacy standards to the student-centered teaching encouraged by the ACRL *Framework*, thus preparing practitioners for careers as academic teaching librarians. In these ways, participating in the Scholarship of Teaching and Learning illuminates a path of pedagogical inquiry and professional development for emerging teaching librarians.

ENDNOTES

1. With sincere thanks to Rachel W. Gammons and Lindsay I. Carpenter for their mentorship and support during my MLIS studies. Regarding LIS pedagogical offerings and academic librarians, see Russell A. Hall, "Beyond the Job Ad: Employers and Library Instruction," *College and Research Libraries* 74, no. 1 (2013): 24–38; Susan Andriette Ariew, "How We Got Here: A Historical Look at the Academic Teaching Library and the Role of the Teaching Librarian," *Communications in Information Literacy* 8, no. 2 (2014): 208–24; Dani Brecher and Kevin Michael Klipfel, "Education Training for Instruction Librarians: A Shared Perspective," *Communications in Information Literacy* 8, no. 1, (2014): 43–49. Regarding SoTL benefits to librarians, see for example, Cara Bradley, "The Scholarship of Teaching and Learning: Opportunities for Librarians," *College and Research Libraries News* 70, no. 5 (2009): 276–78; Michael Perini, "Enhancing Collaboration through the Scholarship of Teaching and Learning," *Collaborative Librarianship* 6, no. 1 (2014): 52–55.

2. Association of College and Research Libraries (ACRL), *Roles and Strengths of Teaching Librarians*, adopted April 28, 2017, http://www.ala.org/acrl/standards/teachinglibrarians (quotations); Association of College and Research Libraries (ACRL), *Framework for Information Literacy for Higher Education*, adopted by the ACRL Board, January 11, 2016, http://www.ala.org/acrl/standards/ilframework. On inquiry-based learning, see Nicole Pagowsky, "A Pedagogy of Inquiry," *Communications in Information Literacy* 9, no. 2 (2005): 136–42.

3. Bradley, "The Scholarship of Teaching and Learning," 276–78; Perini, "Enhancing Collaboration," 52–55; Pat Hutchings, Mary Taylor Huber, Anthony Ciccone, and Carnegie Foundation for the Advancement of Teaching, *The Scholarship of Teaching and Learning Reconsidered: Institutional Integration and Impact* (San Francisco, CA: Jossey-Bass, 2011), 50–51; Janice Miller-Young and Michelle Yeo, "Conceptualizing and Communicating SoTL: A Framework for the Field," *Teaching & Learning Inquiry* 3, no. 2 (2015): 37–53; Peter Felten, "Principles of Good Practice in SoTL," *Teaching & Learning Inquiry: The ISSOTL Journal* 1, no. 1 (2013): 121–25.

4. Mia O'Brien, "Navigating the SoTL Landscape: A Compass, Map and Some Tools for Getting Started," *International Journal for the Scholarship of Teaching and Learning* 2, no. 2 (2008): 1–20.

5. For literature on generalized graduate student participation in SoTL, see for example Nancy L. Chick and Cynthia Brame, "An Investigation of the Products and Impact of Graduate Student SoTL Programs: Observations and Recommendations from a Single Institution," *International Journal for the Scholarship of Teaching & Learning* 9, no. 1 (2015): 1–23; Annetta Tsang, "Reflective Learning as a Student and an Educator: Connecting the Scholarship of Teaching and Learning," *International Journal for the Scholarship of Teaching & Learning* 3, no. 2 (2009): 1–4; April L. McGrath, "Personal Reflection: An Early Introduction to SoTL and the Shaping of an Academic Career," *International Journal for the Scholarship of Teaching & Learning* 6, no. 2 (2012): 1–4. For recommendations from instruction librarians, see Brecher and Klipfel, "Education Training for Instruction Librarians"; Pagowsky, "A Pedagogy of Inquiry"; Hall, "Beyond the Job Ad." For readings in library engagement in SoTL research, see Lisa N. Mitchell and Erik T. Mitchell, "Using SoTL as a Lens to Reflect and Explore for Innovation in Education and Librarianship," *Technical Services Quarterly* 32, no. 1 (2015): 46–58; Jeanette McVeigh, "Librarians, Faculty and the Scholarship of Teaching and Learning," *Pennsylvania Library Association Bulletin* 66, no. 2 (2011): 13–16; Perini, "Enhancing Collaboration";and Asako Yoshida, "Information Literacy and Research Development Skills: Advancing Librarian's Participation in Pedagogical Research," *Qualitative and Quantitative Methods in Libraries* 4, (2014): 865–77.

6. University of Maryland, "About the University of Maryland," accessed December 7, 2018, https://www.umdrightnow.umd.edu/about-university-maryland.

7. On the Research and Teaching Fellowship program, see Rachel Wilder Gammons and Lindsay Taylor Inge, "Using the ACRL Framework to Develop a Student-Centered Model for Program-Level Assessment," *Communications In Information Literacy* 11, no. 1 (2017): 168–84; Teaching and Learning Services, University of Maryland, "Research and Teaching Fellowship," https://www.lib.umd.edu/tl/fellowship; Rachel W. Gammons, Alexander J. Carroll, and Lindsay Inge Carpenter, "'I Never Knew I Could Be a Teacher': A Student-Centered MLIS Fellowship for Future Teacher-Librarians," *portal: Libraries and the Academy* 18, no. 2 (2018): 331–62.

8. Teaching and Learning Transformation Center, University of Maryland, "University Teaching and Learning Program (UTLP)," accessed October 26, 2017, https://tltc.umd.edu/content/utlp; Teaching and Learning Transformation Center, University of Maryland, "UTLP Level Program Requirements," accessed October 26, 2017, https://tltc.umd.edu/utlp-level-program-requirements.

9. The author learned ideas for classroom activities and formative assessments through readings and trainingsee for example Mary Snyder Broussard, Rachel Hickoff-Cresko, and Jessica Urick Oberlin, *Snapshots of Reality: A Practical Guide to Formative Assessment in Library Instruction* (Chicago: Association of College and Research Libraries, 2014).

10. bell hooks, *Teaching to Transgress: Education as the Practice of Freedom* (New York: Routledge, 1994; Maria T. Accardi, *Feminist Pedagogy for Library Instruction* (Sacramento, CA: Library Juice Press, 2013). Maria T. Accardi, "Feminist Pedagogy for Library Instruction," Library Juice Academy course, completed August 2017, http://libraryjuiceacademy.com/065-feminist-pedagogy.php.

11. Library Orientation Exchange,"About LOEX," accessed October 2017, http://www.loex.org/about.php; Erin Durham, "Participatory Learning Strategies for One-shot Instruction Sessions," poster presentation from LOEX Conference, Lexington, KY, May 11–13, 2017, http://drum.lib.umd.edu/handle/1903/19220.

12. Teaching and Learning Services, "ENGL 101: Academic Writing," accessed October 2017, https://www.lib.umd.edu/tl/first-year/engl-101; Barry J. Zimmerman, "Becoming a Self-Regulated Learner: An Overview," *Theory into Practice* 41, no 2 (2002): 64–70; Deborah L. Butler, "Individualizing Instruction in Self-Regulated Learning," *Theory into Practice* 41, no. 2 (2002): 81–92.

13. Teaching and Learning Transformation Center, "University Teaching and Learning Program (UTLP)," https://tltc.umd.edu/content/utlp; "UTLP Level Program Requirements," https://tltc.umd.edu/utlp-level-program-requirements; "Fearless Teaching: 24th Annual Innovations in Teaching and Learning Conference," May 11, 2018, , University of Maryland, accessed May 2018, https://itl.umd.edu/.

14. O'Brien, "Navigating the SoTL Landscape,"1–2.

15. Ibid.

16. McVeigh, "Librarians, Faculty," 14; Bradley, "The Scholarship of Teaching and Learning," 276–77; Hutchings et. al., *The Scholarship of Teaching and Learning Reconsidered,* 2, 12, 45–46.

17. See recommendations by Hall, "Beyond the Job Ad"; Brecher and Klipfel, "Education Training," 46–48; O'Brien, "Navigating the SoTL Landscape," 1–2.

18. Kathleen McKinney, *Enhancing Learning through the Scholarship of Teaching and Learning: The Challenges and Joys of Juggling* (Bolton, MA: Anker Publishing Company Inc.,2007); O'Brien, "Navigating the SoTL Landscape," 1–2; Felten, "Principles of Good Practice in SoTL." On additional case studies and examples, see Pat Hutchings, ed. and Carnegie Foundation for the Advancement of Teaching, *Opening Lines: Approaches to the Scholarship of Teaching and Learning* (Menlo Park, CA: Carnegie Foundation for the Advancement of Teaching, 2000); Miller-Young and Yeo, "Conceptualizing and Communicating." For articles by library professionals, see Bradley, "The Scholarship of Teaching and Learning"; Mitchell and Mitchell,

"Using SoTL as a Lens"; Perini, "Enhancing Collaboration"; Yoshida, "Information Literacy and Research Development Skills"; and McVeigh, "Librarians, Faculty."
19. For conference recommendations see Lauren Hays and Melissa Mallon, "Keeping Up With… The Scholarship of Teaching and Learning," September 2017, accessed October 27, 2017, http://www.ala.org/acrl/publications/keeping_up_with/sotl; McKinney, *Enhancing Learning*, 93; Teaching and Learning Transformation Center, "Professionalization Opportunities for GTA's, https://tltc.umd.edu/professionalization-opportunities-gtas; Lilly Conference Series on College and University Teaching and Learning: Evidence-Based Teaching and Learning, http://lillyconferences.com/; "LOEX," http://www.loex.org/; and LOEX, "Poster Session Proposals," http://www.loexconference.org/posterproposals.html.

BIBLIOGRAPHY

Accardi, Maria T. *Feminist Pedagogy for Library Instruction*. Sacramento, CA: Library Juice Press, 2013.

Accardi, Maria T. "Feminist Pedagogy for Library Instruction," Library Juice Academy course. Completed August 2017. http://libraryjuiceacademy.com/065-feminist-pedagogy.php.

Ariew, Susan Andriette. "How We Got Here: A Historical Look at the Academic Teaching Library and the Role of the Teaching Librarian." *Communications in Information Literacy* 8, no. 2 (2014): 208–24.

Association of College and Research Libraries (ACRL). *Framework for Information Literacy for Higher Education*. Adopted by the ACRL Board, January 11, 2016. Accessed October 26, 2017. http://www.ala.org/acrl/standards/ilframework.

Association of College and Research Libraries. *Roles and Strengths of Teaching Librarians*. Adopted April 28, 2017. Accessed October 25, 2017. http://www.ala.org/acrl/standards/teachinglibrarians.

Bradley, Cara. "The Scholarship of Teaching and Learning: Opportunities for Librarians." *College and Research Libraries News* 70, no. 5 (2009): 276–78.

Brecher, Dani, and Kevin Michael Klipfel. "Education Training for Instruction Librarians: A Shared Perspective." *Communications in Information Literacy* 8, no. 1 (2014): 43–49.

Broussard, Mary Snyder, Rachel Hickoff-Cresko, and Jessica Urick Oberlin. *Snapshots of Reality: A Practical Guide to Formative Assessment in Library Instruction*. Chicago: Association of College and Research Libraries, 2014.

Butler, Deborah L. "Individualizing Instruction in Self-Regulated Learning." *Theory into Practice* 41, no. 2 (2002): 81–92.

Chick, Nancy L., and Cynthia Brame. "An Investigation of the Products and Impact of Graduate Student SoTL Programs: Observations and Recommendations from a Single Institution." *International Journal for the Scholarship of Teaching & Learning* 9 no. 1 (2015): 1–23.

Durham, Erin. "Participatory Learning Strategies for One-shot Instruction Sessions." Poster presentation from LOEX Conference, Lexington, KY, May 11-13, 2017. Accessed October 30, 2017. http://drum.lib.umd.edu/handle/1903/19220.

Felten, Peter. "Principles of Good Practice in SoTL." *Teaching & Learning Inquiry: The ISSOTL Journal* 1, no. 1 (2013): 121–25.

Gammons, Rachel W., Alexander J. Carroll, and Lindsay Inge Carpenter. "'I Never Knew I Could Be a Teacher': A Student-Centered MLIS Fellowship for Future Teacher-Librarians." *portal: Libraries and the Academy* 18, no. 2 (2018): 331–62.

Gammons, Rachel Wilder, and Lindsay Taylor Inge. "Using the ACRL Framework to Develop a Student-Centered Model for Program-Level Assessment." *Communications in Information Literacy* 11, no. 1 (2017): 168–84.

Hall, Russell A. "Beyond the Job Ad: Employers and Library Instruction." *College and Research Libraries* 74, no. 1 (2013): 24–38.

Hays, Lauren, and Melissa Mallon. "Keeping Up With… The Scholarship of Teaching and Learning." September 2017. Accessed October 27, 2017. http://www.ala.org/acrl/publications/keeping_up_with/sotl.

hooks, bell. *Teaching to Transgress: Education as the Practice of Freedom.* New York: Routledge, 1994.

Hutchings, Pat, ed., and Carnegie Foundation for the Advancement of Teaching. *Opening Lines: Approaches to the Scholarship of Teaching and Learning.* Menlo Park, CA: Carnegie Foundation for the Advancement of Teaching, 2000.

Hutchings, Pat, Mary Taylor Huber, Anthony Ciccone, and Carnegie Foundation for the Advancement of Teaching. *The Scholarship of Teaching and Learning Reconsidered: Institutional Integration and Impact.* San Francisco, CA: Jossey-Bass, 2011.

McGrath, April L. "Personal Reflection: An Early Introduction to SoTL and the Shaping of an Academic Career." *International Journal for the Scholarship of Teaching & Learning* 6, no. 2 (2012): 1–4.

McKinney, Kathleen. *Enhancing Learning through the Scholarship of Teaching and Learning: The Challenges and Joys of Juggling.* Bolton, MA: Anker Publishing Company, Inc., 2007.

McVeigh, Jeanette. "Librarians, Faculty and the Scholarship of Teaching and Learning." *Pennsylvania Library Association Bulletin* 66, no. 2 (2011): 13–16.

Miller-Young, Janice, and Michelle Yeo. "Conceptualizing and Communicating SoTL: A Framework for the Field." *Teaching & Learning Inquiry* 3, no. 2 (2015): 37–53.

Mitchell, Lisa N., and Erik T. Mitchell. "Using SoTL as a Lens to Reflect and Explore for Innovation in Education and Librarianship." *Technical Services Quarterly* 32, no. 1 (2015): 46–58.

O'Brien, Mia. "Navigating the SoTL Landscape: A Compass, Map and Some Tools for Getting Started." *International Journal for the Scholarship of Teaching and Learning* 2, no. 2 (2008): 1–20.

Pagowsky, Nicole. "A Pedagogy of Inquiry." *Communications in Information Literacy* 9, no. 2 (2005): 136–42.

Perini, Michael. "Enhancing Collaboration through the Scholarship of Teaching and Learning." *Collaborative Librarianship* 6, no. 1 (2014): 52–55.

Teaching and Learning Services, University of Maryland. "ENGL 101: Academic Writing." Accessed October 26, 2017. https://www.lib.umd.edu/tl/first-year/engl-101.

Teaching and Learning Services, University of Maryland. "Research and Teaching Fellowship." Accessed October 26, 2017. https://www.lib.umd.edu/tl/fellowship.

Teaching and Learning Transformation Center, University of Maryland. "University Teaching and Learning Program." Accessed October 26, 2017. https://tltc.umd.edu/content/utlp.

Tsang, Annetta. "Reflective Learning as a Student and an Educator: Connecting the Scholarship of Teaching and Learning." *International Journal for the Scholarship of Teaching & Learning* 3, no. 2 (2009): 1–4.

Yoshida, Asako. "Information Literacy and Research Development Skills: Advancing Librarian's Participation in Pedagogical Research." *Qualitative and Quantitative Methods in Libraries* 4, (2014): 865–77.

Zimmerman, Barry J. "Becoming a Self-Regulated Learner: An Overview." *Theory into Practice* 41, no 2 (2002): 64–70.

Conclusion

The Scholarship of Teaching and Learning unleashes great potential in librarianship. Consequently, the editors of this book hope this is only the start of a long conversation. There remain many unexplored questions and topics within both information literacy and librarianship. This range of inquiry leaves many opportunities for librarians to jump in to ask (and answer!) these questions. Many of the case studies presented in this book address the open-ended questions related to student learning and information literacy but, as with all good research, they also raise new issues for consideration. As the case studies show, SoTL provides a framework for addressing these issues, but, more importantly, asking more questions in order to improve students' learning experience and to improve our teaching.

Academic librarians are ideal candidates for participation in SoTL projects; we're inquisitive, we're passionate, and we care about student success. If readers are interested in talking the next step and becoming more involved in SoTL, here are a few of our recommendations:

- Talk to your university's teacher center.
- Find a SoTL mentor.
- Develop a journal club and read SoTL literature.
- Conduct a SoTL study.
- Partner with other librarians engaged in SoTL.
- Partner with faculty participating in SoTL.
- Lead in SoTL initiatives.

Whether you use SoTL as a professional development tool, a research agenda, a way to create theory, or for a deeper understanding of your teaching and your students' learning, the editors of this book look forward to the Scholarship of Teaching and Learning being used to grow and enhance academic librarianship.

Recommended Readings

Many of these texts have been cited throughout the book, but the following documents have been instrumental in our understanding of and interest in SoTL:

Barr, Robert B., and John Tagg. "From Teaching to Learning: A New Paradigm for Undergraduate Education." *Change* 27(6) (1995): 13–26.

Bass, Randy. "The Scholarship of Teaching: What's the problem?" *Inventio: Creative Thinking about Learning and Teaching*, 1(1) (1999): 1-10.

Boyer, Ernest. *Scholarship Reconsidered: Priorities of the Professoriate.* San Francisco, CA: Jossey-Bass,1990.

Bradley, Cara. "The Scholarship of Teaching and Learning: Opportunities for Librarians." *College and Research Libraries News*, 70(5) (2009): 276–78.

Felten, Peter. "Principles of Good Practice in SoTL." *Teaching & Learning Inquiry: The ISSOTL Journal*, 1(1) (2013): 121–25. http://dx.doi.org/10.2979/teachlearninqu.1.1.121.

Hutchings, Pat, ed. *Opening Lines: Approaches to the Scholarship of Teaching and Learning.* Menlo Park, CA: Carnegie Publications, 2000.

Kanuka, Heather. "Keeping the Scholarship in the Scholarship of Teaching and Learning." *International Journal for the Scholarship of Teaching and Learning*, 5(1) (2011): 3.

Kern, Beth, Gwynn Mettetal, Marcia Dixson, and Robin K. Morgan. "The Role of SoTL in the Academy: Upon the 25th Anniversary of Boyer's Scholarship Reconsidered." *Journal of the Scholarship for Teaching and Learning*, 15(3) (2015): 1–14. http://doi.org/10.14434/josotl.v15i3.13623.

Mårtensson, Katarina, Torgny Roxå, and Thomas Olsson. "Developing a Quality Culture through the Scholarship of Teaching and Learning." *Higher Education Research & Development*, 30(1) (2011): 51–62. http://dx.doi.org/10.1080/07294360.2011.536972.

McKinney, Kathleen. "Making a Difference: Approaches of SoTL to Enhance Learning." *Journal of the Scholarship of Teaching and Learning*, 12(1) (2012): 1–7.

Miller-Young, Janice, and Michelle Yeo. "Conceptualizing and Communicating SoTL: A Framework for the Field." *Teaching & Learning Inquiry*, 3(2) (2015): 37–53.

O'Brien, Mia. "Navigating the SoTL Landscape: A Compass, Map and Some Tools for Getting Started." *International Journal for the Scholarship of Teaching and Learning*, 2(2) (2008): 1–20. Retrieved from http://digitalcommons.georgiasouthern.edu/ij-sotl/vol2/iss2/15/.

Poole, Gary D. (2007) "Using the Scholarship of Teaching and Learning at Disciplinary, National and Institutional Levels to Strategically Improve the Quality of Postsecondary Education," *International Journal for the Scholarship of Teaching and Learning*: Vol. 1: No. 2, Article 3. Available at: https://doi.org/10.20429/ijsotl.2007.010203.

Editor Biographies

Jackie Belanger is Director of Assessment and Planning at the University of Washington Libraries, where she leads assessments designed to improve Libraries services, resources and spaces for user communities. Her background is in student learning outcomes assessment, and she has published and presented work on critical assessment, design thinking, assessing student learning using rubrics, and the use of assessment management systems in libraries.

Cara Bradley is the Research & Scholarship Librarian at the University of Regina in Saskatchewan, Canada, where her primary responsibility is supporting graduate student and faculty research. She first became interested in SoTL while seconded to the role of Associate Director of the University of Regina's Centre for Teaching and Learning. She has published and presented widely on topics including SoTL, information literacy in the disciplines, information policy, and academic integrity. Her personal interests include gardening and traveling.

Lauren Hays, PhD, is an Assistant Professor of Instructional Technology at the University of Central Missouri. Previously, she was the Instructional and Research Librarian at MidAmerica Nazarene University in Olathe, KS where she enjoyed teaching and being a member of the Faculty Development Committee. She has presented widely on the Scholarship of Teaching and Learning, including at the annual conference for the International Society for the Scholarship of Teaching and Learning and she was the 2017 speaker on SoTL for the Association of College and Research Libraries' Student Learning and Information Literacy Committee's Midwinter Discussion. Her professional interests include SoTL, teaching, information literacy, educational technology, library and information science education, teacher identity, and academic development. On a personal note, she loves dogs, traveling, and home.

Rhonda Huisman is the University Library Dean at St. Cloud State University where she oversees strategic planning, library instruction, collections, and space as well as staffing, professional development, and outreach. Rhonda has researched faculty-librarian collaborations, information literacy, and the first-year experience, but her primary focus has been on collaborating with K-12 librarians, community colleges, and four-year institutions to research college-readiness initiatives. Recent publications and presentations at ALA, ACRL, LOEX, and the IUPUI Assessment Institute have covered high-impact education practices, faculty-centered workshops, and communities of practice. She is an active member of several local and consortia boards, as well as served on many ACRL committees and facilitates for ACRL Immersion and the ACRL Standards for Libraries in Higher Education.

Melissa Mallon is the Director of the Peabody Library and Director of Teaching and Learning at Vanderbilt University Libraries in Nashville, TN. Melissa is involved in several national efforts to promote information literacy, including serving on the steering committee of New Literacies Alliance, a multi-state collaborative effort to create free and open digital modules to teach students critical thinking and research skills. Melissa's research interests include online learning, instructional design, the intersection of critical thinking and digital learning, and (of course!) SoTL. She recently published her first book, on the pivotal role of academic librarians in digital learning. Melissa tweets at @librarianliss.

About the Contributors

Norm Althouse is a teaching professor and teaching fellow at the Haskayne School of Business, University of Calgary. His responsibilities include the development and co-coordination of a business skills class in the undergraduate program and organizational behavior course in the EMBA. He completed his MBA in 1993 and has taught at the University of Calgary since January 1995. Norm is the lead author on one of Canada's premier introduction to the business textbook, *The Future of Business*, currently in its 5th edition and widely adopted at post-secondary institutions in Canada. Norm is actively publishing cases and papers as part of his scholarly activities.

Toni Anaya is Associate Professor and Instruction Coordinator at the University of Nebraska-Lincoln, where she works with the Institute of Ethnic Studies, Modern Languages & Literatures, as well as a variety of pre-college and first year groups on campus. Her current area of research is exploring the recruitment and retention of people of color in the library profession and library instruction for first generation, non-traditional and international students.

Roberto A. Arteaga is an academic librarian in the Pacific Northwest. His research interests include critical information literacy, instructional design, and e-learning. Off work, he listens to a lot of music and tries to find time to play video games, watch anime, do web design, and read. He can be found on Twitter at @irobarte.

Sarah Bankston is the BIMS and veterinary medicine librarian working at the Medical Sciences Library at Texas A&M University. She serves as the subject liaison to the biomedical sciences undergraduate program and the professional veterinary (DVM) program within the College of Veterinary Medicine and Biomedical Sciences.

Jill Becker is the head of the Center for Undergraduate Initiatives & Engagement for the University of Kansas (KU) Libraries. Since 2012, she has worked to integrate information literacy and research skills into first-year experience programs. Jill earned her bachelor's degree in English from KU, and her master's degree in library science from Emporia State University. At present, she is a doctoral candidate in higher education administration at

KU. Her hopes as a librarian and teacher are to help undergraduate students gain a better understanding of the nature of information in today's world so that they can become informed seekers, users, and producers of information.

Catherine Bowers (csbowers@valdosta.edu) is assistant professor/reference librarian and coordinator of library instruction at Valdosta State University. She has taught cultural anthropology courses, interdisciplinary research methods courses, and a course about the information society.

Nancy Chick (PhD, English) is Director of the Endeavor Foundation Center for Faculty Development at Rollins College in Winter Park, Florida. She is also editor of *SoTL in Action: Illuminating Critical Moments of Practice* (Stylus, 2018), co-editor of *Exploring Signature Pedagogies: Approaches to Teaching Disciplinary Habits of Mind* (Stylus, 2009) and *Exploring More Signature Pedagogies* (Stylus, 2012), and founding co-editor of *Teaching & Learning Inquiry*, the journal of the International Society for the Scholarship of Teaching and Learning (ISSOTL). She is also a long-time fan of librarians.

Noémi Cobolet (noemi.cobolet@epfl.ch), teaching librarian, Ecole Polytechnique Fédérale de Lausanne (EPFL). Noémi works at the EPFL Library as a training librarian. She has been part of the publish support team since 2016. Between 2011 and 2014, she was librarian in Madrid (French cultural institute) and at the University of Burgundy in France.

Emma Coonan is a research fellow at the Centre for Innovation in Higher Education at Anglia Learning & Teaching. She carries out individual and collaborative research into innovative pedagogic approaches, including design thinking in teaching and learning, pedagogies of inclusion, and student perceptions of learning gain. A librarian for ten years, Emma's background is in academic, digital, and information literacies in higher education. Her experience includes e-learning course design, leading professional workshops in scholarly practices and support, and developing the highly cited ANCIL curriculum for information literacy in collaboration with Jane Secker. Her chief research interests are in the field of applied pedagogic research and the scholarship of teaching and learning. As editor-in-chief of the *Journal of Information Literacy* she also has a keen interest in scholarly communications practices. She tweets as @LibGoddess and drinks far too much espresso.

Erica DeFrain is assistant professor and social sciences librarian at the University of Nebraska-Lincoln. Erica's research interests focus on asynchronous online learning and information literacy skills development, and she is a research fellow with Project Information Literacy. She holds a master of arts in library science, a master of science in educational technology, and a PhD in educational psychology, all from the University of Arizona.

Leslie Delserone is Associate Professor and Science/Government Information Librarian at the University of Nebraska–Lincoln. Her research primarily focuses on agricultural information, most recently the research practices and needs of agricultural scientists, and the preservation of and accessibility to the publication and data products of agricultural research.

Kyle Denlinger is the e-learning librarian at the Z. Smith Reynolds Library at Wake Forest University, where he supports the development of blended and fully online courses, teaches the library's credit-bearing information literacy course LIB 100: Academic Research and Information Issues, and facilitates special projects related to instructional technology and information literacy. His interests include open pedagogy, citation management, and designing authentic online learning experiences. Kyle earned his MA in information science & learning technologies from the University of Missouri-Columbia and his BS in secondary education from the University of Cincinnati.

Erin Durham recently graduated with an MA in history and MLIS in library and information science from the University of Maryland, College Park, where she worked for two years as a graduate assistant for the Library Teaching and Learning Services. Ms. Durham completed practitioner certification from the Teaching and Learning Transformation Center at the University of Maryland, and her areas of research interest include information literacy, critical pedagogy, and the scholarship of teaching and learning.

Peter Felten (pfelten@elon.edu) is executive director of the Center for Engaged Learning, professor of history, and assistant provost for teaching and learning at Elon University. He has served as president of the International Society for the Scholarship of Teaching and Learning (2016–17) and also of the POD Network (2010–2011), the US professional society for educational developers. He also is co-editor of the *International Journal for Academic Development*.

Amy Fyn is the coordinator of library instruction at Coastal Carolina University. She received an MLIS from Wayne State University and an MA in English literature from Boston College. She has served on ACRL Instruction Section committees and presented at regional, national, and international conferences on library instruction topics, including active learning and assessment.

Raphaël Grolimund (raphael.grolimund@epfl.ch), is the former coordinator of the teaching librarians at the Ecole Polytechnique Fédérale de Lausanne (EPFL) in Switzerland, where he now coordinates the liaison librarians. He is also teaching at the University of applied sciences in Geneva (Information Studies department), where he prepares the next generation of teaching librarians.

Cécile Hardebolle (cecile.hardebolle@epfl.ch) is a teaching advisor at the Ecole Polytechnique Fédérale de Lausanne (EPFL). Originally trained as an engineer, she holds a PhD in Computer Science and she has taught at several engineering schools. Cécile currently works on innovation projects in teaching and learning, with a particular interest in the flipped classroom model and project-based learning. She also develops resources to help students learn how to learn, including a book, a MOOC and an online tool called the LearningCompanion.

Lauren Hays, PhD, is the instructional and research librarian at MidAmerica Nazarene University in Olathe, KS where she enjoys teaching and being a member of her institution's Faculty Development Committee. She has co-presented at the annual conference for the International Society for the Scholarship of Teaching and Learning and was the 2017 speaker on SoTL for the Association of College and Research Libraries' Student Learning and Information Literacy Committee's Midwinter Discussion. Her professional interests include SoTL, teaching, information literacy, educational technology, library and information science education, teacher identity, and academic development. On a personal note, she loves dogs, traveling, and home.

Peggy Hedges is a teaching professor at the Haskayne School of Business at the University of Calgary, teaching in the areas of finance and strategy. She received a BSc and MBA from the University of Calgary and a PhD in environmental planning from the University of Strathclyde. Her background includes education and experience in financial services. Peggy's research interests include classroom and pedagogy techniques, small business financing, alternative funding for defined benefit pension plans and risk analysis of catastrophic bonds. She has co-authored two Canadian textbooks, one on corporate financial management and the other on investments and portfolio management. She is a fellow of the Institute of Canadian Bankers (FICB) and a fellow of the Canadian Securities Institute (FCSI).

Amanda Nichols Hess, PhD, is an associate professor and the e-learning, instructional technology, and education librarian at Oakland University Libraries in Rochester, Michigan. In this role, she works with her colleagues to develop the libraries' diverse and user-focused online learning offerings; she is also responsible for delivering professional learning offerings aimed at equipping librarians to integrate instructional design and technology into their teaching. Amanda's research focuses on library instruction, instructional design/technology, and the intersection of these practices in faculty development.

Eveline Houtman is coordinator of undergraduate library instruction, Robarts Library, University of Toronto and the liaison librarian for economics, geography and the study of religion (despite having a background in music history). She has also been music cataloguer, government information specialist, and department head. In addition, she is a PhD candidate at the Ontario Institute for Studies in Education, where her research explores the contexts and experiences that shape academic librarians' teaching practices.

Siara Isaac (siara.isaac@epfl.ch) is a teaching advisor at the Ecole Polytechnique Fédérale de Lausanne (EPFL) in Switzerland. She is particularly interested in how students develop transversal skills such as inquiry and team work in science and engineering contexts. Siara is concurrently pursuing a PhD characterizing the epistemic development of engineering students. Originally trained as a chemist, she has taught in Canada, China, and France.

Melissa E. Johnson is the electronic resources and serials librarian at Reese Library, Augusta University (Augusta, GA). She is the liaison librarian to the Department of Chemistry and Physics, Department of Biological Sciences, and Department of Mathematics and the embedded librarian in the Department of English and Foreign Languages, where she occasionally teaches freshman composition. She earned her BA in English from Augusta University and her MLIS as well as her MA in English from Valdosta State University. She is active in NASIG, ALA, ACRL, GLA, and SELA, and received a 2015 fellowship for the MLA International Bibliography. Ms. Johnson was a member of Augusta University's 2015 SoTL Fellowship.

Lindsay Johnston (BA, MA, MLIS) has held various positions at the University of Alberta Libraries since 1999. She has been a manager for nine years and is currently the public services manager for the Rutherford Humanities & Social Sciences Library and Weir Law Library. Lindsay is the subject librarian for Slavic studies and philosophy. Her areas of focus include reference, discovery, instruction, and staff training and she values the importance of the continuum of public service which connects all four.

Maoria J. Kirker is the instruction and assessment coordinator at George Mason University. She received her MS in library and information science from the University of Illinois at Urbana-Champaign and is currently completing an MS in educational psychology from George Mason University. Her research interests include librarian-teacher beliefs, communities of practice, and professional development for instruction librarians.

Rebecca Kuglitsch is assistant professor and director of sciences at the University of Colorado Boulder Libraries. She holds an MLIS from the University of Washington. Her research interests include information literacy in the sciences, transfer of information literacy skills, and information literacy in practice.

Denis Lacroix (BA, BEd, MLIS) has been a librarian for the past fourteen years at the University of Alberta Libraries in Edmonton (Alberta, Canada). He has been responsible for managing collections and information literacy services for the romance languages, Latin American studies, Western European studies, film studies, classics, and linguistics. His subject librarian position has slowly developed to encompass research data management, scholarly communication in the humanities, and research ethics.

Corinne Laverty is Teaching & Learning Specialist and Librarian at Queen's Centre for Teaching & Learning. Dr. Laverty plays a leadership role in developing and delivering a campus-wide Scholarship of Teaching and Learning program across campus. She is Senior Editor for the *Journal of Applied Research in Higher Education*.

Elizabeth Lorang is associate professor and humanities librarian in the University Libraries at the University of Nebraska-Lincoln. She directs the Digital Scholarship Incubator, teaches advanced research skills, and co-teaches the Digital Humanities Practicum. For more, see https://elizabethlorang.com.

Margy MacMillan is a Professor Emerita and librarian recently retired from Mount Royal University after over 25 years of working with students staff and faculty on aspects of information fluency. Her research interests are situated at the busy intersection of SoTL and Information Literacy with a focus on how students read and work with academic texts. She is currently a Senior Researcher with Project Information Literacy, working on national, ongoing studies of how students solve information problems in their academic, personal, and professional activities. She retired just so she could keep up with her twitter feed @ margymaclibrary.

Molly K. Maloney, University at Buffalo, UB Curriculum Librarian. Molly is a member of the Educational Services department. Her area of instructional expertise is English as a second language (ESL).

Ann Marshall is an information services and instruction librarian at Purdue University Fort Wayne (PFW), where she is also the government documents librarian and library liaison to several departments within the PFW College of Arts and Sciences. She has co-authored publications in *Library Hi Tech*, *Library Journal* and *College & Research Libraries News* and holds an MLS from the Syracuse University School of Information and a PhD from the Maxwell School Social Science Program, also at Syracuse University.

Pamela McKinney is a faculty member in the Sheffield iSchool. Her research has focused broadly on pedagogy for information literacy and, in particular, the relationship between inquiry-based learning and information literacy. She teaches on postgraduate programs and is the iSchool's departmental employability lead. Prior to joining the iSchool, Pamela was learning developer in the Centre for Inquiry-based Learning in the Arts and Social Sciences (CILASS), a Centre for Excellence in Teaching and Learning (CETL) with a special responsibility for taking forward the information literacy strand of activities in teaching development and research. Further information on publications, etc. at https://www.sheffield.ac.uk/is/staff/mckinney.

Heather K. Moberly holds the Dorothy G. Whitley professorship at the Texas A&M University Libraries and serves as the coordinator of veterinary services for the Medical Sciences Library. She has a joint appointment in the College of Veterinary Medicine and Biomedical Sciences and works with the continuum of education there including undergraduate, professional veterinary (DVM), and graduate (masters and doctoral) curricula.

Christine M. Moeller, as an academic librarian, collaborates with faculty and other campus partners to facilitate students' development of critical-thinking and inquiry abilities. Her research centers on the intersections between information literacy pedagogies and the pedagogies of colleagues across campus. In her spare time, she can often be found playing with her cats or leveling up her character in an RPG. She can be found on Twitter at @ christinemmoe.

Alison Olcott is an associate professor of paleobiogeochemistry at the University of Kansas (KU), where she uses chemistry to quest for and understand fossils, and the director of the Center for Undergraduate Research. She is deeply committed to education, particularly of undergraduate students with a special focus on first-year students. Her ultimate goal is to prepare students to find, evaluate, and apply ideas and information with an awareness of their disciplinary and global context.

Mathilde Panes (mathilde.panes@epfl.ch) is a librarian and the coordinator of the teaching librarians team at the Ecole Polytechnique Fédérale de Lausanne (EPFL) in Switzerland. Her professional interests include the expansion of information literacy, the role of librarians in academics and innovative pedagogy.

Zahra Premji is a research and learning librarian for libraries and cultural resources at the University of Calgary. Her responsibilities include undergraduate instruction for business students. Zahra's research interests include information literacy, assessment of learning, and incorporating learning technologies into practice. Zahra received her BSc and PhD in chemistry from the University of Calgary and her MLIS from the University of Alberta.

Catherine Fraser Riehle is associate professor and learning resources design librarian at the University of Nebraska-Lincoln. Before beginning her current position in January 2017, Catherine served for ten years as a faculty member at Purdue University Libraries. Catherine's research interests focus on the intersection of undergraduate education, information literacy, and scholarly communication.

Lindsay Roberts is assistant professor and education librarian at University of Colorado Boulder. They hold an MLIS from University of Denver. Their research interests include the teaching of information literacy concepts, motivational design, transfer of learning, and metacognition/metaliteracy, particularly for adult learners.

Joan Ruelle (jruelle@elon.edu) is Dean of the Carol Grotnes Belk Library at Elon University. She discovered the world of SoTL through liaison work with the Center for the Advancement of Teaching and Learning, which resulted in opportunities, communities, and collaborations to rethink and deepen the teaching role of academic libraries.

Bryan J. Sajecki, University at Buffalo, UB curriculum librarian, is a member of the Educational Services department. His area of instructional expertise is in assessment of learning outcomes.

Caroline Salamin has acted as a teaching librarian at Ecole Polytechnique Fédérale de Lausanne (EPFL) from 2011 to 2018. Her focus was on the design and teaching of interactive information literacy classes for undergraduate, master and doctoral students. She is currently transitioning to a position of analyst in the private sector.

Nasser Saleh is head engineering and science librarian at Queen's University. Dr. Nasser Saleh's research focuses on integration of information literacy in undergraduate curriculum, particularly in pure and applied science. He plays a leadership role in developing partnerships between faculties and librarians and works closely with curriculum committees in engineering and science departments. His research interests include collaborative information behavior, educational technology, and international librarianship.

Maura Seale is the history librarian at the University of Michigan. Previously, she was a collections, research, and instruction librarian at Georgetown University. She welcomes comments @mauraseale.

Kathy Shields is the research and instruction librarian for history and social science at the Z. Smith Reynolds Library at Wake Forest University. She is the liaison for history, psychology, and Latin American and Latino studies and supports faculty and students in those subjects through collection development and research instruction. She also teaches LIB 210: Social Science Research and Strategies, a credit-bearing information literacy course. She received her MLIS from the University of North Carolina at Greensboro and a BA in English from Mississippi State University.

Jenn Marshall Shinaberger is the director of the faculty development center at Coastal Carolina University and has spent the majority of her career in higher education as a faculty developer. She has presented at international, national, and regional teaching and learning conferences such as POD Network and Lilly Conferences on Teaching and Learning. She has an MSEd from Capella University and MPIA from the University of Pittsburgh.

Bobby Smiley is the associate director of the Divinity Library at Vanderbilt University. His case study emerged from research done for a Lilly Teaching Fellowship at Michigan State University, where he was the digital scholarship and American history librarian. Bobby received his BA from the University of Wisconsin-Madison, an MA in Religion from Yale, and his MS in Library and Information Science from the Pratt Institute.

Nicole Thomas, University at Buffalo, UB curriculum librarian, is a member of the Educational Services department. Her area of instructional expertise is in digital literacy.

Cynthia A. Tysick, University at Buffalo Libraries, Head of Education Services, leads a department of six librarians charged with delivering library instruction throughout the first two years of the undergraduate general education program. The bulk of that instruction is delivered through one credit's worth of advanced library research skills embedded in a four-credit writing and rhetoric course. Cynthia has worked at the University at Buffalo for almost sixteen years and is a subject liaison for classics, anthropology, archaeology, and communication.

Sarah Wagner is an information services and instruction librarian at Purdue University Fort Wayne. She is the liaison to the College of Engineering, Technology, and Computer Science, as well as serving as social media manager and scholarly communications coordinator. She has presented at regional and national conferences on library instruction, information literacy, and student interviews. She also previously co-presented and published a study on the role of the library in the popular Harry Potter series.

Micah J. Waltz is a lecturer at Texas A&M University at the College of Veterinary Medicine and Biomedical Sciences with a joint appointment at the University Libraries in the Medical Sciences Library. He teaches undergraduate writing courses that emphasize reading and writing about scientific literature, with a focus on students learning to critically evaluate articles. Students practice translating scientific information for non-scientific audiences, using clinical skills to guide their discussions for best practices of communication.

Meghan Webb is an instruction and outreach librarian at the Z. Smith Reynolds Library at Wake Forest University. In addition to teaching a credit-bearing information literacy course, LIB 100: Academic Research & Information Issues, Meghan is involved in implementing a variety of library programming and cultivating library outreach efforts. She received her MLS from the School of Information and Library Science, and a BA in communication studies from the University of North Carolina at Chapel Hill.

Sheila Webber is a faculty member in the Sheffield iSchool. She is head of the iSchool's Libraries and Information Society Research Group and director of the Centre for Information Literacy Research. She teaches on the iSchool's postgraduate programs and currently supervises three PhD students. She is a University of Sheffield Teaching Fellow, an Honorary Fellow of CILIP, and is a fellow of the UK's Higher Education Academy. Previous roles have included iSchool director of learning and teaching. Her central focus for teaching and research is information literacy. As well as presenting and publishing articles, she has maintained the *Information Literacy Weblog* since 2005. Further information on publications etc. at https://www.sheffield.ac.uk/is/staff/webber.

Thomas Weeks is the reference and instruction librarian at Reese Library, Augusta University (Augusta, GA). He is the liaison librarian to the Office of Faculty Development and Teaching Excellence, Department of Social Sciences, Department of Art and Design, and the College of Education. He earned his BA in English from Augusta University and his MLIS from Valdosta State University. He is currently working on a MS in instructional design and technology at Georgia State University. He is active in ACRL and is a 2016 graduate of the Immersion program. Mr. Weeks was a member of Augusta University's 2015 SoTL Fellowship.

Justine Wheeler is the director of the Business Library at the University of Calgary. Her research interests include information literacy, transition experiences, and the role of academic librarians. Justine received her BA and PhD from the University of Calgary, and her MLIS from the University of Alberta.

Sara Maurice Whitver is the coordinator of library instruction at The University of Alabama Libraries and liaison librarian for English Department and the Writing Center. She is interested in finding ways to support librarians in the classroom and partner with faculty and graduate student teachers to enhance information literacy within the curriculum.

Shelly Yankovskyy (sayankovskyy@valdosta.edu), instructor of anthropology and sociology, Valdosta State University, earned her PhD in anthropology at the University of Tennessee in May 2013. She is a cultural anthropologist specializing in medical anthropology, specifically the mental health system in post-socialist Ukraine as well as the US.

Donna Harp Ziegenfuss, EdD, an associate librarian at the University of Utah, has over ten years of experience working in academic libraries, twelve years of experience in instructional design and teaching in traditional, hybrid, and online formats, and fifteen years of experience working in the area of faculty and professional development. My research interests focus on library instruction and assessment, technology integration, instructional design, librarian identity, academic leadership, and qualitative research. As a qualitative researcher, I am interested in understanding how student dispositions and perceptions impact student success, as well as how conceptual change theory can be applied to develop reflective and engaged teaching and research librarians.